Working Class Heroes

Working Class Heroes

Rock Music and British Society in the 1960s and 1970s

David Simonelli

LEXINGTON BOOKS
Lanham • Boulder • New York • Toronto • Plymouth, UK

Published by Lexington Books
A wholly owned subsidiary of The Rowman & Littlefield Publishing Group, Inc.
4501 Forbes Boulevard, Suite 200, Lanham, Maryland 20706
www.rowman.com

10 Thornbury Road, Plymouth PL6 7PP, United Kingdom

British Library Cataloguing in Publication Information Available

Library of Congress Cataloging-in-Publication Data
Simonelli, David.
  Working class heroes : rock music and British society in the 1960s and 1970s / David
Simonelli.
      pages cm
  Includes bibliographical references and index.
  ISBN 978-0-7391-7051-9 (cloth : alk. paper) -- ISBN 978-0-7391-7052-6 (pbk. : alk.
paper) -- ISBN 978-0-7391-7053-3 (electronic) 1. Rock music--Great Britain--1961-
1970--History and criticism. 2. Rock music--Great Britain--1971-1980--History and
criticism. 3. Popular music--Social aspects--Great Britain. I. Title.
  ML3492.S56 2013
  306.4'8426094109046--dc23
                                    2012037309

Printed in the United States of America

For my wife, Michele
and my kids,
Bridgette, Brendan, Madeleine
and Sylvia

Table of Contents

Acknowledgments and Sources

Any project this long in the gestation requires handing out thanks to an incredibly long list of people.

This project began as a dissertation at Tulane University more than a decade ago. Dr. Sam Ramer, Dr. James Boyden and Dr. Wilfred McClay were encouraging at important points in the project. I also treasure my friendship with Dr. Ken Harl, who shared ideas, pasta and many laughs that allowed me to look at my advisors as future colleagues for the first time. The graduate school, represented then by Ms. Kay Orrill and Ms. Ruth Barnes, supported me with grants, particularly by allowing me to apply for a second Selley Dissertation Award. Dr. Rick Teichgraeber was essential in pointing me toward readings that would help me place my work in the context of British cultural and intellectual history. Dr. Linda Pollock challenged me and my ideas numerous times, having lived through the period I was writing about, but she also gave me a series of her own music tapes that allowed me to listen to and learn about bands I had only read about in books and journals. Most of all, Dr. George Bernstein, my advisor, surprised me by telling me what a great idea he thought the project was, and he tirelessly pored through my writing and my sources like no one else who has read this book. He and Mrs. Bernstein have been endlessly good to me over the years, and I owe them the academic life I enjoy today.

Many friends also supported me when and where it counted. Michael Andrews, Kent Germany and Marc Eagle listened to me prattle, moan, bloviate and scheme over numerous cups of coffee—truly a hardship for Kent since he doesn't drink coffee. I loved the give and take on our projects and learned as much from them as I did from my own work. Similar friends included, in no particular order: Mike and Dawn Redman, Laura Kelley and Thomas Bayer, Mary Germany, Sue Loegering Daves, Beth Manley, Don Wright, Keira and Lauren Williams, Ursula Vesala, Corey Andrews, Becca Livingstone, Four

Meaher, Dave Dressing, Guillaume Aubert, Gregg Bocketti, members of the Louisiana Philharmonic Orchestra and others too numerous to name. Two further friends I made over email connections are Jonathan Traub, who has sent me numerous useful articles, and Jonathyne William Briggs, now at Indiana University Northwest; I can at last say to these two interested readers, it's done.

In Britain, the Institute of Historical Research has allowed me to meet many prominent British historians, some of whom have been helpful with my work. In particular, Dr. Peter Catterall, who ran the Institute of Contemporary British History's twentieth-century seminar at the IHR, allowed me to present my work in a public forum for the first time. The late Dr. Arthur Marwick could not meet with me but I had a useful email exchange with him over the issue of class in British culture. Dr. Andrew Blake spent most of an afternoon with me, helping me pin down where I might do research and giving me good ideas on the role of music in British history.

Along with the staff at the places I worked, I need to plug a few sources that I consider woefully underutilized. The staff at the British Library, particularly in the National Sound Archive, was professional, friendly and helpful. In the NSA, I found the *History of Rock* series, a three-year run of magazines detailing the history of rock music from its roots to the new wave bands of the 1980s. I was amazed to find that the authors of the articles in this journal were the same journalists, critics, and academics that I had run across in secondary sources and in the music journals I had read from the 1960s and 1970s. Anyone looking to challenge or further this topic would do well to start with *History of Rock*. Besides this, I recently found http://www.rocksbackpages.com/, subtitled "the online library of pop writing"; it has helped me immensely in allowing me to check some of my sources from *Melody Maker*, *New Musical Express*, *Sounds* and other journals. The British Library's Newspaper Archive is located in Colindale, and the staff there was essential to my research too.

Perhaps the most amazing archive molders in the messy attic room of the Edinburgh University Library: the BBC's newspaper archive. This collection came from all over the country, and it allowed the BBC to check its coverage of events in the news with that of other sources. It consisted of shoebox-size boxes with handwritten labels ("Beatles", "Grosvenor Square", "festivals", etc.). Each box contained a stack of articles, clipped, identified by newspaper—not by page number; any footnotes reading "no page number available" came from this archive—glued to tissue paper and stamped with a date somewhere between 1955 and 1975. I spent a week taking notes on a beat-up architect's table, resolving that if I never found an academic job, I would return to Edinburgh and pitch the idea of cataloguing and digitizing this archive. Well, I found a job. However, the fact that this archive remains boxed in an attic in Edinburgh, barely available to the public unless they know about it already, is academically criminal. Its usefulness is impossible to calculate, and I would urge any historian of Britain's mid-twentieth century to look for it. (I could not find it listed online.) I found out about the BBC newspaper archive from the friend with whom I traveled there, Chad Martin, from whom I learned a lot. We shared many a pint and many a laugh, and I wish him luck at the University of Indianapolis, hopefully to see him at a conference one of these days.

As this project became a manuscript, it received more help along the way. *Contemporary British History* published my first article, which is chapter 13 in this book, on punk. *Popular Music History* put out my article on the BBC and the programming of progressive rock, whose material spreads across a few chapters here. The chapter on folk rock was originally a conference paper delivered at the Midwest Conference on British Studies and it received very useful commentary from Dr. Dan LeMahieu, the moderator of our panel. The manuscript itself was placed in front of several readers, some of whom were brutal, some constructive, all of them anonymous, all of them useful. I received great encouragement from the North American British Music Studies Association, two of whose conferences I attended. Amongst the scholars who talked with me about my work were Erick Saylor, Charles McGuire, Alain Frogley, Jenny Doctor and Christina Baade. Here at Youngstown State University, my chair, Dr. Martha Pallante, has been faithful in supporting me as a scholar. All of my colleagues have presented a congenial atmosphere here in which to work, but I am especially grateful to two retired professors, Lowell Satre and Martin Berger, who have read and commented on this work. And of course, my editor at Lexington Books, Erin Walpole, has been a godsend, especially for setting deadlines for me and demanding that I keep them.

My parents are patient and understanding people who never pushed me too hard to finish this so they could brag to my aunts and uncles. My wife, Michele, and my kids, Bridgette, Brendan, Madeleine and Sylvia, have put up with a lot, having me staked out in front of a computer so often and away at the office working on weekends and over vacations. I have talked with Michele about this project any number of times, and gotten excellent ideas every time, especially towards developing a title for this book. The whole family has also been more than patient with my taste in music too. I love them all and dedicate this book to them.

However, I cannot avoid mentioning two other friends who need to be honored with this book. Back when I was twelve or so, my friend Tom Leibowitz convinced me that the Rolling Stones was the greatest band in the history of rock. A few years later, another friend, David Wexler, showed me that the Who was a match for them. I am still in touch with both of those friends, and in most respects, this book would not exist without them.

Youngstown, Ohio
2012

Introduction

In the twenty-first century, class persists in the mindset of most westerners as the preeminent way to describe their economic, social and cultural status—middle class, working class—and for good reason. It's easy to understand, if virtually impossible to define properly. Most people would probably agree, colloquially, that class—social class—is a concept that defines a person's social stratification according to a number of different precepts, most prominently their economic status and prospects, based on their job, their education and their social milieu. There is something comforting about describing oneself as a part of a mass of people who likely share the same political, economic, social and cultural interests. In August 2002, Britain's Labour Party-leaning newspaper, *The Guardian*, published a Mass Observation poll declaring that 68 percent of British citizens agreed with the statement "I'm working-class and proud of it"—this in a nation whose traditional industrial economy has been in decline for nearly a century. Even more, 55 percent of those who responded to the poll said they "claimed to have working-class feelings" even though their socioeconomic standing would have marketing researchers placing them in the middle classes.[1]

If respondents were "working-class and proud of it", how did they define what it meant to be "working-class"? Since the end of the Second World War, it's clear that something has changed in perceptions of class and what it means as a delineator of status in British society. Many institutions have contributed to the equalizing of British society since that time. Education, the National Health Service, the baby boom, Americanization, television and radio, all eroded the easy identification of class in socioeconomic appearance and reality. Yet still, the idea persists, even prospers.

It's the contention of this book that the average person, let alone intellectuals and academics, now defines class in mostly cultural terms, and less in socioeconomic ones. Defining class in cultural terms has always been relevant and necessary, but in the postwar era, such definitions have obscured any real sense of the original socioeconomic paradigm. The cultural divisions in British society are reflected, and in part defined, in their popular media of expression: television, radio, movies, literature, journalism and a host of others. And of all those media of expression, the one that provided the best, most lasting and most explicit forum in which to discuss the changes in British society, and redefine them on new lines, was popular music in the 1960s and 1970s—especially rock and roll, and its allegedly more sophisticated sibling, rock music.

Rock and roll and rock music are treated too often by music historians as mere imports from the United States—not an entirely wrong assumption, but certainly a misleading one. For rock music as a British artistic medium is very illustrative of long-term trends in British cultural history as a whole. From the beginnings of Beatlemania in 1963, rock and roll was more than a reflection of British cultural norms: it was also a catalyst for their transformation. Rock and roll articulated new ideas about a vast array of issues, including class, generation, politics, art, geography, gender and language. Listeners—mostly adolescents and young adults—then used those new meanings to interpret, celebrate or criticize the socio-cultural changes they saw taking place around them. In short, rock and roll provided a rhetoric that helped define and redefine the parameters of British society and culture in the 1960s.

It's important to note here that the music did nothing to assert those parameters all by themselves. It's ridiculous to assert that a stockbroker in London who liked "A Hard Day's Night" in 1964 would suddenly decide that all of his inherited ideas about the realities of the working classes were wrong, and that the stevedore with the grimy hands standing next to him on his Metropolitan Line train home was surely a budding artist in disguise. Popular art did not destroy societal boundaries. What rock and roll did do was provide an environment for young people—Britain's future stockbrokers and stevedores, not to mention teachers, store clerks, small businessmen, coal miners, politicians, rail workers, students, delinquents and everyone else—to rethink received ideas about class and redefine them. Instead, people who grew up with rock and roll in the 1960s and 1970s made class more relevant to their own circumstances in an increasingly professionalized, post-industrial world by basing their ideas of class in cultural tastes as opposed to wage packets and living circumstances.

What's more, they paid a lot of money to gain access to that forum, as did any number of other people around the planet. Rock and roll made British culture seem exciting, new, and exportable. The Beatles' conquest of America in 1964 kicked open a door into the world's consumer market that had just been breached by James Bond movies two years earlier. This was the beginning of a massive outflow of the products of British pop culture, and at the crest of the tide was music. Britain became a major exporter of culture to the world economy in the 1960s, opening up new industries in an era when traditional industries like coal, steel, and shipbuilding were in their dying throes. The British economy benefited as British culture transformed itself: British novels, films, art, and fashion reflected the impact and attitudes inherent in pop, rock and roll and rock music, and exported them too. Popular music in Britain thus was a serious contributor to the nation's future prosperity, in the eyes not just of its own musicians and fans, but also in the eyes of watchers of British culture in general.

Yet all of this cultural power emanated from a series of social and cultural prejudices, stereotypes and misperceptions. From the beginning in the 1950s, fans, critics, managers and musicians considered rock and roll in Britain an exclusively working-class music, much as it was associated as an exclusively African-American music in the United States. Anyone looking into the origins of the music, the musicians, or the music's audience could see that such associations were false. Yet the perception lasted, and it was the most important perception that sustained rock and roll as a vital artistic medium in Britain in the 1960s. Rock and roll represented an alleged rebellion against post-Victorian tastes in British culture, tastes that were often accused of being "middle-class". This too was just a simplified perception of the realities of class. One's class status had little to do anymore with how one perceived that elusive Victorian quality, "respectability", which kept the curtains in people's windows and the drugs and excessive drinking out of their bodies.

The perception lasted because the reaction against rock and roll was so vehement on the part of those people—critics, economic producers, politicians, radio and television broadcasters, newspaper and magazine columnists and vocal members of the public at large, both professional and otherwise—who made up the cultural "establishment". Elite cultural critics' rejection of rock and roll fueled its popularity, both with the working-class school-leavers whom the establishment identified as rebellious and dangerous, and with middle-class adolescents whom the establishment feared would give in to the merit-less, immoral and impoverished values that they believed rock and roll perpetuated. And if a British teenager didn't read the columns of Monica Furlong or pay attention to Mary Whitehouse on TV, she could always substitute the values of her parents as a worthy straw man to burn up.

Merely by being heroes to teenagers, then, rock musicians were associated with their alleged rejection of the establishment's cultural dictates, even though that rejection rarely held up under scrutiny. That rebellion defined the musician's "authenticity", another odd and elusive quality that provided a standard by which rock and roll could be measured as good or bad. Rebellion could come from anywhere, against anything, to provide authenticity—even, in the case of the Kinks' Ray Davies, when he was able to place himself in opposition to the concept of working-class rebellion itself. Rock musicians became spokesmen for young people specifically because they seemed rebellious, and they articulated their rebellion in interviews, humor, fashions, attitudes and politics, not to mention their lyrical content. Critically, these musicians' ability to define themselves in opposition to the "establishment" in itself was sufficient to link them with the working classes—or at least, an invented conception of what it meant to be working-class. At a time when social distinctions were becoming harder to measure, few could determine exactly what it meant to be working-class anyway.

So this book will be mostly about the perpetuation of an image, a rhetoric and a lifestyle, derived from the British audience's conception of rock musicians, that made them seem like rebels against the established rules of British culture, and thus "authentic". The image was almost completely paradoxical. To be "authentic" in rock music, British musicians had to display their rejection of the cultural status quo. They damned the world of technology and industry, suburban lifestyles, conventional morality, national and international politics, eventually even the notion of making money and placing records on BBC and commercial radio playlists. At the same time, they indulged in all of these things, and got rich doing it. The definition of authenticity in rock music changed constantly over the course of the sixties and seventies. The people who defined authenticity—always the musicians themselves, but also an increasing number of music journalists, youth intellectuals and students, eventually even cultural commentators from the country's most respected establishment media—likewise changed, as often as the society in which they lived.

Rock musicians and their perceived values spoke for millions of teenagers in the sixties, and they spoke in what those teenagers believed to be the authentic voice of the working classes. Teenagers adopted values designed to aggravate their parents, and rejected their alleged social striving for comfortable status in a post-Victorian world. It was, quite simply, "cool" to be working class (and proud of it), and coolness could be bought with the few shillings and pence it took to pick up "Can't Buy Me Love", "Mother's Little Helper" or "Substitute". The myth was more important than the reality, the image greater than the background it derived from. To be working class, or more precisely, to identify with an erroneously held but widely accepted set of working-class values, was to be young in Britain in the 1960s, and vice versa. No challenge to traditional British cultural values had ever seemed to be so strong or so precisely defined.

Yet subtly, from the very moment when the Beatles became national superstars in 1963, the post-Victorian cultural milieu in which they operated was in a process of momentous change—change dictated in part by the artistic adventurism of the Beatles themselves and the hundreds of bands who followed them. They all made music that was slightly but distinctly different from that of their

American influences, music informed by the culture they had grown up in and based in their own natural artistic curiosity. British rock and roll musicians created adventurous music in the 1960s that sold millions of records around the world, in some part specifically because they were British.

So as rock and roll became more articulate—and more British—it also became more standardized, less rebellious against cultural standards in a very real way. Such changes manifested themselves in the way musicians talked about the music. To begin with, the very term "rock and roll" started to take on a new meaning. London bands of the mid-sixties at first disdained it in favor of "rhythm and blues"; the lyrical and political influence of the American Bob Dylan also contributed to its falling out of favor. Rock and roll was "pop" music and "pop" music" was the music of the masses, made for commercial intent. As musicians' artistic vision grew, they repudiated any hint of commercial intent, to maintain authenticity. "Pop" music—the music of the singles charts, packaged and sold just the same way that soap or television commercials or automobiles were—became a crass concept. Since "rock and roll" was pop music, and since the ambitions of its musicians went well beyond popularity or financial success (at least, outwardly), British musicians began to claim that they played "rock" music, a seemingly more dignified term that matched their more ambitious artistic purposes.

The change in rhetoric reflected a growing exclusivity among rock musicians. Rock musicians were "artists" who made "art", and not everyone could be an artist, anymore than anyone could operate an industrial lathe, or weld rivets, or teach, or manage a stock portfolio. Like those other careers, there were certain accepted professional standards to becoming an artist. A rock musician in Britain had to write his own music, he had to acknowledge the many sources he tapped to write interesting songs, he had to show a certain ambition toward creating a masterpiece, he had to be proficient on his instrument and he could not care in the slightest about the commercial possibilities of his art, even when it raked in millions of pounds and dollars.

These changes manifested themselves in British rock music with the beginnings of the psychedelic movement and cemented themselves as British rock musicians turned to the concept of "progressivism". Psychedelia narrowed the source of the music's professional values to those of a certain sector of the British youth audience. These were young people who came to define themselves exclusively from other music listeners by their interest in albums rather than singles, their ability to identify drug references in music (which they often made up themselves), and their sense of persecution by a worried cultural and political establishment. "Progressive" rock fused the primitiveness of rock and roll with elements of English folk songs, Anglican church music, exotic Eastern rhythms and classical music. And the rock musicians who pursued these influences popularized the idea that expertise and talent were the keys to making art, which made them worthy of the highest social distinction, whatever their socioeconomic origins or cultural beliefs.

Progressive rock also reflected a newfound political consciousness amongst both musicians and their audience. Like their American counterparts, youthful intellectuals established a "counterculture" based on progressive values. A radical young group of cultural and political leftists in the "London underground" provided a voice for youth culture by organizing newspapers, concerts, and other public displays of the values they believed would overthrow the old cultural establishment. The London underground became, in effect, professional intellectuals in youth culture, defining proper standards by which countercultural values should be measured. Nothing better symbolized the paradox at the center of British mass culture in the late 1960s. The very medium through which so many young people expected to transform their society, rock music, had become one of the engines through which they became members of a new "establishment" themselves. By asserting their leadership in youth culture and measuring their favorite bands against their own vision of a proper British culture, the underground and the young people that followed it created a new vision of British social stratification, based on a revamped, less Victorian idea of professional values and cultural standards. They became like the very people they despised. The musicians they lionized followed an even higher path, into the very highest elite of British culture and society. They met with almost universal admiration for their "high cultural" values, and joined in a rather snobbish mockery of "low" pop music—which happened to be the music of actual working-class teenagers at the time.

Many people recognized this growing elitism on the part of the progressive audience, and tried to fight it. Regional music subcultures defined themselves in part by their representation of "true" working class values, in their love of soul, ska and reggae. The more widespread challenge to progressive rock values came at first from "glamrock" bands, who tried to bring showmanship, a prodigious "pop" interest in cash profits and a large measure of fun back into rock music. In short, they tried to revive rock and roll. Some of their effort might have been undermined, however, by glamrock's most visible exponent, David Bowie, an unparalleled performer who clearly aspired to the higher cultural ideals of many of the progressive bands. If Bowie and other acts created pop music that they saw as glamorous and commercial, they also created "art"—a decidedly un-working-class pursuit. The music of Bowie and other glamrock acts made decadence itself seem artistic, in a way that many rock critics, musicians and listeners liked, but which forced them to question what had happened to the values to which they had once adhered.

By the mid-seventies, British rock music seemed dead, artistically and emotionally. In the midst of a growing economic crisis in which young people were the first to be laid off from work, the music industry offered soft rock and pop music as limp as the British economy itself. The result was the rise of "punk", the last and most powerful challenge to the professionalization of rock music in Britain. Punk was a last gasp effort to assert the alleged working-class roots of British rock and roll. It was reflective of the anger of its youthful audience, dividing itself from earlier rock music by asserting that its musicians openly played "pop" music—and that pop music would soon become the medium through which a vague "revolution" would come to destroy middle-class British society once and for all. The sympathetic music press often lionized punk musicians as the saviors of rock and roll values, a revitalizing element that perfectly captured youth anger.

Yet therein lay the problem. Punk music's anarchic rhetoric was only capable of being mastered by punks used to co-opting texts to suit their needs— mostly art students, university students and others from privileged backgrounds. For a working-class punk like Johnny Rotten of the Sex Pistols, "Anarchy in the UK" was an assertion of his naïvely utopian aspirations. When middle-class punks like Subway Sect asserted that "Nobody's Scared", it was merely another metaphor for a purely artistic anger, like dada or surrealism. Not surprisingly, the rhetorically working-class element in the punk movement quickly transformed when its lack of authenticity was exposed. The rhetoric of punk changed; it became "new wave" in 1977-78, a shift in language considered more sympathetic to the values of a respectable audience.

By 1978, then, the musical transformation of British cultural rhetoric was complete. There was still a middle class, still a working class, but who considered themselves representative of those monikers was harder to tell. The thirteen-year-old girl who had delighted in the Beatles' mockery of their social superiors now frowned upon the Sex Pistols saying "fuck" on national TV in front of her own children. Yet she also was still likely to buy David Bowie's *Heroes*, vote Labour in the 1979 General Election, and show up at a rally of the Campaign for Nuclear Disarmament. And just because she didn't like her daughter hearing such language didn't mean she didn't think it was funny.

It is important to assert what this book is, and what it is not. It is an effort to gain a perspective on the changes in British society in the mid- to late twentieth century through the prism of a popular medium of cultural expression, rock music. Often, however, the subject matter does not really concern the music itself so much as it is about the images that surrounded it in journalism, fashion, television, film, and other commercial and media ventures. It is not really, then, a book about rock music itself inasmuch as it uses the music as a window on British society. For the purposes of definition, the window has until recently been somewhat dirty and in need of cleaning.

Besides being about British society and culture, this book is also an effort to touch what seems to be the "third rail" in studies of rock music in Britain—its role as a medium through which one might perceive class structure. As any number of music historians and critics have asserted before, correctly, rock music has done nothing to change social distinctions in British society. Yet rock music still has provided a way to watch British society change, and provided a language with which to describe how it happens to be that people in Britain still identify themselves in the seemingly archaic fashion of being "working class" or "middle class". In the end, by providing heroes that young people emulated, subcultures that gave direction to their tastes and a counterculture that challenged the norms of British society, rock music helped change the *language* of social stratification—the "rhetoric of class", as the late social historian Harold Perkin referred to it. It allowed young people to think of themselves as belonging to the same social categories as their parents, but also allowed them to define the categories themselves in an entirely different, more culturally based fashion.

On a larger level, this book is about how rock music became British. Of course British rock and roll began as an imitation of American heroes, whether they were pop artists, Chicago bluesmen, Greenwich Village folkies or otherwise. Yet the music changed in Britain because the musicians who made it were products of British culture. They understood issues of folk authenticity, the cult of the amateur, the notion that professionals in a social democratic society served their community, the powerful cultural desire to counter the effects of industrialism with Romantic pastoral values, the influence of empire, and especially the role of class as a delineator of societal values. British rock musicians translated all of these values into their music, and made it their own. Arguably, then, especially with the rise of progressive rock, rock music in Britain became an entirely new and nationalistic cultural medium, separate from its American cousin, reflective of the society that it came from, and profitably exportable besides.

In 1973, Steve Winwood noted, "What happens nowadays seems to be that rock and roll engulfs everything. Poetry's no longer poetry, fashion's no longer fashion, music's no longer music—it's all rock and roll. It seems to swallow up everything, just one big melting pot."[2] This has only become truer over time. Today Coca-Cola sells the idea that someone who drinks the products of a multinational capitalist conglomerate is an iconoclast with attitude; millions of young people pierce and tattoo their bodies to express their individuality, even though everyone else is doing exactly the same thing; obnoxious behavior by public figures is worthy of constant attention by the media because it sells commercials; and rock music itself isn't rebellious enough to survive without the sheen of being "alternative", to separate the derivative sounds of the present from those of the past. Meanwhile, the healthy questioning of authority is a recognized norm, the values of youth drive cultural production, freedom of expression has been upgraded from a privilege to an expected right throughout the western world, and individuality and diversity are increasingly more celebrated than looked upon with suspicion. All of these values, bad and good, translated themselves into people's lives in some way through rock music. This book is hopefully a step toward getting to the root of how the music has translated those values, and more directly, what its impact has been and will continue to be in British history.

Chapter 1
Society, Culture and Music in Britain Before 1963

Rock and roll music was only the latest in a long series of phenomena in the history of industrial and post-industrial Britain that focused debate on the content and direction of British culture. Since the onset of industrialization, intellectuals, religious leaders, professionals, cultural critics and the public at large had struggled with each other for control of popular culture. The higher up one was on the social and professional scale, the more likely their contempt for popular culture; in fact, many denied its legitimacy as culture at all. Generally, people in positions of cultural power suppressed popular cultural institutions they disliked, or at least denigrated them in an effort to assert influence. A select few popular culture institutions, however, became "respectable" despite these efforts. Popular music was amongst these institutions, for a myriad of reasons.

Folk Music and the Music Hall

The intellectual conception of an appropriate British culture was mainly Romantic, in opposition to the industrial economy so many people perceived as an ever-present menace to Matthew Arnold's "sweetness and light". The folk music movement in Britain best represented these values in the early twentieth century, and many of those who feared a decline in cultural standards counted themselves members as a result. Cecil Sharp founded the English Folk Dance and Song Society (EFDSS) as a repository for the music of England's peasant culture, a culture considered endangered by industrialism. In an effort to prove that Britain was not "the land without music", men like Sharp went out into the rural farmlands of England to find and record folk music.

Of course, the first issue for the EFDSS and its members was to establish just who the "folk" were. The emphasis was decidedly on the anti-industrial and the pastoral, and the Romantic values inherent therein. Defining the source of English folk culture so narrowly was of no real concern to the movement's leaders or members—they believed that the earnestness of their mission leant them authority, especially over the people from whom they learned their songs. The EFDSS's goal, in most respects, was not to find an "authentic" folk music (an adjective they would throw around loosely for an entire century); it was to define folk music, and the people who produced it, in the interest of inventing tradition and preserving the national heritage. The "folk", then, were decidedly not working-class in origin; they had no identity in the factory. The EFDSS's idea of "folk" was found in a dying "merrie England", centered on local communities and suspicious of industrialism and central authority. The "people" were a pastoral community of rural artisans and agricultural laborers, simple, religious, pre-industrial, and pre-literate. These "folk" indulged in the spontaneous non-commercial creation of music that they themselves undervalued, but that the EFDSS understood to be the true "authentic" folk music of England. They were an idealized people for the EFDSS—docile, easily directed, and representing the last vestiges of a culture that the English people had drifted too far away from, in the opinions of the movement's members.[1]

This vision was at great odds with reality. The "folk" that the EFDSS so idealized hardly existed by the early twentieth century; mechanization of agriculture and union movements had made rural commoners far more like the urban working classes than like their peasant forebears. Yet the actual existence of the EFDSS'S vision of the "folk" and their traditions was beside the point. The success of the folk music movement depended only a little on the preservation of the national culture that it claimed to have discovered. Far more important and novel was the sense of exceptionalism that a love of traditional folk music provided for the movement's adherents. As the preservationists of the nation's musical heritage, they felt a powerful sense of elitism as respondents to an urgent cultural crisis. Industrialization and urbanization in Britain appeared to be killing peasant culture. The loss of the village lifestyle would be irretrievable in the face of the factory, the machine, German militarism and American consumerism in the twentieth century. The very conception of what was "English" was about to be lost forever. Thus, men like Cecil Sharp, Ralph Vaughan Williams, and later, A. L. Lloyd and Ewan MacColl, saw themselves as cultural heroes, and adherents of the folk music movement seconded their status. These were the saviors of an English folk cultural inheritance, not in the least bit beyond trying to save that inheritance from the ignorance of the English folk themselves.[2]

The EFDSS spread the gospel of these invented folk values to like-minded people all over London and the Home Counties, and later, to the rest of England. The result was a group of comfortable, professional people and their families—lawyers, doctors, composers, writers, teachers, journalists, civil servants—who recreated old peasant songs and dances, peasant dress, peasant instruments, even peasant lifestyles in the interest of preservation. They applied a combination of professional and Romantic values to the way they measured folk music and the musicians who played it. Expertise, amateurism, accessibility, anti-commercialism, artistry, artlessness, subject matter and obscurity were debated factors in determining "authenticity", a hazy concept whose parameters only became more and more vague.[3]

The nature and sources of folk music were not the only aspects of popular culture—a culture of the people—that were debated in the early twentieth century. The Victorian music hall arose in the late nineteenth century with a new abundance of working-class leisure time. In the 1850s and 1860s, entrepreneurs started to build specially designed halls specifically for entertaining a drinking public with popular music. People sat at tables, beer arrived in large ewers, the audience talked back to the performers and the performers answered back to the audience. Sing-alongs were always popular. The audience was mainly a working-class and lower middle-class group, made up of factory hands, artisans, tradesmen, shopkeepers, and occasionally their wives, though not often. They were usually young, boisterous without being rowdy, and noisy, and the sense of community engendered between audience and performer was the most important entertainment value in evidence.[4]

As it happened, the same sort of professionals, businessmen, religious reformers and the like who were inclined to manufacture their own vision of "folk music" out of the "folk" of England were similarly inclined to destroy any other idea of a musical heritage that they had not created themselves. Cultural reformers despised the music hall as a vulgarity, an example of capitalist greed corrupting the popular taste in pursuit of guineas. The vulgar songs, dancing women, risqué jokes and low intellectual content of a music hall evening were unacceptable to the typical Victorian or Edwardian professional family. Worst of all was the destruction of the most civilized of the arts, music. Yet regardless of the efforts of reforming and religious bodies to attack the music halls, nothing eclipsed the halls' popularity.[5]

However, as the music halls continued to prosper, their entertainment standards began to change. As they became rich, the music halls' proprietors came to see themselves as morally respectable entrepreneurs, and wanted British society to perceive them as such. It took little to convince them that the best way to do this was to curb the vulgarity in music hall performances. They lectured performers to cut down on profanities, relax the political commentary, and above all, to avoid interacting with the audience to provoke such responses. They installed dress codes and behavioral policies for the audience as well, and de-emphasized the sale of alcohol as the principal source of the music hall's revenues. Auditorium seating replaced the beer tables, pointing the audience's attention at the stage—and with the added seating, bringing in even larger revenues as well. Prices for attendance went up, and a better clientele began to attend the shows. By 1914, the music hall was a markedly different institution from what it had been in the 1880s, even though it always maintained its popular flavor. The demands of big business had led to cultural reform.[6]

The development of folk music and the music hall represented different ways in which the dominant cultural standards of respectability asserted themselves in the early twentieth century. Those standards demanded a select image of what "the people's culture" should be, and conflicted with other images, especially if they reflected the values of industrialism or commerce. Few things were worse than for a cultural institution to be "popular". Yet paradoxically, the goal of the folk music movement was to recreate what it saw as the people's music, and spread its values on a national basis. On the other hand, the commercial success of the music hall, venue for a true people's music, drove its entrepreneurs to adopt new cultural standards that would prove more acceptable to the reformers who hated their businesses. In short, music as popular culture could not be perceived as popular or it would not be perceived as culture. Popular music could only achieve an appropriate level of cultural respectability if it surrendered its values to those defined by the professionals, critics, intellectuals, religious reformers and politicians, or allowed those selfsame people to define its values to begin with.

Mass and Popular Culture in Britain, 1918-1945

Music halls began the development of an even more insidious danger to the folk culture of Britain—a culture produced for mass consumption, and thus profit. Cultural elites despised mass culture as democratic, meant to appeal to everyone, whatever his or her social standing. That meant it had no standards, other than success in a mass market. In the 1920s and 1930s, members of the cultural establishment tried desperately to control new technology and new media that made mass culture possible, in the effort to uplift people's tastes, the prime example being the BBC. Critics tended to judge mass culture according to its aesthetic value as opposed to its popularity. Thus, the creation of a democratic, truly popular culture was always a struggle between what was commercially acceptable and what was aesthetically acceptable.[7]

The original home of mass culture was the United States, and the "Americanization" of European popular culture began in the era after the Great War. The United States had been the force behind the winning of the war, it had the most powerful economy in the world, the most diverse population ethnically, and a cavalier attitude toward "high" European culture. Mass culture was Hollywood movies, jazz bands and crooners, mass advertising, the Charleston, co-

medic radio shows and sports. America's vision of its own culture was viva-
cious, full of pleasure at a time when Europe was in the throes of mass privations and economic restructuring. On the movie screen, at least, American society seemed boundlessly affluent, a place where abundance and respectability
were the norm.[8] Many educated Europeans feared this process, seeing more bad
than good in American culture. Culture was supposed to improve people, not
cater to their desire for fun or abundance.

The newest mass medium after 1920 was the radio. The British Broadcasting Corporation received its charter from the government in 1927 under its head,
the sober Scottish Calvinist John Reith. His motto was "knowledge, endeavor,
achievement", and his social conservatism and influential drive meant that he
intended the BBC to live up to that motto. Nine million homes had radios by
1939. Radio reinforced and dominated cultural life, and the BBC existed to
shape the cultural development of the nation in the face of the impact of Americanization.[9] Under Reith, the BBC intended to teach the British people what
good taste was in music, by exposing them to the classical tradition. BBC culture would contribute to cultural progress, and the result would be a well-
educated, tasteful listener who was active and discriminating. Popular music was
entertaining but not meaty enough to warrant the public's lengthy attention.
Broadcasts of popular music mingled with broadcasts of classical music, a self-
evidently better music of lasting social significance. The radio should ideally
become the hearth around which a family would gather, and by reaching every
British family, it would become the basis for a national community as based on
the values of a discerning post-Victorian morality. Or so people like Reith believed.[10]

When American jazz swept the Western world in the 1920s and 1930s, the
BBC's directors were determined to diminish its popularity in Britain. The public's love of American big bands and pop crooners like Bing Crosby and Rudy
Vallee, however, forced the BBC to answer for its broadcast policies, almost
from its inception. Listeners wrote in to the service's publicly distributed scheduling magazine, *Radio Times*, mostly to complain about the lack of their favorite
music on the radio. By the 1930s, radio stations on the continent broadcasted to
Britain, especially Radio Luxembourg, which at times reached more than 45
percent of the British radio audience. Many of the continental services played
jazz.[11] The BBC could not maintain its monopoly on the development of British
music culture for long.

The BBC thus resorted to the tactics of the folk music movement, in determining what "authentic" jazz was and what it was not. If the BBC could not get
an audience to prefer classical music to pop music, at least it could direct the
audience's pop tastes. Thus, broadcasting policies distinguished between what
was "real" jazz and what was just "pop". The BBC found a difference between
big band "symphonic" jazz like Glenn Miller or Duke Ellington, and the music
of crooners like Crosby or Frank Sinatra. It was the difference between "light"
and "commercial" music, "real jazz" and "pop", the respectable and the disrepu-

table. To the BBC, popular culture had a hierarchy too. A "common"—as opposed to "mass" —culture meant that a discerning audience needed to define a common set of values for the rest of the British audience. At least a big band was fairly close to a symphony orchestra. When the BBC made a distinction between the "real" and the "inauthentic" in music, its listeners were to assume that such a distinction arose in the interest of their own improvement. Thus, the BBC did not play certain types of jazz in the 1930s, like the scat singing of Ella Fitzgerald or the "hot jazz" of the Cab Calloway or Louis Jordan combos.[12]

During the Second World War, the BBC abandoned its cultural mission and concentrated more on entertainment that would keep the British population focused on the war effort. One result was the development of the Light Programme, devoted entirely to popular music and comedy. The most popular musical image of Britain during the war was Vera Lynn singing "The White Cliffs of Dover". The music of American big bands was extremely popular and in demand on the Light Programme. Ironically, at the very time when wartime government publicists considered a definition of British culture vital to the national interest, the BBC's broadcast of light and popular music acknowledged that Americanization and its values were a stable part of the definition. The broadcast of pop music and jazz increased every year, just as it had during the 1930s.[13]

Youth in the 1950s and the Culture of Consumption

Increasing Americanization brought with it the values of American culture, and to the British public, no quality defined American popular culture as directly as the quality of youth. To Americans, it seemed, youth was a cultural virtue. The first manifestations of what would eventually be called "youth culture" arrived in Britain during the harsh economic conditions of the 1920s, as grammar and university-educated students rejected the society of their elders in favor of an alternative society, undefined but of their own making, to replace the tired institutions that had brought the Great War about.[14] Most such young people were middle-class, however. Working-class adolescents worked. Seven out of every ten fourteen-year-old working-class boys held some form of employment in 1938. Many were apprentices with lifetime careers ahead of them at a decent pay scale, but even an unskilled clerk or laborer with fewer long-term prospects earned comparatively well right away.[15] With their ready cash and dimmer futures, unskilled workers were the most prominent target market for mass cultural production. They were more likely to be dissatisfied with their job prospects, and thus more likely to question the values of the society in which they lived and worked.[16]

Then came the western baby boom of the 1940s and 1950s, and a vastly larger number of these disaffected youth in Britain, America and elsewhere.

Simply by dint of sheer numbers, adolescents became a serious economic force. With the end of austerity in the 1950s and the beginnings of sustained economic growth, British adolescents had more and more money and exercised more and more influence on the marketplace. Gradually, the creation of youth-oriented activities and products and the consumer-oriented culture that resulted gave such adolescents a new name, from American consumer parlance—the teenager. The working adolescent with ready cash to hand had been a cultural phenomenon in Britain since the 1930s at least, but it was not until the 1950s that they became a consumer category worth appealing to all on their own.[17]

To many British adults, the entire concept of the teenager was insidious. Their children's idols, music, clothes, favorite movie stars, their very dreams were all American.[18] To British teenagers, however, the word "American" was practically a synonym for "exciting" or "new". The automobile and the television set were prime symbols of affluence. American artists dominated the British music charts. Programming on the BBC moved away from pop toward folk music in an effort to balance the scales. Nevertheless, little could stem the tide of teenage interest in American music.

Critically, however, the youth consumer of music and other mass commodities in Britain was very different from his American counterpart. Defined as a marketing concept in the United States, the teenager was aged between 14 and 18, in high school, of either gender, possibly working a part-time job but more likely receiving an allowance from his or her parents to spend on products manufactured and marketed for teenagers. The nature of British society dictated that this would not be the case. Instead, marketers defined the British teenager as a young adult male, aged between 16 and 21, the age at which he was likely to either get married or move out of his parents' house. He was usually out of school and working a job that he more than likely considered boring and dead-end. The products he bought appealed to middle-class adults, who were a part of world that he found alien to his experience. The very idea of a teenager was alien to most adults in the 1950s—they had never been teenagers themselves, or so they thought. They certainly had not had the amount of leisure time that their children had, which was the most critical factor in determining what a teenager was as a consumer concept. Above all, in America, the teenager was middle-class by commercial design: in Britain, he was working-class by cultural association. As a commercial image, a teenager in America was carefree and perhaps bored with his or her life prospects, but not dissatisfied. As a cultural image, a teenager in Britain was frustrated, aggravated with his life prospects, and bored with the adult world.[19]

The late 1950s and early 1960s were an era of steady economic improvement in Britain, as the era of austerity came to an end and postwar affluence settled in. Unemployment was low, and the welfare state worked. The future seemed bright, and young people represented that future directly. Correspondingly, youth became recognized as a social grouping, with the hopes of the nation pinned on their proper nationalistic development—along with fears that the nation would sink in a tidal wave of Americanization.[20]

With the standard of living improving, the composition of the working classes changed dramatically too. The old "dirty" manufacturing industries gave way to less taxing labor: transport services, distribution, and public service industries. While the results were generally better for the individual and his or her family, the standards of working-class culture and unity were fragmenting, and many people—especially young people—felt the loss and wanted to document it in their own lives.[21]

The middle classes were now salaried employees themselves, not just independently self-employed businesspersons and professionals. The Conservatives, traditional protectors of the status quo, were the dominant party in politics, mainly because the status quo was desirable. To some people, the development of a welfare state and an improved standard of living for the working classes seemed like the seeds of moral growth; others saw them as the seeds of cultural disintegration.[22] Either way, the very boundaries of class itself seemed to be breaking down.

Rock and roll music came to symbolize many of these changes in British culture. It reflected this new prosperity as well as cultural fears. The music came from America, but it became identifiably British in that it challenged and supported the pursuit of the classless society, mastered British rhetoric, communication and technology, and had the ear of British adolescents at the center of all these changes.

The Advent of Rock and Roll, 1956-1963

Rock and roll virtually created a concept of community among British youth that as yet did not exist in the postwar era. Huge swathes of American commercial culture catered to the youth market. Even if rock and roll's cultural significance grew into the 1960s, in 1950s America, with so many cultural outlets for teenagers, the music was just another commodity along with movies, literature, drive-ins and television that accommodated their amusement and desire to have fun. In Britain, where the dominant culture was not youth-oriented and where many of their parents damned mass culture as a corrupting influence, teenagers found rock and roll a positive godsend, a release for pent-up energies and frustrations. It was their collective unconscious, the common thread, the central constituent of youth culture. All teenagers in Britain understood the language of rock and roll and could connect across it whatever their social or cultural circumstances. Adult fears about rock and roll—that it represented the Americanization of British culture, that it provided their children with bad role models, that it introduced them to inferior cultures emanating from blacks and the working classes—meant little to British adolescents. They craved their own representative culture, and with rock and roll music, they got its first widespread manifestation.[23]

It was also important that the concept of community fostered by rock and roll was a marketable commodity. British rock and roll was exportable precisely because of its ability to articulate the languages of youth, and the image of a rebellious working class that youth identified with. Authentic rock and roll in Britain came from working-class boys or Americans; all other rock and rollers exploited the music for the sake of money alone.[24] This construct was exportable, and influential, in a way that British jazz, classical and traditional music never had been, and at a time of economic uncertainty, this was an asset of paramount importance to the British economy, and therefore also the state and its institutions.

Yet at the same time, rock and roll represented a decline in traditional cultural standards to many intellectuals and critics, and those critics were not ready to abandon those standards. Rock and roll was considered the ultimate example of the ephemeral nature of postwar popular culture: a song lasted three minutes on the BBC, a scant two months or so on the *New Musical Express* (*NME*) charts, and then disappeared into the historical ether. Meantime, unscrupulously money-hungry managers and record executives fattened their wallets by exploiting the dreams of working-class adolescents, and cheapened British culture by making such adolescents rich role models for others who would come later.[25] There was some element of truth in all this, but the totality of the construct was most important in lending the music its rebellious image in Britain and fostering its popularity. This larger vision expanded the music's audience, and eventually expanded its scope and influences well beyond even the imagination of the music's American forebears.

Even in the 1950s, it was easily demonstrable that rock and roll was not just a music reflecting working-class values: the appeal of rock and roll spilled easily over class barriers. Yet the association of rock and roll with working-class culture persisted, because of the nature of the nascent youth market in Britain. Both working-class and middle-class adolescents had money. Yet while the middle-class adolescent was usually in school at sixteen and his money came from his parents—like his American counterpart—the working-class adolescent was at work and his money came from his own pocket. Both lived at home by the 1950s, meaning they had no bills. The working-class adolescent, however, was partly a product of the new welfare state; his family had less need of his income than they would have had in the 1930s. The working-class adolescent had a larger, earned income and no restrictions on how to spend it, and thus had a lot more disposable money at hand. If the British entrepreneur expected to sell records, fashions, ideas and attitudes to a young market, his target audience was the working-class male teenagers who made up one-third of the entire British consumer market in the 1950s. The middle-class adolescent would either follow along or, better yet, adopt the allegedly more sophisticated cultural values of his parents.[26] Gradually, the "norms" of youth culture began to grow around these imagined working-class values, or at least those values that were associated with an imagined working-class life—excitement, cultural risk, self-indulgence, quick-wittedness, autonomy and toughness. All of these stereotypes applied equally to youth culture by the end of the 1950s.[27]

The most powerful manifestations of this representation came in the form of subcultures. Groups of working-class teenagers disenchanted with the predominant respectable cultural values were determined to pursue their own norms within a smaller, more manageable social circle. Subcultures were symbolic challenges to a symbolic cultural order; they provided opportunities for young people, as new members of adult society, to challenge that society's norms and try to reshape them in their own image.[28] Most of the subcultures that arose in twentieth century British history focused on leisure and a crude rendering of working-class traditions, often exaggerating them to the point of caricature. During the 1950s and 1960s, subcultures were the number one source for new fashions, musical styles and values for adolescents of every socio-cultural persuasion.[29]

The first of these subcultures were the "Teddy boys", so called for their taste in Edwardian suits as the emblem of their rebellion—a look they ascribed to partly because it looked to them like the dressing style of villains they saw in Hollywood westerns. They wore their hair in a huge greasy pile in a style called a ducktail. Teddy boys were found most often in working-class south London areas like Brixton or Elephant and Castle throughout the 1950s. The most violent minority amongst them were raw and physical, prone to getting drunk and fighting with switchblades, coshes and bicycle chains. Naturally, media attention focused on this minority and was overwhelmingly negative. The British public feared the Teds as representatives of anarchy and violence, and their occasional dance hall riots were front-page news in London tabloids.[30] However, their very notoriety attracted the attention of adolescents from all classes, and if other teenagers could not bring themselves to carry razors and create a climate of moral panic amongst their neighbors, they could at least look the part by buying Edwardian suits and Brylcreem.

The average adolescent could easily sound like a Ted as well by the mid-1950s, by listening to rock and roll. The Teddy boys were around years before rock and roll arrived in Britain, but their instant adoption of the music as a sure irritant to adults lent the music a powerful credibility amongst other young people. It was not long before rock and roll and the Teds went together as elements in a dangerous new hooliganism—dangerous, in part, because rock and roll became the soundtrack to other teenagers' inarticulate protest against adult culture.[31] And of course, it was cheaper, easier and much safer to rebel against one's parents by buying a Jerry Lee Lewis record than it was to wander the streets of south or east London looking like an extra from a Howard Hawks film.

Rock and roll arrived in Britain, not in the music charts, but in the movies. *Blackboard Jungle* (1955) received intense negative publicity in America for its portrayal of Vic Morrow as a juvenile delinquent rebelling against the school system as a symbol of authority. Adults considered such an image of American teenagers to be too vulgar and potentially damaging for teens to see themselves. However, the film was more popular with teens, especially teens in Britain, for featuring the song "Rock Around the Clock" (1955) by Bill Haley and the Comets in the opening credits. Teddy boys and other teenagers flocked to hear the song, and to the horror of many theater owners, boys and girls danced in the aisles, tore up the seats on occasion and screamed at the screen while the song played. After the first week's showings, there were few similar riots in theaters, but the press trumped up the hysteria to reveal the alleged link between rock and roll, Teddy boys and working-class violence.[32] The Gaumont and Rank Organization theatre chains cancelled bookings of the movie. Blackpool's city council banned it altogether, and their example was followed up in Birmingham, Belfast, Bristol, Liverpool, Carlisle, Bradford, Brighton, Wigan and Preston. Coincidentally, September 1956 was the same month that commercial television began in Britain, bringing with it a number of American shows that arrived in the living rooms of comfortable families all over the country. Anti-American fervor over the invasion and corruption of British culture—not to mention British teenagers—thus rose exponentially.[33]

Most vulgar of all was the acknowledged king of American rock and roll, hero of the Teds and millions of other teenagers in Britain, Elvis Presley. Presley barely existed on BBC radio or television, yet his dominant musical personality asserted itself on the pop charts. His first British hits in 1956—"Heartbreak Hotel", "Blue Suede Shoes" and "All Shook Up"—were a shock to the British public, which had little experience with black singing styles. He never toured Britain, yet because his presence was so huge as an innovator, other artists filled the vacuum. American rockabilly artists Gene Vincent and Eddie Cochran became far greater pop stars in Britain than they were at home, largely because they were accessible. If they copied Elvis's image in America, in Britain they were the image to be copied themselves.[34]

Buddy Holly had an even bigger long-range impact on the British teenaged music audience, however. He was a group leader singing entirely original songs, playing a guitar well and singing with great virtuosity. He even produced his own records, determining not just what he played but how it would sound. In short, Holly was talented, undeniably so. He had a hard, fast sound related to country and western, which was relatively new to the British pop charts too. For people on both sides of the Atlantic, Holly demystified the process of songwriting. He wrote songs that he liked to play, and played them well. Holly was also gangly, with black prescription glasses and a trebly, hiccupping vocal sound; his image might be described as that of the hippest nerd in school. If he could make music, anybody could.[35]

Holly's professionalism was a revelation in Britain. A rock and roll star did not have to be a novice musician with a pretty face who could swivel his hips. Good musicians like Holly not only liked rock and roll, they played it, and brilliantly. They could bring a standard of "quality" to the music that British music critics had previously dismissed as impossible. In other words, it was possible to be respectably professional and still play rock and roll. With Haley and Holly, the cultural values of rock and roll extended beyond their working-class or American boundaries.

Skiffle

In 1956 and 1957, British musicians struggled with the new music, so popular with the youth audience. One musician who found a successful accommodation was Lonnie Donegan. Donegan was a guitarist and banjo player in the Chris Barber Jazz Band, a trad jazz outfit. The Barber band recorded an LP at the Royal Festival Hall in 1955, *New Orleans Joys*, but they did not have enough material to fill out the record. Barber thus allowed Donegan to add two songs he liked from the American folk blues tradition, covers of jugband blues songs by the American folk singer Leadbelly. Donegan outfitted Barber with a stand-up bass, the band's singer played a washboard, and Donegan himself played guitar. Together, they played a pure version of African-American folk music Donegan called "skiffle", an American term. One of these songs, "Rock Island Line", became a hit in late 1956, remaining in the *New Musical Express* singles charts for six months. The song even reached the top ten in America. Donegan followed up with several more hits and thus kicked off the "skiffle craze" in Britain in the late fifties.

The movement derived from American sources, but skiffle was nonetheless music discovered by a British musician, and not merely copied from the American pop charts. For the first time, a British musician had established a comparatively original popular sound. Young audiences responded to the new fad enthusiastically. Skiffle was easy music to learn and play for the average boy who might never have picked up an instrument in his life. Thousands of teenagers bought acoustic guitars and began to learn a few rudimentary chords. In a nation known for its "cult of the amateur", skiffle was tailor-made to appeal to a wide audience. For many adolescents of all social and cultural origins, it became the first reason why they learned to play music. Donegan himself had an open, jovial music-hall personality that sold his music well. He sang with a wild, reedy voice, and shook on stage in a manner not unlike that of Elvis himself playing guitar in front of a microphone. He admitted that his career based itself around three chords, which was the entire point of his popularity. Anyone could play skiffle, and anyone could be Lonnie Donegan. Coffeehouses and folk clubs in London filled with teenagers playing skiffle on stage or dancing in the audience.[36]

Skiffle also opened up new vistas in popular music unexplored previously outside the folk music movement. Donegan's version of skiffle was acceptable to the English Folk Dance and Song Society because it was "authentic"—it was indigenous African-American music, not watered down by Donegan to be popular, but played just as many English folk purists believed it should sound. This was not a minor issue. American blues artists like Big Bill Broonzy, Lonnie Johnson, and Sonny Terry and Brownie McGhee had been to Britain in the late forties, publicized as folk blues acts playing acoustic guitars. Donegan also played acoustic guitar, and he sang with verve and color, if not necessarily with precision, evincing his amateurish passion for the music. Skiffle was acceptable to the most nationalistic repository for popular music in the country, the EFDSS, because it stuck closely to its American folk origins.[37] As a first cousin of skiffle, rock and roll had made an intellectual breach in the critical mainstream of British culture.

A few other groups became popular as skiffle bands—the Chas McDevitt Group, Johnny Duncan, and the Vipers, a folk favorite. The rise of these bands produced a British folk revival. Skiffle clubs opened up in coffeehouses throughout Soho in London, including the Ballad and Blues Club, the Breadbasket, the Gyre and Gimble, the Nucleus and the 2 I's Coffee Bar. The BBC Light Programme on radio launched *Saturday Skiffle Club* with a weekly audience of two and a half million. The Independent Television program *The 6.5 Special* was named after a skiffle hit by Bob Cort, and it featured a national skiffle contest to determine the best skiffle band in Britain.[38] Such exposure was critical in getting British boys to pick up guitars and try their hands at the new music. Rock and roll could not get the same exposure on the BBC; it did not have the blessing of a respectable musical institution like the EFDSS.[39]

Skiffle's popularity waned in the late fifties. Every skiffle song sounded like every other, and a pudgy, flat-faced, middle-aged shuffler like Lonnie Donegan had virtually no sex appeal next to the explosiveness of Elvis Presley. Even the EFDSS turned on Donegan, deciding that anyone playing folk music for money was clearly a "sell-out" himself. The skiffle clubs became "folk and skiffle" clubs, and then simply folk clubs. The BBC's *Saturday Skiffle Club* became *Saturday Club*, a pop show for teenagers.[40] Still, skiffle helped show how rock and roll might become a legitimate British musical form, played by British musicians in British clubs with British values behind their music. As they learned to play guitar, British teenage boys began to learn about the blues origins of both skiffle and rock and roll, and they also learned to measure music according to its "authenticity", the way the folk music movement did. If British musicians did not come up with a popular form of music in their own country, they could at least provide the professional standards by which other music could be measured.

The Elvis Imitators

Elvis was the obvious sterling model for any singer interested in rock and roll. The most obvious response to Elvis was simply to try to copy him, and dozens of teenage boys were trotted out before the music-buying public. A select few became successful long-term music acts. However, the competition they offered to Elvis was tepid at best. The goal of British musical culture since the turn of the century had been to establish music as a representative medium of respectable, nationalistic norms. Rock and roll had to fit into this model. British record companies wanted to make the music palatable not just to British teenagers, but to their parents as well.[41]

The first of the Elvis imitators was Tommy Steele, a nineteen-year-old who was marketed as "Britain's answer to Elvis Presley". His first hit on the pop charts was "Rock with the Cavemen" in November 1956. Steele was actually Thomas Hicks, a semi-professional singer who had been in the navy, and had thus been to America. He had heard rock and roll and bought records before most of his contemporaries. His manager was an impresario named Larry Parnes, who decided to play up Hicks's origins in Bermondsey, a grubby docklands suburb of London. Parnes saw that the music's appeal to teenagers lay in the danger it represented to the cultural establishment. Elvis was dangerous in America (and Britain, for that matter) because he sang like a black man and appealed to white girls and boys. Tommy Steele, it was determined, would be dangerous because he was working-class and would appeal to the children of middle-class parents. Parnes determined that Steele's authenticity amongst British teenagers would come from his class origins.

After six months of chart successes, however, Parnes redirected Steele's career into the more respectable show business circuit. Britain had never had a rock and roll star before; Parnes regarded Steele as the same sort of talent as those that used to emerge from the music hall: working-class and upwardly mobile. Rock and roll was just a little more raw and weird than its earlier counterpart, and it catered to a teenage audience that entrepreneurs like Parnes did not really understand. Steele's hits all had a certain novelty appeal (titles included "Rock with the Cavemen" and "Doomsday Rock") that made them more broadly appealing to an older audience. To Parnes, a booking for Steele at the Café de Paris nightclub was a triumph for rock and roll—it was moving up and out of the teenage coffeehouses. To those selfsame teenagers, Steele lost his teenaged appeal quickly, and by 1958, he played pantomimes and began a career as an actor in West End musicals.[42]

His handlers, meanwhile, continued with the formula, since they were satisfied with the outcome. Parnes, and a host of entrepreneurs like him, decided that Britain needed more than one answer to Elvis. It required little effort to find the requisite singers: Tommy Steele was allegedly discovered at the 2 I's Coffee Bar, and thus dozens of good-looking young men packed Soho looking for a chance to be discovered in the same way.[43] They were given stage names that ran the gamut of qualities that adolescent girls would look for in a boy—Billy Fury, Adam Faith, Johnny Gentle, Marty Wilde, Dickie Pride, Vince Eager.[44] They represented adolescent rebellion in the music but their public images adhered to norms set by people like Parnes in the music establishment. No teen idol would ever display the sort of raw sexuality Elvis Presley exuded when he danced, nor would any ever sing with the abandon Elvis had in a song like "Hound Dog" (1956).

The most popular of these early teen idols was a teenager from a class-marginal family in Hertfordshire. Cliff Richard was born Harry Webb in Lucknow, India, in 1940, where his father was a civil servant. When independence came in 1947, his father and mother moved to England, where neither of them had ever lived before. Having no established roots or a job in waiting, they went from being typically privileged members of the British *raj* to being virtually penniless in England. Thus, young Harry was a perfect candidate to be Britain's first major rock and roll—and cross-class—musical star. His parents were born and raised as members of the highest caste in India, yet Harry himself experienced much of the working-class poverty of England in the austerity of the early fifties as well.[45]

The newly christened Cliff Richard bore a passing resemblance to Elvis Presley and had distinct talent as a vocalist. His first hit was a raw song called "Move It" (1958) that was the B-side to a more traditional pop ballad called "Schoolboy Crush". Jack Good, the producer of the ITV pop music show *Oh Boy!*, heard "Move It" and invited Richard and his band to play on his show in 1958. He wrote a column on them in *Disc* magazine, playing up Cliff's authenticity by describing his family's socioeconomic circumstances. The appearance on *Oh Boy!* and the press attention accorded to Richard prompted "Move It" to become a hit in September 1958, reaching number two in the *NME* charts in a month.[46] By 1959, Richard and a brilliant professional backing group, the Shadows, were touring all over Britain, bringing a little bit of Elvis into people's lives—but only a little.

Cliff Richard's aspirations ultimately were no different from those of his peers. Cliff liked Elvis as a model, but he also liked Bing Crosby and Johnnie Ray. His career soon shifted into a more mainstream direction to accommodate an older music audience. He branched out into ballads, and he made movies as well. A slow ballad from one of these movies, called "Living Doll", became a major summer hit in 1959, and brought Richard into the adult entertainment world of television, movies and theater less than a year after he had broken on the national charts. He was booked to a six month run at the London Palladium in 1960. The Shadows themselves began to record their own instrumental hits, such as "Apache", which also went to number one in Britain in 1961. By 1962, Richard's career had thoroughly shifted gears toward more middle-of-the-road ballads that appealed to a much more refined audience.[47]

That did not mean that he abandoned his teenage audience; Cliff Richard had a mission. He saw himself as a role model for younger teenagers, and presented himself as such to the public. He did not smoke or drink (at least in public), he cherished his parents, and even sold a scarlet colored Thunderbird he had bought in 1962 for fear it would make him seem out of touch.

[Being a music and film star] brings duties along with it. Although strictly I'm not a teenager anymore [he was twenty-two in 1963], I don't feel a division between myself and the kids. I feel it's up to me to set an example. What sort of example? Well, not getting into scandalous affairs, starting little trends in dressing smartly, general behaviour, you know—I suppose you could call it living decently, a moral code. . . .What I work hardest at, apart from the job itself, is being agreeable.[48]

Cliff Richard fit every mold asked of him, offended no one and pushed for adult respectability like any other pop singer of his day. Once, when asked why he had given up his earlier rock and roll days to sing ballads like "Living Doll", he responded, "Well, I wanted a career . . .".[49]

By 1960, the pop music charts in Britain were an indicator of how the record companies, the broadcasting industry and the British audience diverged, and how they coalesced. The charts had traditional light pop music (Perry Como, Ken Dodd, Frankie Vaughan). There was light rock and roll directed at a young teenage audience, largely female (Cliff Richard); some skiffle and the occasional novelty item (Lonnie Donegan) that represented music hall traditions and the occasional folk item (Donegan again, the Spinners, the Kingston Trio). American and British acts vied for the top of the charts, but rock and roll in general was a properly respectable, even nationalistic endeavor. When Elvis Presley's single "One Broken Heart for Sale" (1963) failed to reach the top spot in British singles charts, and Cliff Richard's "Summer Holiday" did make the top spot, music critics hailed the news with relief.[50]

All was not lost for rock and roll in Britain, but it did not have much of a British flavor to it at all by the early sixties. Elvis dominated the British pop charts with a sure-handedness that frustrated and baffled the British music establishment. Other American acts landed chart hits as well—some became even greater successes in Britain than at home. Buddy Holly and the Crickets, Eddie Cochran, Gene Vincent and the Blue Caps, Bill Haley and the Comets, Chuck Berry and Little Richard all had twice as many hits in Britain as they did in America itself. British adolescents were especially attracted to African-American artists; they were the most calculated to irritate the imperialistic and racist sensibilities of the average British parent. And the traffic across the Atlantic was still mostly one way. Cliff Richard and all his brethren had a hard time cracking the *Billboard* Hot 100 music charts in the United States Richard switched labels almost as often as he released singles in the United States, and none of them seemed able to make him a star. It was clearly not due to any sort of prejudice on the part of the American consumer toward homegrown product. Trad jazz artists and bands from the British boom of the 1950s proved very successful both critically and financially on American tours, and in 1961, a British instrumental band, the Tornadoes, went to number one in the United States with their hit song "Telstar". The inability to at least counter Elvis's impact by exporting British stars—essentially, an effort to redress a musical balance of trade—became an obsession in the British music industry by the early sixties.[51]

The moment was soon to arrive. A real new wave in British rock and roll came from local music scenes. By 1962 and 1963, new groups in London and the provinces were so numerous that they amounted to a virtual underground movement. Amateur bands played pubs, dance halls and clubs for enthusiastic audiences. Television and radio ignored local bands, but they were beloved by teenagers in cities around Britain. Critically, since most of these bands had only a limited access to American rock and roll records and singles, they ended up incorporating music hall songs, folk music and jazzy pop into their repertoires. In the early 1960s, British rock and roll built a new identity for itself in front of audiences of teenagers hungry for music that the established music industry would not provide them.

Even more, a new audience grew, mainly in London—prosperously upper middle-class, older, intellectually oriented, and headed into professional jobs. The blues, folk music and rhythm and blues were popular at universities, art colleges and with sixth-form students. American acts like Bob Dylan and Muddy Waters appealed to them. Many of these enthusiasts soon found themselves members of rock and roll acts themselves. Rock and roll had always crossed class boundaries in Britain, but by 1962, the process included not just the appeal of the music but also the makeup of the musicians who made it.[52] In the next two years, from 1963 through 1964, these bands would rise meteorically into the nation's consciousness and change the nature of rock and roll in Britain altogether.

Chapter 2
The Beatles

The years 1963-1966 were the original golden age of British rock and roll, a golden age ushered in by the Beatles. The Beatles started a revolution in the pop music industry that made rock and roll the music of choice for billions around the globe, and made Britain the most watched musical and cultural center on earth. They did this by establishing themselves as talented songwriters and as the most powerful champions of a new assertion of a working-class consciousness in British culture. By being working-class in image, writing their own songs, ignoring the larger adult audience in favor of appealing to youth alone, and expressing their opinions on society, the Beatles created the rudiments of a lasting image of the rock and roll musician—in pursuing these ideas, they became an idea themselves. They thus created a standard for a new version of rock and roll authenticity, that elusive quality that determined what made a musical act "the real thing" or "not the real thing".[1]

Many of the new rock and roll musicians who followed the Beatles onto the pop charts in 1963 and 1964 were from the provinces, and they created a cultural and geographic bridge into London as the center of British culture. Many of these musicians came from the northern industrial cities, and like the Beatles, the British public associated them as members of the working classes. Adults at first perceived them as an amusing if untalented pleasure, or as a mildly disconcerting annoyance. They were also classless in outlook if not in origins, so they were at least representative of positive social change, if not cultural change.[2] Above all, though, by the time they had established their worldwide popularity, all British rock and roll musicians, as representatives of youth culture, were expected to be like the Beatles. Their image was patented as the image of rock and roll authenticity in British culture throughout the 1960s.

Liverpool

Between 1963 and 1966, the English north served the same function in midwifing the new rock and roll scene in Britain as the American South had served in the United States.[3] Liverpool, the home of the Beatles, was a port city in the throes of economic decline, its once-thriving docks rotting away, its people increasingly radicalized by the ravages of the end of the industrial era. As the Communist *Daily Worker* put it in December 1963, "The Liverpool Sound is the sound of crumbling houses and thirty thousand people on the dole."[4] A wealthy shipping-oriented past had given way to a dismally poor present, and Liverpool was as archetypal as any northern industrial city of the depression of the old industrial economy.

Liverpool had always been one of the centers of working-class culture in Britain. By the 1960s, the city was already famous for its football team and fans, its entertainers, and its radical left-wing politics. It had always been outward looking, since it was long the major industrial seaport in Britain. It had a thriving ethnic community of varying influences: Irish, Scottish, Welsh, as well as people of African and Indian descent. Everyone faced tough lives, and Liverpudlians had a reputation for chronicling their lives with a unique, very accessible sense of humor. Many people also learned a hobby like music to pass their time while on the dole. Liverpool thus became the grimy backdrop for the careers of a number of famous entertainers.[5] The lack of employment was even a boon to the music scene; as a member of one band opined, "It is a good thing, the fact that [I'm] on the dole, as far as I can spend all day practicing whereas, if I had a normal job, I wouldn't be able to do that at all."[6]

When the Beatles reached the singles charts in 1963 with "Love Me Do" and "Please Please Me", Liverpool was already reasserting itself as a center of British working-class culture. The television hit *Z-Cars* featured true stories from the files of the Lancashire Police Force. It showed a Liverpool that was central to the eventual appeal of the Beatles: one where "crime and adolescent terror incubate in the kind of atmosphere of immorality one associates with Dickensian England."[7] To see four post-adolescents emerge from the same atmosphere, seemingly in control of the same primal urges of the frustrated working-class male that *Z-Cars* displayed week after week, made it easier to understand the Beatles' appeal. George Harrison summarized Liverpool's cultural energy for a *Daily Mail* reporter: "It's exciting trying to keep alive."[8]

Liverpool was far removed from London's cultural dictates. In early 1963, the music industry in London focused on the development of teenaged heartthrob solo singers who would pursue respectable careers; groups were considered out of fashion and unmarketable. With no corporate direction of the rock and roll scene in Liverpool, groups flourished there. The city had more than 300 clubs catering to rock and roll acts, with about ten clubs being the premier venues in the city, booking 150 local bands on a regular basis. Most of the bands covered American rock and roll hits, especially Motown songs as produced on their British subsidiary, Tamla. The local disc jockey and compere at the Cavern Club, Bob Wooler, also had a large record collection that bands mined extensively for new material. It was from these sources that "the Liverpool sound" was created. Some of the groups—the Beatles most prominently—also wrote music on their own. The publication of a local rock and roll magazine, *Mersey Beat*, brought these bands together under one banner, as it linked the Liverpool fans with their favorite bands.[9] Liverpool, in the words of one writer, was Britain's answer to Nashville, and it produced "a Scouse sound that [even] the Americans couldn't copy back."[10]

The Beatles' manager was Brian Epstein, a novice at the management of music groups who saw the appeal of the Beatles right away. It was at Epstein's suggestion that the Beatles started wearing suits, smoking a higher-class brand of cigarettes, swearing less and acting more professionally on stage. The standards of post-Victorian British culture demanded the maintenance of show business propriety—politeness, tidy dress, musical accessibility without pandering to the lowest common denominator—if a musical group was to succeed nationally. Such changes were critical to the band's success, and to the success of numerous bands around Liverpool, in establishing a standard of respectability for their music.[11] Bill Harry, the editor of *Mersey Beat*, explained:

> When we started *Mersey Beat* two years ago, the Beatles . . . had long haircuts and rather an untidy form of dress. All over Merseyside the groups were wearing jeans on stage, were very sloppy, long haircuts. Worst of all, they were actually swearing on stage. So we wrote some editorials—"Get your hair cut. Don't smoke on stage, stop swearing." And we found that the groups did take notice: smart suits on stage, a more professional outlook, and rock and roll became more of a major industry than just a hobby.[12]

However, the truly remarkable thing about the Beatles, the other Liverpool groups and Epstein's management of their image was how much of their working-class Liverpool personality was NOT purged. Brian Epstein recognized the potential for freshness in their accents, humor and music, and the devil-may-care attitude they brought to a British music scene that was boring. On radio and television, the BBC accent dominated the airwaves; after 1963, the Beatles and other northern bands made having a northern accent fashionable. The Beatles were also exceptional in how little they cared about maintaining conventional social dictates while keeping a high profile. As one journalist described it, they were like "four cats looking at a king".[13] They broke many of the social conventions of polite, public society—smoking, drinking and occasionally even swearing in public, going on holiday (and presumably, sleeping in the same hotel room bed) with their girlfriends, gently mocking their social betters. The Beatles were different because they were still recognizably working-class, and they broke social conventions to assert the fact.[14]

Still, the connection the Beatles made between working-class values and those of youth was implicit rather than explicit. The Beatles never flaunted their class status, like a weapon; they used it as a tool. Their authenticity early on arose from their status as an unconventional music group playing unconventional music. They were a bunch of working-class Liverpool lads, cleaned up just enough to meet public standards of respectability, yet much of their popularity came from their good-natured mockery of those standards. They made music that was mainly American in origin, yet they dared to make that music entirely their own by writing, performing and sounding different from their sources. This became a professional ideal, one based upon their musical talents and their merits as sunny, positive, adventurous artistic personalities. Their authenticity helped them remake the image of British rock and roll. The standards were not accepted immediately—in fact, most British critics in 1963 thought they possessed neither talent nor merit. But by 1966, when they had become smash hits in America, remade British rock and roll and become representatives of British youth, their authenticity and their professionalism became one and the same. The Beatles defined professionalism in rock and roll, and the values they adhered to became the values of British youth culture itself.

Beatlemania

Before all else, however, the Beatles were transformed from being simply a pop group into being a cultural phenomenon as a result of "Beatlemania", the explosion of emotion released by their audiences wherever they appeared. There were millions of teenagers in both Britain and the United States who wanted to exercise their spending power on music they liked, and Beatlemania proved just how great their economic power was. For teenaged girls, the Beatles were one of their first major forays into the open expression of their sexual desires and fantasies, as well as their buying power.[15] Thus, rock and roll in the mid-sixties became a step towards their involvement in the women's movement and the sexual revolution.

Beatlemania really began in earnest in October 1963, when a "riot" was staged for cameras after the Beatles had played the television show *Sunday Night at the London Palladium*. Such rioting was useful in selling newspapers. The publicity soon made the Beatles objects of adoration for their female fans. The audience's shrieking was usually too loud to hear songs at concerts, and the hysteria carried itself into screaming at movies. Audiences even threw jellybeans at George Harrison when a report on the band mentioned he liked them.

The Beatles were dehumanized, their music meaningless in comparison to their image.[16] Harrison addressed the issue politely in an interview.

> Now if you're surrounded by a band of screaming girls who rave over you, you adapt yourself to the situation. You do not think that there is anything sexual about this. They are not lusting after you as some people seem to think. . . . The fact is they rave because they are excited by our kind of music.[17]

The Beatles represented a new role for adolescent girls in British society, but few could define what that role was or how it seemed to have gotten so far out of the control of parents and their cultural expectations so quickly. That did not keep any number of commentators from trying. One psychiatrist attempted to explain Beatlemania in November 1963.

> We admire [the Beatles'] freshness and innocence so much that it's almost like giving birth. Older generations look at them in wonder, thinking "This is what we have given birth to: how marvelous they should have gone so far so soon." With the younger fans, the girls, the adoration is mostly the old story of mass hysteria at a given time. A lot of the feeling among the girls is phoney. But it would not have taken on the magnitude it has if there had not been the need to release sexual urges. . . .
>
> There's no getting away from it—a revolution is taking place under our noses. It amounts to sexual freedom with a sense of responsibility and honesty. The fans recognise the honesty that shines from the Beatles. While other pop stars have thought in artificial terms of reaching out to their audience, the Beatles are giving honestly as well as receiving.[18]

Another doctor claimed that girls were repressed, and that, when performers encouraged them to release the tensions in their lives, they screamed. It was not a matter of sex or appreciation, but simply relaxation. A psychologist disagreed, claiming that screaming by young girls WAS sexual, and a healthy outlet at that. Another psychologist noted that it was teenaged boys who screamed for bands in Eastern Europe, and that release of tension was clearly the most important issue. The American sociologist David Riesman, author of *The Lonely Crowd* (1950), claimed that the Beatles merely represented rebellion against the adult world. And on the debate raged.[19]

Regardless of the reasons for Beatlemania, it marked the distinction between what made the Beatles an extremely popular and original rock and roll act and what made them a major cultural phenomenon never before experienced. The intensity of the audience's reaction to the band, and the pounds that girls and boys spent in acquiring Beatles records and other products, clearly demanded some sort of cultural attention. The response to Beatlemania from critics, journalists, politicians, religious leaders and parents in general was predominantly negative at first. Whatever the Beatles and Beatlemania were about, it surely seemed to represent a serious challenge to the cultural status quo and the continued maintenance of traditional standards of music and conduct in the postwar era.

Most commentators in 1963 and into 1964 saw the Beatles as symptomatic of a decline in the artistry of popular music that rock and roll had ushered in with Elvis Presley in the 1950s. The Beatles were one more example of the contrary, amateurish nature of rock and roll and the Americanized rubbish culture that it represented. The notion that four working-class Liverpudlians should become a national obsession therefore baffled one musical authority after another. Matthew Arnold's dire prediction of cultural philistinism seemed to be realized in the explosion of Beatlemania. Standards for popular culture had surely reached a new low in 1963.

The tabloid newspapers that brought Beatlemania to the public were impressed by the phenomenon, but not intimidated. The first time the Beatles appeared as the subject of an article in a national paper was when John Lennon drunkenly belted a partygoer at a birthday party for Paul McCartney in June 1963, as reported in the *Daily Mirror*. But it was not long before it became obvious that coverage of the Beatles sold newspapers.[20] The newspapers' music critics and editorial columnists, however, did not share in the euphoria of Beatlemania. Most of them found the Beatles at best amusing and at worst nauseating. Most critics thought the Beatles were musical no-talents who had simply turned up the noise level in rock and roll: four silly-looking working-class yobboes who got to live the dream of pop stardom for a while. Anytime now, it would surely come to an end, when they would go back to Liverpool and their workaday lives with a nice nest egg and some great memories.

No newspaper devoted more coverage to the Beatles than the *Daily Mirror*; no newspaper sold as many copies at the time, and the Beatles were a key to maintaining that circulation.[21] Yet its music reporter, Donald Zec, did not warm to their music. In an effort to distinguish between his enjoyment of them as people and his disgust with the music, he called the Beatles

> four frenzied Little Lord Fauntleroys who are making £5000 every week . . . with stone-age hair styles, Chelsea boots, three electric guitars and one set of drums, who know their amps and ohms if not their Beethoven. . . . They are pleasing to look at, friendly of manner, and . . . they are in fact as nice a group of well-mannered music makers as you'd find perforating the ear-drums anywhere.[22]

Zec was apparently surprised to find himself forced to answer a series of angry letters from Beatles fans in a future issue of the paper. "All I wish to say is that it's tough enough having to listen to [the Beatles]—don't tell me I have to love 'em as well."[23] Others felt no qualms in dismissing them altogether, such as Fergus Cashin in the *Daily Sketch*: "But let's face the real truth about Beatlemania—the awful truth. They sound awful—just old rock and roll with the volume turned up."[24] Even supporters of the band in the press felt it necessary to deny that the Beatles were anything close to good musicians or songwriters. *Melody Maker* jazz columnist Bob Dawbarn spent three days on tour with the Beatles in Britain and then wrote an article defending why he liked them by damning their music with faint praise—"The Beatles, I am sure, would be the last to claim that there is anything culturally or aesthetically important in what they do. Nobody needs to compare them to J. S. Bach or the Modern Jazz Quartet."[25]

Even Parliament could get caught up in the phenomenon. Conservative MP Henry Price of West Lewisham believed the Beatles had to be stopped: "[Beatlemania] has a hypnotic effect on [teenagers]. Their eyes become glazed, their mouths gape, their hands wobble loosely and their legs wobble just as loosely at the knees. . . . We've got to beat the beat of the Beatles." Prime Minister Sir Alec Douglas-Home threatened Canada that he would send the Beatles there unless the Canadians bought more British goods.[26] The Beatles took it all in stride. They stated they did not care if people said they were not any good—"because we're not."[27] Apparently, everyone agreed by early 1964 that popular music was not a serious artistic endeavor.

The adult public as a whole were not entirely infatuated with the Beatles either, especially since their cultural impact went well beyond their music. The Beatles' French haircuts became a teenaged fad, and provoked a number of controversies in schools and workplaces. One grammar school went on strike when the headmaster forbade any of the students to wear the new haircut—"It brings out the worst in boys, and makes them look very unintelligent".[28] Swindon's mayor denied another student an award he had won for his mathematics proficiency because the student refused to cut his hair. A sixteen-year-old was suspended from his job as an apprentice in a factory when he refused to cut his hair too.[29]

The Beatles were also a disruption from the serious business of maintaining work and school schedules. A textile shop came close to striking when the foreman shut off the radio playing over the company's loudspeaker. The Beatles' "She Loves You" had come on the radio and the working girls yelped with delight, which the foreman considered a major distraction to work.[30] One school dressed up four boys as Beatles to mime to their records, and 300 girls screamed as if it were the real thing. The headmistress, exclaiming "I don't like the Beatles", cancelled the rest of the show and the Christmas party at which the boys were supposed to play. "And I'm not sorry."[31]

The attacks on the Beatles delineated a fear for the future of British culture in the face of Americanization. The Beatles were another alternative challenge to traditional post-Victorian cultural standards, but unlike other such challenges, their anti-Victorian values seemed in part to be what made them popular. Tommy Steele's class status mattered because it showcased his humble origins in relation to his rise to popularity—a rise predicated on his meeting the traditional cultural expectations of a popular entertainer. The Beatles clearly did not intend

to ever meet those expectations. Instead, it appeared that they were simply reset-
ting them, changing the principles by which cultural vibrancy would be measured in the future—not exactly a surprising turn of events by 1963 and 1964, but
hardly an acceptable one for the majority of the adult audience for music in Britain. In fact, the Beatles threatened even to render the tastes of that adult audience as an irrelevancy. Young people and musicians were clearly enamored of
the values the Beatles represented. The Beatles were unconsciously in the process of establishing a new ideal as to how a popular musician should operate, an
ideal that their critics did not share, at first.

The Conquest of America

However, critics' opinions began to change as they took notice of the Beatles'
impact when they reached America in February 1964. To their amazement—and
to the amazement of the Beatles themselves—Beatlemania turned out to be exportable. The band was a sensation in the land that had given birth to rock and
roll. Slowly, over the course of 1964, music critics in the press began to reassess
their talent as musicians and songwriters. At first, they were lauded as good ambassadors for Britain; then they were recognized for their commercial successes
in America and around the world. But finally, more commentators became convinced that the band's commercial success had to mean that the Beatles must
have a certain mastery of their art. If they could take an American music back
across the Atlantic and have the United States in an uproar, they must be better
musicians than people thought. Anyone counting the incoming dollars could see
that—and a lot of people were counting them in 1964.

Even more, a certain national pride accompanied the reversal of fortunes on
the American and British music charts, as displayed in newspapers and music
journals. The Beatles' record sales helped redress the balance of payments, at a
time when a shortfall in incoming pounds was a nationally-publicized issue.
They had reversed the cultural tide of Americanization—sort of; at least they
were not American. They were proof of the affluence and apparently growing
classlessness of British society; succeeding in the United States, alleged to be
the original classless society, seemed to reinforce the idea. Therefore, they were
the obvious ideal of what a rock and roll musician ought to be. Nothing allowed
the Beatles to establish themselves as the standard for rock and roll professionalism in Britain like their success in America.

Even before the Beatles reached America, their impact on the British music
scene was measured against that of American rock and roll artists. At the end of
November 1963, eight of the top ten singles in Britain were by British bands,
fourteen of the top twenty, and twenty of the top thirty.[32] British artists' renewed
control of their pop music market was inspiring to music journalists. The Beatles
and Cliff Richard topped the *New Musical Express*'s International Popularity

Poll in 1963, a moment marked by *NME*'s news editor, Chris Hutchins, as "reflect[ing] the change in favor from American to British artists and product."[33] Over the course of 1963, not a single American artist reached the top of the pop charts in Britain, an event which *NME* writer Derek Johnson said called for "us [to] frantically wave the Union Jack, for this has been the most incredibly successful year ever in the history of modern pop music for our own British artists."[34] By March 1964, all of the top ten singles in the British music papers were the product of British artists, and British artists produced 77 percent of the top-selling singles in Britain.[35]

So British pounds spent on popular music were being spent at home. But the Beatles accomplished much more. British artists had cracked the *Billboard* music charts in America on rare occasions, but for the most part, the musical traffic had flowed only one way across the Atlantic. In 1963, the year of British Beatlemania, not a single song from a British band even made the American top forty. The arrival of the Beatles changed all that. With their first tour in February 1964, the Beatles took an estimated $2 million home from the United States. Their songs filled the *Billboard* charts by April. Suddenly everything British was popular in America, and thus throughout the world due to American influence. So the Beatles brought home money from abroad, too. Their success likewise opened the door for hundreds of other British artists to cross the Atlantic and dominate the American music scene.[36] The British economy had suddenly acquired for itself an overseas arm from a source—rock and roll music, an American cultural invention and cultural invader—that no one in the country could have predicted a year earlier.

The Beatles' commercial success in America was quickly noted at home in the press. They sold out every single show they booked in the United States on their February 1964 tour before they had ever played a single note, an unprecedented feat at the time.[37] It was a testament to their talent as musicians and songwriters, since the American public had not seen them yet, and their singles had only been on the charts for two months. Clearly, people wanted to see the band play because of the music they made, not because of their looks or some indefinable desire for cathartic release. Beatlemania was one thing, but artistic talent within the boundaries of this crude music was another consideration altogether that made the press take notice.

At first, what the critics noticed was the Beatles' demeanor as Beatlemania spread across the Atlantic. Once on tour, the Beatles remained polite and witty, just as at home, and proved excellent ambassadors. The group thus earned the respect, if not admiration, of cultural pundits back in London. Fergus Cashin of the *Daily Sketch*, a Beatle-basher previously, was one of them.

> Whatever one may personally think about this particular rash of beyond the fringe lunacy, one cannot help but admire the instinctive good manners and the natural wit of these four young surprised ambassadors of Britain. They have remained cheerfully sane in front of the distorted mirror of insanity. They have

kept their heads while all about them crowds were losing theirs and blaming it
on them. In the crazy wax of Pop [music] they have put this country on top
without letting any of us down.

People really like them, and even the serious critics of world affairs cannot help
but admire their refreshing candour and feel duty bound to comment in American opinion columns on the gentle, politely dignified behaviour of these happy
young amateur diplomats from Liverpool.

I salute The Beatles. They are a wonderful example to youth.[38]

Eventually, though, the need grew to define just where this commercial and
cultural success derived from. Over the course of 1964, debate began in the
press as to just how the Beatles could not only make it in America, but sustain
that success for such a long time in the ephemeral pop culture market. With
hindsight, the reasons seem more obvious today. As musicians, they had trained
in tough bars in Liverpool and Hamburg, so their sound was tight and they believed that they could handle any song professionally, whether they had written
it or not. The tightness they developed as a band drove them to be energetic as
songwriters to match that tightness. As songwriters, since they could not read
music, they had no preconceptions as to what "the next chord/note" ought to
be—instead, they were inclined to simply try what they liked and see if the audience liked it as well. Their success in Britain and America leant them confidence in their songwriting too, such that they could afford to disdain the tech-
nical mastery prized by earlier musicians in favor of spontaneity and creativity,
and know by their phenomenal record sales that they prized the right qualities.
The fact that there were three different songwriters in the band—rarely did Lennon and McCartney actually contribute equally to a song's development—with
very different styles meant that they had a wealth of material to choose from to
showcase the best of their abilities.[39]

At the time, though, what made the Beatles so spectacularly popular seemed
more of a mystery, even to their most ardent fans—let alone their nastiest critics.
And by no means was criticism of the Beatles finished. If anything, those people
determined to damn them as a cultural abomination became more vehement, if
fewer in number. Just days after their first appearance in the United States on
The Ed Sullivan Show, Nat Hentoff, a reviewer for *New Musical Express,* wrote,
"Musically, this reviewer cannot understand either the fervour of the Beatles'
admirers or the scorn of their detractors. Except for their visual uniqueness, the
Beatles are a run of the mill rock and roll attraction."[40] Others identified themselves as lonely heroes of a once-vibrant culture now under fire from the stupidi-
ty and hedonism of the modern Americanized world. They felt themselves cou-
rageous for making the point that the four Liverpudlian emperors of pop had no
clothes beneath their tailored suits and outlandish haircuts. One newspaper letter
writer made the effort to be as florid and cutting as possible, as if he could
shame the masses into buying Vaughn Williams recordings.

The fact that I regard the Beatles-and-all-that as a passing incident . . . is of no consequence. I am apparently the only person on these islands who thinks like this and thus I am in a minority of one against 52,000,000. . . .

The fact that their furry twanging is as unskilled as a quartet of chimps tarring a back fence means nothing. . . . The fact that their raucous clumsiness has to be electrically boosted until our eardrums are bursting and that a cut at the power station could reduce them to their correct adenoidal proportions mean nothing.

Although I have lost some of my capacity for surprise in this world of wonderment I am still astonished that such a lack of skill can go so far in the world of popular music. . . .

The verbal content of what these striplings are bawling is one long amorous yowl preferably with a mention of a good blubber, because of some sex contest that has gone awry. . . . Listening to this glutinous slush is like being forced to eat warm putty encased in pink sugar icing.[41]

The *Daily Mail*'s television commentator, Monica Furlong, perhaps went the farthest in her attack on the cross-Atlantic cultural nonsense the Beatles represented. She likewise could not fathom their appeal, and addressed the issue in her regular column after she watched a television interview of the Beatles.

The singing of these boys is pleasant enough, and little more. They are not charming, not handsome . . . they are not witty as Englishmen or (more accurately) Irishmen have understood the term. . . . I would rather have listened to Wilde or Shaw or Chesterton or Sydney Smith talk for ten minutes, than have an hour in the company of these four monumental bores.[42]

Furlong's complaint prompted a deluge of responses in the *Daily Mail*'s letters column in favor of her opinions by five to one, and prompted her to break out of her role as television critic to address the decline of British culture in general. Furlong vented her disgust at the sort of society that could produce an act like the Beatles and be duped into liking them. She wrote a second article a month later detailing what she considered the "seven deadly virtues" which would get one labeled a hopeless square, out of touch with modern life. The virtues were efficiency, hard work, sincerity, modesty, the stiff upper lip, purity and thrift.[43] The stiff upper lip must have come in handy often.

Such complaints were mostly lost on the British record-buying public. Before the Beatles, British rock and roll had been a pallid imitation of its American forerunner. The glamour of youth rebellion went missing, there was very little excitement, and above all, no authenticity. British rock and roll acts simply aped their American models, in most people's opinions, and very badly at that.

Now, with the success of the Beatles in America itself, ambivalence crept into discussions of their import. It was not hard to define differences between the Beatles and their predecessors in both Britain and America. The Beatles were a self-contained act, capable of writing and performing all of their own music. They had an odd sense of humor, they expressed their opinions on current events, however flippantly, they were fashion trendsetters and they seemed to care not a whit for the explosion of attention they elicited from people.[44] Most of all, they had suddenly made it "cool" around the world to be British, and to buy British products, especially records. Adults and intellectuals usually liked them as personalities, perhaps liked their sense of humor and even sometimes liked their music. Nevertheless, such popularity demanded that the Beatles' popularity be justified somehow, that they had to be more than just a pop band, not just to give them respectability but also to maintain that respectability for the critics who assessed their impact on British culture.

Cultural commentators singled out John Lennon in particular as an intellectual worthy, especially as they identified him early on as the "leader" of the group. His book of doodles and nonsensical verses, called *In His Own Write* (1964), was hailed by the *Times Literary Supplement* as being "remarkable; they are a world away from the trite sentiments and underdeveloped language of the Lennon-McCartney songs (heaven knows what the fans are going to make of them)". The book was compared to the work of Joyce, Lewis Carroll and James Thurber, with a dash of Spike Milligan thrown in for good measure. Lennon was asked to be the guest of honor at a Foyle's Literary Luncheon celebrating Shakespeare's 400th birthday; the luncheon sold out immediately. Lennon and the rest of the Beatles had dinner with the master of Brasenose College, Oxford, were praised by Prince Philip, and were bickered about by politicians desperate to harness and use their popularity.[45]

Music critics also acknowledged that the Lennon-McCartney songwriting team was probably as financially successful as any of the century, on either side of the Atlantic. The Beatles were, according to one journalist, "contemporary" and "kn[e]w instinctively the emotional needs of the record buyer."[46] Their talent as songwriters reflected a level of professionalism unmatched by other rock and roll songwriters. Author and literary critic Francis Wyndham noted that "John Lennon and Paul McCartney may be remembered as a song-writing team long after Beatlemania has died down; [but] it is only when their numbers are sung by other (not necessarily superior) performers that their excellence <u>as songs</u> can be appreciated."[47] By 1966, Lennon and McCartney were the most sought-after songwriters in popular music history. Even traditional, non-rock and roll performers clamored to sing Beatles songs. A BBC Light Programme bank holiday special, *The Lennon-McCartney Songbook*, had covers of Beatles songs done by Pat Boone, Frank and Nancy Sinatra, Keely Smith, Ella Fitzgerald, Andy Williams, Peter Sellers, Lena Horne and numerous other adult-oriented entertainers.[48] A number of their songs even sounded like older, traditional pop music, a music they seemed to respect. Popular ballads like "A Taste of Honey" and "Till There Was You" showed up on their first album, and such songs as "All My Loving", "If I Fell" and "Your Mother Should Know" sounded to the untrained ear like music hall songs. Almost all of them sold in the millions. As songwriters, then, the Beatles played a role as middlemen between the old conforming music establishment and a rebellious youth culture.[49]

Intellectuals all over Britain re-evaluated Beatlemania. Many were happy that the sunny images of the Beatles presented a welcome alternative to the messy and uncooperative Oxbridge students who had peopled the Campaign for Nuclear Disarmament, and who were beginning to protest British foreign and domestic policy with an irritating abandon. For once, it seemed, British youth culture had a positive alternative to the destruction of societal norms, one that established new norms with which people could be comfortable. Charles Hamblett and Jane Deverson addressed the Beatles' images in their study of the rise of British youth culture, *Generation X* (1964).

> The general settling down which followed the initial, and healthily brief, frenzies of Beatlemania, has left British youth more free than ever before in recent history to develop a mystique which is not a carbon copy of whatever trends happen to have caught on across the Atlantic.

> Clearly it is in the nature of youth to latch onto a current fad from which to develop its own attitudes, but the Liverpool explosion has widened up the possibilities of increased social tolerance in Britain and given a fresh impetus and glamour to the larger provincial scene. A progressive provincialism is essential to the balanced development of a country, and even at the pop level there is a need for group identification. In fact, the pop culture as fostered by TV and the mass circulation periodicals is helping to unify Britain in a sensationally successful manner and is one of the chief reasons for authoritarian and pro-establishmentarian hostility. The Beatles are knocking the stuffing—and the stuffiness—out of the neo-Victorians.[50]

Members of the British Empire

Politicians now leapt on the bandwagon, eager to enlist the Beatles in their drive to power. Alec Douglas-Home mocked the Beatles' music in December 1963; just months later, Conservatives tried to assert that the Beatles were Tory sorts of people. Dame Barbara Brooke, wife of the Home Secretary in the Home government and a vice-chairman of the Conservative Party, spoke to female constituents in Southgate.

> I welcome [the Beatles]. Not just because they have become a substantial invisible export making a useful contribution to the balance of payments. But also because I believe that they are a healthy sign of constructive activity by young people for young people themselves. Not sitting waiting for other people to do for them, but getting about and doing on their own.[51]

William Deedes, minister without portfolio in the Home Government, commented on the work that went into becoming a pop musician and how it represented positive values for the young.

> The beat groups are not thumbing their noses at society—they are not rebels. The Beatles and their rivals are not cynically striving to shock by being second-rate. Their aim is the first-class of its kind. Failure to attain it is spotted and criticised ruthlessly by their many highly discriminating critics. To be tops in the beat business demands work, skill, sweat. There is no place for the lazy, the incompetent, the slipshod.

> For those with eyes to see it, something important and heartening is happening here. . . . The young are devising their own media to express a standard free of divisions of class or creed.[52]

The Labour administration of Harold Wilson went even further after assuming office in October 1964. Wilson had called for an increase in exports, and the Beatles had successfully met that challenge. The British music industry boomed, and British pop music dominated the world's music charts. Under these circumstances, the Queen and the government should take notice. Thus, the editorial staff at *Melody Maker* launched a campaign in 1965 to get the Beatles awarded Memberships in the British Empire. A few newspapers joined the call, such as the *Daily Express*. Wilson, who cultivated an image of youth and modernity, agreed. The Beatles thus received MBEs in June 1965, for their services to the British economy and for their behavior as ambassadors of British culture.

Here, a cultural line was drawn, however. Many people were angered at what they saw as the cheapening of the MBE. Previous award recipients, many of them soldiers, very publicly returned their MBEs to the crown, prompting John Lennon to note that the Beatles could be proud they did not have to kill anyone to receive their awards.[53] As if testing his cultural status a year later, Lennon described his opinions of Christianity in the *Evening Standard*. It was not the first time the press had solicited his opinions—he was often referred to as having a certain "bite". But these were certainly the most controversial views he had expressed.

> Christianity will go. It will vanish and shrink. . . . We're more popular than Jesus now; I don't know which will go first—rock and roll or Christianity. Jesus was all right but his disciples were thick and ordinary. It's them twisting it all that ruins it for me.[54]

The remarks prompted a bitter attack on Lennon from the religious community in America, and Lennon offered a shaken apology before their 1966 United States tour. But there was little if any reaction in Britain itself—the Beatles WERE more popular than Christianity. Even in the United States, despite a call for the burning of their records and the banning of their music on the radio, not a single American rock and roll radio station pursued the ban. When the Beatles showed up in Memphis, Tennessee, a local religious revival was scheduled specifically to draw young people away from their concert appearance—yet the Beatles outdrew the revival in attendance by a ratio of eight to five, even though the revival was free.[55] More popular than Jesus, indeed.

The Beatles' investiture with MBEs and the impact of Lennon's comments on Christianity marked the end of Beatlemania in Britain.[56] The Beatles were now the established image of the rock and roll musician as a cultural figure and as an artist, to the point that politicians, cultural commentators and the press accepted them as such. That status had even been projected abroad and allowed them to easily weather a storm of moral protest in the United States. To be a Beatle was to be in the vanguard of youth culture and its direction. Other rock and roll acts had to follow the Beatles' lead, on pain of being found inauthentic.

Rock and Roll in the Provinces

Once the Beatles became a hit in 1963, the London-based record companies began scouting northern England extensively for new talent. Previously, it was impossible as a provincial pop music act to obtain a record contract without making the lifestyle gamble of moving to London, working the lilt out of one's accent and finding an agent. Now, every artist and repertoire man in the music business scoured cities for his own version of the Beatles to bring back to London untouched by the mark of Denmark Street professionalism. If Decca, Phillips and Pye were going to compete with EMI on the charts and in the massive profit margins EMI had made off the Beatles, they would have to track down new talent more quickly than before.[57]

Agents, managers and record company representatives mined Liverpool for any band that they could find, often regardless of talent. Even international companies got in on the effort to sign Liverpudlian bands, and bands from all over the northeast moved to Liverpool in hopes of being discovered. Few if any music industry types took the time to understand what made the Beatles and the Liverpool scene popular. They still had little idea why the Beatles had rock and roll talent, or what professional standards they had established for what made rock and roll authentic. To the music industry, Liverpool was a source of working-class scruffs looking to make it big in a primitive and talentless genre, and an audience existed for that genre.[58]

Gerry and the Pacemakers, the Searchers and Cilla Black were some of the Liverpool acts that benefited from this frenzied search. None of them, however, had the long-lasting impact of the Beatles, since none of them was interested or able to meet the standards the Beatles had established for the performance, packaging and sale of rock and roll music. Gerry and the Pacemakers was a vehicle for Gerry Marsden, a dynamic lead singer whose aspirations leaned toward the very same style of pop jazz family entertainment that had been the musical norm before the Beatles. Their hits were traditional Denmark Street pop songs or show tunes, and they only lasted on the charts for a year.[59] The Searchers were one of the first acts to mine American and British folk music for inspiration. Their third single, "Needles and Pins" (1964), became a hit with its jangly folk guitar sound, reaching number one in the U.K. and the top ten in the United States. But their record company, Pye, wanted three albums in nine months, a ridiculous demand that meant that the Searchers never developed enough good material to meet commercial dictates. They dropped from the charts by 1965.[60]

Cilla Black was the hatcheck girl at Liverpool's Cavern Club during its lunchtime sessions, where the Beatles and other Liverpool bands played frequently. She sang occasionally with the different bands that came through the Cavern, and so caught the eye of Brian Epstein. He lavished almost as much attention on Black as he did on the Beatles, but he clearly groomed her to have a cross-generational appeal that would make Black—not to mention Epstein himself—seem more respectable in the entertainment business. The commercial and social dictates of the day would not allow her to sing straight rock and roll songs—". . . they all thought I was some sort of ballad singer and not a real rocker like [the other Liverpool musicians]."[61] However, Epstein allowed her to make a virtue of her working-class background, and the tabloid newspapers loved her for it. She was the polar opposite of the glamorous London image— people who wanted her to change her accent for show business were "snobs". Even when she made it big, her parents refused to move from working-class Scotland Road in Everton, a pride of place in their community that Cilla herself obviously shared. All of these facts meant her music career lasted much longer than that of the other Liverpool acts that arrived after the Beatles. Even when her songs stopped reaching the charts in 1966, she made movies, starred in pantomime and hosted her own variety series on BBC-TV starting in January 1968.[62] She continues to make television appearances regularly today.

Manchester was the next major city mined for its bands by the London music companies. Two major singles acts of the sixties came from there, the Hollies and Herman's Hermits. The city's music scene was much smaller than Liverpool's; it did not have an alternative music press to publicize events, nor did it have an entrepreneur like Brian Epstein to tie a number of the bands together under a business venture. But Manchester did have a local songwriter named Graham Gouldman who wrote a number of hits for Manchester bands, and he helped give both groups a lasting local identity on the national scene.[63] However, their lack of songwriting talent and their focus on making hit singles to satisfy the commercial market meant that the Manchester bands had little cultural impact. They were not innovators; they were interested in making money like any number of older music professionals. Of course the Beatles had no less of a desire to make money, but their imaginative songwriting was precisely how the cultural impact of pop music had been established in the first place. So the Hollies and Herman's Hermits were not the focus of any of the intense devotion accorded to the Beatles in Britain.

Nevertheless, these acts proved that the old professional standards for making music could still work in Britain, with the occasional new twist. Working-class pride was still enough to build an audience off of, just as it had been back in the days of the music hall, but now, that audience recognized such sentiments as being respectable. The Beatles had made new rules for rock and roll—bands needed to write their own songs and play them, and they needed to present their class status as an appealing aspect of their images. As yet, though no distinct line existed between the concept of "popular music" and "rock and roll", so there was no determination—yet—that an act that crossed those boundaries risked losing their entire audience, only their popularity as a rock and roll act.

Other cities also developed their own music scenes in the sixties, the most prominent being Birmingham. The group scene lacked the cohesion of either Liverpool or Manchester, where bands had been playing the same circuit of clubs for three or four years before being discovered by London's music industry. But Birmingham later produced two very strong acts in late 1964 and 1965, the Moody Blues and the Spencer Davis Group. Later in the sixties, the local music scene became more organized, and the Move became a major national hit in 1967.[64] However, by then the initial shock of having bands coming out of the provinces with their accents and fresh sounds was long over, and their class status was no longer of primary interest.

When unable to find a new hive of talent outside London, music industry advertisers and journalists occasionally invented "city sounds" themselves, to make it seem as if a band was the next Beatles. The Dave Clark Five had a distinctive, powerful drum sound—Dave Clark himself was a drummer—and the release of their first single in 1963, "Glad All Over", marked the beginning of the "Tottenham sound". The band was a major success on the American charts, but at home, it had few hits after 1964. Similar efforts were made with the Zombies, one of the most imaginative of the new pop acts and the supposed vanguard of the "St. Albans sound". The Zombies were particularly popular in the press for being the band with members who had turned down going to university in order to make it big in the pop music world. They managed only two major hits in Britain and America, both classics—"She's Not There" (1964) and "Time of the Season" (1968), both written by keyboard player Rod Argent. Before they became a seriously popular act, however, they broke up. A third such manufactured music scene was the "Andover sound" of the Troggs, a fun band that was supposed to represent "the sound of straw bales and manure", rough-hewn and primitive. They produced several mid-sixties hits in Britain, the most famous being "Wild Thing" (1966).[65]

Other acts with higher social origins found success in America, but were failures on the British charts. As British critics attuned themselves to the Beatles' success, the upper classes were seen as an illegitimate source of rock and roll talent. One such example was Peter and Gordon, two boys from Westminster School in London, as pedigreed as pedigreed could be. They were discovered singing the Everly Brothers and folk songs at London's exclusive Pickwick Club—no coffee bars for this duo. Their clipped, crisp accents went unnoticed in America, but in Britain they were call for ridicule in the press. Maureen Cleave of the *Evening Standard* joked about their American success: "They were thought to have a bit of class. The Americans could see a direct line of succession through Drake, Marlborough, Wellington, and Churchill down to Peter and Gordon."[66] Their reliance on Lennon/McCartney compositions for hits also got them in trouble in Britain; they were clearly not an authentic act if they lived off the Beatles for hits. A similar duo, Chad and Jeremy, scored a grand total of one U.K. hit, but a spate of their singles made the *Billboard* charts in the United States all the way into 1966. They inaugurated—and terminated—the "Oxford Sound": Jeremy Clyde was an old Etonian, and a grandson of the Duke of Wellington. Chad and Jeremy essentially abandoned Britain as a market, but their careers finally went into decline in the United States when they tried to appeal to the ultra-serious American folk music audience. Their one attempt at an American college circuit tour was a disaster.[67]

By 1965, bands like Peter and Gordon, Chad and Jeremy, Herman's Hermits and the Dave Clark Five represented a new kind of British pop group—ignored or vilified at home, but exceedingly popular in America.[68] Nothing could be better for the export industry and the balance of payments deficit, but it marked a growing change in musical values in Britain too. Like those acts that crossed boundaries with traditional Denmark Street pop music, none of these acts met the professional standards set by the Beatles for rock and roll either. They seemed oriented less toward artistry than profit, and in the case of the two duos, they were from the wrong class background. These standards changed as the Beatles' career progressed—by 1965, it was no longer expected that an act like Herman's Hermits could sing non-rock and roll pop standards and still be considered a rock and roll act. Thus, those acts that could not meet the new standards failed on the British charts. Some of these artists became successful in America, but music writers in the press took that as proof that anything could be sold in the United States—and proof that the British audience's confidence in its own tastes had matched that of its models.

The Beatles' domination of the British pop charts was challenged in 1964. Even as five of their singles topped the American *Billboard* sales charts in April, their only record in the *NME* charts was the extended-play single "All My Loving", which was falling off the charts at number twenty-six. They were still a phenomenally popular band; in the next week, "Can't Buy Me Love" entered *NME*'s charts at #1. Yet, as some fans and journalists noted, their success had made them remote; their very popularity as international stars had removed them from the audience that had promoted their popularity. Even more, they were no longer symbolic of teenaged revolt by 1964. Other acts that seemed more dangerous had entered the British charts—the Rolling Stones, for example, clearly enjoyed sticking their loutish behavior in the faces of the British public. This made the Beatles more palatable to adults—and thus changed their image with the rock and roll audience they themselves had created. By 1965, one and a half years after their original rise to stardom and still a guaranteed chart success, the Beatles were only the third leading hit-producing band in Britain, behind the Rolling Stones and Australia's Seekers. Other bands had competed with their musical talents and, more importantly, represented new sections of the music-buying public.[69]

None of this lessened the impact that they would continue to have on popular music in Britain and around the world, best likened to that of an earthquake. The Beatles had massive commercial and artistic successes ahead of them in the sixties. Their popularity never truly waned at any point in their careers; instead it expanded as their musical ambitions expanded, well beyond the boundaries of their original youth audience. In large part that was because the Beatles virtually redefined what it meant to be British. Their music swept the globe and ushered in an unprecedented era in which British culture, for the first time since the industrial era began, was considered the most exciting culture on earth. They created a text of social distinctions in their music, their attitudes and their image that defined first what a rock and roll musician was, to a lesser extent what a working-class person was, and finally what it meant to be young in the 1960s. British young people experimented with music, art, politics, sexual morality, fashion and the like, and the rest of the Western world watched, absorbed the changes and contributed to the process.[70] And bought millions of Beatles records too.

The Beatles blazed every path traveled by British bands in the 1960s. They broke down class barriers at every turn. Authenticity was the very essence of their craft, and being seen as working-class was central to their authenticity.[71] They established the ideal that future rock and roll acts would have to aspire to, and build upon, and their social impact on British culture had only just started. They became the very embodiment of rock and roll itself, an American music. If the Beatles performed something, whether it derived from medieval minstrel songs, Indian music, or baroque and classical styles, it was rock and roll.[72] And they were thus the cultural phenomenon of their age.

Chapter 3
London

The rise of Beatlemania and the numerous beat groups from Liverpool, Manchester and Birmingham had given teenagers a vague sense of their own cultural and economic power, and it had made the provinces culturally interesting. But London was the traditional focus of British culture, and it was not long before popular music returned to its center. The phenomenon of "swinging London", as defined in an April 1966 article in the American magazine *Time*, was impossible to imagine without its soundtrack, at first supplied by the Beatles, then a whole series of new bands from London itself.

"Swinging London" was, as most legends are, a term targeting only a small percentage of the happenings in Britain's capital in the 1960s. As a characterization, though, what mattered most was that it gave a name to a social revolution that brought a number of previously marginalized social groups to the center of London culture—especially young musicians. The revolution lay mostly in how they perceived class and other social distinctions, though fashion and the new relaxation of strictures in terms of sex were also critical to the image, especially in districts like Soho and Chelsea. The Beatles themselves moved to London in 1964, and though new bands and musicians challenged their hegemony as youth icons, the Beatles remained the maypole around which the currents of British pop culture and pop music danced all throughout the 1960s. Their arrival on the music scene already represented an opportunity to change the direction of British culture, an exciting opportunity for numerous people in the art and music worlds.[1] Their move to London was symbolic in that it placed them at the traditional center of popular culture.

The Beatles had created new professional standards to which other British rock and roll musicians had to adhere. The press identified them as a group, versus being individual singers like Cliff Richard; they wrote their own material; and the public perceived them as being from working-class backgrounds. But those standards did not last for long. London was a more sophisticated place than the provinces, wealthier, more ambitious and with sharply defined social and cultural divisions. The musicians who grew up in London and the surrounding suburbs lived in this atmosphere, and they reworked the Beatles' professional standards to suit their own cultural values. The Rolling Stones, the Who, the Yardbirds, the Kinks and many other bands who arose in London in 1964 and 1965 changed British rock and roll utterly, and as a collective, at least as much as the Beatles themselves. One thing remained the same with all of them, though. The London musicians might or might not be of working-class origins, but for the purposes of establishing their authenticity—not to mention their marketing value—they promoted a stance in opposition to the hegemony of middle-class adult notions of respectability, and even flaunted it.[2]

British teenagers affirmed those values by buying their records, in Britain itself and around the planet. The London bands, like the Beatles, became a serious cultural phenomenon because they mastered many different markets beyond record industry singles. They spread fashion, style and attitudinal changes, whether by the obvious act of wearing clothing and accessories or simply by talking to the press and critiquing British society, especially its consumptive practices. They thus became London's greatest trendsetters, and the social acceptance of rock and roll musicians at the center of London's cultural elite built a fresh new image for British culture around the world.

Rhythm and Blues

The rise of rhythm and blues groups in London was actually contemporary with that in Liverpool, beginning with the formation of bands in 1960 or 1961. But due to the record industry's initial zeal for signing bands in the provinces, the London bands signed with labels a little later. Plus, the Beatles also had to establish the principle of a band as a marketable success before the London acts could capitalize on it. Thus, the R&B bands rode the coattails of the Beatles and other acts into the British musical consciousness.

This music scene, however, would sweep all others before it. Like their counterparts in Liverpool, London musicians knew each other in an insular but inclusive club world. Indeed, the musicians in London were a fraternity far more incestuous and underground than that in Liverpool. They switched bands often and considered themselves a separate musical community from that of the commercially based pop charts. They inhabited a city full of art schools, coffee bars and jazz clubs, especially in Soho. There were little musical *salons* like this all over Britain—John Lennon himself had gone to the Liverpool Art College, sneered at jazz and played at a local club organized at a nearby pub called Ye Cracke.[3] There were, however, a lot more of them in London, by dint of sheer size, and they thus provided a bigger pool of talent to draw from, and a larger audience to play for. The London R&B groups contained much better musicians than any other city's bands.[4] Most of the musicians and the people who came to see them were slightly older than adolescent and attuned to an affluent culture if they weren't affluent themselves. Most of them were also of university age and educated at a higher level than secondary modern, and so had been exposed to art, literature, fashion, and the ideas behind them.

The rhythm and blues scene in London, then, mostly resembled the older folk music movement of the English Folk Dance and Song Society. This was hardly a surprise—it actually got started under the respectable auspices of the folk movement. British fans interested in folk music noticed the derivation of American folk music and the blues from older sources around the British Isles.[5] However, as usual, folk patrons felt the need to define just what the "authentic" American blues were, just as they had long debated over what was "authentic" British folk music. Similarly, there was little understanding of what the blues was really about as an American folk music. As late as 1969, a columnist wrote in *English Dance and Song*, the EFDSS' journal: "To sing the Blues the negro had to feel unhappy about something, usually bad luck, poverty, loneliness or an unfortunate love affair."[6] No one questioned her interpretation in subsequent issues. As had always been the case, Britain's folk music audience simply did not accept any folk music as received: they demanded instead that it conform to their own standards of authenticity.

To the British folk audience, the blues was the acoustic music of poor blacks from the Mississippi valley, not the electric blues of American cities like Chicago whose musicians and groups filled the R&B charts in America in the 1950s. This could create some rather irritating situations for American blues artists who toured the UK. For example, Muddy Waters toured Britain under the auspices of the EFDSS, and audiences actually booed him for playing electric guitars. To accommodate them, on his next tour of Britain in the mid-sixties, he came with only his acoustic guitar, prepared to cater to his audience's discerning tastes. However, by then, with the rise of R&B-based pop groups like the Rolling Stones and the Yardbirds, British audiences were well-used to the idea of electric blues acts like the Chicago bands. Thus, to his consternation, Waters was actually booed again for showing up on stage without an electric band! To his eternal credit, he showed up a third time in the 1960s, not with a machine gun, but with his electric band, forgetting his obnoxious audiences the first two times, and was a monstrous hit.[7]

Nevertheless, British folk acts played old blues songs on stage and jazz artists considered the blues a source for the development of British jazz. Throughout the 1950s the acoustic blues and its electric cousin, rhythm and blues, remained much more closely associated in Britain with the respectable image of folk music and jazz than it was with less respectable rock and roll.[8]

In 1955, the first rhythm and blues club opened in Soho, the Barrelhouse and Blues Club located in the Roundhouse Pub on the corner of Wardour and Brewer Streets. To the surprise of the proprietors, Cyril Davies and Alexis Korner, a hardcore of blues fanatics kept the club going for a long time. At first, they only accepted acoustic blues as authentic, but when Muddy Waters arrived with his electric band from Chicago, the club converted to electric rhythm and blues in homage to Korner and Davies's American idols. Korner and Davies formed a band, Blues Incorporated, which became a spawning ground for talent all over the London area. Any musicians in London who wanted to play rhythm and blues would sit in with Blues Incorporated and learn the electric blues. Among the enthusiasts who joined Blues Incorporated on stage were Mick Jagger, Brian Jones, Charlie Watts, and Keith Richards.[9] In May 1962, Blues Incorporated became the new house band at London's top jazz outlet, the Marquee Club in Soho. The comparative prosperity of the rhythm and blues audience resulted in a huge spate of clubs like that of Korner and Davies that sprouted up all over London soon after, at Eel Pie Island in Twickenham, the Flamingo in Soho, the ABC Club in Ealing and the Crawdaddy Club in Richmond.[10] Like the Cavern Club in Liverpool, they provided a meeting point for young people around London to share their interest in music that, for the moment, the record companies and the BBC ignored.

The bands that played the clubs absorbed the folk club atmosphere and attitudes prevalent with people like Korner and Davies. The Beatles and other bands from the northern industrial cities were more pop-oriented. Many of the provincial musicians were from dirt-poor working-class families, and music was a way to make a good living. Even the Beatles made music for people to buy, music that an audience would enjoy. The London bands were generally from more prosperous working-class or middle-class backgrounds. They were interested in rhythm and blues for its aesthetic pleasures, for its ability to convey meaning in their own lives even if they were not poor black men from Mississippi, Louisiana or Chicago. Virtually no London R&B musician would consider playing the pop standards and show tunes that the Beatles and the Liverpool acts played on stage—the very idea would be derided mercilessly. To be a musician on the London R&B scene meant being a purist concerned with authenticity, like the members of the EFDSS: audience be damned.

The band that Jagger, Richards, Watts and Jones formed, the Rolling Stones, became the most popular of the London acts playing rhythm and blues. Their first shows were at the Marquee when Blues Incorporated took gigs out of central London, but they did not last long there: the Marquee was a jazz club, and too many purists believed the Stones were a rock and roll act. The manager of the Marquee, Bill Carey, actually laid down guidelines for what constituted the difference between rhythm and blues and rock and roll. The proper London R&B musician had to have a knowledge of jazz, his band had to employ certain instruments (a harmonica especially), and he had to be familiar not just with American blues music, but with the work of Davies and Korner! It was only after their first few singles had reached the charts that Mick Jagger would admit, "A lot of the stuff that we do, like the Chuck Berry numbers, are not awfully different [from rock and roll]. . . . I mean, there are differences between a rock number and a Muddy Waters number, but they are really not so marked."[11]

Defining Terms and Purposes

As more and more bands after the Stones began to identify themselves as R&B acts, an issue cropped up amongst rhythm and blues enthusiasts: exactly what was rhythm and blues? What determined the difference between rock and roll and rhythm and blues, and where did acts that everyone loved—Chuck Berry, Bo Diddley, Muddy Waters, Howlin' Wolf, Jimmy Reed, Little Richard, Elmore James—fall on the spectrum? How could a band like the Rolling Stones play and record songs as disparate as the smooth Motown pop of Marvin Gaye, the country-swinging rock and roll of Buddy Holly, the more rhythmic rock and roll of Chuck Berry and the electric Chicago blues of Muddy Waters, and call it all R&B? According to Keith Richards, the term arose in 1962 and 1963 because at the time, rock and roll was the music of Fabian, Frankie Avalon, Cliff Richard and Adam Faith, and no self-respecting London R&B act wanted to be associated as such.[12] The usual folk music debate, then, over what was authentic and what was not, applied to the Stones and other acts after them, and for the same reasons—to establish the social exclusivity of the musicians and fans that patronized the music.

In numerous articles and interviews, musicians, reporters, folk enthusiasts, blues purists and their fans came up with definitions of "rhythm and blues". By early 1964, the distinction was obvious: London bands were "R&B bands", whereas provincial bands were "beat" bands. Furthermore, the London acts disdained the commercial intent of the provincial bands; they played "rhythm and blues" because they liked the sound, not to get rich.[13] In 1965, singer Steve Winwood of the Spencer Davis Group—a Birmingham act—tried to coin a term by using the words "Negro pop" to describe the music that the R&B bands made, a term alternately inclusive and exclusive at the same time. "Negro pop" seemed to be anything that he thought African-Americans liked in music, a huge territory in which to operate. Yet only a few people in British popular music could claim to know exactly what those tastes were, let alone establish any sort of legitimacy for their claim. Above all, "Negro pop" was not the standard fare on the British pop charts. Essentially, the image of the African-American and his music was a totem. In America, the African-American was oppressed and expressed his frustrations in music; in London, English youth used the same music to express their own alleged class and generational oppression by the dominant adult culture.[14] Only a select few musicians were capable of playing music with a similar "Negro" feel to that of African-Americans, a feel that no other pop music of the day in Britain could match.

However they defined terms, critics in general mocked bands like the Stones for their pretensions as a real "rhythm and blues" act. The notion that a bunch of white middle-class English post-adolescents had anything whatsoever in common with black American blues artists seemed ridiculous to many critics and folk music connoisseurs. Most expected a backlash from American rhythm and blues groups once they arrived to tour Britain. British R&B bands were by definition inauthentic. Sooner or later, African-Americans would step up to re-claim their music, and bands like the Stones and the Yardbirds and the Animals would go back to their small clubs in west London. After all, people tended to prefer the real thing to any cheap imitation.[15]

Yet the expected backlash from African-American R&B groups never came. In fact, Muddy Waters himself said that he liked the Stones, when he heard and met them in 1964.[16] Afterward, no one questioned the Stones' authenticity as an R&B act in the music press. But by then, with the Beatles' arrival on the charts and in America, the definition of "rock and roll" itself no longer seemed so closely tied to Frankie Avalon and Cliff Richard. The point was moot; the Beatles had redefined just what rock and roll was, and the Stones met that definition.

The Rolling Stones

Of more importance was the fact that the Rolling Stones were far more than another rhythm and blues act anyway, by that time. Many people took them as a challenge to respectable culture in Britain. The Stones became the second most popular group in British popular music after the Beatles through the sixties. By decade's end, they had achieved an image of rebellion and cultural power that lasted even beyond the Beatles' break-up—even beyond their definition as a "rock and roll" act.

The Stones started out covering old blues and rock and roll standards; their first hits were songs by Buddy Holly, Howlin' Wolf, Willie Dixon and Chuck Berry. They loved rhythm and blues because it expressed the attitude of the out-sider in society. It also dealt with taboo subjects like sex in a frank and discon-certing way to white ears. Mick Jagger was hardly a brilliant singer. But when he sang "I'm a King Bee" and said he'd buzz all over his girl, or wondered where his "Little Red Rooster" had gone, there was little doubt that this skinny, south London twenty-year-old talked about an illicit sex life that proper middle-class English boys were not supposed to have.

The image created for them, then, by the press and by their manager, An-drew Loog Oldham, was of a bunch of oversexed, loutish, immature post-adolescents, grammar school ne'er-do-wells—rebels against middle-class values. Unlike any other band regularly mentioned in the press—the Beatles in particular—the jobs and schools the Stones had abandoned were almost always listed in early articles about them, to outline how far removed they were from the pursuit of respectability. Keith Richards was from an occasionally destitute working-class family, but he was intelligent enough to earn a position as a student at Sidcup Art School in south London. Brian Jones was from a wealthy family in Cheltenham and attended Cheltenham Art College. Mick Jagger's father was a gym instructor with a television program on the BBC; Mick himself was a student at the London School of Economics. Bassist Bill Wyman was from a bricklayer's family, but had gotten a good job at an engineering firm through connections in the Royal Air Force. Charlie Watts, the drummer, was the son of a lorry driver for British rail, but had also gone to art school and had held a lucrative day job in advertising as a graphic artist. Jagger, Wyman and Jones had attended grammar schools.[17] In other words, all of the Stones were either from respectable middle-class families or were upwardly mobile members of the working classes and should have been obsessed with achieving respectability, in the eyes of most British adults.

Instead, the Stones cultivated an image different from that of the Beatles or any of the other provincial bands—they were vulgar, aggressive and arrogant. The image was as invented as the values on which it was based. In nearly every interview they did, the Stones and especially Jagger came across as polite, pleasant and well-mannered, whereas the Beatles and especially Lennon expressed their bile and "bite", showing a willingness in interviews to reveal their caustic side—hence Lennon's observations on the decline of Christianity. Yet it served the Stones and the press well to posit the Stones as anti-Beatles, to play with the same class and youth values that the Beatles had promoted and turn them on their head. Before Lennon's 1966 statement on Christianity, the Beatles' criticism of the cultural establishment seemed gentle, fun-loving, and perhaps even respectful. From their beginnings, on the other hand, the Stones seemed as if they wanted to pillage the establishment from top to bottom.

Their public attitudes, while not entirely put on, were mostly calculated by Andrew Loog Oldham, who had been a nineteen-year-old publicist with Brian Epstein's NEMS Management when he became the Stones' manager in 1963. Oldham positioned the Stones as anti-heroes, an antidote to the Beatles' sunny façade in the press. As a result, the press saw the Stones as threatening where the Beatles were funny, which served them well since the idea of threat was at the heart of their blues-based music. British society's most uncomfortable subjects—sexuality, misogyny, drugs, and especially the boredom of an affluent life—were the focus of the Stones' work. Jagger especially made for a contrary sex symbol, his big lips and scrawny body in contrast with the bravado he gave off in performance and the licentious lyrics he sang on record. As Oldham put it, "Pop music is sex, and you have to hit them in the face with it."[18] At a time when the adult British public was still trying to work out its position on the sexual revolution, the Stones played Robespierre, in command of revolutionary values and waiting for the adults at the guillotine.

The Stones thus became archetypes of the worrying future of British culture. If British teenagers looked and acted like this now, what of the next generation? The excitement the Stones inspired in adolescents was completely lost on their parents. The Beatles were appealing to most British adults because they were appealing to the journalists that followed their careers. They were witty, enjoyable to be around, and by 1964, one might even consider the idea that they were talented. Few adults would complain if their daughters came home on the arm of a (rich) Beatle. The Stones, on the other hand, were well-known for being the target of a *Melody Maker* front-page headline, as orchestrated by Oldham, "WOULD YOU LET YOUR DAUGHTER MARRY A ROLLING STONE?" Since the image sold newspapers just as well as records, the press was prepared to accept the manufactured idea that the Stones were humorless, loutish and angry. Jagger and Richards' lyrics made fun of their generational and social superiors in a fashion that seemed to lack respect, which only amplified the image.[19]

So from the start in late 1963, the tabloid newspapers treated the Stones in the exact opposite way that they treated the Beatles. A Beatles story, or for that matter any story on the provincial bands, was a featured story of any day that it ran, and the tabloids marketed the story in bold letters on the front page. By contrast, the Stones received only the tiniest of column inches and few pictures in 1963, at a time when their club gigs were the talk of London.[20] Once the Stones' records made the pop charts in 1964, most newspapers buried stories about them in their entertainment pages, or placed them at the bottom of the front page, as if unable to ignore them but still hoping they would go away. Only the *Daily Mirror* put them on the front pages regularly, in headlines as large as those of the Beatles—no small fact, as the *Mirror* had the country's highest circulation at the time. Any material on the band's rebelliousness was enough to get into the *Mirror*, no matter how banal. When a hotel restaurant refused to serve Jagger because he was not wearing a tie, the *Daily Mirror* printed the news in inch-high headline letters.[21]

As with the Beatles, the press was first attracted to the Stones as a phenomenon by the reaction of fans at their concerts. The Beatles on stage were funny and attractive—it was easy to see what adolescent girls liked, if not so easy to decide why their reaction was so intense. On the other hand, journalists could not fathom the audience's reaction to the Stones at all. They were ugly and virtually ignored the audience while they played—why would girls scream in the same fashion?

The result was a change in language by the press. When girls screamed and cried, jumped up and down and rushed the stage at a Beatles concert, newspaper articles waxed on "Beatlemania". The same audience reaction was a "riot", "pandemonium", or "violence" at a Stones concert. The fans of the Stones supposedly "rioted" even more often than they did at Beatles concerts, and with more violent results. In 1964 there were 30 arrests in Wembley, violent clashes with police in Manchester and Liverpool, and in New Brighton a girl pulled a switchblade on a policeman who tried to arrest her. Glasgow fans came to Blackpool to see the Stones and nearly pulled the group off the stage in the midst of a melee in the front row. The band's Belfast and Wiltshire concerts ended within minutes of their reaching the stage.[22] Such audience reactions inspired bewilderment in the papers: who could possibly like these people?

Adults, especially in the press, attacked the Stones' physical appearance regularly. They were actually not particularly slovenly; they merely showed up for interviews, concerts and other public appearances in everyday casual clothes. But such clothing did not meet the professional standard established by the Beatles, who wore suits or at least suit jackets nearly everywhere when appearing in public. The result was a deluge of public distaste over the Stones' allegedly dirty appearance. Never had the word "unkempt" been so abused. Considering the stereotypical image of the working classes as dirty and smelly, the Stones' image as being just this side of "the great unwashed" only added to their reputation as rebels.

The Stones' hair was a particular focus. The Beatles' hair was long, "but it's WASHED, it's super clean".[23] The Stones' hair was longer and seemingly not as straight, and so gave the impression—to anyone searching for such an impression—that it was unclean and messy. The difference showed up in press coverage of schools six months after the initial row over the Beatles' long hair. Suddenly, youngsters now wore "Rolling Stones hair styles". Three such boys wore girls' yellow ribbons in their hair at the behest of the headmaster of their school, basically as an exercise in humiliation. A year later, a judge in Glasgow lectured a student brought before him for breaking a window at a Stones concert in the city, telling him, above all, to cut his hair because he and the Stones looked like "complete morons".[24] Mick Jagger defended his hairstyle, claiming, "[A]rt students and college people have had these haircuts for years. They were around when the Beatles were using Brylcreem."[25] He also attacked the notion that he and his bandmates were ugly: "We could name a few uglier people in the business. Yes, quite a few more."[26]

If Jagger intended to explain away his band's loutish appearance, then he was a complete failure. More likely, he and Oldham realized that such explanations only enhanced the Stones' image as a band that simply did not care about respectability, an image calculated to drive parents to distraction and simultaneously capture their children's attention and keep it. An exasperated parent expressed the attitudes of a nation of parents in a letter she mailed to the Stones personally.

The whole lot of you should be given a bath and then all that hair should be cut off. I'm not against pop music when it's performed by a nice clean boy like Cliff Richard, but you are a disgrace. Your filthy appearance is liable to corrupt teenagers all over the country.[27]

Such attacks earned the Stones instant credibility with their youthful fans. As Ray Coleman of *Melody Maker* put it in 1964: "Young fans now realise that their elders groan with horror at the Rolling Stones. So their loyalty is unswerving."[28] Maureen Cleave of the *Evening Standard* placed their appeal in perspective.

> Parents do not like the Rolling Stones. They do not want their sons to grow up like them; they do not want their daughters to marry them.
>
> Never have the middle-class values of neatness, obedience and punctuality been so conspicuously lacking as they are in the Rolling Stones. The Rolling Stones are not the people you build empires with; they are not the people who always remember to wash their hands before lunch. . . .
>
> Parents feel cheated. Just when the Beatles had taught them that pop music was respectable, just when they were beginning to understand, what happens? Their children develop a passion beyond the comprehension of anybody for these five young men. . . .
>
> "The Rolling Stones are not just a group; they are a way of life." This is one of the wilder statements on the sleeve of their record. I don't know about their being a way of life, but sometimes I strongly suspect they're a figment of our imagination.[29]

When the Stones' first tour of the United States was a commercial failure, British newspapers and music journals crowed with delight. In *Melody Maker*, the more conservative of the two major music journals, the failure of American audiences to accept them was worthy of a two-page spread. The article described how Dean Martin mocked the Stones after they performed on his variety show, and the empty stadiums they played to all around the country. There was some reserved sympathy, as the tour's failure was a result of bad promotion. In comparison, though, Cilla Black, already a greatly loved entertainer, also toured America and bombed, and the press ignored it.[30] A month later, it was front page news in the *Daily Express* when the Beatles' "A Hard Day's Night" knocked the Stones' "It's All Over Now" off the top of the pop charts.[31] Perhaps it would not be long before Britain could finally do away with these cretins.

Yet the Stones kept making the sort of news that sells newspapers and journals. Letters poured into *New Musical Express* after the Stones' stint on television's *Juke Box Jury*, where they dismissed virtually every song they heard; many viewers found such behavior offensive. The Stones had problems with the BBC, which temporarily banned them when they missed a recording session for *Top of the Pops* by mistake. Contract problems got them thrown off shows on ITV as well. Fourteen hotels refused to book the Stones in 1966 because of the ruckus they caused on the premises on a regular basis (a problem mainly with unruly fans as opposed to the group itself). Entertainment writers vilified them in 1967 for refusing to uphold music hall traditions on television by going around the revolving stage on *Sunday Night at the London Palladium* and blowing kisses at the audience. They claimed to find it demeaning and stupid. Upon being reproached, Jagger declared he would never play the show again. Brian Jones faced numerous paternity suits over the course of his brief life, a fact played up often in the tabloids.[32]

The Stones' indifference to the storm of public indignation that pursued them built up their image as well. The Beatles were very conscious of protecting their benign public image, as Lennon's public apology for his remarks about Christianity showed even as late as 1966. The Stones, on the other hand, could not care less about offending people—in fact, they calculated to do so, it was their stock in trade. Jagger's occasional brushes with the law, however innocuous, attracted newspaper attention. In Liverpool, he had to answer for a series of traffic violations for speeding that might have resulted in his license being suspended. His solicitor defended his character before the judge, making the statement that both Caesar Augustus and the Duke of Marlborough were known for having long hair and that both of them had fleas, whereas his client did not, despite press reports.[33] In 1965 Wyman, Jagger and Jones were arrested for public indecency in West Ham for urinating on the wall of a petrol station that had refused them use of the bathroom. The expression of public outrage that resulted seemed to roll off them; in fact, Andrew Oldham made certain that the newspapers knew about their arrest before the evening was out.[34]

The Rolling Stones promoted youth values in opposition to an adult world, but they also connected them to working-class stereotypes—of rebellious, lazy, oversexed, rude, unclean, dumb and petulant males—in opposition to the dominant society. To respectable adults of the middle or working classes, the Stones represented an apocalyptic cultural future: to their vast and growing audience, they represented freedom and license.

There was also an element of racial consciousness to their stance. The adult, BBC-educated journalists that wrote for newspapers and music journals resisted jazz, swing and rock and roll in part because they perceived them as having black origins, and stereotypically, African-derived cultures were considered erotic, narcotic and interested in miscegenating with Europeans. With jazz and the blues, at least some British adults could create an artificial distinction between "art" and "dance" music; with rock and roll, no such distinction could yet be conceived.[35]

For these and many other reasons, the Stones worshipped their rhythm and blues idols in the United States. Musicians like Muddy Waters, Howlin' Wolf and Elmore James were African-American, and faced hostility, violence and oppression as a result, a situation they sang about both overtly and obliquely in the Stones' favorite songs. Clearly, there was something in this with which a bunch of white middle-class twenty-somethings could identify. Britain was a racist society too, debatably more relaxed than the United States but clearly able to distinguish cultural differences between black and white. English culture found blacks outlandish. The Stones could not be black, but they could be out-landish, which was the next best thing.

The archetypal Rolling Stone was Mick Jagger. With his huge lips and petu-lant attitude, he conveyed an image of sexual charisma, capitalist success and excess, revolt and masculinity—or more accurately, anti-femininity, since he was considered unmasculine even by his supporters. He even lived out of wed-lock with singer Marianne Faithfull. To British parents he seemed the embodi-ment of Britain's cultural decline. As Maureen Cleave put it, "When middle-aged, middle-class persons said this country was going to the dogs, they had in mind Mick Jagger."[36] His relatively comfortable background and his high level of education made him far more dangerous than any other representative of the revolt of youth, since he had given up the expected route of a middle-class male to a respectable adulthood in order to become the nation's bugbear.

The record industry acknowledged the power of Jagger's image by trying to capitalize on it. However, the notion of producing the usual carbon copies of a star as nauseating to adult tastes as Mick Jagger was anathema to the average music executive. Instead, they produced new stars, both male and female, that challenged his image. Many people considered Jagger lecherous, sickly, effemi-nate and untalented, so the record companies countered with pop singers who were wholesome, obviously talented with strong voices, and representative of traditional masculine and feminine stereotypes. Tom Jones and Engelbert Hum-perdinck were two of these new singers, both of them known for their macho images. They sang pop and country songs whose lyrics reflected a standard mo-rality, and they appealed to a disaffected older audience.[37] Meanwhile, new fe-male pop singers represented the image of the sort of woman who would seem-ingly never scream at a Rolling Stones concert. Lulu, Sandie Shaw and Dusty Springfield each appealed to a different section of the British listening audience, all of them wholesome and feminine and all of them acceptable to an adult pub-lic.[38]

Nevertheless, the opposing stereotype only made the new standard all that more appealing. The Rolling Stones and Mick Jagger recaptured the original notion of rock and roll as rebellion, and they made it chic and marketable too.

Dylan and Social Protest

Added to this mix in 1965 was the arrival in pop music of the only American musician with an influence as great as that of the Beatles on both sides of the Atlantic, Bob Dylan. Dylan had long had a reputation in Britain as a great folk artist—with everyone except the British folk community. In 1963 he toured the country, to the disdain of a number of British folk artists because of his great popularity in America. The dean of folk song collectors, A. L. Lloyd, referred to

Dylan as a "cabaret artist". A letter writer to *Melody Maker* complained: "Folk was written to last, for people to enjoy for centuries, not to be another 5-minute pop wonder."[39] Ewan MacColl, the country's best-known folk singer, said Dylan was an "anti-artist".[40] Ian Campbell, another mainstay on the British folk music circuit, said Dylan's "Blowin' in the Wind" (1963) was not folk music, and wrote an article for *Melody Maker* arrogantly entitled "Pop and Folk—and How to Tell the Difference".[41]

In May 1965, Dylan returned for a tour of Britain, a tour recorded in the D. A. Pennebaker documentary *Don't Look Back* (1967). Soon after, he went electric, releasing the brilliant single "Like a Rolling Stone" (1965), which became a huge hit in Britain. If the British folk movement was disgusted, however, rock and roll musicians were mesmerized by the possibilities Dylan's topical lyrics and jangling folk guitar sound offered them. At first, the obvious thing to do was to copy Dylan's sound—folk singer Donovan Leitch became a star for looking and sounding like the folk Bob Dylan with his single "Catch the Wind" (1964).[42] In 1965, the Beatles released three new singles, "Help!", "You've Got to Hide Your Love Away" and "Norwegian Wood", all of them influenced by Dylan's sound.

But it was the Rolling Stones who developed a songwriting style that followed Dylan's lead and was original in and of itself. The Stones did not start out as such. As lyric writers, Jagger (who wrote most of his own lyrics) and Richards built a persona of narcissism and arrogance, usually sung in the first person. "Time Is on My Side" (1964) and "Heart of Stone" (1964), the Stones' first self-penned single, were both assertions that the narrator dominated women and that he had the ability to avoid messy entanglements even though women wanted him more and more all the time. Their style was in obvious contradiction to the Beatles' lyrical desire "to hold your hand", and also very much in keeping with the songwriting traditions of their rhythm and blues idols, full of sexual innuendo and braggadocio.[43]

The blues tradition was built on personal experiences far beyond the bedroom, though, as a songwriter as complex as Dylan realized. It was also based on the repression of African-Americans in a racist society. Certainly no young English middle-class post-adolescent could come up with similar experiences to draw from when songwriting. Here, though, the Stones' equation of the values of youth with an alleged class rebellion served them well. Jagger and Richards began writing songs about their own experiences as disobedient and disrespectful post-adolescents under the influence of the experiences of the blues masters they loved.

Their first American number one song, "(I Can't Get No) Satisfaction" (1965), was one of the great rock and roll songs of all time, about a frustrated teenager's damnation of the hypocrisies of the adult world. The lyrics opposed the radio's adult white noise and the ubiquity of commercial penetration of everyday life coming from the television set. The song was brilliant in its ability to describe the mute anger of adolescence, directed against the news media, mass advertising, and the opposite sex. Many listeners believed that the girl described in the third stanza was in the middle of her period, which was shocking for the time, but apparently slipped passed the BBC's censors.

"Satisfaction" was the first of a number of Stones songs to point up the contradictions in the values of respectability in Britain. On the same album as "Satisfaction", *Out of Our Heads* (1965), the Stones included a song, "Play with Fire", mocking the pretentiousness of a wealthy girl whose family had fallen on hard times after a divorce. The girl still rode around in chauffeured cars and dressed in diamonds and fashionable clothes, but the narrator knew that she had lost her financial backing, based on the London suburbs her mother frequented. In later singles, "Get Off of My Cloud" reiterated the irritation with the adult world displayed in "Satisfaction". "Nineteenth Nervous Breakdown" was about a girl's imprisonment in her dull family life; "Mother's Little Helper" was a scathing indictment of a woman's reliance on prescription drugs to get through the day, and secured itself a ban by the BBC for a short time.[44]

In 1965 and 1966, Jagger and Richards became prescient social commentators on the bankruptcy of modern affluent culture, an original answer to Dylan and his influence. Even more, though, the Stones now hobnobbed with debutantes, aristocrats, politicians and artists constantly. Their form of rebellion was a pose, yet it was looked upon as stylish even by the very people Jagger and Richards castigated. Their eloquence and urbanity played well in London social circles. They were rich, but not because they aspired to be rich, as Keith Richards revealed in a 1966 interview in *New Musical Express*.

> We don't ask ourselves what is most commercial. We simply say—we like this one best. What we have liked over the past few years has proved to be what young people like, so this is how to choose a single. This is probably the way that Mozart wrote. He wrote for himself. So do we. And it is a happy coincidence that what we like should also be what our public likes.[45]

By 1966 Jagger was the toast of London's bohemian elite, a rebel who dominated the city's style. He counted among his friends the photographer David Bailey and Princess Margaret. Said literary critic and essayist Francis Wyndham in 1965:

> Mick Jagger is the physical original of his generation; that pretty-ugly appearance has been so widely and so swiftly imitated that it no longer seems eccentric. Just as, a few years ago, girls discovered that they had always looked like Brigitte Bardot without realising it, so today boys' mouths have mysteriously filled to reproduce the Jagger lips. . . . His outline suggests the attenuated, extravagant decadence of a Beardsley drawing, but his personality projects an image of nervous virility rather than one of epicene languor.[46]

With their image, and to a lesser extent, their songwriting, the Stones added to the Beatles' standard by which other rock and roll bands were measured for their authenticity. For a rock and roll band in Britain to be authentic in the eyes of the music press, other musicians and the audience itself, it now had to express rebellion against the adult world—in the Stones' case, most specifically the rich and prosperous middle and upper classes. Nothing in this ideal required them to be working-class themselves. They had to write songs, as the Beatles had established, but now those songs also had to comment on the values that marked affluence in Britain. The result was the commoditization of authenticity—the Stones had become a pillar of an alternative establishment, a youth-based cultural elite that was the very essence of chic in London. Even the Beatles mastered the concept of using pointed social commentary to uphold their own dominance of London's social scene, with brilliant songs like "Eleanor Rigby" (1966), "Taxman" (1966) off the album *Revolver*, and the double A-side single "Paperback Writer" and "Rain" (1966).[47]

Rhythm and Blues: The Aesthetic

The division between commercial success and the earthy aesthetic of R&B caused great tension that tore some bands apart and made other bands question the commercial imperative. A large number of R&B bands became chart mainstays like the Rolling Stones, several of them reeling off single after single between 1964 and 1967 that dominated the pop charts in Britain and America. Critically, none of these bands, including the Stones, made their reputation by placing obscure R&B standards in the pop charts. All of them instead recorded songs given to them by new songwriters, or covered old rock and roll songs [Buddy Holly's "Not Fade Away" (1964) was the Stones' first American hit single] or wrote songs themselves. Usually, their favorite rhythm and blues songs were left to the album.

The bands that learned to write their own material, like the Stones or the Beatles, were the ones that survived the longest with their authenticity intact. Those that never developed successful songwriters—or ignored good songwriters in their midst—feuded over the tyranny of picking hit singles to direct their musical fortunes. The songs they recorded often did not reflect their tastes, or the notion of rebellion that the new standard of authenticity demanded of them. It left them at the mercy of the major record companies, who could then dictate their image to make them palatable to the pop market.[48]

Rhythm and blues bands from outside London were caught in the transition between standards as the audience's tastes shifted on the pop charts. Bands like Them and the Animals had popular hit singles in 1964 and 1965. Them, from Belfast, featured the brilliant vocalist Van Morrison, whose songwriting credits included "Gloria" (1965), a raunchy rock and roll classic covered by many bands over the years. Yet the band relied instead on outside pop songwriters for most of their singles and did not last through 1966.[49] More successful were the

Animals, from Newcastle. They exemplified a working-class toughness that the Stones could only pretend to have—many of their parents were unemployed coal miners, and their Newcastle audience was as roughneck as any audience in Britain. They topped the charts in Britain and America in mid-1964 with an old folk blues number they found on a Bob Dylan album, "House of the Rising Sun". Further cover singles followed, such as "Don't Let Me Be Misunderstood" and "We've Gotta Get Out of This Place" in 1965. They wrote their own material, often about the harsh circumstances they grew up in around Newcastle, but producer Mickie Most would not release their self-penned songs as singles. His success at picking their singles apparently kept them from firing Most, but the band argued over their direction constantly, as they strayed further from their R&B roots. Finally, the original band broke up in 1966.[50]

Another thing that the London bands prized, which the Animals lacked, was excellent musicianship. In a musical genre that had long favored the enthusiasm of the amateur, this was an odd change of focus. The electric guitar became central to the mythology of rock and roll, and lead guitarists became the heroes of the London scene. Previously, the emphasis in rock and roll had been on the singer, though, as usual, the Beatles were innovative in their democratic structure in which no member was dominant. The talents of the musicians didn't matter before—if anything, their amateur status was the source of the music's vitality. This was even the case with the Beatles. Critics ignored their musicianship and celebrated their songwriting talent specifically because they knew nothing about traditional music theory.

In the London bands, however, the guitarists expressed the bands' professionalism. The Yardbirds were the archetypal guitar band. At different times they featured three of the greatest guitarists in the history of the music: Eric Clapton, Jeff Beck and Jimmy Page. The Yardbirds became the top band on the London club scene when the Rolling Stones became a popular sensation and moved out of the clubs. Clapton was their second guitarist, a blues enthusiast and an adept learner who idolized his blues heroes. His obvious passion for the music he made and the men who wrote it came out in his playing. Yet he had also developed a style of blues guitar all his own, unlike contemporaries such as Keith Richards, who made their living copying the sound of American heroes like Chuck Berry. It was not long before Clapton stole the attention of the Yardbirds' audience from singer Keith Relf. He was the first instrumentalist to become the focus of a band. The evidence lay in the graffiti spray-painted or scribbled on walls all over central London—"Clapton is God".[51]

The Yardbirds' live reputation was so great that their first album was recorded live at the Marquee Club rather than in the studio. It was full of Bo Diddley, Muddy Waters and Chuck Berry songs, but none of them was a hit single. So the band turned to Manchester songwriter Graham Gouldman, who penned hits for the Hollies, and covered "For Your Love" in April 1965—a decidedly un-bluesy number with its harpsichord and Latin shuffle beat. It went into the top ten in Britain and the United States, but it cost them Clapton, who left the band because he thought the song was too commercially oriented.[52] The Yardbirds defended their acceptance on the pop charts, claiming, "It was our luck the record sold, NOT our fault!"[53] Apparently, putting out records that became pop hits was becoming something to answer for, instead of proof of a band's talent.

Jeff Beck, Clapton's replacement, was a far less disciplined but much more inventive and adventurous guitarist than Clapton. Beck was an early exponent of feedback, often going on stage without tuning his guitar to get a distorted sound when he tried to bend notes. He was also a major fan of jazz, so he incorporated elements of the jazz repertoire in his playing. The Yardbirds' next single, "Heart Full of Soul" (1965), also written by Graham Gouldman, contained a riff after the chorus where Beck simulated the sound of an Indian sitar. This was one of the first instances of a rock band exploring exotic, non-Western music for influences, and it was due largely to Beck's style. Subsequent singles spelled out their artistic ambitions. "Shapes of Things" (1966) included a wild guitar solo by Beck, a long drone that gave the song a psychedelic feel well before such a sound was popular in rock music. "Still I'm Sad" (1966) was based on a thirteenth century Gregorian chant. But the band fell out once again over musical direction. Bassist Paul Samwell-Smith, the principal songwriter in the group, could not handle the musical indiscipline of Beck, who was prone to showing up on stage drunk or stoned and even more often seemed indifferent to the idea of playing a good show. Samwell-Smith left the band as a result, to become a producer.

Guitarist Jimmy Page arrived to play bass, but soon switched to guitar and the band became a two-lead guitar outfit for a brief period. Nevertheless, Beck's volatility began to wear on everyone. Soon after he tried to hit Relf over the head with his guitar, he was fired for his erratic behavior, and Page became the group's focus. Without a true songwriter after the departure of Samwell-Smith, however, the group foundered. While in the United States they were an exciting exemplar of swinging London, in Britain they were still a singles band without a great songwriter. The Yardbirds finally broke up in July 1968. Numerous groups grew out of the Yardbirds' demise, evidence of the overwhelming talent in the band. Beck went on to form the Jeff Beck Group with Rod Stewart on vocals, Page formed Led Zeppelin, and Keith Relf and guitarist Chris Dreja created one of the most popular folk rock outfits in Britain, Renaissance.[54]

The Kinks

Every major rock and roll band conformed to the new standard in one way or another in the mid-sixties. Not all of them were comfortable with every aspect of the standard, however, especially as it rested on a specious understanding of the nature of working-class values. The Kinks were a very successful singles act on the British charts, but they only hit the American charts occasionally, a rarity among acts with a similar hit-making ratio. Perhaps this was because Ray Davies's songs were about traditional English cultural concerns, the concerns of respectability. The Kinks and their songs stood out on the pop charts from 1964 through 1967 in their open defiance of the new conventions in youth culture, and their espousal of the values of their parents.

The band made their name with a pair of commanding singles in 1964, "You Really Got Me" and "All Day and All of the Night", which were hits on both sides of the Atlantic and established the Kinks as a powerful, driving rock and roll act rivaling the Stones. They wore hunting jackets, frills and lace—hence the band name, which made them somewhat notorious in 1964. In a musical climate where the Beatles and Stones pictured the working classes as the natural social origin of rock and roll in Britain, the Kinks were as working-class as a band could get. Brothers Ray and Dave Davies were from the north London suburb of Muswell Hill; their father spent plenty of time on the dole in the 1950s, with eight children to feed.[55]

As it turned out, however, no songwriter had more affection for the hoary old clichés of Victorianism than Ray Davies. If respectability was a concept the Victorian middle classes had once used to keep the working classes in line, then the Kinks seemed to accept its dictates wholeheartedly. Davies was simultaneously considerate of and satirical of respectability, an ambiguity that drove the success of his band on the British charts.[56] Of all the pop stars of the era, Ray Davies displayed the most cynicism for the explosion of British youth culture and its new representation of cultural rebellion. He knew poverty, dirt, anger and resentment, but he also knew contentment, deference, uncertainty and the value of hard work. It made him a particularly authentic voice railing against what he saw as the cultural establishment—an establishment that, by 1965, included the Beatles and the Stones.

For example, Davies lambasted the dandyism of the London fashion explosion in "Dedicated Follower of Fashion" (1966). Ostensibly about his younger brother Dave, the song was a harsh put-down of a man who has to have the absolute latest in everything immediately, only to cast it away within a short time in favor of the next fad. The song was a surprise among the hits of the year for its obvious mockery of current youth culture, but it was also lacking in much of the toughness of the earlier singles: it sounded almost like an old music-hall song, with its sing-along chorus. Ray Davies's target was the nouveaux riches of the new youth culture and the decadence of London. One biting attack was "Sunny Afternoon", about a drunk reclining in the sun after abusing his wife, and it went to the top of the pop charts.[57] Apparently, many people saw the same contradictions in the new youth culture that Ray Davies did—or they simply did not see themselves in the lyrics.

As the rest of the London rock scene became more and more enamored of spectacular instrumentalists and complex musical arrangements, Ray Davies retreated still further. He asserted, "People should realise that things like food and tea are important."[58] Bassist Pete Quaife celebrated Davies's songwriting focus—"You still can't beat going to the pictures, a couple of pints and a fag. The Kinks all agree that Sunday dinner is the greatest realisation of heaven."[59] The single "Autumn Almanac" (1967) was the epitome of such pleasures, a lovely song about enjoying the simple routines of the fall season—raking leaves, watching football, neighbors meeting on Friday evenings and ruminating over the end of the summer season.

Critics pegged Davies as a throwback to old Denmark Street songwriters. Other rock and roll musicians would have chafed at the tag; Davies loved it, while Paul McCartney, Pete Townshend of the Who and Paul Samwell-Smith of the Yardbirds cited the influence of his music on their own compositions.[60] The Kinks were in some ways the exception that proved the rule—Davies's songs rebelled against the cultural standards of youth even as they were being defined. Youth values had assumed greater importance in the development of British culture, focused around "rebellion", whatever that was. The Kinks, one of the best bands of the era, showed that the alleged working-class values behind that rebellion were a myth, and found originality in upholding respectable values as they had actually lived them—and they were beloved for it. Their authenticity and their popularity only grew over the rest of the sixties.

Clearly, the Rolling Stones' conception of what a rock and roll musician had to be was very complex. The Kinks' name, their backgrounds, their public pronouncements, their refusal to kowtow to the dictates of youth culture only made them that much more exemplary of the ideal. The Stones made it possible for anyone to be a rock and roll musician, so long as he did not conform to the old standard of how a musician should act. It was possible for a middle-class adolescent to aspire to be a rock and roll musician, so long as he was willing to challenge the societal values his parents had instilled in him. In the case of Ray Davies, he could even challenge the new values, as rewritten by his peers, so long as he maintained the image of being rebellious.

British teenagers and young adults could use rock and roll as an outlet for their energies and anger, and be accepted, even lionized for it in London, the epicenter of Britain's emigration of commercial culture. The acceptance of new values, based on invented conceptions of the nature of youth, class, gender and race, seemed stronger than ever. Together, the London bands advanced the Beatles' ideal by establishing a new concept of authenticity in rock and roll. The audience and critics now expected the rock and roll musician to be as attuned to license and bohemianism as his poetic comrades of the early nineteenth century. They considered their artistic output to be free of the dictates of commerce and industry, and openly mocked those dictates in their songs. Yet simultaneously, the development of an original brand of popular music made these artists and the audiences that listened to them the members of an exclusive elite, defined by its commercial tastes and yet denying that they had any artistic affinity to commerce whatsoever. In short, the dictates of authenticity were very similar to familiar Romantic notions of English culture, notions advanced as an alternative to the post-industrial norm. Rock and roll music—or as its practitioners increasingly referred to it, "rock" music—had begun to take on an entirely British identity, while its musicians also began to contribute to the transformation of that identity by changing how people talked about it.

Chapter 4
Mods

The rise of rock and roll in the 1950s coincided with a renewed emphasis on adolescents as juvenile delinquents whom adults could blame for most of the ills of modern British society. The Teddy boys were the most obvious manifestation of this problem, the logical antecedents of a coming cultural apocalypse. This was hardly a British-specific phenomenon. The coupling of juvenile delinquency with youth culture was an issue everywhere in Western society, associated with its emphases on masculinity, consumption, hedonism and irresponsibility. In the postwar era, however, as Western economies boomed, masculinity, consumption, hedonism and irresponsibility were all marketable characteristics as well, nowhere more than in Britain, London in particular. To be a Ted, a teenager simply had to look and act like one—and that meant buying a lot of clothes, records and other necessary accoutrements, on top of affecting a delinquent attitude. Nothing represented a Ted's consumer interests—indeed, nothing represented a teenager's consumer interests—like rock and roll music. Adolescence might be a time of troubles, but there was a lot of money available to the entrepreneur willing to capitalize on those troubles.[1]

Adolescent troubles in Britain in the early 1960s were, as would be usual anywhere in the Western postwar world, a combination of simple emotional angst and real live changes in the culture surrounding them, of which a group of people just making their way into adulthood would be particularly sensitive. The working classes in Britain had a greater political confidence after the political victory of 1945, yet at the same time, the spread of affluence seemed to promise the eventual erasing of class distinctions. National service ended in 1960, but the

threat of nuclear war was a continuing threat to western Europe. Americanization brought with it a popular culture that emphasized teenaged concerns and
consumerism, though it also seemed to be another reason to fear for the future of
the distinguishing characteristics of Britishness.[2] Just as they had in the 1950s—
and for decades before besides—young people in Britain and especially London
created numerous subcultures to negotiate these distinctions and define an alternative to a mainstream culture they found uncomfortably adult.

Subcultures

Subcultures grew out of the collective recognition that class and youth were
distinguishing characteristics in an increasingly faceless urban society. In the
postwar era, they fed off images brought to them through the media of movies,
newspapers, radio and television, which in turn used them as a source to find the
latest styles in fashion and music. Teenagers in subcultures mixed and matched
ideas and values according to certain indefinable rules to make a statement about
their lives.[3] However, the very definition of a subculture meant that most youth
were not involved in them—they defined their uniqueness by their exclusivity.
In fact, conflict within a subculture usually arose between those who considered
themselves full-time adherents and those they accused of being only part-time
adherents. Eventually, the death knell for any subculture sounded when younger
age groups, often from differing social circumstances, appropriated the styles of
a subculture without any regard to the meaning of those styles.[4]

Everything in an English—and perhaps British—teenager's life gained definition through social divisions, especially in London. Schools upheld traditional
class distinctions, via social groups, relationships with teachers and the like. The
building of council tenancies after the war to replace bombed homes in east and
west London meant the break-up of working-class neighborhoods, kin networks
and local economies. British adolescents' existence in a generational void, coupled with these institutional dislocations, made them into a quasi-class in and of
themselves.[5]

The experience of an adolescent in a shifting adult culture, then, was often
unnervingly alienating and lonely. As a result, they often rejected the values of
the school and the council tenancy for pop music, fashion, and the fantasy world
of the cinema. The British entertainment industry depicted these cultural pursuits as the glamorous height of working-class culture. Yet many adolescents
resented having to fit the societal norm of respectable adulthood, and a select
few turned to juvenile delinquency.[6] The delinquent tended to be someone who
felt a greater loyalty to his locality and the solidarity of his friends than he felt
toward the law or morality. Many simply would not knuckle under to the conventions of the adult world, regardless of the values they might share with it.
They conceived of class as a form of hypocrisy, as one teenager opined.

I failed the 11-plus, and I felt bitter, my parents were disappointed in me and instead of getting the bike I was promised, I was bagged for the next six weeks. On the other hand the boy who sat next to me in class passed with flying colours, got a bike and became a snob, and who wants to be one of those? From then on it was if you can't beat them with your brains, beat them with your fists.[7]

Subcultures were borne of these expressions of frustration. Different gangs of delinquents established alternative cultures through the articulation of their tastes in fashion, music, organization, definitions of masculinity and femininity, and especially in class attitudes. Postwar British youth culture traced a line of descent through a series of subcultures—the Teddy boys being the first—which were all born of working-class frustrations in London. The mass media focused on subcultures as evidence of the nation's moral decline, delinquency gone rampant amongst youth and a sure sign that this American emphasis on youth culture was getting far out of hand. With the coming classless society that many politicians and intellectuals seemed determined to bring about, many adults feared that ethical standards would be lowered to the level of cretinism, if the children of Britain had their way.

Yet at the same time, subcultures were proof of the endurance of the ideals of class amongst British youth, especially in London. It was no accident that subcultures arose in the affluent south of England, rather than the more working-class north. In the south, there were more jobs and more money was available, yet aspirations to a higher living circumstance were also likelier to be frustrated as well. There was more exposure to an affluence that working-class adolescents in west or east London believed they could never be a part of, no matter what jobs they got or how much money they made—and a greater ambivalence as to whether they wanted any part of that affluence regardless.[8] The school system that had promised upward mobility had failed many of them; the welfare state seemed stagnant; even the Labour Party seemed uninterested in the revolution of everyday life that would level social distinctions. Subcultures, then, were a way of opting out, of telling their social superiors that they had no desire to pursue respectability as their parents and social superiors defined it.

Subcultures became marking points from which teenagers of every social circumstance took their cues in fashions, music, politics, even their views on society itself. The media focused on groups like the Teddy boys because they were "folk devils". Yet their exposure in the press spawned identification with subcultures amongst British teenagers, who often saw them for the first time in the nation's newspapers, radio and television programs and above all, rock and roll.[9] As adherents of subcultures discovered, if their lifestyles could not be easily emulated by the average British teenager, the trappings of those lifestyles—the music, fashion, attitudes and ideals they adopted—could be easily copied.

Once a teenager could look like a Teddy boy without actually being one, the essence of a subculture as an alternative culture had disappeared.[10]

This was especially true once middle-class teenagers bought into the styles of a subculture. Consciousness of the distinctions between classes never disappeared from the mind of an adherent to a subculture—in fact, the distinction was all-important. A subculture provided a context for the development of a collective working-class identity and individual self-esteem.[11] Once that distinction was lost, the subculture's style had disseminated into the mainstream. This was because, to the adolescent in White City, being a Ted was the very definition of working-class style, and what made him different from an adolescent in Winchester. To an adolescent in Winchester, however, being a Ted was a symbol of youth community, of being one with the adolescent in White City. Subcultures, then, took standards similar to those rock and roll had spread in the 1960s, constructed their own working-class values and style, and eventually defined values and style for youth across the entire social spectrum in Britain.[12]

After the Teds melted into the pop culture mainstream, two new subcultures arose reflecting different visions of the rebellion Teddy boys represented. One manifested itself in a heavy machismo punctuated by conservative values, an identification with alleged working-class norms. The other revealed itself in a cool sophistication to rise above the perceived bankruptcy of commercial mass culture. Adherents of the first of these subcultures called themselves the Rockers. The second group called themselves the Modernists, or Mods.[13]

Mods and Rockers

The Rockers were more directly derived from the Teddy boys than the Mods. The Rockers' musical and fashion tastes remained locked in the 1950s. They clung to the purity of rock and roll, and to the image of misfit and delinquent adolescents whom they had observed in American movies, like Marlon Brando in *The Wild One* (1953) or James Dean in *Rebel Without a Cause* (1955). The Rockers wore their hair in a pile on top of their heads, they wore leather and denim almost exclusively, and they drove motorcycles. They emphasized their own masculinity, in part by hanging out with girls and forcing them to conform to outdated standards of sexuality and femininity. They were swaggeringly macho, and when they met up with Mods—often, since they came from the same primarily working-class neighborhoods—the results were often violent.

Much more than the Mods, the Rockers expressed their contempt for respectability openly. They saw themselves as the epitome of the working classes and were determined to hold onto their class identities in the face of a growing classless society. To them, the present and the future were dominated by hypocrites, and therefore the only thing worth maintaining was their own rather hypertrophied sense of their own past. A pair of Rockers, one girl and one boy, summarized the Rockers' attitudes.

> They can say what they like about us, we know what the score really is. Call it a Welfare State? The only welfare they're interested [in] is in building bigger detention centres for Rockers. . . . Even the blacks in America aren't standing for any more pushing about from the old geezers who think they can run everything. And we're hated as much as the blacks are.[14]

> I'm just a wild Rocker, a menace to society. I'm not ashamed of it. Why should I be? Ever since that Profumo lark I've come to the conclusion that we working-class yobos, as they like to call us, have less to be ashamed of than those establishment geezers.[15]

The Rockers were doomed as a subculture, however. Their style was merely atavistic without being innovative, so they had a hard time attracting committed adherents in their neighborhoods.

The Modernists were much more influential. The Mod was the English version of Norman Mailer's "white negro", a west Londoner, often Anglo-Irish, with an ambivalent conception of what it meant to be working-class, white, and masculine.[16] Fashion and music were the critical components of the Mod lifestyle. They wore sharply tailored Italianate suits, French haircuts neatly and closely cropped, and they drove scooters. Style was all-encompassing: being cool was more important than being alive. The latest popular clothes or music could change from one week, one day, even one hour to the next according to what one saw or heard on the street. They preferred a select group of British rock and roll bands, Tamla/Motown singles, Stax/Volt soul, and a new Afro-Caribbean music called "bluebeat" or "ska". They despised Rockers as much as the Rockers despised them, seeing them as greasy, primitive thugs, whereas the Rockers saw the Mods as sissified dandies. Together, they practiced a nightly ritual of gang violence in the streets of west and east London, and quickly established themselves with adults as the latest threat to Britain's future.

The Mods' obsessions with fashion involved more than merely dress. A teenager's image as a Mod came from how his clothes were tailored, how he danced, the scooter he rode, even just the way he walked or stood around looking bored.[17] Mods lived in a world of perpetual motion, always trying to keep one step ahead of the trends, because a Mod above all wanted to be a trendsetter and not a follower. It was not unusual to see a Mod boy wearing makeup, especially eyeliner, largely to stand out in the crowd. For a short period in 1964, originality was even displayed on the Mods' T-shirts: they wore numbers on the back designating how important they were in the hierarchy of trendsetters and followers. More often, a true trendsetter amongst the Mods—the boy who bought the smartest suit before anyone else, and had it tailored just so—was known as a "face". People who followed his lead, depending upon how soon and how often, were ranked as "tickets", of a first class, second class, and third class variety. Very few Mods were faces. The entire goal in being a Mod was to be seen in the right place at the right time with the right look, no matter how or where you got it. Marc Bolan, later famous as the leader of the band T-Rex, was a Mod face in the early sixties. He remembered the Mods' obsession with style in an interview.

> What turned me on about that period of time was the total involvement materially with what was going on, because it was a complete involvement with perhaps seven people that one respected and really being important to be the leader of that materially. It was very material, down to clothes, totally. . . . Levi's seven or eight years ago in England were unheard of, . . . and there was a place in Leman Street, Whitechapel, which used to have them. . . . I went there and there were about forty people that all looked like Dickensian urchins, . . . [a]nd there was a big pile of Levi's and we just stole the lot. . . . It was great knowing we were only one of a few people in England who had them.[18]

The scooter became the most important way for a Mod to be immediately recognized as a Mod, and not just as a well-dressed adolescent. The Mods even rode their scooters in a faddish manner. At first everyone rode them with their toes pointed outward; later, they rode them with their heads tilted to one side. The scooter was simply an extension of the Mod's fashion style: a good one had chrome, lots of mirrors and an alpine horn. It was not a good idea to ride around with a girl on the back—"it makes the machine look untidy to have a girl on the back."[19] No one really cared how well it ran: no Mod would get his hands dirty cleaning and fixing his scooter. That was a pastime for Rockers.[20]

Mods were slightly more gender-inclusive as a subculture than Rockers. Girls contributed heavily to Mod style; to the Rockers, girls were strictly subordinate and inferior, an accessory to a motorcycle. Mod girls had their own fashion icons, such as the models Jean Shrimpton and Twiggy. They particularly liked the image of Greta Garbo; a London cinema festival was crammed with teenagers when it showed a few of her films. The most important style-setter, however, was Cathy McGowan, a co-host of Independent Television's pop music show, *Ready, Steady, Go!*, which ran from 1963 through 1966. McGowan became a fashion plate and fantasy girl, with her slightly-older-than-teenage appeal. She hailed from Streatham in east London, and counted herself as a Mod. Given a list of three things important to teenagers—music, sex and clothes—she stunned an interviewer by ranking clothes the most important, and sex the least important, saying "It's what you look like that really counts." When asked if there was anything that bothered or frightened teenagers, she said "Yes. They're all terrified of growing old."[21] The *Daily Sketch* spent a week in October 1963 sampling McGowan's opinions as an exemplar of youth culture.

> Politicians, clergymen, welfare workers, teachers—they often seem to us like a lot of silly kids. And if there's one subject they get mixed up about more often

than another it's this one—the Teenager of Today. They'll say, for example, that Britain's teenagers are becoming more Americanised every day.

They couldn't be more wrong. Just now it's great to be as English as you can get. And if you're from the North of England, like Liverpool, that's even better still. . . . At one time, . . . some kids would pretend that their father was a doctor or a solicitor to impress their friends. Now they're more likely to boast that their Dad works in the meat market or on the roads, particularly if they really do some dull desk job. Teenagers who come from wealthy homes are always trying like mad to prove that they're working-class.[22]

Basically, though, girls were outsiders to both the Mods and the Rockers. There were women who were a part of the action, and they followed their own style trends as well. But the Mods and Rockers never accepted them as insiders; if anything, a girl was a distraction from fashion trends and music, which were the real important things in life.[23]

The lifestyle of a Mod demanded money. The clothes themselves were usually not overly expensive, but a Mod bought new clothes virtually every weekend to keep up with the trends. Most Mods, then, had jobs, usually as clerical workers of some sort. A Mod spent most of a Saturday afternoon shopping in Soho to find the right clothes to wear that night. Such shopping could get rather unusual. It was not unheard of for young Mods to go into women's stores to buy, for example, "a polka dot blouse, to match the eye make-up, a smart lady's jacket, with a red lining, four-inch high-heeled shoes, and a shoulder strap bag."[24] Such were Mod priorities—it did not matter what you wore, or how you got it, as long as you stood out in the crowd.

The best crowd in which to stand out was usually located in a club playing rock and roll. Every west London town had a central club that catered to, or was taken over by the Mods. Soho had the Scene, the Marquee and the Flamingo, the three top clubs in London with the best bands and the highest-ranking faces. Dance at the clubs was again a matter of appearance: it was okay what one looked like on the dance floor as long as it looked right. Dancing was a sexless activity, largely because the Mod doing the dancing was usually on amphetamines while he was out on the dance floor. In fact, it was rare to even have women on the floor, especially since the dancing could become quite manic and violent.[25]

Mods wanted a musical sound as distinct as their style in clothing. Tamla/Motown and Stax/Volt records were popular, but only because they were hard to find in London, not because the music was unusual—the Beatles, Stones and other R&B acts played Tamla/Motown songs often. The goal in being a Mod was to be original; having the original American singles that London bands played was one manifestation. Another was simply to patronize original acts around London, to find a band that no one else knew about, yet. The Mod was as elitist in his musical taste as he was about his fashion sense. They tolerated bands like the Stones at first, then mocked them for their copies of American rhythm and blues. The Beatles were a joke, a teenybopper group and worst of all, a girls' band.[26]

The press began to identify the Mods and Rockers in late 1963, mainly by their fashion sense. The *Daily Mirror* published a short article on "this West Side Story rivalry" that identified the two "cults" by their styles in clothing and transportation. It even included a pair of columns entitled "How to Spot Them", as if Mods and Rockers were rare birds recently sighted in the London area. The columns came complete with descriptions of indoor and outdoor wear, and the looks of both girls and boys.[27]

But the Mods and Rockers really came to media attention in spring 1964. Adherents to both gangs traveled to the seaside on holidays: to Clacton during Easter weekend, and to Bournemouth, Margate and Brighton for the May bank holiday of 1964. Local adolescents objected to the presence of these potentially unruly outsiders from London, and clashes resulted. The press, however, attributed all the fights to gang wars between Mods and Rockers, of which there were only a few. By most accounts, the Mods "won" these skirmishes, beating up the locals and the Rockers due mainly to sheer numbers, and overwhelming the local police.[28] Said one Mod, an eighteen year old from London:

> I was at Margate. . . . It was a laugh, I haven't enjoyed myself so much in a long time. It was great—the beach was like a battlefield. It was like we were taking over the country. You want to hit back at all the geezers who try to tell us what to do. We just want to show them we're not going to take it. . . . I felt great, part of something important instead of just being something they look down on because you haven't passed GCE. . . . I suppose it's because I don't have a chance. I don't talk right and I haven't been to the right schools—I haven't had the education. That makes you sick—to see them preaching at you.[29]

Because of these clashes, the Mods were transformed in the British press. Once they had been an interesting group of fashionable trendsetters; now they were the leading moral panic of the time. What made the Mods seem particularly dangerous to the adult world of 1964 was an inability to spot them easily. Most of the time, a Mod looked like a well-dressed teenager, and usually, a well-dressed teenager was a comforting sign of the future in waiting. The message of violence the Mod lifestyle advertised was roundly condemned, but another message, a message of youth consumption, was also represented and absorbed. Suddenly, everyone in London seemed to be designing and buying sharp Italianate suits, getting French haircuts, listening to London rock and roll acts on pirate radio stations and frequenting the Soho clubs. The Mods themselves, indeed the very word "mod" itself, became the top symbol of 1960s consumption. It was not long before the concept of the Mod and the concept of the teenager seemed to be one and the same.[30]

Yet there was a problem, because above all things, Mods hated commercialism. The Mod who spent all of his paycheck on clothes, scooter accessories or records did so to be ahead of the tickets, to be exotic and new. Once anyone else picked up on the idea of wide side vents on trousers or an extra mirror on the scooter, it was passé and commercial, and was slagged off as boring. In its essence, Mod was rampant consumerism in pursuit of the unattainable, an item that could not be marketed. A Mod face had to have an R&B or soul record, or an Ivy League jacket or a target T-shirt *first*. Likewise, the Mods parodied the fast pace of modern life and the fly-by-night nature of modern culture. To the Mods, too many people cared about what others thought of them, and these people bought new things in order to be seen as respectable—to keep up with the Joneses, as it were. By taking the consumption of new items to a pace properly described as frenzied, the Mods made fun of their social superiors, even as they found themselves caught up in the same pursuits.[31]

Critically, though, a Mod was a Mod because he felt like a part of a community, a rebellious underground that defined itself as outside the cultural mainstream. When a Mod managed to find himself the right jacket, a cool new band, a new club, a weird accessory for his scooter or just a quirky way of standing on a street corner that looked menacing, it meant little unless a whole group of his friends copied him and adopted these items and ideas themselves. In short, his individuality had to be recognized as a part of a larger movement. Mod was a series of paradoxes, surrounding the collective expression of individual identity, particularly through the purchase of consumer goods in the pursuit of an anti-commercial life.

Therefore, a Mod's individuality, and his community itself, was ruined once too many people began to copy Mod styles. Once thousands of teenagers began buying the same items he did, the Mod face was at sea in an ocean of tickets. The Mod subculture really only lasted for a few years, because it became impossible to define oneself as different if everyone else did so in the same way. Yet the Mods had helped to define the parameters of youth culture in Britain more than any subculture previously. They established youth fashions and tastes, and provided a model for communal organization that was lasting.

Pop Art

The maintenance of such a subculture, defining itself through a paradoxical consumerism, was almost a living artistic work on the fast-paced bankruptcy of bourgeois affluence in Britain in the 1960s, in particular for the working-class adolescents who ascribed to its philosophy. Life as a white-collar clerk or an apprentice in a shop lacked any currency for a working-class teenager who aspired to a fantasy life of Jaguars, fast and beautiful women and minimal toil as sold by a highly developed capitalist economy in which "you never had it so good". Amphetamines fueled the fire; the effect of a high on speed was to make one's speech and movements as mechanical and fast-paced as a telephone call from one City of London skyscraper to another. As such, the Mods were well named. More than simply modern, they were Modernists, unconsciously ascribing to many of the same ideals of speed, technology, and machine-like living that the Italian Futurists and the British Vorticists had defined in the early part of the twentieth century. The Mods' mockery of bourgeois affluence and emphasis on youth and the masculine reflected trends found in artistic and intellectual Modernist movements.

In fact, an art movement had started in Britain in the 1950s that saw such paradoxes in everyday life, and chose to depict them as a commentary on the beauties and horrors of postwar popular culture. In the early fifties, a few artists wanted to break out of the rigidity of artistic pigeonholes, to explore high intellectual ideas in the twentieth century as a whole, but also work in the development of popular culture. They wanted to show how magazines, movies, television, radio, music, car designs, posters and advertisements conveyed their artistic ideals, and the ideals of the mass of the English public. Many of their intellectual contemporaries—George Orwell, Graham Greene, Harold Pinter— saw the collapse of Victorian security in the era of postmodernism after 1945 as apocalyptic; the new artists saw postmodernism as exciting and liberating. Deconstructing British culture was unnecessary—the war had seen to that. The war had left the British identity moored halfway between America and Europe. The tethers to the empire may have been falling away but they left behind a culture that was richly cosmopolitan and international. These new British artists were determined to depict the world they found in the war's wake, to open a door between the world of art and the world of life to show that they were one and the same.[32]

Thus was born Pop Art in Britain. Amongst its practitioners were Peter Blake, Richard Hamilton, David Oxtoby, Eduardo Paolozzi, David Hockney and others. Like most artists since the Romantic era, they were determined to live their art; unlike other artists, they decided that the best way to do so was to find art in everyday life, rather than to create and impose it on an indifferent world.[33] Hockney, for example, took all of his life's inspirations from the mass advertisement surrounding him. Typically, having seen an advertisement for hair coloring reading, "I have only one life; let me live it as a blonde", he went home immediately and dyed his hair blonde.[34]

Pop Art and its adherents were obsessed with the influence of American culture in Britain, but in a mostly visceral way—academic arguments about the nature of Americanization meant little in comparison to defining why it was so emotionally energetic and exciting.[35] Like the Mods, artists like Peter Blake constructed a version of America and its cultural power in their works, trying to define the cultural contradictions they saw around them through their lifestyles, since they could not really articulate the contradictions in their heads.

Students all over Britain absorbed Pop Art ideas at the numerous art colleges that flourished during the postwar era—colleges attended by dozens of future rock and roll musicians of the sixties and seventies. John Lennon attended the Liverpool College of Art; Keith Richards and Charlie Watts of the Rolling Stones were art students in London; Eric Burdon of the Animals went to the Newcastle College of Art; Ray Davies attended Hornsey College of Art in north London; Eric Clapton was expelled from Kingston College of Art. Art colleges were meant to train students to become graphic designers, but they also served as educational halfway houses for later adolescents who clearly had brains and talent, but refused to conform to the dictates of the school system—almost a job description for the average British rock and roll musician.[36]

As taught at the nation's art colleges, Pop Art made the greatest effort to capture the images that flashed across Britain's television screens and magazines in the 1950s and 1960s. One of the occasional instructors at Ealing Art College was the Austrian/English artist Gustav Metzger, who practiced "auto-destruction". Metzger was obsessed with the fast pace of modern life, and how so much of modern pop culture was designed around the concept of planned obsolescence. An auto-destructive work of art demonstrated its own decay and collapse before the viewer's eyes. For example, Metzger dipped photographs in acid so they would dissolve as one looked at them. He created statues that crumbled at the base from the moment they were finished.[37] He also designed an apparatus that would deliver drops of water one at a time to a hot plate so that as soon as one drop evaporated another took its place. Auto-destruction was an excellent depiction of the ephemeral nature of modern culture, how anything could be planned, celebrated and destroyed right before the observer's eyes.

Pop Art broke down the distinctions between high culture and what would earlier have been termed *kitsch*. The result was popular culture—or more properly termed, pop culture. English pop culture, in comparison to American pop culture, was far more of a class phenomenon, a rebellion against the public taste. Yet for all the references and roads between the high and the low in pop culture, there was always an element of cheek and irony in it. Referencing pop cultural images like women's bras, cars, bodybuilders, a series of pop records or a scene from a comic book usually involved a certain amount of ambivalence toward the subject. Pop Art broke down the distinction between high culture and popular culture, and in the process invented a paradoxical appreciation of both. Popular culture was mass-produced, yet placing one item on a canvas made it into a work of art.[38]

In such an atmosphere, it became obvious that rock and roll musicians, especially those trained at art colleges, would take many cues not simply from art movements, but from the concept of art as everyday life, and of everyday life as art. The intersection between art and life was the essence of Pop Art, and rock and roll musicians determined to live their music, to adopt lifestyles that made an artistic statement.[39] Pop Art's principles were also the essence of Mod, and the essence of the culture of London in general. Those principles, intersections and essences all came together in the musical career of the Who.

The Who

The Who pursued both Mod and Pop Art as defined through the medium of their guitarist and songwriter, Pete Townshend. As the son of a musician, Townshend had led a comfortable and solid middle-class life in Chiswick. Nevertheless, he grew up in the working-class atmosphere of west London, particularly at Acton County Grammar School. There he met singer Roger Daltrey, later a sheet metal worker, and bassist and songwriter John Entwistle, a post office worker. Upon completing his secondary education, Townshend moved on to Ealing Art College, where he sat in on lectures given by Gustav Metzger and was exposed to Pop Art concepts. Townshend, then, was perfectly placed to see the similarities between the lifestyle of the average west London Mod and the artistic concerns of the average Pop artist. He became obsessed with the connection between his own upbringing, his reflection on the lifestyles of the Mod audiences he played for, his education as an art student, the links between art and life in the mid-sixties, even his status as an Englishman.[40]

The Who's first manager was a Mod, Pete Meaden, who shaped their image, briefly renaming them the High Numbers and dressing them in the flashiest clothing Carnaby Street could produce. Their visual image was critical to their authenticity as Mods. Their most famous clothing accessory was a suit jacket made out of a Union Jack that Entwistle and Townshend shared on stage and in photographs. They made the Union Jack seem like a representation of a new nationalism, based not on a union of three nations in their domination over most of the world's non-European population, but of a new pop culture that had spread itself so far that it could accommodate any image, no matter how sacrosanct. Drummer Keith Moon even took to wearing t-shirts with the Royal Air Force's target symbol as well. The flag and its colors changed from being a symbol of national pride into a pop culture icon around London and beyond, and the Who helped inspire that conversion. The Who presented an aggressively masculine image as well, particularly in the person of Roger Daltrey, who had a reputation for punching his bandmates if he did not like their antics. They even had a logo made up of the band's name with an arrow rising from the "o", seemingly an assertion of the band's almost exclusively male audiences. They appeared at famous Mod hangouts like the Goldhawk Social Club in Shepherd's Bush, the Railway Tavern in Wealdstone, the Marquee in Soho and the Scene Club in Soho's Ham Yard, the red-hot center of Mod culture.[41] Their reputation as a stage act and as Mod faces made them a huge draw throughout London.

As a Mod band, the Who became famous for their fashion sense, for the Union Jacks they draped over their amplifiers and their shoulders, and for the power of their stage presence. But most of all, they became the top rock act in London because they destroyed their instruments on stage when their concerts ended. The ritual began as most such ideas do, as a simple mistake. On stage at the Railway Tavern, Townshend broke his guitar neck by shoving it into a low ceiling in the middle of a song, and in order to save face when the audience laughed at him, he thrashed the instrument to pieces as if he had meant to break it. Offstage, though, Townshend recognized the potential hidden in this atavistic act. Auto-destruction fit in nicely with his own "incredibly glamorous" image of the Who's destroying themselves financially by wrecking their equipment. Mod was about speed and violence; the Who's music and stage act were approximately a rendition of that speed and violence in music. Initially, Townshend and the band agonized over the destruction of Townshend's guitar, a very expensive piece of equipment. They found, however, that their audiences came to demand that Townshend destroy his guitar every time they played, and the band obliged, extending the destruction to Moon's drums and their amplifiers in the process.[42] By destroying their instruments, the Who not only expressed the aggression inherent in their Mod audiences; they commented on the ephemeral nature of pop culture. (They also ran themselves into massive debt.) Current mass-produced items, however tailored to suit the consumer's needs—like side vents on a Mod's pants, or a Rickenbacker electric guitar—could come and go so quickly that one might never know they had been there, even though they had seemed essential just moments before.

Ealing Art School's head tutor was Roy Ascot, who turned over the school to the principles of a new movement called cybernetics. The idea was to study communication and control in living bodies and mechanical systems, to understand how they interacted on an automatic basis. Essentially, it was about how a machine could become, in the hands of an artist, an organic thing, a tool of the artist's vision as useful as his own limbs and digits, and just as reflective of his own ideas. Townshend used these ideas throughout his career, always obsessed with technology and the possibilities it raised for expressing his ideas. The destruction of his guitar was frightening and exhilarating precisely because Townshend was destroying a part of himself, at the same time as he reminded the audience how transient a piece of laminated wood with a pickup and strings could be. As he put it, "I smash guitars because I like them. I usually smash a guitar when it's at its best. I don't have a love affair with a guitar—I don't polish it after every performance. I play the fucking thing."[43] Pop Art and Mod were of the same root in popular culture, and Townshend meant to exploit that connection. He described how in an interview later in his career.

> I was really into that thing of the Who destroying themselves and chopping away at their own legs and all that and just ending up nowhere and perhaps even blowing themselves to bits one day. . . . Before the Who got big I wanted them to get bigger and bigger and bigger and bigger until a number one record and then wrap dynamite around their heads and blow themselves up on TV.[44]

The rebellion inherent in such an exaggerated vision appealed to the intellectual in Townshend. Auto-destruction became a Mod ritual, a moment at which all of the audience's frustrations of growing up working-class and stifled in London came to a crashing explosion on stage. When Pete Townshend rubbed his mikestand against the strings, smashed his guitar's neck into the speaker stand, or simply splintered the guitar by crashing it down on the stage again and again, he articulated the rage of kids all over London, and eventually, all over Britain.[45] He also built them into a community, at first based on their own mutual affinities for music, and later based on their willingness to allow music to lead them into rebellion against the surrounding pop culture.

Rock and roll was a force to the Who, a force reflecting the frustrations of youth. The Who adopted the Mod image and style to find and save the spiritual roots of their own civilization, that of their generation and of their mates in working-class west London. Townshend talked often in terms of "getting back to the streets", and rock and roll to him was the music of the streets of west London.[46] He equated Mod with his roots in west London, and he was determined to reflect and preserve those roots in his music. Townshend became a spokesman for the Mods, a musician capable of articulating Mod concerns.

> We communicate aggression and frustration to the audience musically and visually. We want to show the audience that we are frustrated characters, that we do want to get something out of our system and we wanna do it in front of them.[47]

> [Our fans] are in a crummy predicament, having to work to live, in respectable places like Brown and Polson. They envy our music. They would love to get hold of a £300 guitar and wallop it. They would like to jump up on stage and yell about why can't the kids have pills and how the youngsters are being put down by people of 40 who want to be 20.[48]

Such statements made Townshend the most prominent player of a new role for rock and roll musicians in Britain—the working-class intellectual. Whatever his true socioeconomic circumstances, Townshend's association with the Mods made him a representative of teenaged values, rock and roll values, and in the fashion of 1960s London, working-class values. The fact that Townshend had attended art college while the Mods themselves worked grubby clerks' jobs in London did not change this fact. It only enhanced his image: he had learned articulation there. Townshend and the Who were better suited to represent the Mods' rage through their raucous, chaotic music, by smashing their equipment, and by writing about the Mod lifestyle.[49]

Townshend as Songwriter

Songwriting was the most important way a rock and roll musician could express his status as a working-class intellectual, and Pete Townshend was in the process of developing a distinct songwriting personality. He was brilliant at taking the problems of adolescence and expanding on them to baroque proportions. He established the universality of male teenage angst across social boundaries in a way that no other songwriter of the day could match. Townshend addressed some of the most sensitive issues of adolescence in a straightforward, often humorous, but always sensible fashion. Primary in his music was a search for identity, a search similar to that of the Who balancing itself between the dictates of the Mods, the dictates of popular success, and the dictates of "art", whatever that meant to the rock and roll fan of the 1960s.

The band's third hit single, "My Generation" (1965), made them fixtures on the pop music scene. Christopher Booker, then editor of *Private Eye*, said that Townshend's mockery of getting old was the first time that the "death wish" of English popular culture had revealed itself.[50] Later, Townshend characterized "My Generation" as the first truly British rock record, "the first one that should have been sung in a cockney accent".[51] The song made the Who's reputation as prescient commentators on teenaged values. Other songs captured different nuances of the adolescent—and Mod—experience, particularly "The Kids Are Alright" (1965), about a Mod immersing himself in the dance floor and in fights once his girlfriend had been shunted safely aside.

The Who's songs combined Mod concerns—identity within the collective, masculinity, working-class frustration and release—with the common themes of being a British teenager. Townshend accomplished this by writing about unusual teenagers in extraordinary circumstances, and his descriptions of their strange lives amplified the sort of concerns that any teenager would find commonplace. "Happy Jack" (1965) was a novelty song about a donkey at a seaside resort and how he was able to bear the taunts and abuses of children. Its message was an appeal to the adolescent outsider to defy the torment of his existence with a smile. "Substitute" (1966) described a boy whose entire life is second rate, especially his relationship with his girlfriend. "I'm a Boy" (1966) was a lament by a boy who was treated like a girl by his mother, and who dressed him as such. "Pictures of Lily" (1967), perhaps the culmination of all these singles in its harnessing of the Who's powerful stage sound on record for the first time, was an ode to masturbation while looking at postcards of Lillie Langtry.

Each of these songs revealed a different part of the vision Townshend had of his audience. Conditioned by the Mods, he saw all youth as a collective. The Mod subculture and youth culture in general were alike in their aspirations, their desire for release, their private concerns. He noted in 1965, "People of a certain age have to identify with something, don't they? Two wars gave youngsters before something to identify with. Our generation had to find something else."[52]

As a songwriter, Townshend himself provided that identification. By writing about teenagers on the fringes of a normal life, he was able to make his listeners feel an even stronger sense of community—at least their problems were not that weird, in comparison to a boy whose mother dressed him up like a girl. Townshend conceived of youth as a community, made up of individuals with similar problems across the social and cultural spectrum. It would take very little to transform this vision into a community with a common purpose, like that of the Mods in working-class London. By 1965, young people had remade British society in their own image and the image of the music that they lionized, made by people like Townshend himself.

Mod tastes, then—including their love of the Who—spread across London, Britain and the rest of the Western world in 1965 and 1966. As exemplars of a rampant consumerism in pursuit of a style no one could copy, the Mods were simultaneously rebellious and conformist at the same time—which was exactly what made them popular. Mod as a subculture became the essence of British youth culture, a culture that spread across Britain and the world through media exposure.

The Mod Aesthetic

One should not overemphasize the Mods' love of British acts. They loved American soul music, especially Tamla/Motown and Stax/Volt records. Mod bands generally tried to cater to them by playing covers of American soul songs or writing their own versions. Even the Who billed themselves on their early posters as "Maximum R&B", and covered songs like "Heatwave" by Martha and the Vandellas. But the Mods' taste for American music was not all encompassing. What they really wanted was music of their own, music just as trendy and exotic and new as their clothes and their clubs and their scooters. The Mods felt superior to the Stones and the Beatles, the bands of the masses, and wanted a distinctive music to go along with their distinctive images. The result was a select few new bands whose style and image reflected the originality that the Mods prized. The Mods saw these bands as trendsetters—musical faces, if you will. The Who were the first of these bands, but others retained the Mods' respect on the same principles: the Small Faces, the Yardbirds, and the Kinks were a few.[53] The Yardbirds and the Kinks quickly passed from Mod obsessions to national ones, and like the Who, abandoned their Mod roots. The Small Faces were the most successful at maintaining careers with their links to the Mod subculture intact.

The Small Faces were mainly from east London; well-versed in Cockney, they made the most of their accents and lingo. They were a band of, quite literally, "small" faces: they were all elfin in size. It was an odd little quirk that made them perpetually fashionable: no Mod could shave five inches off his height to be a face. (They were so small—all under 5'9"—that they went on their second tour in a single Jaguar, with three of them stuffed in the back seat.) Their manager signed them to a promise of £20 a week and all the clothes they wanted from Carnaby Street boutiques. Guitarist Steve Marriott and bassist Ronnie Lane developed a talent for songwriting, and 1966 saw them achieve four top ten hits in the UK.[54] Unlike the Who, which had been groomed to meet a demand for a Mod band, the Small Faces were Mods already, who happened to play instruments. The difference made them a new favorite at a time when the Who was moving on to Pop Art and auto-destruction as a focus. As a result, their Mod image was everything to the band: when their managers asked them to hire Ian McLagan as a new keyboard player, they did not question his professional abilities—they wanted to know how tall he was.[55]

Other groups attained local popularity, occasionally breaking the national charts but generally sticking close to their roots in Mod clubs around London. Each of them emphasized something different about the Mod lifestyle. The Action performed excellent, soulful covers of Motown singles and Chicago soul bands like the Impressions. The Creation's lead singer, Kenny Pickett, in imitation of the Who's auto-destruction, would spray-paint lightning quick pictures on canvasses while on stage and then set them alight; their guitarist, Eddie Phillips, dragged a bow across his electric guitar. John's Children featured the Levi's-pinching ace face, Marc Bolan; they emphasized their use of psychedelic drugs and amphetamines. Even a few provincial bands became Mod favorites for brief periods. Two Birmingham bands, the Move and the Spencer Davis Group, became popular in 1966, though they soon moved on to bigger things on the national charts. Spencer Davis featured sixteen-year-old Stevie Winwood, known for his uncanny Ray Charles impression as a singer and his talents as a keyboard player and guitarist too. The Move destroyed TV sets on stage and burned political figures like Harold Wilson in effigy.[56] Mod tastes had clearly spread beyond London to shape rock and roll music everywhere in Britain in 1965 and 1966.

The Mods patronized the music of London's Afro-Caribbean community as well. A few soul acts in London competed successfully for the Mods' attention as British versions of the American music they bought and loved. Geno Washington and the Ram Jam Band covered up-tempo singles from the Stax/Volt stable in America, by artists like Wilson Pickett, Otis Redding and Aretha Franklin.[57] But imitation was never accepted for long as worthy of the Mods' patronage. What the Mods really wanted was a sound that was exclusively their own, that they could claim as original. So they instead became patrons of a new rock and roll music called bluebeat, or ska.

Ska was the music of the Jamaican community in Britain. It melded the sounds of Caribbean calypso with American rhythm and blues by combining rhythm guitar chords with the drums on the upbeat. The resulting hurry-up sound had a sense of urgency that kept an amphetamine-fueled Mod dancing all night long. It was particularly appealing in its insistence on audience participation, yelling "yeah" at the right moment or moving in time to the movements of the band. The sense of community and action required of such a stage show appealed to the Mods' sense of unity. Identification with Afro-Caribbeans also drew upon the Mods' stereotypes of blacks, in their desire to be seen as cool and detached. As a Mod art student stated, "At the moment we're hero-worshipping the Spades—they can dance, and sing."[58]

All of these acts became popular in London because they were associated with the most notorious subculture of the mid-sixties. Being a Mod was a way of life for a teenager in Hammersmith. Being a Mod was a marketing strategy for a clothing designer in Mayfair, however. Whatever their efforts at alternative community, the Mods and their styles and fashions were virtually designed for imitation. Of course, the Mods despised the reduction of their separatism to a profit motive, but there was little they could do about it. As rock and roll bands took up the Mod banner, and teenagers across London and across Britain embraced their styles, the attitudes and the class values of the Mods became synonymous with the concept of being young and rebellious. Indeed the very word "mod" itself was twisted and blanded. It became the simplest adjective to use commercially as a signifier of being youthful, hip, cool in demeanor and classless in attitude.

As the Mod image spread across the landscape of British culture in the sixties, it seemed classless. To most young people who adopted Mod styles and fashions, the celebration of working-class culture that Mod represented made them feel as if they were a part of a community, in rebellion against the social divisions of the industrial past. They were a part of a youth community that challenged the hegemony of adult values by adopting what they believed were working-class values. It seemed like divisions between generations had replaced those between classes, and that youth culture was classless culture.[59]

In fact, the perception of classlessness and the paradoxical placement of working-class values at the center of that classlessness was precisely what made London's youth culture so exciting.[60] Under such circumstances, to be working-class in origin and upwardly mobile in lifestyle—like the Mods—was positively trendy. Margaret Forster, author of the popular sixties novel *Georgy Girl* (1965), noted how her origins as the daughter of a factory worker from the north of England had made her a hero to her friends.

> I'm terribly pleased to be working-class because it's the most swinging thing to be now, and so it was all my time at Oxford—a tremendous status symbol really. People were always asking with a sort of envious reverence "Do you really live in a Council house? Does your father, excuse me asking, but does he really wear a boiler-suit and work in a factory? He does—oh, how super!" . . . No, I'm very conscious of it, because I know it's a good thing and makes me seem all the brighter and cleverer and more super to have come from the muck of the North. People are such comic inverted snobs nowadays. All the mass media are biased in favour of anyone young and working-class, it's like having a title

must have been a hundred years ago. I wouldn't have been born anything but working-class whatever you'd offered me.[61]

Thus, Mod began to die out as the look and sound of the London originals began to spread around the country. Any adolescent could watch *Ready Steady Go!* in 1965 and see the new styles in clothing, the new types of music emanating from London. Teenagers emulated what they saw on the screen, and to them, Mod meant the Who and the Small Faces, not a way of life. It meant Townshend in his Union Jack jacket, Moon with a Spitfire target on his T-shirt, Daltrey with tape and symbols on his sweaters, Entwistle wearing military medals and buttons on his jacket.[62] It did not mean fighting in the streets with Rockers, keeping up with the trends at a frenetic pace, or establishing a sense of community in defiance of the expectations of respectability. Mod was fashion to the average teenager, and bands like the Who and the Small Faces were the most prominent exponents of that idea, whatever their intentions.

In fact, both bands eventually abandoned their Mod audience in the end. Even before they released "My Generation", the Who put out "Anyway Anyhow Anywhere" (1965). Townshend called it their first "Pop Art" single, full of guitar effects that sounded like Morse code, a jet engine and the tuning of an AM radio. According to Townshend, Pop Art was to "represent something the public is familiar with, in different form".[63] In reality, there was no difference in the sound, only in how Townshend characterized the sound. Meanwhile, within only six months of reaching the charts, the Small Faces became one of the first bands to write psychedelic hit singles, such as "My Mind's Eye" (1966) or "Itchycoo Park" (1967). It worked well for the Who and the Small Faces, and badly for Mod—suddenly, Mod itself was old-fashioned, a taste for tickets. The subculture dissipated in 1966 and 1967, though it has experienced numerous brief rebirths up to the present day.[64]

Mod was all about immediacy, an emphasis on being as current as was humanly possible. In such a situation, there was no time to reckon for a future; most Mods did not think they had one anyway. For a band to consider a future beyond Mod was twice as ridiculous. A Mod band's status as flavor of the moment was doubly in jeopardy if they stopped having hits, or if the Mods stopped liking them. The fact that the Who and the Small Faces survived Mod and the pop culture of the sixties is a tremendous testament to their talent as acts.[65] Their local brethren remained in local clubs all throughout the sixties, but stood less and less of a chance of breaking through to the national market as time wore on.

What Hath Mod Wrought?

Yet the movement of Mod bands into the mainstream also represented a move into a more respectable vision of youth culture. Mod was dangerous, a working-class movement of the west London streets and frightening to a cultural establishment that had waged war against such movements since the beginning of the industrial era. To adolescents who did not understand it—and even to some intellectuals who did—Pop Art was not dangerous at all. It was bohemian, elitist, a movement accessible to patrons of Soho art galleries and now, listeners to the radio playlist; it certainly did not hold Britain's cultural future in its hands only to throw it away, as the Mods did. The Who had changed the rhetoric of their music, but they had also changed the rhetoric of youth culture. Pop Art was art, and art was classless. The art school backgrounds of Pete Townshend and so many other musicians like him brought rock and roll into a new cultural realm, as a medium by which rock and roll musicians could become respectable, intellectual, wealthy—and thus create their own cultural norms.

Townshend and his bandmates certainly did not intend this. They did not consciously want to abandon their working-class roots in west London, and they remained, rightfully, heroes to the Mods and to any number of teenagers across London and the rest of Britain as representative of their values. But the Who's success as a music act, as fashion plates and as working-class intellectuals revealed them—and their audience—to have different cultural aspirations than groups like the Beatles, the Stones and other acts. The Who aspired to be artists, and being an artist was not a working-class occupation, whatever their sympathies: it was a bohemian one.

To be an artist was to have talents that others could not easily duplicate. Yet rock and roll seemed at bottom to be as non-artistic an occupation as there was; much of its charm and virtue had lain in the belief that anyone could make this music if they set their minds to learning the mere rudiments of musicianship. The Beatles were certainly great songwriters, but in 1964, they would sooner have referred to themselves as craftsmen instead of artists. Most of the critics who raved about their music would agree—pop music was not art. On the other hand, Gustav Metzger himself loved the Who, asking them to destroy their instruments at one of his academic seminars. In 1965, a number of French avant-garde musicians asked the band to play a musique concrete date in Paris.[66] Townshend himself could not determine exactly how seriously he should take his art—if indeed he made art at all. "I'm not afraid of calling anything I do an art form. I've just never thought of it further than it being something that personally I got pleasure out of, and which made me money."[67]

But now, in 1965 and 1966, a music form once defined by the amateurism of its musicians was far more serious in its artistic ambitions than anyone in Britain had ever realized. The music of a band like the Who was clearly "pop" music, made for a popular audience, meant to sell lots and lots of units. Yet now, the Who made it seem as if the mass production of singles, an ugly industrial process, could have a certain art to it. In fact, its very popularity was what made it "Pop Art"; there was a certain cleverness behind Townshend's ability to make music that serious artists like Metzger considered worthy of attention, and managing to foist it upon the public. It almost seemed as if someone was being fooled into liking pop music and considering it art, whether it was a bunch of French artists seeing a vision of themselves in the destruction of the Who's instruments, or Mods in the Goldhawk Social Club finding a certain elitism in the notion that their favorite music was recognized as Pop Art.

The Who's musical ambitions were high, and they changed the professional standard for rock and roll musicians just as the Beatles and the Stones had. Townshend himself denied that the concept of professionalism could ever be applied to rock and roll music.[68] Nonetheless, the view that rock and roll musicians were talented artists who maintained certain ideals prevailed amongst the musicians themselves. Even more, as the music became more professional, it became more accessible to a larger public, in particular as the musicians themselves matured. Respectable people had learned to tolerate and even like the Beatles, they still despised the Stones, and the notion that an act such as the Who were artists still seemed ridiculous to most. But a wedge forced itself into such perceptions, and with that wedge came the realization that the British cultural establishment could claim this raucous American music form and shape it to project its own values—even as its musicians became a newer and more raucous cultural establishment.

Chapter 5
Marketing a Lifestyle

Class rebellion was not the only aspect of the Mod subculture that proved commercially viable. The central paradox of the Mod lifestyle—that one bought things to be as anti-commercial as possible—became the central paradox of youth culture in general. This was hardly a new phenomenon in British culture; in fact, it had defined bourgeois culture since the advent of the industrial era. The idea of buying one's originality, of consumption being the road to bohemianism, was as old as the idea of Romanticism as the antidote to industrialism. The Mod subculture had proven merely that the working classes made such value judgments as well. Now, in the mid-1960s, youth deified the working classes as the true representatives of the national soul, much as the EFDSS had created its own vision of the peasantry a century earlier. The construct had no weight to it; in fact, young people demonized the industrial world as priggish, soulless and dull, like the factories and mines where the working classes worked—priggish, soulless and dull, like their own parents. Americans and American products took the place of the exotic, a new alternative standard to which British youth aspired. Band managers capitalized on these values; record companies promoted them in music; independent radio and television played the music for young people all over the British Isles. Entrepreneurship went bohemian in London, as alive and well as it had ever been in the 1960s, despite a supposed decline in the entrepreneurial spirit.

The eclecticism of British culture was a large part of what made it so marketable. British bands began to explore the historical sources of English culture in the mid-sixties, once London regained its position at the center of the music industry's talent production. Many of them found inspiration in folk, classical or religious traditions. Some thrust a radical social realism on the listener. Still others explored the musical influences of the old empire, especially Indian, Middle Eastern and West African music. Of course, any band could trade on all aspects of these cultural values in certain songs. The tapping of common sources for inspiration established strong nationalistic roots in British rock and roll, and was entirely in the alternative Romantic tradition as well. Such artistic efforts were what gave British rock and roll an identity different from that of American rock and roll, and they made it marketable all over the world.

These attitudes also defined new values in rock and roll. The artistic temperament assumed that a rock and roll musician, like any musician, had a certain level of expertise in music. In the mid-sixties, this sort of expertise—a new professionalism—manifested itself in a musician's desire and ability to work beyond the average rock and roll vocabulary of rhythm and blues, pop, 1950s rock and roll, and country and western influences. The battle between the artistic license involved in being a musician and the marketability to make good in the pop music industry provided rock and roll with its vitality in Britain, and ended up redefining the musical genre itself.

The values of youth lay squarely in the middle of this battle. The talents of acts like the Beatles, the Rolling Stones and the Who had established the rock and roll musician as a professional. He now had to have a suitable musical background. As groups like the Yardbirds made explicit, he had to be good at playing his instrument. He should be a songwriter with something to say, or he should be in a group that had one. If he was not working-class in origin, he had best act rebellious in opposition to the cultural values that dominated British society. He should consider himself an artist, trying to express the ideals and values of his youthful audience in words, music and performance, and he could measure his success through his ability to get the youth market to buy his music. Many of these musicians had been to art schools, particularly in London, so they were well acquainted with combining bohemianism with professionalism. They carried their values out of the art schools, out of their working-class neighborhoods or middle-class suburbs, and into the clubs, studios and arenas where they performed. By asserting a new professionalism for rock and roll musicians, they reasserted the ability of professionals to dictate the values of British culture to an entirely new generation of people, whether they realized it or not. Young people began to measure their favorite artists against this standard, and began to base their own tastes as consumers on the professional values of rock and roll too.

Swinging London and Its Businesses

These values had found their most articulate expression in the Mod subculture, and the Mods thus became trendsetters for youth all over Britain. But music was not the only area in which Mod tastes triumphed, particularly in London. In fact, the most outstanding display of Mod trendsetting came from the fashion industry. In the late fifties, the first Mods began to frequent Soho menswear stores to get the latest Italian fashions tailored to measure. A small strip off Regent Street called Carnaby Street catered to their tastes. The shops there sold to a West Indian and gay clientele in the fifties, but by 1962, more and more Mods began to show up, looking for Italian suits, American Ivy League sweaters, and any sort of variety to distinguish themselves from everyone else around them. Mary Quant became the first fashion designer to design specifically to their tastes at her shop on the King's Road in Chelsea.[1] The stores catered to girls as well—the miniskirt was originally a female Mod fashion. Boutiques spread to every High Street in London, carrying the new fashions made popular by working-class teenagers, now sought after by every teenager who identified with the Mods.

The world of fashion, then, adopted the values of the lifestyle dictated by rock and roll music, and profited upon it. For example, the model Lesley Hornby, a.k.a. Twiggy, was the most widely recognized face in London, and the most popular British model of the era on the international circuit. She was the queen of high fashion in one of the most elite and sophisticated industries. But as her manager, Justin de Villenueve noted, her popularity was due to the fact that "She's the epitome of the modern working girl. Because she's working-class and not one of those country types like [Jean] Shrimpton, ordinary girls feel they can identify themselves with Twiggy." Twiggy herself was the image of the British teenager, and knew how to maintain the proper image. Villenueve kept her on an expense account of £10 a week, "[b]ut that means I can buy all the records I want, the Stones, the Beatles and all, and to me that's rich."[2]

Once an adolescent had kitted himself or herself out in the latest fashions, the next thing to do was go to the right place to be seen in them. The clubs in London's West End became the center of London's musical development and the places where all young people went to find the next major acts on the British and world pop charts. The Marquee Club, on Wardour Street in Soho, was one of the greatest breeding grounds of talent in London in the 1960s, and the most talented acts of the era passed through its doors, playing for two million customers in ten years. The Who, the Rolling Stones, the Yardbirds, the Spencer Davis Group, the Animals, the Small Faces and hundreds more bands all had gigs or even Tuesday evening residencies at the Marquee.[3] Essentially a dingy basement with a low ceiling, the Marquee was nevertheless the womb of London's rock scene in the mid-sixties.

Because it was at the center of the new youth lifestyle, music became a huge business in Britain. British teenagers contributed £1 billion a year to the

British economy—more than the manpower costs of the armed forces. Teenagers bought 90 percent of the fifty million singles sold in Britain every year. Fashion changes made it so that clothing purchases amounted to a tenth of a young wage earners' pay per year. Young working teens bought record players and radios on hire purchase; the more enterprising bought electric guitars and drum sets. Purchases defined identity in London in the 1960s, and no one was better defined than the teenager. The fact that so many had the money to buy what they wanted, and that their purchasing power did not seem to depend on their class background, was a major factor in leading people to believe they were entering into an era in which class itself would disappear. Age seemed a more appropriate divider of people, at least in a consumer society. The classless society seemed to be giving way to the generation gap. Young people had the sort of money that could demand the development of consumer trends that would reflect their interests.[4]

The media contributed to the spread of youth culture as a business by reporting on fashion and music changes in an almost obsessive manner. The national press reported the cultural goings-on in the capital breathlessly, as a way of selling newspapers and advertisements. Advertisements especially trumpeted the new fashions. Radio stations and television programs broadcast the latest bands to an insatiable teenaged public. Movies made all of the new styles seem glamorous and powerful. And all of it sold extremely well on the continent, in the Commonwealth and in America. From 1964 through 1967, there was little question that London was the hippest city in the world, for perhaps the first time in its ancient existence.[5]

Pirate Radio

The media focused on rock and roll musicians, fashions and lifestyles because the images sold well. Television, radio and the film industry fed off rock and roll music and musicians just as much as the musicians needed television, radio and films to make them popular. The music broke through the strict controls imposed by guardians of the national taste over the entertainment industry. The British Broadcasting Corporation was the avatar of cultural standards in entertainment, and rock and roll did not meet such standards. The BBC's priggishness could be daunting. In 1963 the corporation banned the Cougars' "Red Square" because it was based on a theme from Tchaikovsky's First Piano Concerto, and was thus "a distortion of a major classical work".[6] Under such circumstances, the promotion of music for a youth audience interested in escaping the BBC's standards inspired a level of creativity and entrepreneurship in the music industry that was unprecedented. A huge market existed for rock and roll in Britain, and if the BBC would not cater to it, other media and business groups were more than willing to try.

Before 1963, the BBC always made a modest effort to accommodate its teenaged audience's thirst for the new American music. The Light Programme had a show called *Saturday Club* that broadcast plenty of rock and roll and interviewed a number of British teen idols, plus the occasional American star like Gene Vincent or Eddie Cochran. But it only lasted for two hours, despite the audience's love of the show and demand for more. The BBC had long hoped to shape the tastes of the public; by the 1960s, it had settled into the role of mainly broadcasting to the tastes of a mainstream adult audience, and catering to what it considered minority eclectic tastes as much as possible around that audience. Rock and roll was one of these minority tastes. There was only so much tolerance and airtime that the nation's cultural arbiter could spare when its producers debated whether the Coasters' "Charlie Brown" should get on the air because its lyrics contained the word "spitball".[7]

After 1963, however, with the demand for the Beatles' music so high, it was inevitable that someone would challenge the BBC's monopoly. That challenge came in 1964 in the form of pirate radio. "Pirate radio" got its name from the fact that most of its stations broadcast from ships in the North Sea or the Irish Sea. They were commercial channels broadcasting to nations with state-run radio services, and were thus illegal. They exploited a loophole in international telecommunications law that allowed broadcasting from international waters. In early 1964, an Irish entrepreneur named Rohan O'Rahilly borrowed £250,000 from various family and business sources and bought a former passenger ferry named the *Frederika* to start the first pirate radio station off the coast of Britain. He outfitted the *Frederika* with two transmitters and a 168-foot-high radio mast, and anchored it four miles off Harwich. O'Rahilly's station, Radio Caroline, debuted on March 29, 1964, with disc jockey Simon Dee at the helm, broadcasting rock and roll and pop music exclusively.[8] The response from the audience was immediate, according to Dee.

> We didn't know how it was going, because on the ship we had no outside communication of any sort. . . . When the first boat came out to us it had these enormous sacks on it which we thought were food, but they were mail. It was fantastic! All you had to say was "It's very cold out here" and you'd get sent sweaters and ski hats. They sent us everything, they were even sending us record vouchers! It was a fantastic success right from the start.[9]

Within weeks, Radio Caroline had millions of listeners who were excited at the prospect of a radio station broadcasting popular music all day long. Revenues came from advertising, and for the moment, British companies faced no reprisals for placing advertisements on Caroline. Shell Oil, Weetabix, VP Wines, the *News of the World*, and Alberto VO5 Shampoo all broadcast commercials. Even the National Coal Board and the Egg Marketing Board, government sponsored bodies, placed commercials on Radio Caroline to reach a sizable audience. Within six months of its debut, Radio Caroline had expanded to two ships, reaching an estimated thirty-nine million listeners in Britain, and sold advertising space at an average cost of £90 for a thirty-second spot. With so much money at stake, it was not long before new stations arose to compete with Radio Caroline. Radio Sutch started in May 1964, operating out of abandoned World War II gun towers at the mouth of the Thames. Its manager soon bought out the owner and rechristened it Radio City. Radio Invicta opened in another fort in June 1964. In January 1965, Radio London began operations, with three times the kilowatt power of Caroline, and made a profit within eight weeks of its debut.[10]

Both the Conservative Home Government and the incoming Labour Government of Harold Wilson threatened to outlaw the pirate stations, but feared the potential reprisal of young voters in the coming elections. Instead, they left the matter to the European Economic Community's Council of Europe, which the government expected to make it illegal to advertise on or finance pirate radio stations. But when the Council's ruling came in January 1965, the Wilson Government was shocked. The Council did not rule that the pirates were illegal; they only had to operate on wavelengths that would not interfere with ship frequencies. Neither did the Council place any stigma on advertisers or the pirates' business operations. The pirates now had virtual impunity of operations, and an audience of British teenagers that would keep them in business for years to come, with a listenership three times that of the BBC.[11]

The phenomenal successes of Radio Caroline and Radio London allowed them to buy out many of their competitors. They modeled themselves on their commercial counterparts in the United States, with radio jingles, disk jockey prattling and non-stop music twenty-four hours a day. Because of their profit-first format, the pirates all made a practice of getting record companies to pay to have their records played on the radio, a scheme known in America as "payola". Since the pirates operated in international waters, such practices were perfectly legal, if dangerous to expose to the public. Radio Caroline even allowed record companies to pay to have records played a certain number of times a day, starting at £8 per single. More importantly, just about any record could get played on pirate radio if record companies wanted to pay for plays and people subsequently wanted to hear it. Thus, dozens of new acts got radio exposure that the BBC surely would not have given them, especially those on small, independent labels. Before the advent of the pirates in 1964, the two biggest labels, EMI and Decca, produced a full 80 percent of new chart acts. Now, smaller labels could get their artists promoted on the air, even if they had to pay for the privilege.[12]

The proliferation of the pirates prompted an examination of the BBC's broadcasting policies, and its directors announced scheduling changes that upped the hours of the Light Programme to twenty-one per day. Yet the BBC was still determined to adhere to its traditional cultural dictates. Light Programme chief Tom Sloan angrily denounced the poor musical standards of British music artists in general, and lambasted his own producers for not promoting more "imaginative" artists on pop programs. A late night pop music program named *Top Gear* was cancelled in May 1965 after four months of competition with the pirates, and the BBC replaced it with brass band and cinema organ music.* Ridiculously, considering the phenomenal success of the pirates, the BBC's producers claimed there was not enough interest in Britain to sustain another two hours of pop music programming.[13] A BBC insider revealed that programming goals were to play 52 percent classical music during the day and 48 percent everything else. As Bob Dawbarn of *Melody Maker* noted, "Apparently the BBC regards its average listener as a churchgoing intellectual, who likes brass bands and cinema organs in the brief intervals of relaxation."[14]

The BBC stood little chance of competing with the pirates' popularity as long as it refused to adopt the same pop music playlist. The battle over the commercialization of British radio was a battle over the class standards of British culture itself. By May 1966, one out of three people in Britain listened to pirate radio stations on a regular basis, according to a poll conducted by Radio London. The pirates accordingly attracted more than £2 million in advertising revenue.[15] Radio London landed £200,000 in advertising revenue in its first year alone. It did not seem as if the pirates had anything to fear, as the BBC clearly offered no musical alternative.

The whole situation was an inherited embarrassment for the new Labour government. The balance of payments crisis was reported widely in the press, but a government committed to public nationalizations apparently found it impossible to consider legalizing pirate radio as a private enterprise that could bring in revenue by broadcasting to the continent. Thus, in August 1966, the government introduced a bill in the Commons to punish all figures associated with pirate radio stations, other than listeners, with a two-year jail term. The pirates united in opposition to Postmaster General Tony Benn's efforts to shut them down. Radio Caroline began to negotiate with American record companies to have them buy space on the air during which their discs would be promoted exclusively.

At this point, however, the pirates went through a series of seedy and suspicious incidents that made people wonder about the honesty of the businessmen involved. The worst was in 1966, when the owner of Radio City, Reg Calvert, was murdered under mysterious circumstances at the home of Major Oliver Smedley, a part-owner in Radio Caroline. The affair made the operation of the pirates seem sordid, especially when Smedley's trial exposed the "payola" scheme to the public. He was acquitted, but the pirates' public image was severely damaged. Both public and governmental opinion was now firmly against the continued operation of the pirates as an illegal operation.[16]

In December 1966, the Wilson Government announced its solution: the BBC got permission to begin an exclusive pop music service, broadcasting

---

Top Gear would return on BBC's Radio One in October 1967.

eighteen hours a day. The government moved to prosecute all the pirates it could get its lawsuits on, but the BBC also promised to hire many of the pirate deejays for the new service. The Wilson Government accordingly passed the Marine Broadcasting (Offences) Act, which made it illegal for British companies to advertise on the pirates' frequencies. The government also planned to demolish the forts that the pirates had operated from as soon as possible. Without advertising revenue, the pirates became too expensive to run, and by the end of 1967, only Radio Caroline was still in business, and only barely.[17]

The BBC's Radio One and Radio Two debuted on September 30, 1967. Featuring disc jockey lineups culled from the defunct pirates, the two stations split the old BBC Light Programme's playlist, Radio One handling rock and roll-oriented pop music, Radio Two providing an easy listening format. But the youth audience considered Radio One a crashing bore in comparison to the pirates. With the collapse of the pirates, Britain had to rely again on the BBC as its exclusive radio service. The death of the commercial competition meant that the new stations simply settled back into the corporation's conservative broadcasting habits. Radio One played station identification jingles for no obvious reason—there was no other station to distinguish themselves from—and their commercials were for other BBC shows.[18] Many people missed the pirates. American FM stations were just beginning to play album-oriented rock and roll music twenty-four hours a day, a format that Radio One made no effort to duplicate. The result was a paucity of airplay in Britain for some of the best British and American rock and roll bands of the era.[19] Nevertheless, the pirates, and the enterprise they represented, showed the power of youth culture in Britain, its values so popular that they could swamp the pretensions of a cultural totem like the BBC.

The battle over pirate radio's continued existence was a battle over the tastes of the youth market, one that the BBC could not win without legal action. But it was also a battle that displayed rock and roll's ability to transmit its alleged working-class tastes to a huge audience. British rock and roll's ability to exercise its economic muscle made it an important forum in which to view the changes inherent in postwar British society and culture. Pirate radio, as an illegal enterprise, and the battle over its continued existence, showed clearly the influence rock and roll had gained in the mass market. In the end, rock and roll compromised the BBC's cultural purpose, at least as far as radio broadcasting was concerned. The very existences of Radio One and Radio Two meant that the British music audience, now dominated by teenagers, demanded catering to its tastes.

Rock and Roll Management

No medium displayed the power of the youth market like pirate radio. Nevertheless, other business enterprises reflected the values of the youth market and rock
and roll as well. Rock and roll inspired new entrepreneurship, in the management of rock and roll bands and clubs, and with the establishment of new record
labels. Already-established media, such as television and the movies, came to
reflect the tastes of the rock and roll audience too. The continued adaptation of
the mass market to the values of rock and roll represented a shift in the rhetoric
of British culture, toward a language that presaged the breaking down of traditional social distinctions. Many people found the changes in British culture more
exciting than at any other time in their lives, indeed at any time in the nation's
modern history. Others were frightened of the possibilities inherent in a classless, gender-less, teenaged and presumably standard-less culture. All recognized
change in the air, if adults did not necessarily recognize rock and roll as the vehicle through which the expression and language of change revealed itself.

Working-class culture traditionally meant soccer, pubs, dancing, and just
hanging out in the street. It was a collective culture, a culture where bonds of
community provided meaning. Middle-class culture was more individualistic,
found in one's purchasing tastes in music, fashion, or magazines, later in the
patronage of television, radio and the movies. All of them were individual experiences, where meaning came from a personal reaction to the medium. Which
class one derived from usually dictated which form of culture was more prominent in one's life.[20] But now, in the meeting ground of pop culture, it was possible to mix both. A young person's expressions of individuality connected him or
her to a wider youth culture that defined itself by its sense of community, of
youth as "my generation". Once an entrepreneur like Rohan O'Rahilly recognized the dual individualistic and communitarian principle inherent in these
youth ideals, it was easy to sell them to a wide audience. In the case of pirate
radio, a teenager listening to an illegal radio station felt like a rebel. It provided
him or her with an identity, separate from law-abiding parents who wanted that
rock and roll garbage turned down or off. But contact with his or her friends
who listened to the same stations provided a sense of community, especially in
the face of governmental condemnation. Most of all, for an entrepreneur like
O'Rahilly, the same kid could be inundated with commercials for acne creams,
deodorants, baked beans, even the records themselves. Dozens of similar entrepreneurs entertained similar notions of the potential of rock and roll as an economic and cultural phenomenon.

The London music scene had its business patrons, just as Liverpool had
Brian Epstein, but they were a very different group of businessmen. Epstein's
management of the Beatles was entirely financial after 1964. He no longer directed their images or their music and became more of a hanger-on—one of
many people accorded access to the Beatles' inner circle, but not one of the peo-

ple involved in their development as artists. His tastes and expectations simply did not fit the standards of development for rock and roll music in Britain; Cilla Black was much more his idea of a proper entertainer. London's music moguls were very different. In general, they were younger, they appreciated rhythm and blues and rock and roll as much as the artists themselves, and they knew what young people wanted. As a result, they managed new bands, started record labels, managed clubs, pressured the most powerful record labels and radio stations to play a wide variety of music, and generally promoted the values of the music they loved just as much as they tried to profit off of it.[21]

For example, Giorgio Gomelsky ran the Crawdaddy Club at the Station Hotel in Richmond. He offered the Rolling Stones a residency on Sunday nights, and when they amassed a following, he became their unofficial manager. When they moved on to bigger venues and a pop chart career, Gomelsky found the Yardbirds and gave them the Stones' spot on Sunday nights. They in turn made him their legal manager, a capacity in which he remained through 1966. As manager, he produced their songs in the studio to create a distinctive Yardbirds sound, raw and raucous but also precise and defined. He also encouraged experimentation in their choices of songs and instruments. After splitting with the Yardbirds, he picked up a few other bands and even started his own record label, called Marmalade Records, to break other new groups in Britain. He later moved to France to establish a circuit of clubs for British bands to play there. Gomelsky's model was typical—a music enthusiast whose continuing interest spawned new businesses, new geographical venues, and the endless search for new talent.[22]

Andrew Loog Oldham, the next manager of the Rolling Stones, was perhaps the best-known manager in Britain after Epstein. Once a member of Epstein's press team, he quit to manage the Stones after seeing them on stage in Richmond. He produced the band's records and directed their rebellious image until 1967, when the Stones fired him.[23] He then became the manager of the Small Faces, and took his profits from management to start an independent label, Immediate Records. He signed the Small Faces to the label in 1967 and secured the release rights to the catalogs of other American independent labels.[24] Immediate became one of the most successful independent labels of the sixties in Britain.

Guy Stevens was a similar entrepreneur. He was the disk jockey at the Scene Club, playing rhythm and blues and American soul records in between band sets for the Mods in the audience. Stevens put pressure on Pye International, the company owning the catalog for Chess Records in Chicago, to release old singles and albums by Chuck Berry, Muddy Waters, Howlin' Wolf and other fifties blues acts, so that people could buy them in the London area. Chuck Berry's "No Particular Place to Go" (1964) became a hit single in Britain as a result. Stevens became co-owner of a record label, Sue Records, with another disk jockey, Chris Blackwell. Through Sue Records, Stevens acquired the rights to dozens of old American blues albums from numerous labels, by artists like Elmore James, James Brown, Bobby Bland and others. Stevens's partner,

Blackwell, managed and produced the records of the Spencer Davis Group in 1966, and later started the most successful of Britain's independent labels, Island Records, in 1968.[25]

Kit Lambert and Chris Stamp were the Who's management team, and their show business and class backgrounds made them a perfect complement to the band's artistic pretensions. They were originally film producers; Stamp's brother was the actor Terence Stamp, one of the biggest British stars of the sixties. His father was a tugboat driver from the east end of London, as working-class a pedigree as possible. Lambert, by contrast, was the son of Constance Lambert, a composer, conductor and music critic who wrote reviews of classical music releases for *The Times.* They were looking for a band to make a movie about the swinging London scene, in the vein of the Beatles' *A Hard Days' Night* (1964), when they came across the Who. They soon became the band's managers and helped direct them through their Mod and Pop Art phases. Each cultivated a sense of outrageousness that became the Who's calling card. Far from discouraging their destruction of their instruments, Lambert and Stamp quickly came to see it as integral to the Who's stage act, even when it ran the band into hundreds of thousands of pounds in debt. Lambert and Stamp also established Track Records in 1966, signing the Who, the Jimi Hendrix Experience, John's Children, The Crazy World of Arthur Brown, and numerous other successful acts of the late sixties.[26] Chris Stamp defined their role with the Who in an interview.

> Being a manager is like being a member of the group. One exercises some sort of control but socially one is on the same level as the group. There's no longer any "Mister" relationship between a good young manager and his group, and indeed there couldn't be. We produce and edit the records, we give the ideas for what to wear on stage and on TV appearances, we help the group with their personal problems such as flats, girl-friends, emotional troubles and so and, of course, on top of that we do all the setting up of bookings and contracts. You couldn't do all these things if you weren't on exactly the same level as your group. We take 40 per cent of the groups total earnings [an outrageously exorbitant rate at the time and now] and I reckon if anything we're still underpaid at this rate.[27]

Television

Most rock and roll managers learned to push their bands beyond the medium of radio, to television and film. Both media were far more interested in profits than they were in maintaining any sense of cultural mission. On television, rock and roll meant ratings, so the competition between the BBC and Independent Television was fierce from the beginning. Shows such as ITV's *Cool for Cats* and *Oh Boy!* vied for attention with the BBC's *6.5 Special, Dig This!* and *Drumbeat.* With the advent of the Beatles, the two competing shows were *Juke Box Jury* on the BBC and *Thank Your Lucky Stars* on ITV. *Juke Box Jury* invited pop stars, celebrities and the occasional audience member to review the records released that week and decide whether they were future hits or doomed to failure. *Thank Your Lucky Stars* had a similar format, and was most famous for the Birmingham accent—a rarity in London-dominated television at the time—of Janice Nicholls, who would announce "Oi'll give it a foive" if she liked a record (five out of five being the highest possible score). Neither show was particularly exciting visually, featuring merely a series of people bobbing their heads or snapping their fingers in time to songs while they waited to review them when the songs were over. Yet teenagers would watch just about anything to get an opportunity to see or hear their favorite rock and roll stars.[28]

Family variety shows were the other staple of rock music programming in the early sixties. *Sunday Night at the London Palladium* was the British equivalent of *The Ed Sullivan Show* in America. It aired on ITV on Sunday evenings, with an old-time music hall format and one big star to close the show. The show pitched itself to an adult audience, so the rock and roll bands who played on the show, and whose phenomenal commercial success almost invariably made them the show-closers, were very much out of place. At the end of the show, all of its stars stood on a revolving stage and waved to the live television audience as the credits rolled, an old show business tradition. When the Rolling Stones refused to take the revolving stage, considering it hopelessly old-fashioned, most rock and roll acts stopped being booked and appearing on variety shows.[29]

The most important show in bringing rock and roll acts to the teenaged audience was *Ready, Steady, Go!*, which started in 1963 on ITV. The show recreated the atmosphere of London's Mod clubs on TV. The audience was selected for its dancing ability, and Cathy McGowan conducted interviews with musicians while the music played and the dancers danced in the background, as if the viewer was in on an inside conversation in a smoky club in Soho. The show brilliantly captured the feel of Mod London, and it was the only thing worthy of keeping a Mod home on a Friday night. Every major pop group appeared on *Ready, Steady Go!* (except Cliff Richard, who was considered passé), and it helped to launch the careers of a number of bands, the Who among them. It ended in 1966 before its format became tired with the onset of the psychedelic era.

The BBC ran to play catch-up. *Top of the Pops* debuted in January 1964; it was a music news show of sorts, reporting on the state of the pop charts. Leading London disk jockeys rotated as presenters from the show's studios in Manchester. The Cathy McGowan figure was a fashionably Mod girl named Samantha Juste who put records on the turntable but never spoke: she only occasionally giggled. It lasted all the way to 2006, adopting the approximate format of *Ready, Steady, Go!* when that show was cancelled by ITV.[30]

Movies

The British film industry was far less attuned than television to rock and roll, particularly in comparison to the American film industry. British films had always catered to the tastes of the adult public, and when *Rock Around the Clock* and *Blackboard Jungle* arrived in Britain, it seemed that the rock and roll film was doomed. If this was how teenagers behaved in a theater when watching such films, there was no way a major film producer would consider offending the wider public by distributing a British version. Instead, the rock and roll film became a vehicle for a number of small, independent film companies to make profits. Most of them were far less concerned with the public taste than they were with making pounds. On tight budgets and fast schedules, they produced pictures in the late fifties to capitalize on the latest craze in music. Most early British rock and roll films, like *Beat Girl* (1960) or *Expresso Bongo* (1959), were tame affairs featuring Cliff Richard or one of the Parnes stable of boy singers.[31]

A Hard Day's Night (1964), like just about everything in the Beatles' career, marked another turning point, this time in the history of rock and roll on film. Its style, humor and mixture of innocence and worldliness set it apart from all of its British and American predecessors. A Liverpool playwright named Alun Owen wrote the film, as he was well acquainted with the Beatles' music and understood their sense of humor. Richard Lester directed the story of a day in the life of the Beatles, as they traveled to London (from Liverpool, presumably) to make an appearance on a TV show. Paul McCartney's cantankerous grandfather was brought along and lost during the film, providing an opportunity to show the group engaging in various shenanigans as a unit and as individuals in the effort to find him and get him back to the studio. The film was something of a combination of a comedy and a documentary, and it worked quite well—a watcher did not have to like the Beatles' music to like the Beatles themselves. It was a major critical and commercial success, though viewers in 1964 could rarely hear the dialogue over the screaming of girls in the audience.

A Hard Day's Night also helped established the Beatles as darlings of the British intelligentsia, thus enhancing their professional status. Critics compared them to the Marx Brothers, and their comedy seemed avant-garde, especially in its gentle mockery of the self-important pomposity of stand-in symbols of the respectable establishment like fashion marketers, TV directors, bowler-hatted professionals and the like. Their next film, *Help!* (1965), was designed to place the Beatles at the center of swinging London's Pop Art world, right where the intelligentsia had placed them. Its comedy was more hackneyed as a result, with a poorly-conceived plot about Ringo Starr being stalked by a murderous Hindu cult for the retrieval of a religiously symbolic ring on his hand. The characters were the same, but the humor was merely silly without being clever—the movie lacked the aura of gentle social sarcasm that had made *A Hard Day's Night* so

much fun. The Beatles themselves disliked the movie, and not surprisingly—
they were hardly the intellectually challenging comedians they were made out to
be. Their contract with United Artists called for a third movie, but as John Lennon said, they did not want to be extras in their own picture.[32]

The Beatles' irritation at having to play a role unlike their daily lives on film
did nothing to dissuade other managers from pushing their own acts into movies,
however. Almost every pop act of the era either made a movie or considered
scripts, in an effort to capitalize on their success. Traditional show business
standards decreed that musical success had to lead to success as all-around entertainers, and it took many musicians a long time to dismiss the notion. A formula was quickly established for the British rock and roll movie. Middling level
pop groups would be paired with chart toppers like the Dave Clark Five or the
Animals in inexpensive, amiable little farces that were really more a mockery of
youth culture in their exploitative plots than a celebration of the music. *Catch Us
If You Can* (1965), a film featuring the Dave Clark Five, was directed by the
then-unknown John Boorman. *Dateline Diamonds* (1966) was a crime thriller
with the Small Faces and a setting aboard Radio London. Peter Noone of Herman's Hermits starred in a Hollywood picture, *Hold On*, in 1966, in an effort to
break into films permanently. The Who did not dismiss Lambert and Stamp's
plan for making a film for several years. Even the Rolling Stones entertained
film scripts and at one point were scheduled to play parts in an adaptation of the
Dave Wallis novel, *Only Lovers Left Alive* (1964).[33] None of these efforts was
particularly successful critically—it would not be until the later sixties that film
became as much an artistic outlet as it was a commercial boondoggle for the best
British rock and roll bands. But these early films brought rock and roll stars to a
teenaged public that craved them. All contributed to the proliferation of rock and
roll values in youth culture, and the huge expansion of profits inherent in their
spread.

Making Records

With so many media outlets, the music industry in Britain made huge profits.
Independent record companies catered to new markets, every music company
invested in new artistic talent, and a large number of the new acts became exportable commodities too. Despite this, though, the music business was not usually seen as an important growth industry. Jonathan Aitken, then a reporter with
the *Daily Mail*, maintained an attitude typical of the times. In *The Young Meteors* (1967), Aitken tried to define the nature of youth culture and the people at its
center in sixties London. As a rule, he found the new trends in British culture
disastrous, but in particular, he damned the "young meteors" as an unadven-
turous lot when it came to business. Aitken did not see the music industry as a
legitimate enterprise, despite its huge profits.

Young Londoners may be amusing in conversation, enterprising on the dance floor and adventurous in the double bed, but when it comes to big commercial enterprises they are naïve innocents.

This is of crucial importance, for after all we are a capitalist country and we depend for our living in the world on the success of capitalist enterprises. Yet the fields of business and finance, which need new talent more than any other, are being sadly neglected by the younger generation, and the quality of young people in London engaged in any aspect of commercial life (a pretty wide field after all) is very poor when compared to their international contemporary competitors. . . .

I was disappointed to find large numbers of intelligent people who had drifted off into cosy, fashionable occupations, such as promoting pop groups, buying for fashion shops, or managing bistros. In such occupations they are little better than idle hangers-on; if properly trained they could be making some real contribution to British business, earning much higher salaries and having far more interesting lives.[34]

Yet rock and roll was a huge industry in Britain, earning extremely valuable export dollars from the United States and helping to redress the balance of payments deficit. The Beatles alone earned more American dollars in 1964 than the exports of the entire British automobile industry to the United States.[35] Aitken and people like him disdained such production because rock and roll was not a respectable business to be in—it was a business that thrived on the proliferation of non-respectable values. Thus, the music industry's profits were not taken seriously or promoted, though business statistics might dictate otherwise.

Music industry profits began to explode with the rise of the Beatles in the 1960s, and the Beatles continued to dominate record sales throughout the decade. Before their records had even reached the world's top music market in the United States, the band grossed £6.25 million in record sales around the world in the last six months of 1963.[36] Upon arriving in the United States, their singles and albums were released on four different labels that had purchased distribution rights. By March 1964, in just three months of airplay, they represented 60 percent of all singles sales in the United States.[37] "I Want to Hold Your Hand" sold 2.6 million copies in six weeks, and the LP *Meet the Beatles* sold a million copies too. Royalties were said to exceed £90,000, the highest in the history of the music industry in Britain and America.[38] They also made around £357,000 in personal appearance fees. These sales were topped by the profits of merchandisers who took home an estimated £17,875,000 from America in 1964, in wigs, t-shirts, hats, guitars, boots, even snack cakes like the immortal "Ringo Roll".[39]

In 1965, the Beatles' publishing company, Northern Songs Limited, was put on the market. It was estimated that Lennon and McCartney would continue earning royalties on their songs through at least 1980—there had already been

674 different cover versions of their songs made around the world by the end of 1964.[40] Northern Songs was worth £2 million in 1965. It was broken up into 1.25 million shares, to be sold by Midland Bank in minimum blocks of two hundred at 7s 9d a piece. Most financial gurus in the City of London, plus the *Financial Times* and the *Investors' Chronicle*, advised against buying into the company, as the Beatles' hitmaking potential was unquantifiable and the resulting gamble could not be risked by most investors.[41] Yet every single share was sold, almost immediately, and Lennon and McCartney reaped an immediate profit of £400,000.[42] By 1967, shares were up to 17s 9d, and the company had more than doubled its profits to £842,000.[43] The Beatles were a solid investment.

Singles were the starting point for the music industry's sales in 1963 and 1964. However, the effort to bring back the "class" performer in response to Mick Jagger's persona was only one effort the industry made to try to change the trafficking of singles to teenaged stereos and rescue the adult music buyer. British retailers and manufacturers instead tried to promote "better music" by improving the quality of the LP market, hoping to keep the music boom of 1964 rolling into the coming year.[44] If the record companies emphasized a more expensive form of record, they believed, then only a wealthier music-buying public—namely, adults—would be able to afford it. Their tastes would eventually come to dominate the market, and the music industry would again be able to reconcile its profits with its cultural values.[45]

The industry's efforts to emphasize LPs in 1965 and 1966 backfired completely, though their profits skyrocketed anyway. In late 1965, the Beatles released *Rubber Soul*, the first serious effort by a rock and roll act to produce an LP as an artistic statement. *Rubber Soul* was a complete artistic package—an artsy photo of the band without any name identification on the front of the record sleeve, and no obvious filler songs between the hits on the record. As usual, other rock and roll artists followed the Beatles' lead; in 1966, the Stones released *Aftermath*, the Who released *A Quick One*, the Beatles released an even better album, *Revolver*, all considered classics. Numerous American bands were inspired by the Beatles too, most notably the Beach Boys with *Pet Sounds* and Bob Dylan with *Blonde on Blonde*. Since so many rock and roll musicians wrote their own music, and rather prolifically, it became clear to teenaged music buyers that they could not hope to keep up pace with their favorite bands' output by purchasing singles alone. Albums soon became a much larger proportion of total sales than ever before. *Rubber Soul* set world sales records by selling 1.2 million copies in only nine days. Meanwhile, while they sold a lot of singles, none of the "class" artists the British music industry counted on to overtake the teenaged consumer's tastes released an album that sold even remotely as well as any of the most important rock and roll artists.[46]

The major labels quickly abandoned their efforts to promote non-rock and roll artists and catered to what the market dictated. The growth of the LP market opened up even more avenues of profit. In early 1966, smaller labels owned by the majors began to release "budget LPs", albums by groups whose luster had faded but whose product might sell to the nostalgic at a lesser price. Labels such as Music for Pleasure, owned by EMI, and Pickwick, owned by Decca, would place racks in shops full of LPs by rock and roll artists that had been deleted from the main manufacturer's inventory for at least a year. The buyer could then go through these bins and find records by Gerry and the Pacemakers, Adam Faith, the Searchers and other top-sellers from three or four years earlier. They all sold well at a cheaper price, both in Britain and abroad.[47]

Selling overseas was especially important for the music industry. In an era when the balance of payments was a major problem for the British economy, export profits from British records rose higher and higher throughout the decade.[48] Despite grim economic forecasts in the beginning of the year, sales in 1967 were up 11 percent from 1966.[49] British manufacturers profited £3.5 million from record exports in 1967. By 1968, London's metropolitan record market was the largest producer in the world outside the United States, with one hundred million records grossing approximately £40 million. A 50 percent export purchase tax on records brought home even more money added to the earnings of British acts performing in overseas markets.[50] Rock and roll may have promised rhetorically to create a new society in postwar Britain, but the best reason anyone might take it seriously—as many young people did increasingly in the 1960s—was because it created serious adult profits too.

Going "Commercial"

Commercial success, however, was dangerous to British rock and roll musicians in 1965 and 1966. They were poised on the brink of being accepted as artists, in touch with a bohemianism that lionized youth values and working-class values. Yet the bohemian lifestyle at London's high society parties, art galleries and exclusive clubs found them far removed from youth or the working classes. A popular sound or group stood poised between the appreciation of a selective audience that defined itself to the exclusion of the wider pop audience, and the demands of that wider audience as manifested in ever-expanding recording profits. Bands like the Beatles, the Stones, the Who and a few others could define popular taste by their own taste. They put out records that reflected their own artistic inclinations without worrying about whether the record would be popular—because records by the Beatles, the Stones and the Who would be popular no matter what. Few other bands were so lucky.[51] Spencer Davis noted as much when describing the success of his band's third single "Keep on Running" (1965): "It's just great. But we hope our fans don't think we've gone commercial! That's one thing we're worried about, all of us!"[52]

"Not going commercial" seemed like a ridiculous notion at a time when the music industry and pop culture in general produced such a huge profit. But the paradox involved in being an "artist" was as old as art and commerce themselves. The level of artistic development in rock and roll was a concept that re-quired a rejection of the standards of commercialism, even as that rejection be-came necessary in order to make even more money. The contradiction existed everywhere in the capitalist world, but it had existed in British culture through-out the industrial era, and it found its roots in the Romantic image of the artist—a loner, an expert at his craft with the heart of an amateur, interested in com-municating deep emotion and meaning that would connect him with a wider community that needed such communication to find its own bearings.

Rock and roll musicians embraced these categories of authenticity whole-heartedly, as signs of their rebellion against the cultural status quo. They held to new standards by which they measured culture, since their own cultural back-grounds were increasingly diverse. Many of them were former art college stu-dents, and by 1966, they had grown up listening to rock and roll since before the Beatles hit the pop music charts. The music they made lay on the verge of its most creative and brilliant period of development in 1966 and 1967. The combi-nation of youth values, entrepreneurial spirit and musical adventurousness made rock and roll one of the most exciting cultural outlets in Britain.

Nevertheless, a social and rhetorical Rubicon was being crossed. Being a professional rock and roll musician in 1967 was very different from what it had been just four years before. Rock and roll in 1963 had been a celebration of spontaneity, amateurism, working-class roots and working-class values. Now, such values were taken for granted, if not ignored altogether. In fact, rock and roll had strayed so far from those values that the very term itself seemed to need redefining. Increasingly in 1966, such musicians referred to the music they played, not as "rock and roll"—spontaneous, amateur, loud, working-class—but as "rock", a term that somehow conveyed a greater seriousness of artistic in-tent—crafted, professional, often quieter, but still rhetorically beholden to the same non-existent working-class values. Rock musicians—artists—were a dif-ferent group, more like their Romantic forebears than like the parents or neigh-bors amongst whom they had grown up. Their wealth alone brought them to a level of classless affluence that belied their roots; their cultural outlook changed accordingly.

Chapter 6
Psychedelia

Kevin Macdonald was the founder of Sibylla's, a popular discotheque on Piccadilly. He was the great nephew of Lord Northcliffe, founder of the *Daily Mail* and owner of *The Times*, and so had inherited a huge personal fortune along with a recent aristocratic pedigree. Macdonald cared little for his gentrified origins, however. Rather, the sort of celebrity and status that he courted was membership in a new classless aristocracy.

> This is Psychedelphia man, it's all happening. . . . Sibylla's is the meeting ground for the new aristocracy, and by the new aristocracy I mean the current young meritocracy of style, taste and sensitivity. We've got everyone here, the top creative people, the top exporters, the top artists, the top social people, and the best of the PYPs [pretty young people]. We're completely classless. We're completely integrated. We dig the spades man. Relationships here go off like firecrackers. Everyone here's got the message. Can you read it man? Sibylla's is the message. We've married up the hairy brigade—that's the East End kids like photographers and artists—with the smooth brigade, the debs, the aristos, the Guards officers. The result is just fantastic. It's the greatest, happiest, most swinging ball of the century, and I started it![1]

The elite that Macdonald catered to revolved around the music scene in England, which had entered a new phase of development in 1966 and 1967. Aldous Huxley coined the term "psychedelic" in *The Doors of Perception* (1958) to explain the mental experience of taking LSD, mescaline and numerous other mind-altering drugs.[2] When musicians began to try such drugs themselves, they adopted the term to describe the music they made, and it reflected the moment.

Psychedelia was a dual-headed sound. One was a jangly, folk-oriented version of pop music, similar to that conceived in San Francisco, the American home of psychedelia. It was bright and colorful and sported trippy lyrics espousing a natural, childlike joy in the effort to "blow your mind". The other version was much heavier and louder, derived from the blues, and was accompanied by a menacing drone usually obtained through the distortion of the sound of the electric guitar. It tried to depict the feeling of a psychedelic trip in the listener, the hypnotic effect of drugs on the brain. The Byrds, an American act, released "Eight Miles High" in April 1966; due to remarks made by David Crosby in an Associated Press article on the band's use of psychedelic drugs, "Eight Miles High" became the first song labeled as "psychedelic" to hit the pop charts in America and Britain. The Yardbirds' "Shapes of Things", released a month earlier, achieved the same status, the first British band to have the term applied to one of its songs. Soon after, the Beatles' double-sided single, "Paperback Writer/Rain" (1966) helped to usher in the era amongst British rock musicians. "Rain" in particular reflected John Lennon's ingestion of LSD, as represented with loud, echoing guitars and thumping drums.[3] The Rolling Stones' "Paint It, Black" (1966) and the Small Faces' "My Mind's Eye" (1966) were also major chart hits. By 1967, with the identification of San Francisco and London as centers of the movement, psychedelic rock dominated the album and pop charts for a brief year.

Psychedelic bands made music for the mind, music for thinking people. And there was a lot to think about. The phenomenon of drugs fueled the cultural establishment's notion that the world of rock and roll music was one of decadence and immorality. The differences between age groups, social groups and cultural groups became stark and polarized. The authorities attacked the music and musicians like never before, which only enhanced its appeal as a form of rebellion. Thousands of fans and musicians turned to a hitherto unnoticed musical and cultural underground, looking for guidance in building a new lifestyle, an alternative to mainstream culture.[4]

The distinctions that developed between mainstream culture and the new psychedelic lifestyle were mainly rhetorical, though by no means entirely so. "Pop" was a trade term for all popular music, initially, but by 1966, it had become associated with the whole of youth culture. "Popular" culture was all-encompassing, spanning everything shared by every generation, class, gender, or sexual orientation—it was basically the same as "mass" culture. But "pop" culture had now become a transitional term for a culture based on music and art, youth-oriented and incorporating what adolescents thought were working-class values in their vision of a future classless society. It was oriented toward protest against the dominant class-ridden mass culture. "Pop" culture invited working-class participation, in an effort to establish that society. "Rock and roll" was its most prominent medium, music so popular that it seemingly tore down the walls that pop culture wanted to scale.

Most rock and roll musicians who had become popular since 1963 had little problem referring to their music as "pop", with its connotations of cleverness and class tolerance. But by 1966 and 1967, in both Britain and America, the artistic aspirations of musicians made it seem somewhat limited to refer to a complete musical package like the Beatles' *Revolver* (1966) as merely "pop" music. It was not music made for the *NME* charts, but for the artistic satisfaction of the musicians involved. This was especially the case as rock and roll musicians began to indulge in drugs, exotic musics and religions, and folk whimsy, hinting at the sort of artistic self-indulgence worthy of Romantic poets. The image of songwriters as craftsmen measuring their music success in terms of units sold was now passé. To make that change, in a process so subtle its starting point could not be pinpointed, serious rock and roll artists began to refer to their music by the somehow more dignified term "rock".

"Rock" musicians continued to pay homage to rock and roll, especially bands that became popular after the Beatles. They referred to their singles as "pop"—after all, they were popular. But by identifying themselves as "rock" musicians, and being identified by critics, journalists and the audience in the same manner, they codified the new seriousness that their music had taken on in the past two years, with the growing artistic adventurousness of so many bands. Rock musicians had a lot more in common with the seriousness of classical, jazz or folk musicians than they did with the raucousness of Elvis or Buddy Holly. "Rock" became more than just a convenient abbreviation; it distinguished their music for its authenticity. Rock was art.

In the psychedelic era, the differences between bands like the Hollies, the Rolling Stones and Pink Floyd resolved themselves in the rhetoric used to describe each band. The Hollies made pop music—they wrote singles rather than albums. They seemingly had no interest in subverting the cultural establishment: they were pleasant but irrelevant to the alternative lifestyle. The Stones made rock and roll, but they also seemed to be serious about their artistic direction, choosing singles only from a plethora of strong songs that would make up a coherent, thematically designed album. Their authenticity was unquestioned, but could always be in danger of cultural or political heresy. Pink Floyd never came near an approximation of rock and roll. Their act was too intense for them to produce anything but rock music, whether it made the pop charts or not, and rock, as art, was inherently authentic.

The whole rhetorical distinction between "pop", "rock and roll" and "rock" was facile. All three of these bands wrote singles for the pop charts, and all three of them sold millions of units for record companies whether they were singles or albums. None of them wrote songs with the desire to please the marketplace more than themselves. Nevertheless, the distinction grew with the flowering of psychedelic rock. The audience which had grown up with the Beatles now expected the Beatles and their successors to be the vanguard of a social revolution geared around youth and its values—values originally derived from rock and roll, now articulated in a new version, "rock" music, particularly psychedelic rock.

Romantic Themes in the Psychedelic Lifestyle

Romanticism has a dark Dionysian side, full of foreboding and menace, and a light Apollonian side, sunny, structured, shiny. In 1966, rock music reflected these two sides of the Romantic vision completely. Psychedelic drugs contributed most heavily to the way musicians and their audience experienced rock music, marijuana and LSD being the drugs of choice. But young people began to have an almost religious response to psychedelic rock and its message. If drugs could free the mind, where would it go? British rock musicians experimented with dozens of new influences and instruments in trying to depict where acid took their brains. Psychedelia was about escapism as social commentary and protest, a return to Romantic spirituality in opposition to the perceived materialistic soullessness of late sixties Britain.[5]

British rock musicians had already started to use Eastern instruments for color in their arrangements. The Beatles were exponents of the Indian sitar, courtesy of George Harrison, who was fascinated with the playing of a bunch of Hindu musicians on the set of the movie *Help!* (1965).[6] He added sitars first to John Lennon's "Norwegian Wood" (1965), then wrote his own songs based exclusively on north Indian ragas, such as "Love You To" off *Revolver* (1966) and "Within You Without You" on *Sgt. Pepper* (1967). They were hardly the first group to tap into Indian sounds, however. The Rolling Stones' Brian Jones used the sitar to perhaps its best effect on "Paint It Black" (1966). The Kinks' "See My Friends" (1965) and "Fancy" (1966) employed a strong droning effect borrowed from the sitar, and the Yardbirds' "Heart Full of Soul" (1966) had Jeff Beck simulating a sitar at the end of the chorus on his electric guitar.[7] British bands made Indian folk music an exotic ingredient in rock music's Romanticism, along with the primitivism of African-American blues and the nationalistic peasant worship of European/American folk music.[8]

Exotic instruments led to a fascination with the cultures that produced them, and the Eastern religions that were the bases of those cultures provided powerful inspiration for numerous songwriters. With only a dilettantish understanding of Eastern religious and philosophical systems, many songwriters found simplicity and an appealing irrationality in them. The East seemed to value nature, the unexplainable, the supernatural, the fantastic—all things that musicians and their audiences found in their minds when they took drugs.[9] Many people found the same things (erroneously) in Islam, Buddhism, and Hinduism. In August 1967, the Beatles visited with the Maharishi Mahesh Yogi, who enjoyed a brief vogue as a hippie guru as a result. Pete Townshend and Ronnie Lane of the Small Faces subscribed to the Hindu ideas of Meher Baba, the author of the famous quote "be happy—don't worry". Eastern religious texts were a source for lyrics and inspiration, such as the *Egyptian Book of the Dead*, the *Tibetan Book of the Dead*, or the *I Ching*. The pilgrimage to Marrakesh in Morocco and the rest of North Africa for marijuana and Islamic spiritual enlightenment became a cliché in the sixties, the Rolling Stones being amongst the pilgrims there.[10] Some made pilgrimages to Istanbul, Ankara, India's numerous cities and Katmandu in Nepal on *bildungsromans* inspired by Eastern religious leaders and ideas. Of course, many went mainly for drugs, and they were sorely disappointed to discover that Eastern religions vehemently opposed the use of substances to find any form of enlightenment. But as more young people from Britain went east and came home, the mixture between British and non-Western cultural ideals grew stronger.[11]

Those who did not wish to travel to find enlightenment either dropped acid to leave their bodies or searched around themselves for Western ideals untainted by materialism. Many were fascinated with the simple philosophy espoused in children's books like A. A. Milne's *Winnie the Pooh*, Lewis Carroll's *Alice's Adventures in Wonderland* or Kenneth Grahame's *The Wind in the Willows*, and their language and characters showed up in numerous songs. Fantasy literature was popular too, like J. R. R. Tolkien's *The Lord of the Rings*, and C. S. Lewis' *Chronicles of Narnia*. Indeed, Tolkien's work became a virtual Bible to many young people in Britain and America, representing everything that British psychedelic rock stood for in the late sixties. *The Lord of the Rings* was a reaction against industrialism, rejecting the contemporary world for an alternative one that was environmentally sound, anti-technological, and balanced between the needs of the individual and the community. In Tolkien's book, the hobbits won the war with Mordor—little people needed to work together to stop the madness, a message taken to heart by British musicians and British youth.[12]

The search for inspiration beyond reason and materialism took many to astrology. The late sixties were the "dawning of the age of Aquarius", the beginning of a new era in which man would enter his greatest period of creativity, peace and happiness. Psychedelic rock used numerous symbols of this coming age in the music. Sunshine symbolized beauty, happiness and strength, and was a continuingly recurring theme in psychedelic music—the Beatles' "Good Day Sunshine" (1966), "Sunshine of Your Love" (1967) by Cream and "Set the Controls for the Heart of the Sun" (1968) by Pink Floyd being examples.[13]

Since Romanticism had both Apollonian and Dionysian sides, the Apollonian vision of the Age of Aquarius was in opposition to the Dionysian vision of religious apocalypse and death. In America, this dichotomy in the Romantic outlook even had a geographical dimension: if San Francisco generally emphasized the Apollonian side of psychedelic rock, Los Angeles was the home of the Dionysian vision, as represented by the Doors and Love. Arguably, Andy Warhol's New York-based traveling performance art spectacle, the Exploding Plastic Inevitable, with the Velvet Underground offering music to accompany the stage show, was another example of the Dionysian vision in psychedelic rock (though many rock critics question whether the Velvets could be labeled a psychedelic act, when "Heroin" was one of their most famous songs). British musicians read Aleister Crowley's works on the occult world (or "Magick") and used them to pursue a hedonistic lifestyle. Everyone's favorite quote from Crowley's *The Book of the Law* was "Do what thou wilt shall be the whole of the Law. Love is the Law, Love under will." One such musician was Graham Bond, a mainstay on the London blues scene.

> . . . I am concerned with the propagation of music in alignment with the Astral patterns. . . . Nearly everything in the galaxy is based on vibration, a force that technologists are only now, in this second age of Aquarius, beginning to realise the potential of. . . . Music is vibration, an essential part of the galaxy, a means of affecting and influencing life, or matter.[14]

The most basic theme in the psychedelic lifestyle was that nature was sovereign over all. The Eastern world was less industrialized than the West; English fantasy and children's literature was focused on nature as a battleground and a playground; the age of Aquarius and the dark side of astrology mirrored day and night. The Romantic desire to break down the industrial world, to get back to nature and a folk lifestyle in touch with the natural world, was at the heart of psychedelic music and the psychedelic lifestyle. British psychedelic rock pined away for Jerusalem against the horrors of the dark satanic mills as vigorously as William Blake had a hundred and sixty years earlier. Even the taking of drugs was about escape, the effort to leave a world of suffering for a "natural" world of ecstasy and pleasure. Donovan, for example, was the original flower child, and nature was his drug of choice.

> Everything that you see is beautiful, it's been made not to be looked upon, it's just been made to be beautiful, it is beautiful and the sea is deep and heavy, but it wasn't made and it really influences me so much. The whole world is so fantastically beautiful.[15]

Adherents to the new psychedelic lifestyle were called "hippies". The hippie movement took sociologists by surprise, especially in Britain, where they were lumped in as yet another subculture in opposition to mainstream culture. Yet hippies were more properly labeled a "counterculture", adherents to an entirely new lifestyle that could be easily joined by anyone in British society. Indeed, many Mods became hippies in late 1965 and 1966, as the Mod subculture lost its exclusivity. However, hippies were dramatically different from their subcultural predecessors in their social origins. Most of the counterculture's loudest and most visible exponents were students, ex-students and dropouts—a decidedly middle-class group.

Thus, the counterculture, as it styled itself, was not the serious break with the principles of the adult cultural establishment that it wanted to be. In fact, it might even be said to extend certain traditional post-Victorian middle-class values to their extremes. Where the hippies called for people to "do their own thing", Victorians emphasized individuality and self-expression. Where the middle classes reveled in a capitalist commodity culture, hippies built a lifestyle around the commodity of rock music. The emphasis on Christian virtues in Victorian culture metamorphosed into the hippies' fascination with Eastern religions. Clothes were particularly important in London, and hippies shopped at all the right boutiques (e.g., the Beatles' Apple Boutique) in order to display the bankruptcy of consumer culture on their bodies. In short, to be a hippie was to be a missionary to the capitalist world, trying to convert unhip heathens, rather than to be a pirate out to destroy and plunder it.[16] Most of all, hippies bought records in droves, especially LPs. The fan had to have enough money to be able to buy an album he might know only on the artist's reputation, and believed himself to have a discerning ear for artists of taste.[17] One might venture to say that hippies took the authenticity they perceived in their favorite musicians and extended it to their own lives. The deeper a hippie could delve into an anti-materialistic lifestyle with an appropriate rock music soundtrack, the more admiration he or she deserved from other hippies.

Sgt. Pepper's Lonely Hearts Club Band

Not surprisingly, all of the themes of psychedelic music could be found in the music of the Beatles. Because of three albums in particular—*Rubber Soul* (1965), *Revolver* (1966), and *Sgt. Pepper's Lonely Hearts Club Band* (1967)— the Beatles became standard bearers in rock who legitimated the sounds of other bands and taught mainstream pop listeners about new sounds and ideas in music. Each album's release was a milestone, its songs copied by artists all over the world and its lyrics dissected for meaning by fans everywhere. The Beatles were rarely instrumental innovators themselves: their creativity was usually expressed in the uses of the studio to enhance sound. Instrumentally, they usually observed and used ideas from other artists in their own music. But the sheer range of their influences, the way they used them and their very popularity as an act assured that their music was the way most listeners heard innovations in rock music. By the time of the release of "Eleanor Rigby" (1965), a song recorded with a chamber music group and without a single Beatle playing an instrument, rock music gained a definition—if the Beatles played it, whatever it was, it was rock music.[18]

The Beatles thus became purveyors of psychedelic rock too. When "flower power" became mainstream in 1967, it was the Beatles singing "All You Need Is Love" that heralded its status; likewise, it was the release of *The Beatles* in

1968, with its stark white cover and tired sounding music, that seemed to bring the psychedelic era to a close. They had been in the vanguard of advancing the new sound on *Revolver*. It included George Harrison's "Love You To", a song played by Harrison and an Indian sitar and tabla ensemble; and John Lennon's stunning "Tomorrow Never Knows", a song based on his interpretation of phrases from *The Tibetan Book of the Dead*, which he read about in a book by Timothy Leary called *The Psychedelic Experience* (1964).[19]

In early 1967, to keep the band in the public eye, Brian Epstein insisted that two new songs from the band's current studio sessions be released as a single before the next album came out. "Strawberry Fields Forever"/"Penny Lane" (1967) was an even more outrageous step than "Tomorrow Never Knows" in establishing the Beatles as the most avant-garde composers of the postwar era. The A-side, "Strawberry Fields Forever", was a John Lennon composition describing his own feelings of being trapped in an unsympathetic adult world and longing to return to the carefree days of his childhood in Liverpool. It linked two very different studio versions of the song together in its center. The first half was a virtually acoustic version that featured a pipe organ as the sound of innocence wistfully lost; the second half was an orchestral arrangement loaded with tape loops played forwards and backwards, improvised speech and other unworldly tools of the recording studio, emphasizing the confusion of adulthood. "Penny Lane", a Paul McCartney composition, was also a paean to a lost Liverpool, rendering what is in reality an incredibly drab little street close to Lennon's childhood home into a bright slice of psychedelic whimsy, full of unusual characters and scenes from a day in the life.[20]

With this double-sided single, the Beatles planted the flag of Romanticism squarely at the center of psychedelic rock. They emphasized innocence, childhood as purity, improvisation, and the spirits of individuality and community united as one. For the next three to five years, these ideals would dominate rock music on both sides of the Atlantic. The Beatles' vision dominated the entire rock music world. The impact of the music on the rise of a so-called classless society, however, was also monumental. By referring back to their old days in Liverpool in a nostalgic fashion, Lennon and McCartney signified just how far removed they were from their allegedly working-class roots. And if the Beatles were removed from their roots, so was British rock music.

Six months after the release of "Strawberry Fields/Penny Lane", the album *Sgt. Pepper's Lonely Hearts Club Band* came out in June 1967. Critic Simon Frith aptly called it "the last great pop album, the last LP ambitious to amuse *everyone*."[21] "With a Little Help from My Friends" was self-explanatory, a description of community. "Lucy in the Sky with Diamonds" took the child Julian Lennon's drawing of "tangerine trees and marmalade skies" and echoed the sensations of an LSD trip. "She's Leaving Home" was about a girl fleeing the domesticity of her parents' lives to find excitement on her own. "Within You, Without You" expounded the exotic values of Eastern philosophy to the materialistic Western listener. "A Day in the Life" was a series of dream-like vignettes that swooped to orchestrated crescendos while conveying the overarching idea—"I'd love to turn you on". That line got the song banned by the BBC, who believed that "it goes a little too far" towards advocating drug use. The corporation also did not appreciate the references to the suicide of the aristocratic socialite Tara Browne —a financial backer of Sibylla's—who was killed in a traffic accident in early 1967.[22] The whole album was sensuous, a document of sex, drugs, community and good times. It was a celebration of what it meant to be young and British in 1967.[23]

The Beatles refused to let any song on the album be released as a single for the pop charts.[24] They intended *Sgt. Pepper* to be a unified conceptual piece, where a series of songs were strung together using a lyrical theme (the music of a band led by Sgt. Pepper). Whereas the Beatles' first album had been recorded in a day, *Sgt. Pepper* took three months and 700 hours of studio time to produce.[25] It fused rock music with classical, jazz, folk, and Indian music, drawing on the influences of avant-garde composers like Karlheinz Stockhausen.[26] Radio stations all over America and Europe played the album nonstop, sometimes for days. If ever a moment might be defined when the concept of Romantic youth culture took flight in Britain, this was it. Across every boundary of class, age, gender, race and geography, the Beatles had defined the most important cultural moment of 1967—arguably the most important cultural moment of the late sixties in England next to the World Cup win of 1966.

The album soon received laudatory praise as the best rock album ever produced, from some unusual sources. Leonard Bernstein declared it one of the best albums he had ever heard; William Mann, the reviewer for *The Times*, said that its songs were as expertly constructed as any Schubert *lieder*. Drama critic Kenneth Tynan stated, "This is a decisive moment in the history of Western Civilisation."[27] The *Times Literary Supplement* called the album's lyrics "the barometer of our times". The *New Statesman*—edited by Paul Johnson, a notorious curmudgeon on pop music—called the album "a song cycle cunningly devised by the Beatles to transform old-style camaraderie into a new aloneness." The *New York Times Book Review* said *Sgt. Pepper* was the beginning of "a new and golden Renaissance of Song". *Newsweek* reviewer Jack Kroll said that "A Day in the Life" was tantamount to "the Beatles' *Waste Land*".[28]

The album achieved a reputation as art, which in and of itself was entirely new. *Sgt. Pepper's Lonely Hearts Club Band* was by the Beatles, a group identified as working-class. It was rock music, which defined itself as anti-establishment, and gained currency with youth because the cultural establishment, and their parents, hated it. Yet these people liked the album too, or at the very least, the ambitions that the album represented, and they shared its Romantic values. Even more, reviewers did not accept the Beatles as purveyors of pop music—they accepted them as artists worthy of the highest merit in the art world. As artists, they were well above the parameters of something as crass and commercial as pop music. If the doyens of Western art criticism accepted the Beatles and *Sgt. Pepper*, then the Beatles had to be associated with serious art. It was inconceivable to critics and intellectuals that pop music could have aesthetic standards of its own separate from those of the rest of the art world—it was popular, and thus intrinsically debased. To be art, rock music had to be associated with elite ideas and elite art, not pop culture. The usual standard was classical music, and people like Paul McCartney were more than willing to play the game of establishing rock music as high art.

> I was always frightened of classical music, and I never wanted to listen to it. . . . [A] taxi driver the other day had some sheet music of a Mozart thing. And I said what's that? you know, and he said, oh that's the high-class stuff, you won't like that. . . . That kind of way I always used to think of it, I used to think, you know, well, that is clever, all that stuff, and it's not. You know it's just exactly what's going on in pop at the moment. Pop music is the classical music of now.[29]

Every other band that had survived on the charts since the Beatles' breakthrough adhered to the standards set by *Sgt. Pepper*, standards that again became the measure of professionalism. If they did not necessarily make the same kind of music as the Beatles, they certainly admired the values behind the concept album and recognized the drug-induced, expansive qualities that psychedelic rock offered them. Though most of them still released pop singles, they universally denied the need to find popular support for their art—true artists expressed their visions despite the commercial outcome, like the Beatles. The new standard required British rock musicians and songwriters—as opposed to rock and roll or pop musicians—to pursue a certain artistic progression in their music, to have the sort of vision that *Sgt. Pepper* evinced and try to make it explicit on albums as opposed to singles. In short, the rock musician was expected to be a serious, progressively minded, anti-commercial artist in the Romantic mold.

The Psychedelic Vanguard

Numerous British rock musicians understood this logic implicitly, even before *Sgt. Pepper* was released, and pursued it in the Beatles' wake. Donovan went from being an earnest folkie to being the original British flower child, a mystic and innocent with folk roots and a love of nature. "Sunshine Superman" (1966) topped the charts in Britain and the United States with its evocations of the sexual prowess of Donovan as nature boy. Subsequent hit singles like "Mellow Yellow" (1966) amplified this character.[30] He continued to maintain a high hippie standard of Romantic whimsy, tapping into Arthurian legend, Milne's Winnie the Pooh stories, and the writings of Aleister Crowley on his album *A Gift From a Flower to a Garden* (1968).[31] The second side of the Small Faces' *Ogden's Nut Gone Flake* (1968) was a children's fairy tale narrative read by comedian Stanley Unwin, about one Happiness Stan, who goes on a fantasy trip into a

Lewis Carroll-inspired world to find the dark half of the moon. In keeping with the effort to release a fully realized conceptual art piece, the album was released in a circular cover to look like a tin of tobacco. The gatefold sleeve opened up to reveal a photo of cigarette papers, used for smoking marijuana. Unfortunately, the record cover came with a handicap: it kept rolling off the shelves of the shops that sold it.[32] The Who, the original "art" band, released *The Who Sell Out* in 1967. Its first side was a loving parody of pirate radio, complete with commercials between songs and radio jingles. As a Pop Art concept, it was based on Townshend's theories about art as a commodity, a mockery of the Who as a product just like the pimple creams, deodorants, baked beans and bodybuilding programs they jokingly advertised on the cover.[33] The album included the stunning single "I Can See for Miles", the best psychedelic hit ever produced in Britain. Even the Rolling Stones, always the Beatles' antithesis, released their own version of the psychedelic concept album, the underrated but still vastly inferior *Their Satanic Majesties' Request* (1967). It had a hologram on the cover and tracks like "2000 Light Years from Home", a description of space travel with a menacingly distorted guitar from Keith Richards.

The new psychedelic sound spawned dozens of new bands. All of them were accustomed to the standards necessary to be respected musical artists: some of the musicians had set those standards themselves. They concentrated on albums as opposed to singles, explored jazz, folk and exotic music for new influences, and espoused a lifestyle that challenged post-Victorian values. Each of them pursued one of the two Romantic visions of psychedelic music—either an Apollonian folk/classical/rock hybrid or a Dionysian electrical drone. Most of all, they all believed their music was representative of a new morality, a new vision of Western society that was more in touch with nature, the limits of the mind and the depths of the soul. In reality, they had simply discovered an affinity for the values of their nineteenth-century Romantic predecessors—the same values that any number of cultural intellectuals in the sixties said should provide the basis for the moral uplift of British culture. The fact that many of these same intellectuals denounced rock music as the soundtrack to cultural collapse only made the psychedelic bands more popular with young people.[34]

In March 1966, *Melody Maker* published a poll of a few dozen pop stars asking them to name their favorite instrumentalists. Eric Clapton won as best guitarist; the drummer was Ginger Baker of the Graham Bond Organisation. Both he and Clapton had played at different times with bassist Jack Bruce, at the time the bassist for Manfred Mann. Within three months, Clapton, Baker, and Bruce formed what became known as the first "supergroup", Cream. Cream became the band against which every great group of musicians had to measure themselves. They became known for their long, jazzy jam sessions on stage, three musicians simply pleasing themselves with their craft and incidentally pleasing their audience along the way.[35] Their artistic output was likewise based in large part on this self-indulgence. Their second album, *Wheels of Fire* (1967), was rock's first double album—a two-record set, half recorded live, half in the studio. It was a masterwork produced with the expectation that the public would accept it because of the almost self-professed genius of the musicians involved. And the public did accept it: *Wheels of Fire* was a massive success on both sides of the Atlantic.[36] Yet the members of Cream claimed to not to care a whit about the money, about pleasing their audiences, about anything other than the experience of playing together. A hippie poet named Pete Brown wrote the lyrics to their next album, *Disraeli Gears* (1967), and he understood the mentality.

> We actually wrote a thing which was much worse [than our released singles] which was so blatantly commercial that it was good in fact, but if it had been done by someone like the Chiffons or the Ronettes or something like that it would have been great, it was so bad that it was good. It was a thing called *My Beauty Queen*, but thank God that never reached the light of day.[37]

Traffic was another band formed by a refugee of the R&B scene, Steve Winwood. Perhaps more than any other popular rock musician in Britain, Winwood questioned his image with the British audience. He wanted to be taken seriously as an artist no matter what musical direction he pursued in the sixties. In part this was due to his music education—he went to the Birmingham School of Music—and in part it was due to his extremely young age: he was only eighteen in 1967. For this reason, he left the Spencer Davis Group in 1967, and founded a new band that would be more worthy of merit as a rock act and less interested in producing commercially-oriented pop music.[38] In the best Romantic tradition, for their first album in 1967, Traffic retreated to a cottage in Aston Tirrold in Berkshire to write songs and record demos. They wanted to, as they put it, "get it together" in the English countryside, expecting to find inspiration.[39] The album they produced, *Mr. Fantasy* (1967), was a classic of its kind. It was full of jazzy instrumentals, whimsical odes to "Coloured Rain", a girl with "No Name, No Place, No Number", and sitar-based drones on how "Stupidly Simple" the world is, if only men would abandon the workaday world and explore their inner beings. Regardless of Winwood's anti-commercial bent, the single "Paper Sun" went to number five in the UK, featuring sitar, tabla and flute over an R&B beat.[40] Another single, "Hole in My Shoe", became a number two single in 1968.

Steve Winwood and Eric Clapton both basked in the praise accorded them for their talents, and were determined to maximize those talents in bands worthy of their professionalism. Neither of them was the most brilliant instrumentalist on the British rock scene, however. Jimi Hendrix quickly eclipsed Clapton, Jeff Beck and Pete Townshend as London's top guitarist in 1967. Hendrix, an African-American, came to London from New York in September 1966. His manager, Chas Chandler, late of the Animals, outfitted Hendrix in the latest Carnaby Street fashions. Then Chandler found him a pair of musicians, the fabulous Mitch Mitchell on drums and Noel Redding on bass, to form a band. On stage, Hendrix had an assured sexuality that was a match for Mick Jagger. He sang wild lyrics about drug experiences and Romantic subjects, and most of all, he played guitar like no one else on earth. At a time of weird experimentation and wild lyrical themes, no one was as spaced out as Hendrix. *Are You Experienced?* (1967), released two months before *Sgt. Pepper*, was by far the most outlandish album of the year. "Purple Haze" compared achieving the high off barbiturates to a girl's love. "I Don't Live Today" was about the execution of an American Indian; "Third Stone from the Sun" was a mostly instrumental vision of earth through the eyes of an alien visitor. The album closed with "Are You Experienced?", less a question than an apocalyptic promise of the comparison between Hendrix's guitar playing and his lovemaking abilities.

Hendrix's exoticism as an African-American in London exposed many contradictions in British youth culture. Part of the reason Hendrix had come to London was to escape the racial stereotypes he experienced on the music circuit in America—African-Americans were not worshipped for their artistic talents in the United States, they were enjoyed for their entertainment value. Hendrix came to London because he was told correctly by his future manager, Chas Chandler, that Britain was a much more amenable place in which to establish himself as a great musical artist.[41] Yet upon making a splash on the London club scene, Hendrix was soon confronted with the London tabloids giving him offensive tags like the "Wild Man of Borneo" or "musical Mau-Mau" to emphasize his blackness on the lily-white London circuit.[42]

But the tabloids were hardly the only offenders. The long-established professional concept of authenticity in British music was applied to Hendrix, creating a stereotyped image of him that was impossible to live up to. If the original danger of rock and roll in Britain came from its association with an alleged culture of working-class rebellion, the original danger of rock and roll in America came from its association with alleged racial sexuality and violence. And Hendrix's audience definitely believed he was capable of racially-based sexuality and violence. To be an "authentic" black performer, Hendrix had to be seen as wild, sexually uninhibited, dangerous and arrogant. He played the role on stage to the hilt—rock music has probably never seen a greater showman in its history. But as a person off stage, Hendrix was naturally very quiet, creative, gentle and sometimes uncertain of his unbelievable musical talents. (He was known to sing in the studio while hiding behind a sonic divider or a speaker, so no one could see him recite lyrics in a voice he considered terrible.) Hendrix faced racial stereotypes in Britain that exposed the ignorance and unconscious racism behind the identification of British working-class values with those of African-Americans. Interviewers played up Hendrix's ethnicity as exemplary of his primitiveness and psychedelic consciousness, and regularly questioned him in a way that they did with no other artist of the era. In Romantic terms, Hendrix was the 1960s' version of Rousseau's noble savage. In one interview, Jane de Mendelssohn of *International Times* delved into Hendrix's Cherokee heritage.

JANE: Tell me about your Indian heritage.

JIMI: Well, my grandmother's a full-blooded Indian, that's all. . . . yeah, she's
a full-blooded Cherokee.
JANE: And is she still around?
JIMI: Yeah, up in Seattle [-] Vancouver, British Columbia now.
JANE: And does she live on a reservation?
JIMI: No, she lives in a groovy apartment building. She has a television . . . and
a radio and stuff like that. She still has her long silver hair though.
JANE: Can't you tell me something about the whole Indian heritage scene, I
don't know much about it.
JIMI: It's just another part of our family, that's all. There's not too much to
know. There's a lot of people in Seattle that have a lot of Indian mixed in
them.
JANE: Do they still take peyote?
JIMI: Oh yes, it's all over the place. . . .

De Mendelssohn tried to flatter Hendrix by saying that "[your music] seems
to me to be moving down to the animal, and that's what you are. The Beatles
aren't animal." She prompted Hendrix to call himself a violent man, in the mold
of the American Black Panthers, after he specifically denied it.[43] Hendrix never
managed to live down this reputation, and it wore on him more and more as his
career continued. Unfortunately, before he could remake his image, he died in
September 1970 from the complications of an accidental overdose of barbiturates.

Drugs were an ever-present part of the experience of both musicians and listeners in the psychedelic era. Both Hendrix and Clapton, not to mention any
number of other guitarists, recorded their guitars in a fuzzy drone when they
were in the studio, to echo the heightened sensory awareness of an acid trip.
Rock music became a synesthetic experience for the listener, a combination of
sight and sound especially—the music buzzed in the ears while the listener studied the record cover as a work of art. But beyond the obvious, the art school
training of so many rock musicians manifested itself in the work of the best
bands of the era. If the professional rock musician aspired to be an artist in the
psychedelic era, he certainly had the experience necessary to discern what art
was and how to produce it.

Two such bands were Pink Floyd and the Soft Machine. Pink Floyd was
formed in 1965 by a pair of childhood friends from Cambridge, bassist Roger
Waters and guitarist Syd Barrett. Barrett was a student at the Camberwell
School of Art; Waters studied architecture at Regent Street Polytechnic, where
he met drummer Nick Mason and keyboard player Richard Wright. No band
reflected the artistic professionalism of the British rock musician more than Pink
Floyd. Some musicologists believed that Pink Floyd's songs had an architectural
structure to them, rising and falling in set musical lines, punctuated with feedback experiments and weird soundscapes.[44] They released two high-selling singles in 1967, "Arnold Layne" and "See Emily Play". Their debut album, *The
Piper at the Gates of Dawn* (1967), was named for a character in *The Wind in*

the Willows, a favorite of the psychedelic period. Barrett wrote songs with a weird lyrical content that were as menacing as they were amusing. The Floyd's stage shows, especially at small clubs, were indicative of Barrett's inner mind, as depicted through the technological advances of the time—space sounds, long instrumental pieces, and atmospheric blob shows projected on movie screens behind the band.[45] Pink Floyd was a complete audio-visual experience, and journalists fell about themselves trying to put the band's psychedelic sound into words.

> Pink Floyd . . . play music which might aptly be described as post-apocalyptic—beyond the critical point of transition between realities. It's there already, on the other side—and Pink Floyd is inviting you over with its incomparably seductive Sirens' call. But their music is no escapist Utopianism, it isn't concerned with a new social order: It represents a striving for union with the universe, a metaphysical perfection that transcends human existence. It hovers, shimmering and reflecting like the monolith in *2001*, turning through space and time.[46]

The Soft Machine was a band from Canterbury, where keyboard player Mike Ratledge and drummer Robert Wyatt attended the Simon Langton School. The school was created for the children of the large local community of artists and intellectuals, who wanted their children to learn in a free environment specifically geared to self-expression, and it exposed its students to modern jazz, avant-garde music and experimental art and literature.[47] Ratledge and Wyatt formed the group in this atmosphere, adding a local singer and songwriter named Kevin Ayers to the line-up. Their improvisational style was heavily informed by jazz, and their quirky compositions made them a hit in London, where they regularly opened for Pink Floyd at clubs. Amazingly, they survived as an act without the requisite guitarist, sometimes recruiting someone to play with them on stage, sometimes not. Like Cream, they became known for virtually ignoring their audience's existence, as if the people who came to see them were not nearly as important as their own artistic self-expression.[48] No band seemed to take themselves as seriously in their musical intent as the Soft Machine. As drummer and singer Wyatt put it, "We're contemporary classical musicians".[49]

Numerous other acts arose through the London club scene or the pop charts, each emphasizing different elements of the Romantic vision. Procol Harum and the Moody Blues were engaged with Anglican church music, with its loud organs, fanfares, full orchestral arrangements and choral vocal arrangements. The Moody Blues even recorded with the London Festival Orchestra. Their album, *Days of Future Passed* (1967), was a song cycle that followed the periods of a single day, from morning to night, linked with banal poems and long instrumental passages.[50]

"Something Happened to Me Yesterday"

One of the most obvious things that any young listener could discern easily about the most important record of the era, *Sgt. Pepper's Lonely Hearts Club Band,* was that the Beatles had been high as sparrows when they made it. If all of its references did not necessarily involve drugs, the writing and recording of the album was positively drenched in marijuana and LSD. Psychedelic music like *Sgt. Pepper* thus lent itself to the cultivation of a drug-induced elitism in some listeners. Only a taker of mind-expanding drugs could understand all the references in psychedelic music, or so it was said. A non-drug user heard "Fixing a Hole" and thought it was about the daydreaming effect that dripping water had on people; a drug user heard it as a reference to shooting up heroin through an arm vein when the "hole" of a craving hit the user.[52] For the first time, the youth community had a "hierarchy", based on music and the Romantic conception of the artistic vision. If you "got it" and found drug references in psychedelic music, you were an insider. If you "didn't get it" and listened to music just as before, without the added stimulation of drugs, you did not understand everything there was to know in music, youth culture, its values or society in general. Thus, as the declaration went out to the adult world that youth was a universal and classless community, the audience divided between listeners who shared real or feigned drug references in music, and listeners who could not care less about such references.

But if drug references divided British youth between a stoned elite and a "less aware" majority, they positively guillotined the elite audience's relationship with the cultural establishment. Drugs and their ingestion by so many British kids created a political division between old and young, between rock music and society in general. Rock music's politics were radical, if vague. The music seeped into the consciousness of youth, making certain ideas current and acceptable, particularly that youth were capable of accomplishing anything. The increased use of mind-expanding drugs was a part of this change in mindset—to accomplish anything, kids needed only to free their minds to pursue their dreams. Drugs seemed an obvious escape from the prisons of everyday life into the realm of the possible and impossible. LSD was the most prominent of these drugs, advocated in the early sixties by Aldous Huxley, Timothy Leary, Richard Alpert and a number of other leading psychiatrists and psychologists as well. LSD's potential for expanding the individual's awareness was celebrated and tapped by millions of people around the globe. It seemed to symbolize the decade: a mass-produced substance and commodity distributed to people to improve their spiritual and creative lives. And rock music, of course, was the favored soundtrack for this expansive trip, with its loud, simple, repetitive and rhythmic beat.[53]

The experience of drugs led a number of young people—student intellectuals, artists, journalists, and rock musicians themselves—to question normal societal boundaries. LSD and other drugs made boundaries seem useless before the potential of the mind—why should everyday people accept such limits, whether they took drugs or not? Rock musicians and a cultured youth elite began to attack the old shibboleths of traditional morality, adding an even more dangerous anti-Victorian aura to the psychedelic era. Many of these people were convinced that drugs could expand the consciousness of everyone in the world, and the experience would change the world entirely for the better. Rock musicians espoused such ideas in their music, and their audiences absorbed them and disseminated them themselves. An equal number of press reporters, cultural commentators and members of the public at large saw such commentary as a vision of cultural Armageddon. One regular voice against the vicissitudes of youth culture was Anthony Burgess, author of *A Clockwork Orange.*

> I remember an old proverb which says that youth thinks itself wise just as drunk men think themselves sober. Youth is not wise, youth knows nothing about life, youth knows nothing about anything except a mass of clichés which for the most part, through the media of pop songs are just foisted on them by middle aged entrepreneurs and exploiters who should know better. When we start thinking that pop music is close to God, then we'll think that pop music is aesthetically better than it is. . . . We don't regard Wagner, or Beethoven or Shakespeare or Milton as great teachers when we start claiming for Lennon and McCartney or the Maharishi or any other of these pop prophets the ability to transport us to a region where God becomes manifest. Then I see red.[54]

It was not hard for such people to blame the questioning of traditional cultural values on the proliferation of drugs. Certainly, drug use among youth was not nearly as widespread as the cultural establishment believed. But that did not mean that the influence of drugs was not widespread across the youth community—any adolescent listening to his favorite Jimi Hendrix song was proof of that, whether he took drugs or not. That hardly meant that every rock music listener was on the verge of charring brain cells and then torching British society; but authorities from the British state and around the globe often acted as if that were precisely the case.[55] Overreacting without knowing the extent of the dissemination of drugs in youth culture, they assaulted the psychedelic rock community, sometimes fairly, sometimes not. London police regularly raided psychedelic clubs and underground newspapers to search for drugs.[56] Record companies banned numerous songs from albums in 1967 that glorified drugs, as they were afraid such songs would bring a public backlash.[57] The Lord Chief Justice condemned the spread of "beat clubs" in the mid-sixties, complaining that they were "nothing more than common lodging houses . . . [with] a flourishing drug traffic." He introduced a bill in the Lords to curb the licensing of such clubs, and the Government announced its support.[58] The United Nations produced a report on narcotics stating that rock bands like the Rolling Stones and the Beatles promoted drug use and abuse, and that youth around the world emulated their example.[59] Pop music had once been a challenge to the norms of post-Victorian culture—now it was taken to be a positive threat. The *Sun* expressed as much after conducting a series of interviews with pop stars in 1967, seeking their views on the impact of the music business in the lives of adolescents.

> The world of pop music has come a long way since the Beatles created their scrubbed and shining image of four short years ago. And the route seems, on the surface, to be mainly downhill. Many adults associate pop with little other than long hair and way-out clothes. Many claim that the alarming increase in drug peddling and addiction can be traced to swaying, half-lit clubs that are the grass roots of the beat groups. Still more see much of today's juvenile delinquency as traceable to the influence exerted on the young by their pop stars.[60]

More than any other group, the Rolling Stones were still the clear targets of press and public fears. Whereas the Beatles quickly became "untouchables" in the press not unlike the royal family, the Stones were considered the embodiment of youth culture's evils. This was not without reason: no band was more attuned to the drug culture than the Stones were. The album *Between the Buttons* (1967) was loaded with songs like "Something Happened to Me Yesterday", an account of Mick Jagger's first encounter with LSD.

The *News of the World* did a series of articles on "Pop Stars and Drugs" in February 1967, and responsibility for the quotes in the series was conveniently misattributed to the more controversial Mick Jagger, as opposed to the less newsworthy Brian Jones. Jagger promptly sued for libel and won. Determined to "get" Jagger after this incident, the paper tipped off the police to a party involving drug use at Keith Richards's mansion in West Wittering, Surrey, called Redlands. The police raided Redlands during a party at which marijuana had been smoked. Police searched the house and found four pep pills, which Jagger admitted were his, and a bag of marijuana, which the band members and many other sources believed was planted on the scene. Jagger and Richards were arrested, handcuffed and brought to jail. Jagger was convicted of possessing the pep pills and was sentenced to three months in jail, despite the fact that most people in a similar first-offense situation would simply have been fined. Richards was convicted for allowing cannabis to be smoked in his house, a more serious charge, and received a year in Wormwood Scrubs.[61]

The sentences were outrageous, and public vilification prompted a reexamination of the ruling. *The Times* condemned them in an editorial by William Rees-Mogg, entitled "Who Breaks a Butterfly on a Wheel?" Rees-Mogg argued that Jagger received unfair treatment at the hands of Judge Leslie Block because of his status as the top symbol of psychedelic London's "new hedonism".[62] The musicians were even defended on the floor of the House of Commons by Dick Taverne, an undersecretary at the Home Office, claiming that press coverage of the case was biased against the defendants. The case against them was finally dismissed in July 1967. Brian Jones also faced conviction for possession of drugs at his London flat. The pressure of the inquiry drove him to a nervous breakdown, and his sentence of nine months in prison was overturned on appeal as well.[63]

Young people protested these verdicts, and much besides. The later sixties was an era of protest as youth took to the streets against the Vietnam War, university regulations, destruction of the environment and the general complacency of affluent capitalism. Occasionally such protests turned violent, but establishment violence directed toward youth protests was completely out of proportion to the violence of the young people themselves. They were accused of "anti-British" behavior when they protested the Vietnam War in Grosvenor Square in 1968, even though the war was not even a British undertaking. Young people attacked lingering Victorianism in economic, psychic and sexual culture. Given Britain's many problems in the post-imperial era, such as militant unions, racism, a failing mixed economy and Rhodesia's declaration of independence, youth protest seemed like a fifth column. Enoch Powell MP referred to hippies as "the enemy within", along with the numerous immigrant populations he defamed.[64]

Because of the press and public attack on drugs and youth culture, many young, creative people, musicians and otherwise, came to the conclusion that post-Victorian culture needed to be debunked, ridiculed, or better yet, destroyed. If heroes of youth culture like the Rolling Stones could be harassed, then it was necessary to define a new vision of the future in Britain where police were circumscribed, individual expression could run free, and the old morality would fall by the wayside. Most of all, the values of working-class community, espoused by educated middle-class students who invented and craved such community, would create a real classless society, free of the demands of the post-Victorian establishment.

The London Underground

The bourgeois-bohemian background of the youth elite lent them a sense of self-importance that made them want to spread their values, and impose them on a defiant adult society. Numerous organizers came together to start clubs, newspapers, events, protests, and rock bands to provide an alternative community for young people in London, similar to that growing in San Francisco. They wanted to celebrate youth, music, drugs, tolerance, the expansion of the mind, the freedom of the body, the awareness of the spirit. This "underground", centered in London, was an effort to institutionalize a counterculture opposed to the strictures of the mass cultural norm in Britain. Youth culture, for these people, was not a passage to adulthood, but an alternative conception of how society ought to be run.[65]

The most common medium that bound them together was rock music; it defined the differences between this generation of Western youth and their parents.

Songs were immediate and ephemeral, yet they expressed the spontaneity that youth culture aspired to and the values that they intended to foster in a future utopian society. They had grown up with rock and roll, and rock musicians to them were intellectuals with a gift for defining their audiences' desires. Again and again, throughout the psychedelic era and beyond, rock music defined the direction of youth culture. What a listener read into the lyrics and music of a song, album, live performance or the like became the most vivid vision of the alternative society. At every event organized by the London underground, the soundtrack to the individual and communal expression of youth was rock music, not as background to the event but often as the event itself.

Many of the most prominent members of the London underground contributed to the establishment of the Notting Hill Free School in Notting Hill Gate in 1966. The Free School was a community self-help establishment run by a poet, John "Hoppy" Hopkins, to teach classes and provide legal and medical assistance to the poor ethnic communities and hippies of the area. Located in Powis Square's All Saints Church, the school became a major focal point for the underground.[66] Hopkins decided to launch an alternative newspaper, *International Times*, or *IT* as it was usually referred to, in order to publicize the Free School. The launch was announced with a party in October 1966, held at an old railroad engine shed called the Roundhouse in Chalk Farm. Two thousand people showed up, including many rock musicians. They came to hear music by Pink Floyd and Soft Machine, to roll around in gigantic vats of jelly, and to gobble handfuls of drugs, many of them handed out by the doormen. Critically, this was the first counterculture event covered by the mainstream press, as represented by the *Sunday Times*.[67] Similar events took place over the course of the next year, some at the Roundhouse, some at other venues. It soon became clear that there was a need for a single club where events could be held on a regular basis. With that in mind, in December 1966 Hopkins bought time on Friday nights in the basement of an Irish dance hall on central London's Tottenham Court Road to set up a club called UFO. UFO became the epicenter of the underground's projected cultural earthquake, where London hippies came to buy drugs and the latest fashions, where donations were made to the various community projects the underground promoted and where Pink Floyd, the Soft Machine and Fairport Convention held musical court.[68] The alternative society was off to a rousing start.

However, organization brought attention from the establishment. UFO was continually in the headlines as the center of degenerate culture in London, and police raids were common. In April 1967, a police raid closed down the offices of *International Times*, and an event was necessary to provide the funding for legal bills. The result was the 14-Hour Technicolor Dream, held at Alexandra Palace on April 29, 1967. It attracted forty-one bands to play its huge stage before ten thousand people. The 14-Hour Technicolor Dream was proof of the widespread impact the underground had across a large spectrum of the rock and youth communities. This would be the last major event for the underground, however. Hopkins was arrested for drug offenses in June 1967, and UFO's lease was revoked.[69] Other psychedelic clubs opened in central London to replace UFO, notably Middle Earth in Covent Garden, where Fairport Convention moved in to become the house band.[70] But it was not long before the psychedelic ambiance had disappeared from the clubs and the counterculture. As people all over the country began to wear bells and beads, caftans and sandals, the aura of excitement in the new hippie culture disappeared beneath a wave of price tags. Clearly, more radical measures were necessary to build an alternative youth culture. Only a stronger political commitment could accomplish what the underground wanted to do—subvert the existing post-Victorian society in the interest of building a classless youth utopia.

Rock music in Britain and America still carried the banner of rebellion into a future where youth values would be triumphant. But for all their hyperbole about the unity of youth, most counterculture figures were still university-educated and entirely out of touch with the working classes whose values they believed themselves to be in harmony with. By 1968, "youth culture" as they knew it was very different from the culture of adolescents who were still leaving school at age sixteen to join the union and work at the local plant. In America, far more young people at every social level were going to college, and they often saw the working classes—for many of them, their parents—as a conservative enemy.[71] In Britain, there was no notion of the working classes as the enemy. But the elitist rhetoric of British youth culture, derived from the aesthetic standards adopted by rock music, meant that a social divide grew anyway, between the music and values of an "underground", "authentic" music audience, and the audience that kept bands like the Dave Clark Five on the charts through 1968. Psychedelic music was a revolt in the name of artistic, individual vision, and it teetered British pop music on an artificial ledge between an escape from capitalism or support of it.[72]

By 1968, the rock music world was leaving the teenaged audience behind in favor of an audience of college educated post-teens and young adults. The advent of psychedelia thus brought about a telling decline in the power of British music on the nation's pop charts. Whereas British bands had dominated *NME*'s Top 30 week in and week out for five years, by May 1968, the charts were split between American and British artists, as they had been before 1963. The mainstays of British rock and roll, who had dominated the pop charts for years, now were in the process of abandoning them in favor of Romantic self-indulgence.[73] The emphasis on albums as opposed to singles, on *gesamtkunstwerks* borne of artistic genius rather than a maintenance of the connection with an audience, alienated the old constituency for rock and roll, now growing up and finding they had less and less in common with their musical heroes.

Because of the exploitative nature of record company contracts, no band in the early sixties could survive simply by releasing singles and albums. Groups had to go on the road, playing a string of concert dates all over Britain. Ballrooms and dance halls were prime venues at the time, and bands honed their

craft playing to different crowds in different cities every night. Between 1963
and 1966, it was possible to pay one fee and see eight or ten bands on the UK
pop charts play in a nearby city every week. But eventually, the sheer success of
British bands in America and on the charts meant that they could afford to play
to bigger crowds in bigger venues, and the ballroom circuit began to collapse in
1967. Besides, it was odd and disconcerting for a working-class teenager to
waste a few pounds and shillings on his weekend to go to a dance hall and end
up seeing Pink Floyd, a decidedly undanceable band. Instead, the newer rock
acts tended to play at universities and colleges—to students who were directed
by the youth elite to worship the working classes as the modern-day version of
the Romantic peasantry, but who were hardly about to catch a bus to see a band
in a pub on the grimier side of town. The psychedelic bands marked a repolari-
zation of rock and pop music along class lines.[74]

Two months after the release of *Sgt. Pepper*, the Beatles were chosen to
represent Britain in the world's first live global satellite hook-up. They sang
their latest single, "All You Need is Love" (1967). The show, *Our World*, was
broadcast in thirty-one countries to more than five hundred million viewers. The
Beatles were chosen to represent Britain since, in the words of a BBC producer,
"they are the best of their kind that world has known for many years. They are
particularly and peculiarly British."[75] Such status was a sure mark of the changes
in British society and its sociocultural image, now drenched in psychedelic colors. Those changes were hardly all for the good, however. By the time *Our
World* was broadcast, Kevin Macdonald, the founder of Sibylla's, had thrown
himself from the roof of the building to commit suicide.

Rock music was now clearly identifiable in Britain as the medium of rebellious youth. A relationship had grown between the sounds musicians produced
and the drugs they took. An alternative culture had arisen to expound the values
that musicians and their audience believed in. It seemed the "revolution" might
have just begun. Yet the revolutionaries themselves were not what they seemed.
The image of the psychedelic rock musician was bohemian, with no concern for
monetary gain. He was creative, with little concern for the outside world. He
was blessed with special talents that allowed him to describe his audience's values and those of the society they lived in. His honesty and integrity were his
most crucial link to the audience. In short, he earned merit according to his special talents—he was an artist. Artists created culture. Rock music was in the
process, not of creating a culture for an alternative classless society, but of redefining mainstream British culture instead. The psychedelic era loosened British
rock music's grip on its own social roots, not to mention loosening the grip of
both listeners and musicians on reality.

Chapter 7
Folk Rock

The Dionysian side of Romanticism was well-represented in British rock music during the psychedelic era. The Apollonian side was more long-lasting though, and in its mixed audience, more influential on British culture and society. This was because the musicians who founded rock bands based on folk influences in the late sixties had to deal, inevitably, with the standards of the folk music audience. With the backing of the English Folk Dance and Song Society (EFDSS), its leadership, journalists and musicians, the folk audience had maintained its lofty standards for what folk music was, and by their definition, folk was not popular, unless they said it was. Yet in the psychedelic and progressive eras, English folk music became a legitimate source to add color to popular sounds. Under the circumstances, such standards could not possibly last much longer.

The elitism of the folk music audience had seeped into British popular music anyway, numerous times since the advent of rock and roll. Skiffle had been a staple in folk clubs in the 1950s. The rhythm and blues movement in London had gotten its start in folk clubs too, and its followers learned from club members how to draw an artificial distinction between "R&B" and "rock and roll". More than a few folk singers such as Donovan and Dusty Springfield had crossed the magical line of popularity, and seen a simultaneous end brought to their folk circuit careers. Now, rock musicians were listening to English folk music and using it to define themselves as artists. In many respects, then, the folk music movement had taught rock music how to define its own elitism. Due to the much-revered nationalism and respectability of the folk movement, its attitudes were highly influential on rock musicians, folk musicians who played rock music, and the audience that listened to them all.

This had a great deal to do with the social origins of the critical audience for both musics. Folk music's audience in Britain was professional and educated; the London underground was oriented toward professionalism in their journalistic, educational and business pursuits, and largely university-educated. While the folk music audience was post-Victorian in its cultural and moral outlook, its members at least pretended to sympathize with the alleged bawdiness and bohemianism of the peasants and working classes from whom their favorite music originated. Rock musicians, journalists and critics alike identified rock and roll and rock music as the music of the working classes. Most acutely, the folk audience had long hoped vaguely that a revolution in culture might arise from folk music, if only they could provide a positive example to people of the national worth of a common, as opposed to mass, culture. Now, the counterculture arising during the psychedelic moment also hoped to promote a hazily-defined revolution, of youth against materialism, bohemianism against anachronistic moralities, and working-class culture against the established society, largely through the medium of rock music.

So it was little surprise that rock musicians would find folk music a source of inspiration in the later sixties. It was only slightly less surprising that folk musicians aspired to create rock music themselves. But of no surprise whatsoever was the fact that a huge proportion of the folk music audience despised the aesthetic mixture of folk and rock musics, at least at first. From the folk music movement's standpoint, the rise of folk rock was a disaster. The folk audience, long used to picturing itself as an exclusive repository for the development of Romantic British values, had to confront its own conception of what those values were and its role in British society. If a bunch of ignorant adolescents (as they imagined) could co-opt this music and commercialize it for a wide audience, what was to happen to the movement's exclusivity? Likewise, the intransigence of the folk movement toward rock music baffled the musicians who thought of folk as a popular music style. Numerous folk rock artists tried to gain acceptance from the folk audience, only to see that audience divide before them. They also never became popular enough with a mainstream audience to break down the barriers established between the commercial music world and the alleged anti-capitalist authenticity of folk music.

Karl Dallas, the folk music writer for *Melody Maker*, made a state of the union address in the Communist newspaper *The Morning Star* in September 1968.

It is about time that the British folk-music revival stopped cutting itself off from the broad mainstream of new popular music. . . . [T]he   most   creative people in the revival, the traditionalists, have kept to themselves, so it is quite possible for the unaccompanied solo singer in an upstairs room over a pub to have no real contact with the boys with the 100-watt amps in the concert room downstairs. The results of such contacts could be exciting as pop and not irrelevant as folk. . . .

What I'm trying to say is that the revival doesn't have to throw away its greatest strength—its knowledge and respect for tradition—to come to terms with the new pop. Quite the contrary, in fact. . . . Some people maintain that the true British folk music of this century is the Beatles. It isn't, . . .[b]ut undoubtedly the Beatles have produced the most distinctively British popular music since the death of the music-hall, and despite their success and removal from their home ground, Liverpool, it continues to have the true Liverpool twang to it. That twang has grown out of Irish balladry, the Anglo-African choral tradition of the sea shanty, and a dozen different strains of urban popular music. It doesn't turn its back on the past, and it doesn't live in the past either.

Too many people in the revival spend too much time trying to be folkier than thou. In fact, the folk people and the new pop people are basically in the same business, revitalising popular music. The folk people are independent of the mass media (a good thing) but the new pop people are virtually in control of the mass media (an even better thing).

It's nice and safe up there in your room over the pub. The pressures are less and so are the temptations. But it's time we came back down to the marketplace.[1]

Clearly, Dallas was among those who tired of the desperate bohemianism of the folk music movement and its efforts to maintain its elitism in the face of popular music's interest in folk as a source of influence. Yet Dallas might have been surprised to find the same elitism rampant in the counterculture that chastised pop music for its commercial intent too.

The Folk Music Movement in Britain

The attitudes and values of the folk music movement itself were central to the development of folk as a source of influence for rock musicians in Britain. Yet rock music was a major indicator of the decline in national and folk values that the adherents of folk music feared every day. They saw the movement as a direct response to an urgent cultural crisis. Industrialization, Americanization and urbanization in Britain appeared to be killing the national culture, especially peasant folk songs and dances passed down through generations almost entirely by word of mouth. The loss of these elements of the national lifestyle would be irretrievable in the face of television, Elvis Presley and the council estate.

After the Second World War, British politics and culture went through a surge in the popularity of socialist values. The folk movement was one of the institutions caught up in this flow, as folk music, its presentation and its associations became the political province of the British left. Leaders in the postwar

EFDSS like A. L. Lloyd and Ewan MacColl promoted the music of the industrial working classes to go along with the agricultural songs emphasized in the early part of the century. The spread of education meant that the workers themselves better understood the invented value the collectors placed on their folk heritage.[2] Thus, the popularity of folk music in Britain and the values inherent in the movement began to spread to a wider audience as well. This larger audience knew more of the realities of working-class culture, but was no less acceptant of the EFDSS's Romanticized conception of what that culture ought to look like. In fact, such ideas became so widely accepted that it became possible to determine what a "real" folk song was—a song spontaneously produced, of ancient lineage, with no obvious concessions to the musical marketplace. Folk was the root of a future common culture, in opposition to mass culture, and if the British people didn't understand what that common culture should be about, then the intelligentsia in the folk clubs would be more than willing to show them. By the 1950s, folk music had become an exclusive alternative to British popular culture, a cog in the development of an alternative culture based in Romantic traditions.

Folk culture manifested itself in the communal principles observed in the presentation of folk music. The folk club was a place where the audience participated with the performer in singing the music, denying a pop star system of celebrity. Performances took place in small venues with voluntary staffs for low fees. It was little surprise, then, that considering the anti-capitalist bent of the folk movement, few working-class adherents could afford to either perform or get otherwise involved in the movement for any length of time. Instead, most members of the EFDSS and most people who patronized the folk clubs were middle class, professional, and working in the public sector (teachers, civil servants, social workers etc). Only moderately wealthy persons could afford to volunteer their time in a club as either staff or musicians.[3]

If the folk audience was limited in social scope, however, it had plenty of potential adherents who seconded its values. Folk music was the soundtrack to a general movement against the democratization and Americanization of British popular culture. Historians, novelists, essayists and academics came out with works calling for a rebirth in English cultural traditions very similar to the invented folk traditions of the EFDSS. The emphasis, well before the coming of psychedelic or progressive rock, was on the Romantic. English culture needed to emphasize its pastoral roots, a sense of spirituality and the value of community. Technology had gone too far; it needed to be harnessed and subordinated in the interests of the preservation of the pastoral. Above all, the values of the peasantry and workers of Britain needed respect. Such values seemed to be everywhere—in the rise of the Campaign for Nuclear Disarmament (CND) and the Green movement, in E. P. Thompson's *The Making of the English Working Class* and Richard Hoggart's *The Uses of Literacy*, and of course, in J. R. R. Tolkien's *Ring Saga*. The folk movement also became a powerful ancillary part of the CND and any number of green and protest movements throughout the latter half of the twentieth century. Many of the members of all these groups were ecological protesters, adherents of New Age philosophies, enamored of Celtic and other pagan rituals and legends, and fiercely opposed to most efforts at modernization, such as road building.[4]

The EFDSS made a conscious effort to accommodate these people's interest, opening up its definition of folk validity to include industrial work songs, sea shanties and the music and musicians of Scotland and Ireland. The BBC had broadcast British folk music during the war in an effort to pump up nationalist pride, and its popularity after the war was thus unprecedented.[5] Many fans and organizers of the folk music movement seemed prepared to capitalize on that sentiment. Instead, however, the music remained the dominion of a select group in Britain, whose membership certainly expanded, but whose values barely wavered.

Mostly this was due to a challenge coming from new performers on the folk circuit, influenced not just by rock and roll and skiffle but their American folk music counterparts. If British folk music adherents were generally left wing politically and Romantic in cultural orientation, so were their American counterparts. The connection between left wing politics and folk music occurred in the United States at the same time, so the music of American folk singers like Leadbelly, Pete Seeger, the Weavers and Woody Guthrie became popular in Britain in the 1950s too. In 1949, Leadbelly was the first of a series of American artists to tour Britain, and more crossed the Atlantic during the 1950s.[6] A particular revelation was the populist, democratic performance style of American artists. The Weavers startled their British audiences on their 1951-52 tour by inviting them to sing along to the songs they played on stage. Guitars in American folk were also a revelation. Most British folk singers performed songs a cappella, with no musical accompaniment. Such differences in presentation made English folk enthusiasts wary toward the popularity of the American folk singers in their midst.[7]

So long as English and British folk music remained a little-heard alternative to twentieth-century popular music, the folk music movement's belief in its own role as the definer of folk values remained unchallenged. No one might question the EFDSS's dominance of the folk club and dance circuit, and if certain artists did not conform to the movement's dictates (particularly Americans), the folk audience could deride or ignore them. This began to change gradually, though, as the influences of American folk and blues performers began to have an impact on British popular music.

The Rise of Rock and Roll and the Folk Movement

Skiffle excited many members of the folk music movement—if teenagers liked this authentic version of American folk music, they might dig into its roots in

Britain. Rock and roll was a different story, even though its roots were mostly the same. If folk music was the "music of the people", "the people" did not include a bunch of London kids with tumbledown hairdos, skinny ties and swiveling hips. Rock and roll acts played the same folk clubs as skiffle acts, and thus became doubly irritating for taking over the movement's venues too. A letter writer addressed her complaints about this break with tradition in the folk clubs (often referred to as "cellars", since they often met downstairs in large pubs) to *English Dance and Song*, the EFDSS's official journal.

> At the cellar, I gather, the young generation can come along with their guitars and banjos and enjoy themselves. Now a young people's song and guitar club is an excellent thing but it seems questionable whether the organization of such a group is proper to the EFDSS. . . . Folk song is, I am aware, a living tradition and not a museum piece. By its nature it must evolve. But if this evolution leads to colourless and undistinguished melodies linked to dreary words, only made acceptable by tricky guitar accompaniments, we shall have reached a stage where our musical heritage is not worth preserving. . . .We do not want to breed new songs of poorer quality than our sires.[8]

Over time, however, the real issue did not seem to be the quality of the music, so much as it was a matter of the values the new music represented. Rock and roll was music that was raw, exciting, disposable, sexually charged, spontaneous and all-encompassing, all characteristics that no one would apply to English folk. The more rock artists mined English folk songs for influences, the stronger the debate grew over the social values of the folk music movement. Was folk still the "music of the people", and thus open to whatever the people decided it should be? Or, was it the music of a nationalistic middle-class, professional elite that should teach "the people" what folk ought to mean? Musicians and audiences followed this debate in the pages of the music journals over the course of the 1960s. On one side were folk music's "pop" enthusiasts, who welcomed the new interest in folk and the changes it wrought. On the other side was the "trad" audience, determined to hang onto folk music's purity and uncomfortable with a new popular audience that did not seem to know what a true folk song was.[9]

The division first showed up in the music journals as folk enthusiasts discussed the Beatles and their impact in British music. Some of the most prominent voices in English folk came out in support of the Beatles as a real expression of the folk sensibilities of the British public. "They may not make the corn grow higher", wrote Sydney Carter, the editor of *English Dance and Song*, "but they certainly promote vitality." He believed the Beatles reflected older folk origins, in the way they moved on stage and the response they elicited from the audience.[10] At the Royal Albert Hall's Folk Festival in 1964, director Roy Smedley shocked the crowd by having a Morris dance performed on stage to the tune of "She Loves You". Another anonymous reader of *English Dance and*

Song wrote in to describe how useful the Beatles were for getting the excitement going at a Morris dance practice.

> [The practice was] like a funeral march: the original basic excitement had all gone. 'Now', I said, 'supposing I was a Beatle and suddenly found myself doing the Morris, how would I go about it?' So for three seconds we turned ourselves into Beatles and out again and then charged straightaway into another dance and we still don't know what came over us. The effect was electric. Those sitting out were scrambling to join in.[11]

Other folk fans were delighted with the experimentation the Beatles pursued in their music. Their use of traditional instruments—harmonica, sitar, tambourine, harpsichord, double bass, recorder—and less traditional "folk" instruments—comb and paper, packing case, Coca Cola can—made them kindred spirits to the folk movement in the opinions of many of its members. As one member put it in 1969, "One day we will have the courage to admit The Beatles are Folk."[12]

The debate between "pop" and "trad" folk mattered because interest in folk music reached a peak of popularity in the 1960s. Folk's association with the CND lent it a certain political edginess that enhanced its esteem with young people in the early 1960s.[13] Then, the coming of Bob Dylan and his multiple tours of Britain excited further interest in British folk music, and intensified the debate as well. Folk music was supposed to be popular, but to the trad audience, it was not supposed to have any commercial potential. Worse, Dylan then went electric, and his rock and roll single "Like a Rolling Stone" (1965) was a huge hit on the pop charts. Folk music had never been as popular with a mainstream audience as it was in 1965. Pop fans bought folk-derived singles by Val Doonican, the Springfields, the New Seekers and the Watersons. American artists made their mark as well; Peter, Paul and Mary, Joan Baez, Ramblin' Jack Elliott and Pete Seeger all met with success in British clubs and on the British pop charts. Yet the traditional folk enthusiasts despised the scene's explosion in popularity. If a record made money, it surely could not be a true folk song. Only a true folk fan knew what a folk record sounded like, and it certainly never sounded like a pop hit. The explosion in folk clubs—some 300 in 1965 around Britain, half run by the EFDSS itself and more than a tenth of them in London—attested to the growth of folk scenes all over the British Isles. "Folk in Britain has never had it so good. Ironically, fervent folk fans seem concerned at the prospect of the music being discovered by too many."[14]

To maintain the movement's elitism, and despite the evidence, numerous prominent members of the folk circuit denied there was anything like a folk boom in Britain. Most simply did not like the idea. They preferred their folk music on the local level, in clubs, as opposed to on the pop charts. As singer Rory McEwen put it, "Pop music tends to be dance music. You can often twist a folk song till it fits a fashionable beat, but to do so you may have to kill the poetry."[15] Ewan MacColl openly wanted the folk revival to end. "What the pop-folk boom does is give people a false idea of what folk music is, so that when they hear real folk music, they can't recognise it. They say, 'where's the beat?' The best thing would be for the folk boom to end as quickly as possible so that the clubs should continue their steady development. . . . [A] packed club is not always the best club."[16] To negate the English folk tradition by commercializing it was to negate the basis on which the traditionalists defined their importance in the postwar world. Folk music provided them with an exotic niche in an increasingly homogenized mass culture. To reduce that niche was to reduce the listener: better for folk music not to become popular than for it to be debased.[17]

Folk Rock and the New "Authenticity"

In the mid to late sixties, a number of folk-oriented rock and pop acts further divided the folk movement between its "pop" and "trad" elements. They also had a significant influence on the rock audience, which opened up to the idea of a more relaxed, earthy, acoustic and yet urgent sound that could still be classified as rock and roll yet was derived from folk elements. Some of these acts met with considerable popular and commercial success. More importantly, however, all of them adopted the Romantic principles established by the folk audience as the definition of authenticity. They emphasized the pastoral in their music and lifestyles, played up their precision as musicians, and touted their lack of interest in the dictates of the music market and the pop charts. Almost invariably, a loud section of the folk press and public derided them for abandoning the folk movement's traditional values for commercial popularity. The effort to combine a perceived working-class music—rock and roll—with the invented traditions of the "music of the people" proved irritating to the folk audience's sensibilities.

For their part, the rock audience embraced the contradictions inherent in folk rock with abandon. The music's forthright sound, its impeccable leftist credentials and its pastoral imagery lent itself easily to the counterculture's attack on capitalist values in the later 1960s. The "music of the people" could be returned to the people (or at least, the right people) through the medium of rock music. The fact that a significant proportion of the staunchly middle-class folk movement abhorred this development was beside the point: they were the enemy anyway.

Many newer folk musicians came to embrace rock and roll as an influence. They saw the attraction of rock audiences as an opportunity to popularize their musicians' skills and make a decent living at their profession. They wanted to switch folk from an acoustic to an electric medium, to use rock music as an influence and as a catalyst to their own aesthetic, professional and economic lives. Martin Carthy, a guitarist, and Dave Swarbrick, his partner and a fiddle player, "brought the house down" at the London Folk Festival in October 1966. Carthy's second album received a favorable review in *English Dance and Song*.

Carthy and Swarbrick were some of the liveliest performers at the annual Folk Festival at Royal Albert Hall in 1967, performing Tom Jones's "What's New Pussycat" to the delight of the audience. Other albums by guitarists Bert Jansch and John Renbourn also received high praise. The recording debut of Maddy Prior and Tim Hart heralded new blood on the folk scene as well.[19] There seemed reason to believe in the mid-sixties that folk music in Britain had a future even if it removed itself from the commercial excesses of the pop music world.

These young folk artists insisted on intruding on the movement's serenity, however, reminding them that pop music and folk music were both popular musics, "music of the people". A number of musicians outside the folk movement in the mid-sixties also decided that the next great source for rock music was English folk song, influenced by Bob Dylan. Dylan's popularity and the growth of folk rock in America made it seem logical that if Britain were to continue as a major home of rock music, its musicians would have to mine their own folk roots to find their own Woody Guthrie, Robert Johnson or Leadbelly. Nevertheless, only a certain group in their audience listened. The folk artist who wanted to expand his audience was sure to encounter charges of "selling out" his artistry and audience for a pound. So the mixture of rock and folk music in Britain, while plentiful and fruitful, was hazarded with pitfalls.[18]

The Folk Rock Bands

As psychedelic rock was at its height in the mid- to late sixties, several folk rock bands rose out of the folk clubs to mine British folk sources and electrify them for a more receptive rock audience. The folk music movement was dismayed to see some of its most promising young acts turn electric. True to form, folk music festivals and *English Dance and Song* sniffed at the new bands searching for commercialism—even though not one of these bands had regular hits in the pop charts. The bands themselves tended to be alternately annoyed or solicitous of the folk movement. Mostly they rejected the snobbish elitism of folk music devotees, yet it was also clear that these same people were their likeliest permanent audience.

Into the seventies, the folk movement found that it needed new blood and new ideas in order to maintain its vitality. Many people damned the development of new folk songs, having preconceived notions of what a folk song should sound like that should not be tampered with. But with the rise of the counterculture, protest songs in rock music and the call for working-class revolution, the leaders of the EFDSS tried to shed the movement's stuffy professional elitism. They urged the membership to "Go round the clubs, and you will hear songs of real value about student revolts, poverty, love".[19] The leaders of the folk movement clearly wanted to open up its appeal by the end of the sixties, and the rise of the new folk rock bands offered such an opportunity.

The Incredible String Band began as an adventurous folk trio, for the folk music club scene, anyway—Robin Williamson played guitar, Clive Harris took banjo, and a third member, Mike Heron, was a multi-instrumentalist. But the band's stay in the folk clubs did not last long. A folk club in Aberdeen banned Heron from performing as a solo artist for not singing folk songs in the traditionally approved manner.[20] When the band finished its first album in 1966, they split up: "having made a record it seemed that that was as far as you could go at the time."[21] In other words, they found the folk movement stifling, as Williamson admitted in an interview.

> I had a great love for traditional music, and of course I still have, but it is very hard to do creative things and still move in that circle—it tends to be very staid because the people are not into creation so much as preservation. I prefer to float, because I consider what I am doing now to be valid folk music.[22]

After splitting up, Williamson toured Morocco and absorbed musical influences from other parts of Africa and India as well. He and Heron got back together to record a second album, *The 5000 Spirits or the Layers of the Onion* (1967). The album and its follow-up, *The Hangman's Beautiful Daughter* (1968), were Romantic hippie masterpieces, full of odes to the countryside, vegetarianism, new age religious ideas, the spirituality of nature and mind-expanding drugs. They mined British folk for material, especially Welsh legends. The albums were packed with exotic instrumentation, especially from the north African sources Williamson had acquired during his journeys.

The Incredible String Band was the embodiment of the hippie ideal in Britain in every respect—anti-establishment, simultaneously earthy and spacey, exotic, obsessed with nature, oblique and weird. *Melody Maker* referred to them, rather aptly, as "a folk Sergeant Pepper".[23] In interviews they often reinforced this status with their bizarre pronouncements on themselves and the state of the universe. If Williamson and Heron found artistic status as modern-day Romantics, they also might have been recognized, and celebrated, as a pair of strange people.

> Our music isn't consciously gentle it just comes out like that . . .violence is a hang-up . . . my kind of music is ripply and floral . . . I have a love of ancient sounds—Eastern, Chinese, Kabuki music & African drums. . . .
>
> I want to communicate my experience of the glory of life & how we all share in making our lives what they really are. Communication is an end in itself. I say buzz and you say bleep—that's a communication. Starting from that basic theory a lot of things can happen . . . The amount of time we've all lived in the uni-

verse is incalculable what does this instant of talking matter except that we are communicating?

You name it I've tried it like the mysterious ancient things—tarot, magic, astrology . . . I am fascinated by places where there's memory of druids, the magic stones, & ancient towers, woods & sacred groves. Art is the creation of beautiful space artists in living life in it. . . .

A year ago I'd have said I was in touch with the Spirit which wrote all the songs I would have said I wasn't responsible for their existence it was the music but now I'm starting to take responsibility for actually creating them.

Revolution is thinking you've got to fight something—Government isn't there to be fought they're there to be educated. If anything I'm the opposite of revolutionary—reactionary—evolutionary. I don't want to control people. That's not my trip. But I think there has to be some kind of Government, but it has to be done by people individually. Maybe there has to be some kind of code which everyone'll agree to . . . the way I'm approaching politics is by improving myself to a point where I don't need law.[24]

Regardless of their rock audience and spacey aesthetic, the folk establishment accepted the Incredible String Band, if grudgingly. The band was the first folk group to cross over to a rock audience during the heyday of psychedelia, and some critics saw them as a breach in the wall of Americanization and mass culture. *The 5000 Spirits or the Layers of the Onion* and *The Hangman's Beautiful Daughter* were given recommendations in *English Dance and Song* as albums useful toward educating children about English folk song. While much of the Bob Dylan-influenced "folk/pop fringe" was dismissed as being full of "raucous sentimentality", Heron and Williamson were important in getting young people interested in folk music and in contemporary issues as well.[25]

Heron and Williamson had been minor performers in the folk movement, though, and came from Scotland. Not so Bert Jansch and John Renbourn. They had been performing folk clubs around London and had several well-reviewed solo folk albums to their combined credit. In 1967 they formed a band, the Pentangle, which was meant to fuse folk, rock, jazz, and classical elements into a coherent whole, especially in live concert.

The Pentangle fused together the blues, English and American folk music, exotic influences like the sitar, and jazz, and when they succeeded (e.g., "Train Song" from 1969's *Basket of Light*), they succeeded brilliantly. The band's main fan base was rock audiences; bassist Danny Thompson and drummer Terry Cox had played in Alexis Korner's Blues Incorporated, so their credentials with London rock aficionados was impeccable. The band found this appreciation disconcerting; they played in a folk style, sitting down, with no announcements and little amplification, rarely acknowledging the audience at all.[26] Yet the folk circuit the band longed to attract instead ignored them. To add electric instruments, sitars, and jazz elements to the old traditional folk songs was inauthentic, and folk magazines and enthusiasts were apparently uninterested in the direction that the Pentangle had pursued. Said Jansch, "The people on the scene don't really know what's going on and I don't think they ever will."[27]

Following up on Jansch and Renbourn's alleged defection, two more stars of the folk circuit, Martin Carthy and Dave Swarbrick, joined an electric group named Fairport Convention in 1970. Fairport interpreted old folk songs through the medium of rock music. They obtained gigs, however, not on the folk circuit but in clubs like UFO and Middle Earth, where their folk pretensions and Richard Thompson's guitar playing made them a favorite of the counterculture. With powerful vocalist Sandy Denny fronting the band, Fairport Convention recorded three albums, *What We Did On Our Holidays* (1969), *Unhalfbricking* (1969) and *Liege and Lief* (1970) that became landmarks in British rock music. They played old folk ballads and modern songs as well, some of their own creation and others by people like Bob Dylan and Joni Mitchell. Above all, their approach to folk music was as a basis for expansion—to Fairport Convention, a folk song, Romantic in its traditional appeal, was a focus for an equally Romantic indulgence in musicianship and exploration of greater musical themes. Furthermore, the grounding in traditional peasant songs meant that the band's work never had the ponderous egotism of the work of progressive rock bands of the same era.[28]

Classifying Fairport Convention as a folk rock band was an instant sign of a lack of seriousness in the eyes of folk purists. There were no real folk bands, particularly if they had electric instruments and drummers. Carthy and Swarbrick joined Fairport Convention in an effort to bring folk music to a wider audience. Their audience reacted with utter shock. Carthy and Swarbrick seemed to be selling out traditional values in folk music, yet their vast repertoire of folk songs brought all the more influence to Fairport as the greatest of the era's folk rock bands. Denny and Thompson emerged as the band's best songwriters. Together, they brought British folk music to a vast new audience.[29] Some people were excited about the changes in folk music that they thought the band represented. One such was a letter writer in the pop music journal *New Musical Express*.

> In the last week or so I have had the pleasure of seeing the new Fairport Convention and [some of] its contemporaries. . . . What I found remarkable . . . was their extensive use of material of a British nature. Here was the "True British Sound", based on our long history of traditional music, not a third rate, overamplified carbon copy of American Blues and Soul. It could be that these new bands will spark off a whole new trend and balance our whole set of values.[30]

Yet they received no support from the folk music movement for ruining their idea of what folk music meant. Fairport Convention never made the pages of *English Dance and Song* in the late sixties and early seventies, and the band didn't play any of the regular folk music festivals.

In part due to Fairport Convention's poor reception with the folk crowd, bassist Ashley Hutchings, a founding member of the group, left to pick up with new musicians. Crucially, Hutchings wanted to work toward a stronger emphasis on the folk elements in the music, whereas Fairport Convention's emphasis on rock beats made that more difficult. His next band, Steeleye Span, featured a duo, Maddy Prior and Tim Hart, who had made their name on the folk circuit in recent years too. It was particularly important to Hutchings that "the basis of Englishness [w]as . . . not buried" in his music. He recognized what he saw as an upsurge in interest in English folk music as a result. Yet the music he intended to make was not rock and roll.[31] Importantly, however, Hutchings said, "I still think that I'm a rock n' roller." This was largely because he viewed "the way we play, the way we work on things, [as] certainly not academic."[32] English folk music was an academic pursuit: rock and roll was fun.

Steeleye seemed to be the only major folk-rock band that the EFDSS considered acceptable enough to feature on its pages occasionally, obviously, for their emphasis on folk rhythms rather than rock. The more a band strayed toward the rock spectrum, the less the EFDSS was interested in its output. The "trad" element in the folk movement barely tolerated the band's existence— Steeleye Span was a distasteful compromise to the needs of the commercial market.[33] If there was any question about the fact, it was resolved when Hutchings gave up after two albums and returned to the folk circuit. According to Hutchings, British traditional music had had a "very minimal effect" on popular music styles: "all the influence has been in the folk scene", and so he expected to work the folk clubs instead.[34] Without Hutchings, the band itself became more of a rock outfit, touring the United States for almost a full four years with folk-influenced bands like Jethro Tull or Procol Harum. Ian Anderson of Jethro Tull made several suggestions to broaden their appeal, including the addition of a drummer, and the resulting album, *Now We are Six* (1973), met with critical acclaim in the rock music press. They also instantly lost credibility on the folk scene; clubs stopped booking the band and folk enthusiasts lost no opportunity to tell Prior that they did not like her singing for a rock outfit.[35]

As might be expected under the circumstances, a sizeable number of musicians simply would not put up with the folk audience's snobby nitpicking. Largely, they were musicians and bands that already had rock music credentials, and thus did not need a folk audience to accept them in order to get gigs. Many of them had had little if any long-term contact with the EFDSS and its London-based clubs, so they were hardly inclined to accept the folk audience's pretensions. Critically, several of the musicians were of lower social origins, often from the north of England—they knew what "working-class culture" really was, and it certainly did not match up with the limiting caricatures that the folk audience cared so much about.

One such act was Lindisfarne. Formed in 1967, Lindisfarne was a folk act from Newcastle that put Ashley Hutchings's distinctions between the academic and the fun to shame. The music audience in Britain identified the band as a legitimate working-class folk outfit: most of their fathers were unemployed workers in the Tyne valley. Their concerts in Newcastle and the northern circuit were boozy sing-alongs with uptempo numbers in a rock mold, a sort of jug band for the younger crowd.

Lindisfarne toured the circuit of folk and rock clubs, playing electric music in rock clubs and acoustic in folk clubs, whatever made them money. There was never any major question over authenticity or the sanctity of folk music to the band members: they played what they liked, the way they liked, where they liked. One of their favorite songwriting themes was the toughness of life in the crumbling industrial centers of north England. With this attitude firmly in place, they came up with a pair of hit singles in 1972, "Meet Me on the Corner" and the re-released "Lady Eleanor" (from 1970). Their album *Fog on the Tyne* was a best-selling hit, and they toured all over Britain's clubs and festivals. The band split after a third album, mainly due to the inability to come up with new material—there was little question about simply mining the "authentic" old folk songs as album filler. [36]

Roy Harper was another successful maverick. He played folk clubs largely because he would be tolerated there—to an extent. "I was never really in with [the folk movement's audience]. I spent most of my time being thrown out of folk clubs for not being Ralph McTell." [37] His first album, *Sophisticated Beggar* (1966), topped the folk charts, and he was the star of that year's Cambridge Festival. But it was only with his second album, *Come Out Fighting Genghis Khan Smith* (1967), that he began to receive widespread attention in rock circles. He had an intelligent and biting sense of humor, and he was adventurous—one cut on the second album, "Circle", ran for a full eleven minutes at a time when extended songs were rare in rock and nonexistent in folk. He began to appear regularly at rock events, especially in Hyde Park, but he soon got a reputation for arguing with his audiences over music, politics and other issues. Harper was one to speak his mind regardless of the audience, and a loud denunciation of the BBC on *Late Night Line-Up* in 1969 got him banned by other BBC programs for the future. Writing and singing songs like "I Hate the White Man" (1970) to an audience made up of former members of the British Empire was not only provocative, but asserted an artistic integrity higher than any folk act then extant. [38] In no time he was out of the folk clubs and into rock venues, and his audience went with him.

Similar acts were also placing folk songs, both traditional songs and their own, in a rock context. Among them were Renaissance, the post-Yardbirds project of Keith Relf and Jim McCarty; Matthews' Southern Comfort, led by Steeleye Span's Ian Matthews; and Fotheringay, Sandy Denny's post-Fairport band. Other groups like Traffic threw folk elements into a jazz/rock fusion, to create a more melodic sound identifiable to a folk audience. [39] No matter how hard the movement tried to stifle it, the sound of British folk was everywhere by 1970.

"The Long-haired Folkies Syndrome"

Finally, an advertisement in the Winter/Christmas 1970 issue of *English Dance and Song* listed concert dates for Fairport Convention, the Pentangle, the Incredible String Band and Fotheringay. No other mention had been made of the bands in the journal to that point, though their individual musicians had often been discussed and reviewed.[40] The comparative popularity of the folk rock acts had paved the way for a relaxation in the folk movement's strict determination of the respectable in folk music. The folk audience and its leadership learned to welcome rock bands interested in folk music, partially because the audience for folk music had changed, and partly because the audience's idea of what folk music encompassed had changed too.

On the other hand, if a folk revival was in full swing, it had apparently beaten away most attempts to popularize the music. Folk music had influenced rock bands in Britain, but for every rock band mixing its blues with its ballads, there were other acts that the traditionalists turned to for purity and authenticity. Steeleye Span, Fairport Convention with its adjusted lineup and others were acceptable at folk festivals because their members had made their names on the folk circuit before turning to rock as an inspiration. If folk rock musicians would challenge the authenticity of the folk movement's definitions of what the "folk" were, then the movement would have to learn to be accommodating. Another letter writer to *English Dance and Song* tried to rally the troops.

> Get into the public bars; mix with the regulars . . . join in the choruses of "Yellow Submarine" or "Take These Chains From My Heart," learn some "pop" songs yourself and don't be afraid to sing them; finally, when you do get a chance to sing some genuine folk songs, perform them as part of the normal evening's entertainment—not as illustrations to a lecture on "traditional folk culture". . . . [T]he people must be weaned away from "pop" music gradually, not have folk song forced on them.[41]

More and more, though, folk music came to be a big part of a folk lifestyle, of dances, folklore, crafts, and individual interests that came to separate the true folk enthusiast from the dabbler in folk music. Much like rock music, folk music became the center of an entire counterculture itself. If listeners and musicians did not understand what "folk" was, an increasingly larger group of folk enthusiasts chose to live their lives in such a fashion as to show them. These people were holistic, earthy, maybe even Luddite—in short, approaching the supposed concerns of the working classes. A columnist in the *Morning Star* was encouraging.

While the 1960s gave us the folk festival, the period has also crystallised the facts and myths cloaking the great divide between the music served up and its true origins—the working people. Although by no means so exclusively profit-motivated as the rock festival, the not-so-good type can differ drastically from the integral, community-oriented style it ought to be aiming at. Whether the folk festival is built around the people's working-class culture or whether it is merely an annoying disruption of their ordinary life, depends upon the organisers' attitude toward the music as a true people's culture. . . .

Though in the past, the exuberant overflow [into the pubs] has aroused sometimes justified resentment and not always of the long-haired folkies syndrome. It's just that no one had consulted the people or found out what they had to offer. They are surely not at fault to expect that if you propose invading their pub you might first find out and learn from what they do there—and will hopefully continue to do long after the festival has packed up and gone. . . .

Folk music is the exclusive cultural heritage of working people, so let your participation in this year's festivals help continue the living tradition and keep the music alive where it belongs.[42]

No one condemned folk songs for being contemporary anymore; they simply lived different lives to match the standard set within the songs themselves. This often meant ridicule, but at least it meant that folk music would remain a living tradition as opposed to a division between conceptions of what a proper British culture ought to be. Andrew Means of *Melody Maker* summed up the changes.

There is a superficial aura that is sometimes preserved by "folkies" under the false impression that traditional music is necessarily tied up with the working class, which means that to enjoy it, you have to drink beer with religious reverence, sing dirty choruses with loud guffaws, and laugh a lot. . . .[I]t is apparent that this class rigidity will become absolutely outmoded.[43]

Rock music journalist Bob Dawbarn went to a folk club to see Martin Carthy after he too returned to the folk clubs. Dawbarn was struck by the reverence accorded the performer on stage. No one in the audience went up to the bar while he performed, no one went to the rest room, no one even talked while Carthy performed. The audience likewise waited expectantly for songs to sing along to, and participated lustily, in a staged fashion that was miles away from the more spontaneous invitations of the American folk singers who had introduced the idea of the sing-along to Britain in the 1950s. Dawbarn came away highly disillusioned, certain that the stodginess displayed by Carthy's audience was exactly what kept folk music from reaching a wider audience.[44]

Surely, that same audience would have told him that they had no need to display the sort of reckless abandon found at the shows of a rock group like Steeleye Span—it would not be authentic. The very definition of authenticity itself changed in rock music and amongst rock listeners in the 1960s, and it changed to correspond with the definition of authenticity to which the folk music movement adhered. Rock and roll musicians had adopted the movement's exclusivity, respectability and nationalism as early as the development of rhythm and blues in London. Rock music was the music of the masses, modern and disposable music, American music. Likewise, the eventual efforts of the folk audience to accommodate rock musicians' interest in folk changed irrevocably the definition of folk, the definition of rock, and the values inherent in both by the later 1960s and 1970s.

Chapter 8
The Counterculture

By 1968, Britain had developed an alternative youth culture based around rock music, Romantic values, the experience of drugs, and a general desire to explore the limits of human experience. Since governmental and cultural authorities had tried to stem the development of that culture—not just in Britain but all over the Western world—the effort to establish an alternative society became political. The goals of the alternative society were hardly ever spelled out, however; no one seemed to know what it would look like. One Herbert Lomas, a poet and critic, made a rare proposal in the pages of the *International Times*. His goal was the Workless Society, where machines took the place of human labor.

> [A] flower revolution . . . [would deliver] an aristocratic society for everyone[,] to be fully operative in the first two decades of the next century. . . manifesting itself gradually in institutional changes, delivering a society of aristocrats out of the present bloody and constricted bourgeois womb. . . . [Human beings] will be intensely active and creative, pursuing self-realisation because that's what human beings are like when they are free, as we can see from the glimpses we've had of some artists, creators and aristocrats.

Lomas would achieve the "Workless Society" through the creation of a "New Party"—apparently, and ironically, Lomas did not know that Oswald Mosley had used the name in 1931 to start the party he would eventually christen the British Union of Fascists. Lomas's New Party would attract adherents to his ideals by getting its members elected to Parliament. The first New Party MP would be "age twenty-five and he's got that slightly Schuberty, harmless, intellectual look that John Lennon has. He has charm. Old ladies and young girls like him. . . . He's the first of a bunch." Once the New Party took over Parliament, they would abandon the monetary system, build their machines and live a life of leisure, "like eighteenth century aristocrats."

Such an enterprise might want to destroy all money but it would need money to begin with, lots of it, to publicize candidates through the electoral process. And Lomas had no doubt as to where the monetary contributions for his party would come from.

> The commercial interests, the pop clothes and music industries, were the first to realise that most of the free money available nowadays was in the hands of the young—those people who have just started earning and haven't yet hostaged themselves with the responsibilities and expense of marriage and family life. . . . Many of them—the Beatles, say, Mary Quant, the Rolling Stones—are in powerful sympathy with the aims and attitudes of the new movement. No doubt they would be willing to contribute something to a serious and well-thought-out party aiming to realise the kind of society they themselves would enjoy.[1]

In the last years of the sixties, Lomas may well have been right about the willingness of English rock musicians to finance the creation of a new society, however utopian. The psychedelic era had produced hallucinations, but it had also produced dreams—of a classless society of youth, peaceful, adventurous, steeped in Romantic values and disdainful of the values of post-Victorian society. Indeed, the whole of youth culture in Britain since 1963 appeared to be leading to this point. Numerous underground journalists repeated a favored paraphrase culled from Plato's *Republic*: "When the mode of the music changes, the walls of the city shake". By 1968, many musicians, journalists, critics and fans saw rock music as the vehicle that would soon tear down the walls of traditional middle-class culture altogether.

By now, however, the creation of the new classless society—a society conjured up in rock music lyrics and proselytized by British rock musicians—was a project taken up almost entirely by middle-class youth: university students, leftist radicals of Marxist, Trotskyite and Maoist persuasions, alternative journalists, poets, potheads and postmodernists, not to mention rock musicians. Some of them even disdained the working classes' ability to join in the revolution—one need only look at the pop charts to tell whose records they bought, as Mick Farren, a musician and editor of the *International Times,* noted.

> [The workers] are presented with—and they very eagerly accept—a set of beliefs that gear them to [a conformist] kind of living and make this kind of living tolerable to them: just check the top 20. The majority of top 20 singles— property, death, revenge, fidelity. All this is pushed into them, they go out and consume this stuff as fast as they can. There is such an enormous re-education problem.[2]

It was a utopia dripping with the Romanticism of the psychedelic era. Yet paradoxically, it was based almost exclusively on consumerism and the dictates of the market: young people showed their values by buying albums, clothes, newspapers, books, movie tickets, and by patronizing radio programs, music clubs, concerts, vacation spots.[3]

In the 1960s, British society assumed a rhetorical radicalism matched only by Chartism in the modern industrial era. Unlike Chartism, though, the emergence of youth culture and the alternative society was in opposition to affluence and the affluent culture, thus creating a paradox: for however much the London underground and the counterculture wanted to hide it, their survival in connection with the affluence of the West in the 1960s was virtually parasitical. Adult norms were opposed in favor of what was thought to be a strong individuality, yet the only difference was that individuality was usually found in a thrift shop as opposed to a department store. There was a fantastic amount of conformity in the new bohemian culture, a demand by its elite that all of youth culture express its individuality by acquiescing to the counterculture's dictates, at the risk of critical opprobrium. The numerous contradictions involved in matching the rhetoric to the reality were not lost on the countercultural elite: many people recognized the problems inherent in trying to achieve a "flower revolution". There was always an implicit, yet only occasionally expressed understanding that the relative strength of the capitalist adult world was exactly what made the bohemian counterculture possible. Yet even their own recognition of their hypocrisies didn't stop the so-called radicals of countercultural London from demanding that the affluent society bend to their will, even if the result would be the exposure of their weak efforts at changing British society. As a result, the London underground had virtually none of the political significance to which it aspired. With all the professed desire for revolution, virtually no one associating themselves with the counterculture was going to sell their Incredible String Band albums to get the money to buy weapons to overthrow the state.

This was precisely because the real revolution was not taking place in the streets—it was taking place on records and in studios, in vast meadows and stadiums, where fans listened to and absorbed the counterculture's values through rock music. The most defining characteristic of the new society, in conception, in rhetoric, in music and in attitudes toward music as well, was the idea of "progress". The new youth society was a progression from the stultifying oldness of the post-Victorian world, and it needed a new music to proclaim its values—after all, the values of the youth society had always been articulated in rock music. The result, as the psychedelic era ended, was the concept of "progressive" rock music, a music particularly English in its conception of itself as art. Progressive values meant that musicians were politically committed to "the revolution", whatever that meant. They played their instruments well, wrote their own songs with the intent of producing art, disdained the dictates of the music market at the same time they made money in bucket-loads and adhered to Romantic values in their music and in every presentation they made to their audiences. The audience held up older, established rock musicians to this new standard, whatever type of music they made; newer musicians adopted such standards naturally, as naturally as they had grown up with them.

The Politics of the Counterculture

The youthful mavens of the London underground—journalists, acidheads, artists and musicians—were under assault from the British establishment, the London police in particular. The first half of the sixties had been about the leveling of class distinctions. Youthful intellectuals who felt themselves the beneficiaries of social change wanted to entrench the classless society and expand its zeitgeist to the limits of the mind and body. Yet the more that musicians and the counterculture tried to publicize their ideals, the more repression they faced from authorities in London and around Britain. It thus became clear to the leaders that they needed to find an appropriately rebellious politics to overthrow the adult bourgeois establishment. In 1968, the hippie mentality of peace, love and understanding gave way to a more hardened politics informed by their perceptions of the ideas of Mao Tse-Tung, who had recently tried to launch a permanent "Cultural Revolution" in China. European radical leftists flocked to the Maoist banner.[4]

Since rock and roll and rock music had done so much to create an atmosphere in which such social and cultural change could take place in Britain, youth spokesmen in radical newspapers and beyond expected rock musicians to reflect their changing politics. Rock music, especially as it had progressed since 1966, *was* leftist youth politics, even if it was a politics of leisure, whatever anyone's pretenses at Euro-Maoism. Rock musicians were supposed to be cultural icons and spokesmen for youth.[5] Mick Farren explained the mentality behind this process in the pages of *International Times* in 1967.

> There was a time, long ago, when pop stars were nice, albeit thick young men, who were safely kept in check by their managers. The worst things they were ever accused of was a certain preoccupation with death/sex/movements of their hips and possibly homosexual relations with the aforesaid managers. But there followed the less acceptable brigade, the long-haired ones, the ex-art students, the university drop-outs, the beatniks trying to make it rich.
>
> This lot knew a few things, they hadn't come straight from the building site or secondary modern. They knew where things were at. They produced what was probably the most honest music since the start of the rock 'n' roll era. . . . Townshend smashed £200 guitars almost nightly, Jagger's body spelt "Fuck you if you don't know" in semaphore, the Beatles refused to remain loveable mop-tops, and Dylan wrote songs of violent anarchy. The kids of course loved this; if Townshend, Jagger, etc., could get away with this, then just maybe the revolution that began with James Dean and Presley was getting somewhere.[6]

That this was taking place at the same time that rock musicians were becoming more and more professional in outlook was not cause for embarrassment to young Maoists: instead it was to be celebrated, and used for the purposes of obtaining power. Basically, the better musicians became at their craft, the more respect they would earn from the wider society, and thus the larger the platform that they would provide for launching the revolution. Mark Williams, a pop music reporter for *International Times*, tried to describe why and how this was the case.

> Pop is a medium which in this country and, to a lesser extent, in America, is only realising half its potential, like a man who has learnt to walk but hasn't yet mastered running. Any art form, once it utilises the techniques of product marketing and planning, ceases to be a recreation, it becomes a commercial culture and a medi[um] with all the concomitant communicative powers that are intrinsic to media. This power is either ignored or misused and everyone in progressive rock ought to own up and evaluate the possibilities and then start using them in a constructive way. . . .

> I want to see a band who can scream and shout about the dangerous thoughtlessness of the great grey society, about the brutality of our cops and the stupidity of our laws. I want to see a group inciting a riot. I want to see some action. This summer is the time, the mood is right for us to fight politics with music in the same way the press and the tel[ly] can (but rarely do) fight it, because rock is now a medi[um]. Sure it's basically a recreation, a pastime, for most people but because we've now applied new rules to the way it's run—it's also a weapon. Let's use it.[7]

By 1968, the misidentification of working-class values with rebellion had so permeated the wider culture that they had been adopted by middle-class youth, complete with their alleged revolutionary potential. Rock and roll had introduced these values into the lives of young people, and now, in 1968, musicians like John Lennon, Mick Jagger, Pete Townshend and Ray Davies were supposed to line themselves up behind the coming revolution. Their image as working-class intellectuals was now to be put to the test, both politically and artistically. The resulting contradictions between their true sociopolitical ideals and the utopian vision of the London underground redefined the role of the original British rock musicians, and rendered them less and less relevant to a British audience that was going through a process of redefinition too.

The immediate result was these same heroes became targets for criticism because they did not meet the standards of the new Romantic youth utopia. In October 1968, columnist Roland Muldoon of *Black Dwarf,* a radical leftist newspaper circulating mainly in London, analyzed recent singles in the *NME* Top Twenty for their revolutionary content. Whereas the Stones and the Who represented the "violent pulse of the hard Rock world", whose singles "constitute[d] the seed of the new sub-cultural revolution", the Beatles were the consciousness of the enemies of the revolution. "Engelbert [Humperdinck] keeps the old in sugary slumber in Coronation Street, while the Beatles are trying to beguile us with their 'in-ness'". The Beatles had recently released John Lennon's "Revolution" as a double-sided single with "Hey Jude", and Muldoon damned them for trying to fool the youth of Britain into believing that "all you need is love" when John Lennon did not "'dig Mao'".[8]

"Revolution" was Lennon's effort to distance himself from advocates of violence like Muldoon. Its lyrics were a rebuff to the notion that violence could solve anything in Western society, and Lennon thought long and hard over them before he decided to release the song to the public. It was a brave effort to force the counterculture in Britain and America to reassess the means necessary to achieve societal change. Lennon wrote the song to address the May 1968 student revolts in Paris, and he equivocated endlessly about whether the "destruction" to come from the revolution would see him "in" or "out". Eventually the Beatles released three different versions of the song, one on the album *The Beatles* with the word "in" ("Revolution 1"), one on the single with the word "out" ("Revolution"), and one with no lyrics whatsoever, an avant-garde composition inspired by the original song ("Revolution 9").[9]

From 1967 through 1972, the most popular political voice in rock music belonged to John Lennon. Lennon's political ambiguity was an effort to match his music—and his money—to the times. His first solo single release, "Give Peace a Chance" (1969), a sing-along recorded with a pick-up group he called the Plastic Ono Band, was a formative event in youth culture in America and Britain. It made explicit his own leftist political commitments, ideas he did not think the Beatles were capable of espousing.[10] Yet the counterculture attacked him at every turn for his pacifism. The short-lived counterculture art paper *Ink* derided him for his wealth, quoting an exchange he had with a crowd at an anti-Vietnam rally: "'War is over if you want it!' shouted Lennon to the crowd. 'Bullshit', came an anonymous cry. 'What you mean John, is that war is over if you can afford it. You can. We can't.'"[11] Lennon's status as a "working-class hero" was very much in question, among young radicals who had been inspired to their own political rhetoric in part by the very freedom of expression that he had represented to them as a Beatle. Now that they felt as if they had a grasp—however fleeting—on a true youth politics, they castigated Lennon as a tool of "the system". In answer to "All You Need is Love" (a McCartney song), John Hoyland, a radical journalist, countered that

love and kindness between human-beings [cannot] grow in such a society. In order to change the world we've got to understand what's wrong with the world. And then—destroy it. Ruthlessly. This is not cruelty or madness. It is one of the most passionate forms of love. Because what we're fighting is suffering, oppression, humiliation—the immense toll of unhappiness caused by capitalism. And any "love" which does not pit itself against these things is sloppy and irrelevant.[12]

Despite the pedantics of the counterculture, Lennon continued to identify himself, and be identified by his audience, as a "working-class hero" into the 1970s. Not so Mick Jagger, who went from countercultural hero of 1968 to despised hedonist of the early 1970s. In September 1968, the Stones released the single "Street Fighting Man"—just after the Democratic National Convention had been torn apart in Chicago, a few months after the student riots in Paris, and a few months since an anti-Vietnam demonstration took place in Grosvenor Square in Mayfair, a demonstration in which Jagger himself had participated. In the song, Jagger tried to address the frustration he apparently felt after viewing such events—"Well, what can a poor boy do, except to sing for a rock and roll band?"

The album the song came from, *Beggar's Banquet* (1968), contained the Stones' most overtly political work so far. "Sympathy for the Devil" was based on Mikhail Bulgakov's novel *The Master and Margarita* (1967). In it, the devil demanded respect for his role in history as the destroyer of dreams, and asserted that the listener was a willing dupe to the process. The last song, "Salt of the Earth", was a salute to the working classes. But taken as a piece, the statements on *Beggar's Banquet* were not radical calls for the violent overthrow of the establishment—calls that the Stones, more than any other band of the past five years, might be expected to make after all the harassment they had faced. Instead, they were admissions that countercultural politics were hopelessly utopian and doomed to failure in their effort to eradicate hatred, violence, death and evil. "Street Fighting Man" said that radical sentiments were channeled into music instead of action; "Sympathy for the Devil" asserted that evil was a more powerful force in the late sixties than good. "Salt of the Earth" admitted that the Stones had no understanding of the working classes they saluted. The Rolling Stones were wealthy and lived lives of virtually unbridled hedonism, and they admitted that they did not understand the working classes, or the allegedly revolutionary sentiment that the counterculture believed they possessed. Like Lennon's "Revolution", "Street Fighting Man" was a brave statement by Jagger, and a far more honest assessment of personal politics in the late sixties than any made by the vast majority of his peers.[13]

Just about every radical journalist and music critic noticed the ambiguity of "Street Fighting Man", but no one seemed to care. They did not castigate Jagger, as they did Lennon, for not getting into the street to try to tear down the walls of the city with music. Instead, underground newspapers like *Black Dwarf* and *Oz* asked Jagger to write out the lyrics to "Street Fighting Man", where young radical journalists took it as a call to revolution. Obviously young radicals did not care that the song denied that a revolution was possible in London—they instead seemed to see it as a challenge, that Jagger wanted a revolution but that conditions simply were not right yet for it to happen. Jagger proved willing to play the revolutionary hero in interviews.

> I think you are more likely to be anti-Establishment coming from a middle class background than working class. These people have a sort of family to-getherness and life is rougher and tougher—you're able to let off steam more. Middle class people tend to encourage their children to read more and learn more and from this you get discontented as your horizons widen.[14]

Yet Jagger never lost sight of his true role as a half-hearted minstrel enter-taining the true movers and shakers at the countercultural court. He claimed he was "an anarchist", but he denied that he was a spokesman for youth values, saying "Too many people are becoming obsessed with pop music. The position of rock and roll in our sub-culture has become far too important, especially the delving for philosophical content."[15]

In July 1969, on the eve of the release of *Let It Bleed*—an album named in purported mockery of the Beatles' long overdue *Let It Be*—Brian Jones died in his swimming pool. The Stones performed an already-scheduled free concert at Hyde Park in his honor, to introduce the new songs from the album. Like *Beg-gar's Banquet*, it included a number of politically charged songs that became anthems for the counterculture, especially "Gimme Shelter". The Stones were hedonists, however, not politicians. If the London alternative press fooled them-selves early on, they turned vengefully on the Stones when they noticed that the band had never done anything to further the "revolution". Germaine Greer summarized the Stones' "betrayal" after the Hyde Park concert, damning them with her pity at their decline from the rebellious days of "Satisfaction".

> What then is the mode of revolutionary music. . . ? Why did Mick Jagger not tell those quarter of a million people to take over the city? . . . They were cele-brating their togetherness, boasted the underground. They showed the parent-generation how they were gentle and loving and co-operative. . . . No one need be afraid of the Rolling Stones any more. They couldn't change a thing. They didn't want to change a thing.[16]

The Stones ended their subsequent tour of the United States with a free con-cert at Altamont, a one-day, multi-band affair held at a racetrack outside San Francisco. Meant to be a second Woodstock, Altamont was instead a disaster from beginning to end, marred by violence, drugs and chaos. At the height of the Stones' stage show, a young black man named Meredith Hunter drew a gun on Jagger and was stabbed to death by the Hell's Angels security troupe in front of the stage. All of it was captured on film by a crew making a documentary of the tour and the concert. Regardless of intentions, the Stones' lifestyle had proven to be deadly, and their radical politics nonexistent. Their next two albums, *Sticky Fingers* (1970) and *Exile on Main Street* (1972), both reflected their weariness, with songs about aging, the search for spiritual sustenance and the hard truths of lives saturated with drugs and alcohol. The tragedies of their drug arrests, Brian Jones and Altamont had taken their toll, and the Stones withdrew to Nice, France, with their millions, and with the hostility of critics in hot pursuit. The Rolling Stones were finished as role models of youth culture. Jagger's marriage in St. Tropez to Bianca de Macias, a Nicaraguan model, was denounced in the countercultural press, as if Jagger owed the music-buying public his single status and radical lifestyle.

> The wedding was stark public confirmation of the growing suspicion that Mick Jagger has firmly repudiated the possibilities of a counter culture of which his music is part. . . . Jagger put his signature on a declaration of allegiance to the system, spreading his velvet arse for the ruling class, wedding himself to the lethal values of property, personal power and the perpetuation of an oppressive mythology. . . . Mick Jagger is a rebel of convenience. If he was ever an anarchist . . . then it was the anarchy of the child's tantrum, the misbehaviour of a spoiled clot. . . . If rock music is to have any future relevance in the context of underground/left politics, then its practitioners had better start putting their money where their mouths are.[17]

The Stones could not fulfill this role because they never wanted to; at core, like almost any other popular musicians, their political stance was more about show business than shaking down the city's walls. By the early seventies, they were also irrelevant to a British population now trying to deal with unemployment, union disruption, a collapsing currency and inflation. Rather than battling these forces by making a cultural statement, the Stones were the first of a number of musicians to decamp to other countries to avoid losing all of their earnings to Inland Revenue, and they toured the United States often. The highs of swinging London were hangovers by 1972.

Musical Progression and Countercultural Values

Other bands besides the Beatles and the Stones felt pressure to match up to the counterculture's vision of "progress". However, rather than concentrating on politics in their lyrics, they pursued artistic progress through changes in the format and focus of their musical output. The original London bands tended to abandon the singles format after 1967, concentrating on albums, which made more "progressive" artistic statements.[18] As a result, in an economic climate that was beginning to become pessimistic and unprofitable, they found themselves— like the Stones and the individual Beatles after their break-up—removed from their original audiences in Britain, and much more popular in America than ever before. Even as the counterculture drifted away from interest in groups like the Kinks and the Who, the Kinks and the Who found themselves lionized as artistic geniuses in America, capable of selling out gigantic stadiums when on tour and selling millions of records with every release. The result seemed clear: the most

artistically adventurous groups ended up expending most of their energies trying
to reach out to an American audience instead of a British audience.

Of the old British rock bands, the Who remained the most heroic to the
counterculture, working-class heroes by association with the old Mod cult and
the grubby atmosphere of working-class west London. They had made a statement as explicitly revolutionary as "Revolution" or "Street Fighting Man", and
"My Generation" had come out in 1965, no less. The Who were simultaneously
the representatives of revolutionary violence in rock music and its most avant-
garde pop band. Townshend flaunted his power as the original working-class
intellectual.

> I'm today's powerful young man. I'm today's successful young man. . . . It is
> us and people like us who dictate the musical formula, we dictate changing hair
> styles, the way people dress. This is what art is, this is what our music is. It in-
> volves people completely. It does something to their whole way of existence,
> the way they dance, the way they express themselves sexually, the way they
> think—everything. . . . For this reason alone, pop music and its effect is crucial
> to an understanding of today's art. It's crucial that pop should be considered as
> art. It's crucial that it should progress as art.[19]

To aspiring revolutionaries in 1969, however, the Who was a band that still
had not abandoned the "pop" format. If Townshend was an articulate spokesman
for rock and roll and British youth, he was also the proud master of the pop single, which was anathema to the stuffy standards of the underground because true
artists should not make records to make money. In the United States, however,
their image was very different. The Who had made their name, along with Jimi
Hendrix, at the non-profit Monterey Pop Festival. In America, far from being a
pop band, the Who were identified as an underground band from England, un-
der-appreciated by the wider American audience and loved by an elitist hippie
sect. Some sort of balance needed to be struck in both countries, between the art
of making hit singles for a broad audience of allegedly unsophisticated teenagers
and the university student counterculture that bought albums and expected serious revolutionary intent from its favorite bands.[20]

The necessary balance was abandoned with the release of *Tommy* in 1969.
The Who were almost destined to create a spectacle like an opera, with its bom-
bast, ridiculous storylines and over-the-top performances. Townshend cited
Wagner and Mahler as his greatest operatic influences—"Italian opera completely pisses me off."[21] The opera received favorable reviews in the quality
press; as the *Sunday Telegraph* noted, "[the] libretto is as intricate as anything in
classical opera. . . . The story line emerges intact, and the young find it compre-
hensible, aesthetic and entertaining."[22] As a complete piece, meant to be listened
to and understood through a storyline that went from the first through the last
song, *Tommy* was the end of the Who's status as a "pop" band, even as "Pinball
Wizard" became a hit off the album in both the United States and Britain. As the

Who's bass player, John Entwistle put it, "Overnight we became snob rock—the band that Jackie Onassis came to see and all that rubbish."[23] Entry into Europe's top opera houses gave *Tommy* a legitimacy that was in conflict with the Who's image as the band of working-class Mods. *Tommy* was not "pop", or even "rock and roll"—it was "rock" to the core. It cemented Townshend's status as the most articulate spokesman for youth culture. Yet Townshend had little faith in the coming youth utopia.

> When the Revolution comes in England the first to get his head cut off would be Mick Jagger, the second would be John Lennon and the third would be Yoko Ono. Tom Jones would be made prime minister.[24]

The need to follow up *Tommy* with an equally articulate and germane artistic statement occupied Townshend's energies for the next two years, finally culminating in *Who's Next* (1971). The album was an unqualified artistic and commercial success. But "Won't Get Fooled Again", with its damning indictment of the counterculture's elitist politics and the resulting failure of any sort of youth revolution, was apparently as lost on the critics as Jagger's message in "Street Fighting Man". They lionized Townshend as yet another "working-class hero", even as he and his bandmates made their reputations—and a lot more money—by touring America far more often than their native Britain.

As for the Kinks, they simply did not match the counterculture's ideal of how working-class people were supposed to think. After releasing *The Kinks Are the Village Green Preservation Society* in 1967, a concept album with songs that described numerous people in a small village, Ray Davies concentrated on his own "rock operas". *Arthur, or the Decline and Fall of the British Empire* (1969) was commissioned by Granada Television as the soundtrack for a television movie that never aired. It described the feelings of Arthur, a character based on the Davies brothers' uncle, whose children were about to emigrate to Australia to find a new life as Britain's world and economic power slowly declined. Arthur longed to return to the Victorian era, when Britain was still the most powerful nation on earth and his prospects in life would have been more certain. The way Davies carefully laid out Arthur's sense of nostalgia seemed to be in willful defiance of the counterculture's desire to eradicate everything Victorian. Davies even penned a song for Arthur called "Victoria", about a young man pining away for the opportunity to fight for the expansion of the empire. "Some Mother's Son" placed Arthur as a soldier in the trenches of the Great War. "Shangri La" was an evocation of the British dream to own a home, at the same time mocking Arthur's belief that a comfortable middle-class life of respectability would solve all his problems. The mockery was most biting in "Brainwashed", which proclaimed that Arthur was a dupe of the ruling classes, but in the end, the entire album was a sympathetic portrayal of a man lost in the post-imperial twentieth century.

But despite the brilliance of Davies's depictions of everyday life in a society as class-oriented as ever before, there was little question that the Kinks were out of touch with their times. Nostalgia made for brilliant and complex hit singles, but in an era of psychedelic drugs and radical politics, Ray Davies harked back to an older Britain that seemed alien to the average rock listener, let alone the elitist politics of the counterculture. Put out at virtually any other time, *Arthur* would have been hailed as a masterpiece; in 1969, it was a rehash of values in which the counterculture and the buying public were no longer interested. A review in *Oz* commented on Davies's anachronism.

> Ray Davies' appetite for middle-class suburban "Nowhere Men" seems to be almost as insatiable as it is predictable. . . . [I]f we hadn't heard it all before, this album would probably be heralded with blaring trumpets and ecstatic acclaim . . . but we all know what familiarity breeds. . . . [Arthur is] non-progressive and full of Yorkshire pudding. I can't help feeling, though, that while Ray Davies' lyrical coat is undoubtedly many coloured, surely by now it must be wearing slightly shiny at the elbows and egg stained round the lapel. After all, he's been wearing it for nearly four years.[25]

The Kinks's record company, Pye, was ready to drop them after *Arthur,* determined to find a commercially stronger product. Faced with the prospect of being unemployed and in need of a new artistic direction, Davies chose to get more in tune with the times, without giving up his ironic eye. The next album, *Lola Versus Powerman and the Moneygoround* (1970), was about the band's problems with their record company and with society in general. Davies attacked the record companies, unions, the band's manager, anybody greedy. The single "Lola" was a standout, describing an encounter with a transvestite, and it became a major British and American hit.[26] But thereafter, the Kinks lost their audience in Britain. Touring America, they became wealthy and popular, even as Davies found the old image of the band limiting. He mused on how he could go back to simply writing songs for albums without a central underlying theme, while his band went out on the road outfitted with costumes, actors, stage sets and multiple-piece horn sections and orchestras trying to flesh out works like *The Village Green Preservation Society* for a demanding audience.[27] It was a long way from the raw energy of "You Really Got Me", or even the harsh commentary of "Sunny Afternoon"

The Counterculture in Practice

The criticism of earlier rock acts was hardly the most prominent way that the counterculture expressed its leadership of the British youth community. Instead, most of its efforts were focused on trying to make the utopian society it envisioned into a reality. Rock music was always a focus of such efforts—it was the rare commentator in the alternative press who seemed to notice that pounds spent on records might be better spent on financing the revolution. Instead, rock music was the way most countercultural efforts at organization were advertised, the surest and most popular way to get counterculture values across to the youth audience. If the new youth-dominated society was going to be a reality, in a world with no wars, free love, unlimited expansion of the mind, a tolerance for all moralities and an understanding of the role that youth played in establishing the ideals that society should pursue, then rock music was the most important medium in making that society a reality.

Nowhere were the principles of the counterculture better realized—and nowhere was their failure more profound—than in the proliferation of rock festivals in the later sixties and early seventies. Originally an American creation, festivals featured a large number of bands gathered on one stage in an open, natural space in front of an audience supposedly imbued with the spirit of peace and love. They lasted for one to three days, sometimes offering the music for free, sometimes not. Festivals were a vision of the alternative youth community in action. A rock festival was an opportunity to commune spiritually with nature, and to listen to rock music as the center of that communion. The counterculture's rhetoric of peace and love was to be translated into practice, the ultimate Romantic venture. Yet rock festivals also displayed the link between the counterculture's Romantic spirit and its elitist separatism. Only a comparatively well-off teenager could afford to pay to get in to a for-profit festival, or to spend more than a day away from university or work at a free festival. Not surprisingly, then, the audience was usually made up of college students.

The first rock festivals were derived from jazz, folk and blues festivals in both America and Britain. In 1967, there were ten of them operating on an annual basis.[28] The first important festival for the counterculture was a commercial event held in August 1967, when the Duke of Bedford hosted the Festival of the Flower Children at Woburn Abbey, his ancestral home. Thousands of hippies showed up to line the Duke's pockets with their pounds and listen to the pedestrian bands on stage, to the surprise of the bemused Duchess of Bedford, who declared, "I thought it was going to be a flower show with competitions, prizes and lots of flowers."[29]

Woburn Abbey inspired further festivals, with greater social and cultural intent. Peter Jenner, the promoter behind UFO, began booking free concerts in Hyde Park. Pink Floyd, Traffic, and the Rolling Stones all played to crowds of thousands to celebrate the counterculture and its vision. To Jenner, music was the vanguard of a movement to radically alter British society, to tear it from its industrial roots and give it back to a pastoral world where little England would not have to worry itself with profit or class. The Hyde Park free concerts successfully promoted youth ideals and highlighted the ideal of youth community. The gathering for the Stones' free concert in July 1969 was the largest the park had seen since the days of the Chartist rallies of the 1840s, and the House of Commons even commended the concerts for their peaceful nature and called for more to be held.[30] Too many people in one place, however, seemed to spoil the London underground's party—they could not get close enough to the stage. Members apparently felt that their values privileged the underground to a special place in the coming youth utopia. A reader of *International Times* even suggested that the concerts not be advertised in the local press to keep audience numbers down.[31] Jenner castigated her for her "implicit elitism" in the next issue of *IT*.

The counterculture was far more critical of the more prolific profit-oriented festivals, which attracted massive numbers of fans and bands without necessarily promoting the idea of community and idealism. Such concerts lacked the all-important element of anti-institutional anarchy that permeated the Romantic ethos. To the youth elite trying to use festivals to present its vision of a new society, the method by which a festival was organized was even more important than the music itself—only a free festival was worthy of its values.[32] Not so the average teenager or university student in Britain, who was there to hear the music whether it was free or not.

The most successful for-profit festivals were held on the Isle of Wight in 1969 and 1970, with Jimi Hendrix headlining both concerts. Yet the Isle of Wight Festivals were also notable for exposing the problems behind such massive events. Thousands of pounds simply disappeared when the concerts were over—capitalism and greed were more important than community. In 1969, Bob Dylan surprised the crowd by showing up to play unannounced, and of course, everyone in 1970 expected similar excitement. (Conveniently ignored was the fact that Dylan had earned $75,000 for his "surprise" appearance.) However, the stadium site of the 1970 Isle of Wight Festival was too small to accommodate the overflow of people. The sound system was bad, few people could even see the stage, and rain left the field a muddy mess. Some fans actually left the stadium to climb into trees outside to watch the concert, which turned out to be a better place both to see and hear the bands, for free. Thousands of people left before Jimi Hendrix closed the concert, and a contingent of French anarchists made themselves a nuisance by tearing down fences and smashing shop windows nearby.[33] So much for community.

Some festivals were successful enough to become annual events. Glastonbury began in 1971 on Worthy Farm in Pilton as a celebration of the summer solstice.[34] It was followed by a festival at Reading to commemorate the town's eleven hundredth year of existence, which also went down relatively well despite police harassment. The two festivals' parade of bands, free food and alcohol, and festive atmospheres prompted one reviewer to call it "part of a progression that must lead to a permanent rural community. . . . The time for planning the festival where you don't have to go home is now."[35] But the beginnings of annual festivals like Glastonbury and Reading meant that much of the festival spirit had disappeared. Promoters had hoped to reap large profits off the huge audiences; audiences had paid to experience the ultimate youth community, focused around the music that made it all possible. Neither was successful. The adult public tended to associate pop music festivals with political rallies, demonstrations, protest marches and the like, and they disliked them heartily. Locals especially hated the mess that a festival created: despite the counterculture's pastoral rhetoric, most festivals were environmental disasters, between the damage to the festival grounds, the litter and the sewage left behind. One man even suggested in a local newspaper that the 1969 Isle of Wight Festival was calculated to overthrow Anglo-Saxon civilization.[36] Whatever the occasional hysterical reactions of adults, the rock festival exposed all of the counterculture's hypocrisies and failures to the wider society, through a haze of pot smoke and pound notes that floated by.

Certain acts like the Edgar Broughton Band made their reputations at free concerts, as acts dedicated to presenting their music for free and casting out the moneychangers from the alternative society's temple. Broughton's band was known for their dabbling in magic and the occult. The bandmembers used mime and magic rituals on stage as a part of their act, and in the festival era, they were a three-piece—guitar, bass, drums—so they based all of their creations as an act around the symbolism of a triangle. Broughton became known for chanting "Out, demons, out!" from the stage, as if he could personally destroy the aura of profit at a festival.[37] Accused of bringing evil to the hippie culture, Broughton tried to turn the tables on the critics in his audience.

> People have told us that parts of our act are evil . . . they overlook the fact that the ultimate evil destroys itself. They dig the magic, but in sort of a guilty way, and because of this guilt they put us down as evil. We don't want to stop the audience turning on to things they are already turning on to. We want them to do their own thing, as long as they do something.[38]

They were also known for their commitment to "the Revolution". At Hyde Park they collected £100 to give to the London Street Commune, a group of squatters who had occupied the premises at 144 Piccadilly in summer 1969. Broughton himself was seen as a countercultural leader, a role he strenuously avoided accepting in fear that he would be selling out his communalist principles.[39] Said Broughton: "The old middle-road liberalism and apathy is disappearing and I think the masses will become active together against the system. If people aren't prepared to believe that, I think they are foolish, like the guy who says 'I'm only a musician.'"[40] On tour in Germany, the band tried to avoid accepting fees from promoters who, in the band's collective opinions, charged too much for tickets.

Determined to put on free shows in order to uphold the hippie ethic, bands like the Edgar Broughton Band booked town greens in a number of small British communities in 1971, often to be turned down at the last minute for a permit. Yet they persisted; the Broughton Band even showed up at Redcar to play one of the cancelled gigs in autumn 1971, determined that the show go on despite the authorities' opposition. They were arrested instead and jailed overnight. The scene was repeated several times in other communities, with other bands, usually lesser name acts. It did not seem to occur to anyone involved that the message of the music could just as easily be spread at paid gigs played in the controlled setting of a club or theater designed for the purpose, with the proceeds going to the cause of their choice. The hippie ethic of peace, love and understanding dominated the arena rock circuit in the early 1970s. But such concerts lacked the spectacle, the all-important element of anti-institutional anarchy that permeated the Romantic ethos of the day. Part of the show for the Edgar Broughton Band involved the method in which the bandmembers presented themselves. In some respects that presentation was even more important than the music, since the band played fewer gigs as a result. At first, this worked to great advantage, and the band trumpeted their lack of commercial intent in the press.

> [P]eople just can't believe that we don't want to make a lot of money. Of course we do want to make money, but that's not our primary objective, and when we do make money we want to do something with it, not just keep it for ourselves.[41]

But by the end of 1970, like most bands, the Edgar Broughton Band proved unable to reconcile their revolutionary principles with the basic need to make a living as musicians and lead a comfortable life. The band's promoters, Blackhill Enterprises, began to charge £500 a concert for gigs, an average sum for the day. Peter Jenner of Blackhill, always under assault for his desire to make a profit, answered Broughton's critics.

> We've all grown up. I think that Edgar's much more involved with the revolution now than he was—in the sense that the Stones are. I mean, the Stones all drive around in their fuckin' Jaguars or whatever they've got. No one suggests that Jagger is anything but loaded, & he has never come out & said that he's in favour of revolution. But the things with Jagger is what he stands for, the way he acts, has done more for the situation than any number of young long-haired stoned freaks running around talking about revolution. Now, in a sense, that's the same with Edgar. He stands for various things, just by what he looks like, what he does & his attitudes. He works, does more free gigs than any other bands I know, Edgar pays his revolutionary dues. . . . We do a fair number of things, but it's a rock 'n' roll band man. It's a rock band whose members have strong political views, but over the years these views have changed. In two

years, Edgar's grown up a lot, the band have. They're not denying the need for
a revolution, but they've been burned too often by these bloody revolutionaries.
They've appeared at too many benefits that have been a wank in all senses—
like no one enjoyed themselves, the bands didn't play to anyone, nothing happened. So what they're gonna do—I mean they've got some bread now;
they've got to the stage where there's some bread around. . . . Now Edgar's going to be around in 2 years. Say Edgar's around with £5 million in the bank, &
you go to him & say "We need some bread to get so & so out of jail or to get
some bombs" & he does nothing. Or even now, when he's only got £50, & you
go round to him & he elbows you. *Then* you can criticise him, right? [42]

Such were the vicissitudes of pursuing the counterculture's politics as a
British rock band at the turn of the seventies.

In early 1969, BBC television producer and pop music aficionado Tony
Palmer discussed the development of pop music in the sixties and its impact on
British society.

Pop music, if it is to achieve any respect at all (and without such respect, it may
as well just cease to be), has to be made to stand on its own two feet alongside
the best that other forms of artistic achievement can offer. . . . It can only be
from an aesthetic standpoint that a worthwhile estimation can be made, and if
pop music is not prepared to be reckoned in these terms, then it deserves its
worst criticisms—of crass banality, music illiteracy and moral debauchery. [43]

Palmer had identified a trend, one the counterculture and the London underground identified as political, but which most rock music listeners would
identify, like Palmer, as mainly aesthetic. A convergence was taking place in the
late sixties, between the cultural interests of educated middle-class teenagers and
the cultural interests of intellectuals and the artistic avant-garde. The counterculture of radical journalists, artists and students badly wanted those interests to be
dedicated to some vague revolution; plenty of rock musicians were more than
willing to accommodate them rhetorically. The reality behind the rhetoric, however, would prove less than radical—in fact, it would be rooted in some of the
deepest, most conservative cultural roots of English culture. As it turned out, it
was one thing to demand that older rock musicians who had been around since
1963 and 1964 had to adopt a new set of values to match the rebellious rhetoric
of "progress" toward the revolution to which the counterculture aspired. It was
another thing entirely to patronize and produce bands that actually were "progressive", rooted in those values lyrically, musically and in journalistic print.
"Progressive rock" itself would prove to be a journey back to the future.

Chapter 9
Progressive Rock

The counterculture mixed students, journalists, radicals and intellectuals with pop musicians, and the resulting exchange of ideas brought a fresh and exciting vibrancy to swinging London. That vibrancy began to fade, however, as the decade moved along. After a while, it became commonplace to see rock musicians cavorting with artists, academics and authors, far removed from their expected social and cultural milieu. Christopher Booker noted this change as a sign of the "disintegration of the youthful collective fantasy into a more fragmented and inconsequential phase".

> An even more revealing aspect of this disintegration was the wide-spread and rapid merger that was taking place between the cultural interests of teenagers and the avant-garde intellectuals. Eight years before, there would still have seemed an almost unbridgeable gulf between the concerns of, say, the teenagers jiving to Tommy Steele in the basement of the Two I's coffee bar and those of the audiences for Ionesco at the Royal Court Theatre. Now, . . . the coalescence of one form of fantasy with another to make up a sort of overall "pop culture", was taking place so fast that. . . no one would be surprised to see the pages of the "quality" press regularly taken up with the rapturous reviews of the latest pop records, or prominent pop singers being starred in plays and films by directors of impeccable "intellectual" credentials, such as Peter Hall and Jean-Luc Godard—any more than they would be surprised to see Paul McCartney advertised as spending his leisure hours with the latest electronic fragment from the pen of Stockhausen.[1]

Rock and pop music were clearly the media of a new culture, albeit one whose import remained indeterminate. Many members of the adult cultural establishment were more willing to reassess their opinions of rock music in Britain and its impact on British culture, especially between the releases of *Sgt. Pepper* in 1967 and *Tommy* in 1969. Not everyone had the attitude that popular music had made the transition from the BBC's conception of a "mass" cultural medium to that of a "common" cultural medium—its lack of complexity precluded any such transition, as a correspondent for the *Times* pointed out, rather diplomatically.

> Some people want to find in today's ephemera what others get from the works of Britten, Tippett and Shostakovich. The gulf between popular and what is, often ludicrously, called "serious" music is so wide that it denies the majority on either side the enjoyment to be found on the other.

> Popular music is always socially important because it arises immediately from generally held ideas and attitudes. It accepts limitations which (as the Beatles' interest in orchestral instruments and flirtations with Indian music show) not only force musicians to deal in vigorous rhythms and easily singable tunes but also prevent its composers from transcending them. There is simply no point in pretending that the last thirty records to be "number one in the charts" contain as much knowledge, skill or human experience as, say, the *St. Matthew Passion*.[2]

Yet the popular music charts were not where growing numbers of rock music fans were looking for knowledge, skill or human experience in the late sixties. Rather, they were found on rock albums—a far more expensive medium than singles, and thus less accessible to the average working class teenager—and from artists who increasingly were interested in finding that "seriousness" that the *Times* correspondent would deny them. A music critic for the *Guardian* believed that rock music had achieved that "serious" status already by 1970.

> [R]ock musicians are creating a great new field for serious music. In the next century the musical world will hail the Moody Blues with their *Days of Future Passed* [1967] as the first serious composition where nineteenth and twentieth century instruments and styles were successfully related, and also The Who for their very successful opera using purely contemporary instruments and style. . . . It is time to give Rock a more acceptable title—perhaps we should call it the electronic era.[3]

A convergence was taking place in the late sixties, between the cultural interests of educated, upwardly mobile teenagers and young adults, and the cultural interests of intellectuals and the artistic avant-garde. By 1970, the year the Beatles broke up, the coalescence of "serious music" with rock music led many cultural commentators to see rock music as an art form within the realm of pop culture. This was in part because "progress" in rock music led to efforts to combine it with the pretensions of classical, Romantic and modernist music. English rock musicians wanted to create "serious" art. London was now a major center for avant-garde musicians from around Europe and America, many prompted to come by the city's now well-established reputation for producing brilliant popular music. Several of these classically trained musicians began to turn to rock music as a way of achieving their artistic goals. The resulting "progressive" rock music they made was a mixture of rock and the classics, or at least, of classical music forms. Two more opposed music styles are hard to imagine, but the marriage of the two seemed more and more possible by the later sixties.[4]

The Progressive Aesthetic

This was the music of the counterculture, arty and intellectual, matching its vision of rock music's role as the leader of a cultural revolution. The people who made progressive rock, however, did not look or act much like revolutionaries. Most of its musicians were from the English south and had been educated at grammar schools, public schools and universities in southeast England and London, as opposed to art schools. Some studied at the Royal Academy of Music. Their educations made them familiar with the European classical repertoire. As a result, the most distinctive element of progressive rock was its multi-movement programs and symphonic poems, essentially updating program music for the later twentieth century. Many of the bands even recorded with symphony orchestras at one time or another.[5] The messages they conveyed in their music offered two alternative visions in opposition to material culture. Both visions were direct descendants of the psychedelic era's Apollonian and Dionysian Romanticism. Psychedelia's "Apollonian" ethic became progressive rock's "Aquarian" vision, focused on fantasy utopias, whether medieval, Eastern, or futuristic. The "Dionysian" element in psychedelic rock morphed into an "existentialist" vision depicting the bleakness of material society. Nearly every progressive rock act adhered to one or the other of these visions in their music, and since they were hardly mutually exclusive, progressive rock songs often displayed some hybrid of both.[6]

They made some great music, but progressive rock musicians abandoned the original social impetus behind the proliferation of rock and roll in Britain. Its musicians made little pretense to being working-class heroes, and they did not chronicle working-class disaffection in any way. They seemed more interested in bringing traditional English values into rock music, as if they wanted to tame it, to make it respectable and comfortable as art. The music's lyrical disdain of material culture was ingrained in the Romantic traditions of British culture, traditions any educated person in the country would be well familiar with as alternatives to industrialism and materialism.[7] In short, progressive rock represented the mainstreaming of rock music in British culture, an unconscious effort to make the music acceptable to a dominant, established, middle-class audience.

The musicians that audience listened to composed mainly on keyboards instead of guitars, keyboards being much harder instruments to learn and play. In fact, with the advent of electronic synthesizers, particularly the Moog synthesizer in the 1970s, a group could now remain small but still have the full sound of an orchestra, so composing on a keyboard became something of an essential to the progressive sound.

The audience built a cult around progressive rock musicians and their talents, and the musicians wrote "extended compositions" to highlight their musical dexterity. It was not uncommon for songs to last for half an hour in concert. The opportunity to improvise was ubiquitous in long songs, and to satisfy the ego of every band member, *everyone* had his solo. Of course, such improvisations could result in brilliant musicianship, but it was always self-indulgent. The effort once expended trying to capture the feel of an acid trip on record now went into professional experimentalism. Instead of displaying their talents in London's dance clubs, the bands made their reputations on college campuses, where wealthier students were prepared to spend the money to listen to musicians explore their inner musical dimensions. Many of the musicians were excited to get out of the rigors of the working-class pub and club circuit as a result; one such was bassist Lee Jackson of the Nice.

> That! I came through a lot of THAT scene in the North East. They were the only places we could play were working class clubs. . . . A lot more people in the groovy, groovy pop scene, man, wouldn't like to admit that they've ever seen inside a working man's club, I mean but . . . whew, it's frightening, I mean, that's all there is in the North. I mean you just can't exist, well, I haven't lived there since 1965 but in those years prior to that, you had to work in them they were your stable diet for earning bread. It was more like what colleges are now you know. Imagine a group trying to work without doing a college gig? Impossible![8]

Progressive rock concerts, at universities and in larger arenas, were practically a religious experience, a manifestation of the youth ethic of community and brotherhood. The performers controlled the experience and their professional images so powerfully that they were expected to behave in an aloof fashion, only casually acknowledging the audience's existence.[9]

The Moody Blues and Pink Floyd

No single act could be said to have birthed progressive rock, but Pink Floyd and the Moody Blues had the largest claim, as survivors from the rhythm and blues and psychedelic periods. The Moody Blues were an Aquarian rock act, more commercially-oriented than their progressive rock brethren. Their album *Days of Future Passed* (1967) was the first prominent attempt to wed rock music to an orchestra, and by extension, to the seriousness of orchestral music. Their use of orchestration and their emphasis on albums kept them lumped in with the art rock pantheon, even as their singles topped the British and American charts.

The Moody Blues were from industrial Birmingham; saxophonist Mike Pinder had worked as a toolmaker and percussionist Graeme Edge had been a draftsman in a local factory. They started out playing rhythm and blues and skiffle. They moved to London and were one of the many bands discovered playing at the Marquee Club on Wardour Street in 1964. Soon after, they topped the British singles chart with a comfortable ballad, "Go Now" (1965), which also went to number 10 in the American charts. It was hyped by no less a personality than Paul McCartney, who called it one of his favorite songs of the year. But the band's original success was not matched with further singles in the next few years, and it was clear that it needed some sort of a change to remake its popularity. A lineup change added a pair of session musicians, guitarist and singer Justin Hayward and bassist John Lodge, and the band embarked on a new direction in 1967, during the height of the flower power era.

The band's idea was to record a concept album with a symphony orchestra, describing the hours of the day in words and music. They happened upon this idea at just the right moment. Decca had put out a new label, Deram, which was supposed to maximize the use of stereophonic sound by recording musicians that emphasized the uses of the studio. The Moody Blues were thus signed by Deram to record a rock version of Dvorak's Ninth "New World" Symphony with the London Festival Orchestra as conducted by Peter Knight. To the eternal credit of both the band and Knight, the band members convinced the conductor that their own work would be more interesting.[10]

Days of Future Passed was a landmark in rock music. Between the songs, the orchestra added filler material that echoed the themes of the songs by Hayward and Lodge, carrying the songs forward as if through time, on a clock, and subtly changing the musical themes as each new song started. The most famous song, "Nights in White Satin", brought the Moody Blues back to the charts—significantly, with a sound that any number of music critics recognized as more "serious", not to mention far removed from the band's rhythm and blues roots. *Days of Future Passed* took the experimental tone of the Beatles' "Eleanor Rigby" and "Strawberry Fields Forever" and made it an aesthetic, providing rock and pop music with a connection to nineteenth century Romantic music that an adult, educated, usually middle-class listener would find comfortable. "Nights in White Satin" even concluded with a somewhat banal Romantic poem called "Late Lament". The song remained at or near the top of the charts in Britain for three months in late 1967 and early 1968. Also released from the album was "Tuesday Afternoon", which was more of an immediate success in the United States and made the album a chart topper as well. Thus the Moody Blues became the most commercial and visible exponents of Romantic values in rock music, placing their stamp on British culture in the late sixties.

Future albums continued and expanded on this trend. The next album, *In Search of the Lost Chord* (1968), focused on the exoticism of Indian religion and philosophy; one song was even entitled "Om". *On the Threshold of a Dream* (1969) had liner notes written by the composer Lionel Bart.[11] *To Our Children's Children's Children* (1969) was a concept album that explored the moon landing in August 1969 and the human quest for knowledge about the universe. If there was a general theme to the Moody Blues' Romanticism, it was the relation of modern people to the fleeting concepts of space and time. For example, flautist Ray Thomas discussed the use of electronic instruments in rock.

> I'm really the wrong person to talk to about electronics, because I'm a sucker for trad instruments. It takes generations to develop anything fully. Look at the modern flute. When Mozart was composing, people said you could never use one and he was the first to compose properly for flute. And it's taken from then until now to get the thing perfected. Yet it's really a very ancient instrument: only a pipe full of holes.[12]

Pink Floyd, meantime, were exemplars of an existentialist vision in progressive rock. The band released three singles during the psychedelic era, but also made a major change in direction after 1967. Songwriter Syd Barrett became more and more bizarre and unreliable as he gobbled LSD. His old friend David Gilmour was brought into the band as a second guitarist, but within weeks of Gilmour's arrival, the band asked Barrett to leave the group. He was too stoned to be useful. The loss of the band's principal songwriter proved a blessing, however, as the other band members learned to write songs themselves. They turned their backs on the singles market, choosing instead to concentrate on albums while maintaining a relatively constant live presence. Said Gilmour, "We thought, 'All right, "See Emily Play" was a nice single, but not the sort of thing a chap wants to play', so we wouldn't play it, and [the audience] threw beer and coins at us. We cleared more halls than you've had hot dinners."[13] Their record company, EMI, was not pleased.

> The company wanted the whole thing to be a follow-up to the first album. But what we wanted to do was this longer piece [the twelve minute title track]. And it was given to us by the company like sweeties after we'd finished; we could do what we liked with the last twelve minutes. . . . [W]hen we'd finished the album, Norman Smith, our producer, said . . . "After this album they will really have to knuckle down and get something together."[14]

With the development of new technology and the abandonment of the singles format, Pink Floyd became a group dedicated to the exploration of the limits of rock and roll as a genre. On the album *A Saucerful of Secrets* (1968), they wrote a series of conceptual pieces, atmospheric and spacey, but certainly not anything that could easily be described as rock and roll. Songs like "Set the Controls for the Heart of the Sun" amounted to a series of instrumental variations on a central theme, where lyrics were ancillary—in concept, somewhat similar to classical music, using rock instrumentation and rhythms to illustrate ideas.

The next album, *Ummagumma* (1969), included more experimentation, something of a blueprint for future work and songwriting talents. Every band member was given equal space to present his own compositions. The song title of Nick Mason's piece, "Several Species of Small Furry Animals Gathered Together in a Cave and Grooving with a Pict" said enough; few of his compositions would show up on later work. Meanwhile, Waters's and Gilmour's songs were tight and intense, and their talents would be further tapped on future recordings. The back cover of the record showed the band sitting among their equipment in a huge open space—the technology they used seemed as important to the overall outcome of the music as the personalities of the band members themselves.[15] Several years later, Gilmour would describe the album as what it was—"ego trips".[16]

Unlike many other bands, Pink Floyd was prescient enough to understand that rock music as they conceived of it could become pompous and boring. In danger of cliché in the early 1970s, the band retreated into the studio to create a new direction. The result was *Dark Side of the Moon* (1973), an album that realized all of the band's potential and became one of the great albums in the history of progressive rock. It was so masterfully produced that high fidelity buffs often bought it simply to test the quality of their equipment. The album was aptly named; it covered the dark side of life with a clinical detachment worthy of science, with titles like "Breathe", "Time", "Money" and "Brain Damage". The concept, created by Roger Waters, was to do an album based on the things that drive people mad.[17] David Gilmour considered the album somewhat more "conventional" than most other material the Floyd produced, and critics as well saw the album as leaning toward the rock "mainstream". A true progressive artist could not remain accessible however; as David Gilmour noted after the success of *Dark Side of the Moon,* "I think strategically our best thing to do next would be something weird, far out and the kind of thing that nobody could possibly understand."[18]

Progressive Rock in Practice

King Crimson was an act interested in following a similar aesthetic, by making the connections explicit between rock instrumental technology and classical composition. They were led by guitarist Robert Fripp, one of rock's most innovative stylists and a powerful spokesman for progressive ideals in music. Rock critics compared him to Bax, Britten and Walton.[19] Fripp was heavily influenced by Hendrix, the Beatles' *Sgt. Pepper*, Ornette Coleman, Antonin Dvorak, Karlheinz Stockhausen and the Romantic poets, and he hired lyricists who wrote about depression, despair, fear and anger at the height of the hippie ethos of peace and love.[20] His first album, *In the Court of the Crimson King* (1969), became a model for the works of later progressive rock acts, and over the years Fripp played with numerous musicians with whom he would collaborate on increasingly studied compositions laden with studio tricks and inventive instrumentation.[21]

King Crimson's introduction to a national audience came when they opened for the Stones at the Hyde Park concert of July 1969. There was intense debate after the concert over why it seemed that rock musicians—heralds of the coming working-class youth revolution—were losing touch with their audiences. Fripp wrote a letter to *International Times* to explain the transformation of the "underground" ideal of "music for the people" into progressive rock, "music for the art".

> It would probably be true to say that many people connect commercial success with a lack of ideals and integrity. No doubt this is because many of the groups and artists who collect enormous fees play shitty music and show little concern for the values expressed implicitly or explicitly in their work. . . . With the rise of the "underground" there has been a growing concern with the attitudes expressed in and through the music. But what do we mean by "underground"? . . . I think we expect "underground" to be synonymous with honesty, with seeking after a brave new world, and that the values inherent in this ideal tend to be associated with and reflected in, the development of and a greater consciousness of, different art forms; e.g., music, probably the most important in terms of wide appeal. The dissatisfaction of different people with conditions over a wide field of subjects, whether it is housing conditions in Notting Hill or the war in Vietnam, is seen in (or composes) "the underground" and is therefore mirrored in "underground music". Could we perhaps say that the word "underground" is synonymous with the word "improvement"? If so, it would seem that true "underground" music is concerned with improvement. If nothing else were sufficient proof, the [Hyde Park] concert has shown that the "underground" is definitely overground, but yet we still use the word. Perhaps by using it we are seeking to convey an attitude—that much is wrong in this crappy world but that we would like to do a little to put things right.[22]

Though they were hardly obscure, Crimson and Fripp were never astoundingly successful at selling records, lending more credibility to Fripp's contentions. In many respects, the less a progressive band courted the possibility of large album sales and big budget trans-Atlantic tours, the likelier they were to meet with critical success. The intellectuals in the counterculture and the journalists driving the popularity of progressive rock in the music press—few of the progressive rock bands were covered in the regular newspapers as rock and roll bands had been in the heyday of swinging London—clearly favored Fripp's conception of an "underground" concerned with improvement. Fripp tried to convey that popularity was not necessarily a hindrance to the desire to enlighten the music-buying public's tastes. Yet the respect garnered to obscure acts like Hawkwind, Henry Cow or Curved Air was far greater for their perceived disdain of the pop charts, especially since, at one time or another, nearly every major progressive act had a popular hit song. The unspoken disdain for the working-class teenagers who bought pop singles and ignored albums would have been flatly denied by anyone associated with these bands. Yet such a dilemma settled on Curved Air, when a song from their second album, "Back Street Luv", actually made it to number four on the singles charts. The accomplishment rent the band in two, especially after an appearance on the BBC's *Top of the Pops* to support the single.[23] The issue of progressive rock's popularity became more and more of a concern to the counterculture's mouthpieces, like the *Oz* music critic Charles Shaar Murray.

> Once the only part of the pop scene concerned with honest music and real people, there's now more hype, bullshit and hustling on the so-called progressive scene than anywhere else. The straight/commercial pop scene is simple and honest: put it on the radio and people hear it and if they like it, they buy it. That's all, that's how they sold a million "Love Grows" and five million of "Sugar Sugar". The music is crap, but the people are honest. With us, half the music is good, but half the people are dishonest.[24]

"Dishonest" was a rhetorical way of saying that the bands made music for money—every band, progressive or not, made music to make money, but the progressive mindset demanded otherwise. As such, any number of popular, classically-oriented bands became critical whipping boys in the music and underground presses. The youth revolution demanded a lack of commercial intent and a lack of commercial success, and somehow, any band that seemed to cross that barrier—an entirely arbitrary barrier, determined by the writers themselves—was a "sell-out". The working-class adolescents would benefit from a revolution in culture when they stopped buying Gilbert O'Sullivan singles and started scrutinizing the lyric sheet included with Pink Floyd's *Echoes*.

Emerson Lake and Palmer were perhaps the most castigated of the progressive bands, and Keith Emerson embodied the idea of self-indulgence. He was a brilliant pianist who had been classically trained and aspired to composing classical pieces himself. Instead, he formed a rock group in the late sixties, the Nice, which was one of the first bands to try to marry the classical repertoire with rock music. The Nice differed from the Moody Blues in that the arrangement of an orchestra was central to the music, as opposed to an addition to the overall sound. Bass player Lee Jackson addressed the band's marriage between rock and roll and classical music, and threw in a racial stereotype for good measure.

> We improvise like a blues group, not blues you know. . . . the basic policy of the group is that we're a European group, so we're improvising on European

structures. Improvising can be around any form of music, so we're taking European work. We're not American negros, so we can't really improvise and feel the way they can.[25]

Emerson made a name for himself as a brilliant showman, plunging knives into his electric piano to hold notes and sometimes setting his organ on fire while he played it. The Nice became best known for their rousing version of *West Side Story*'s "America", a song performed as a protest against the American war in Vietnam. During its performance at the Royal Albert Hall, the band burned a huge American flag on stage at the end of the song, and earned a ban from performing the Albert Hall in the future.[26] The Nice's credentials as an act representative of the ideals of the counterculture seemed well assured. But Emerson's efforts to marry rock music and classical compositions met with critical indifference. He decided that the problem was with the band—he broke up the Nice and teamed with Greg Lake of King Crimson and a powerful drummer named Carl Palmer to found Emerson Lake and Palmer in 1970. Emerson explained later that the idea was to keep in touch with the times.

> I think this band's music represents possibly the way things are today. If you go back to classical music, you have like the romantic era, the revolutionary era, and each has been created out of what happened in its time, as a response to the surroundings. You can't help being affected by your environment when you write music. If anything ELP's music reflects a lot of what's happening now.[27]

If ELP was the standard to measure by, though, what was happening in the early seventies was a growing focus on the glorification of self. ELP was an exercise in the aggrandizement of Emerson's ego. The band did not even have a guitarist: he handled all of the melodic parts himself on a larger and larger keyboard set, full of synthesizers, organs and electric pianos. ELP's first, self-titled album was released to commercial success in the United States and Britain, but it lacked excitement. Though the single "Lucky Man" (1970) was an interesting combination of organ, acoustic guitar and Lake's strong vocals, most of the rest of the album was a series of ponderous exercises in the uses of a synthesizer. The band was an instantly successful live attraction, but its work on records remained generally vapid. All of Emerson's energies and showmanship seemed dedicated to making classical compositions fit rock instrumentation. Such a marriage warmed the heart of neither the youthful rock audience that wanted rebellion against the conventions of the adult bourgeois world, nor the classical audience whose certainty that rock music was dull, crude and obnoxious was readily affirmed. Emerson Lake and Palmer became the focus of hatred for the critical rock audience in Britain, many of whom tired of the elitism of progressive rock and its pretentious claims to musicianship, seriousness and artistic merit. One of them was Mick Farren of *International Times*.

A band like Emerson Lake and Palmer seek to impress the audience with the fact that they (the audience) lack the ability to do what the musicians are doing; their end product is that the audience feel inferior and isolated. . . . We are being forced to think of our culture in commercial terms. We are being reconditioned to think like capitalists.[28]

Yet ELP was a terrific concert draw, and their albums sold well too. Rock critics despised progressive rock acts that aspired to a faux elitism, especially when the audience appeared to love the music anyway. Emerson Lake and Palmer thus made for a handy critical target.[29]

Genesis, on the other hand, was a band steeped in the Romanticism that became progressive rock's signature, and were thus much more popular with critics. The band's songwriters reveled in nostalgia, ancient legends, medievalism and fantasy, and their music had a sense of continuity and significance. The band members were all from affluent backgrounds: Genesis was formed at Charterhouse, an English public school in Surrey. Genesis's songwriters, singer Peter Gabriel and keyboardist Tony Banks, were very ambitious—their first album, *From Genesis to Revelation* (1968), was no less than the Bible rendered as a concept album. When it was a commercial failure, the band retreated to a cottage in Dorking to record the more successful *Trespass* (1970), a quiet acoustic set full of images of nature's power in winter, decay and ruins. In concert, Gabriel began to introduce spoken narratives between songs to string ideas together, and he wore costumes to play up the narratives of his lyrics. The album *Selling England by the Pound* (1973) was the band at its most eccentric. A series of songs lamented the destruction of English traditions—the Thames, Shakespeare, London, the countryside, working-class life in the East End. In concert, to dramatize the theme, Gabriel would dress up as Britannia herself.[30]

The most commercially successful of the progressive rock acts—and thus, one of the most widely hated by journalists—was Yes. The band lacked the subtlety and rhythmic virtuosity of Pink Floyd in composition, and the band members's undoubtedly fine musicianship often inspired them to ponderously lengthy solos in live concert. Few bands seemed more self-indulgent. Few bands were also more connected to the Romantic, pastoral, fantastical image popular in progressive rock. Yes lived up to every ounce of its own hype, either good or bad.

Yes began as a series of musicians in club bands in London who came together around a mutual interest in the experimentation of classical composition's marriage with rock forms. The collective became a progressive supergroup of sorts as classically-trained musicians floated in and out of the lineup with each album, but the band's vision was the province of Jon Anderson, their vocalist and a hippie mystic who was steeped in Tolkien. The band received positive reviews early on, based on the classical music principles of musical precision to which it adhered.

The main trouble [with the band's first album] is that for some reason the final mixes of some of the tracks on the album . . . are a little "fuzzy" and if you've witnessed their stage appearances which are usually uncannily well-balanced, you're somewhat disappointed by the sound of the album and may not be able to fully appreciate to the full all the instrumental intricacies that are an important part of Yes's work. . . . Yes are a British Music Band. They'll appeal to pop audiences and progressive freaks with equal effectiveness.[31]

The Yes Album (1971) proved a breakthrough, dominated by three extended compositions. "Yours Is No Disgrace" featured a jagged but simple series of related chords from guitarist Steve Howe as a central theme, similar to a symphony. "Starship Trooper" was a patchwork of three different related movements dreamily surrounding Anderson's fantasy lyrics about communication with a sort of organic space vehicle. "All Good People/Your Move" was simply two songs strung together, one a beautiful, mostly acoustic number about chess as a metaphor for life, the other largely a rocking electric instrumental. The album broke the band as a progressive rock act in the UK and in America, and Yes quickly became Pink Floyd's main rivals as a live act.

But Yes had a stridency that Pink Floyd always lacked. The bandmembers' elitist distance from their audience did not immediately show up in their album work. The next album, *Fragile* (1971), opened with probably the band's best track, "Roundabout", a perfect example of the dominance of the Romantic ethic in progressive rock. It opened with a baroque acoustic guitar flourish from Howe, then became a rhythm-driven electrical workout, marked by the keyboard playing of new member Rick Wakeman, another classical pianist. Howe also plucked out the melody of the song on his acoustic, creating a sound comparable to that of a lute. Anderson's lyrics, a sort of promise that his poetry would amaze and amuse his woman, were weird in the extreme.

Fragile also included the album's cover, a picture of an imagined earth as viewed from outer space, by a graphic artist and sometime guitarist on the London scene named Roger Dean. His artwork became associated with Yes, his album covers evoking images of watery, inhuman worlds where machines, if any, were organic and fit in with the surrounding landscape.[32]

Drummer Bill Bruford, a later member of King Crimson, described the Yes philosophy toward music at this time: "It was held that the best thing you could do at a Yes concert was to play the notes perfectly. As far as I could gather from Chris [Squire, the bassist], that was what was required of me, to play the notes that we'd decided I should play accurately."[33] Tellingly, Bruford mentioned nothing about the emotions behind the music, how it should feel: Yes was a band interested in professionalism and precision, not the amateurish delight in producing a great song. In translation, there was nothing "working class" or "rock and roll" about Yes—its musicians were professional, rock, and artistic in total.

Close to the Edge (1972) followed *Fragile*, an album of only three tracks: the title song, the ethereal fairy tale "And You and I" and "Siberian Khatru". Many people saw the album as Yes's apogee. Drummer Bill Bruford was not one of them. He left in irritation with the growing sense of inflated importance in the band—Squire had been known to spend hours tuning his bass for the album's recording sessions. Guitarist Steve Howe asserted that Yes's music demanded attention: "[E]very important move that has to be made is thought out very carefully. . . . I'm talking to you now but if *Close to the Edge* was playing I'd have to stop and listen. I couldn't relax doing anything else."[34] Apparently Howe's audience of pot-smoking adolescents dreamily perusing the details of Roger Dean's album covers was missing the point entirely. Keyboard player Rick Wakeman was also disenchanted with Yes, and more interested in exercising his ego as a flamboyant stage personality. A former student at the Royal College of Music, he left the band under acrimonious circumstances, annoyed with the pomposity of Howe and Jon Anderson.

> One of my ambitions is to send all the pop musicians to the Royal College for a week and watch them die a death, and send all the classical students on the road with a band for a week and watch them die a death too. Those that manage to survive both are the musicians worth taking about. . . . You have to feel pop, not just read the notes.[35]

Wakeman clearly thought of himself in the survivors' category. He left to become a solo artist, making albums of long, classically inspired pieces with Romantic themes at their center. Beginning with his second album, *Journey to the Centre of the Earth* (1974), Wakeman's works became gigantic on-stage spectacles rivaling the concepts of Wagnerian opera, or at least an Andrew Lloyd Webber musical. *Journey to the Centre of the Earth* was a full-fledged concert piece staged at the London Festival Hall with the London Symphony Orchestra, and featured actor David Hemmings narrating from Jules Verne's novel. Clips from the 1950s movie version were projected behind the musicians. The entire project ran at a cost of approximately £20,000—apparently, if you didn't die a death, the pop/classical musician found money raining from the heavens.[36] *The Myths and Legends of King Arthur and the Knights of the Round Table* (1975) was even longer than its name, and performed by ice skaters at London's Empire Pool.[37] Included in the production were a band assembled by Wakeman, the 58-piece New World Symphony Orchestra, the Nottingham Festival Singers, the English Rock Ensemble and a number of ice skaters. The pressure of such a huge undertaking actually caused Wakeman to have a heart attack at the age of twenty-six.[38] Having rejected Yes for its grandiosity, one wonders how Wakeman could have missed the irony.

Progressive Rock on the Radio

The audience for progressive rock was an audience of hippies that considered progressive rock to be elite music, and they believed their own musical taste for progressive rock made them elites within youth culture. Whatever the counter-culture's rhetoric, there was little interest in opening up that elite to a wider youth community. Progressive rock listeners were as sophisticated as the music they enjoyed; they disdained the commercialism of the pop charts. Taking the place of radio exposure were album cover art and the concert experience, in an effort to get the listener to buy the album, listen to it and construct a music listening environment that could rival even hallucinogenic drugs.[39]

Progressive rock's status as "art" made the concept of "pop" music become associated with the crassly commercial. Bands with little commercial potential whatsoever on the charts were capable of commanding huge performance fees based entirely on their authenticity as musicians.[40] The market was subordinate to the process of making music for the proper rock musician—he was expected to separate himself for the most rigid ideological reasons from the business of popular music. Concurrent with this idea, the live concert—necessary in order to reach an audience—became less important than the development of an artistic consciousness in the studio. What was more, the audience adopted these values too, in Britain and especially in America, where the money was. Rock was folk music, made for a youth audience, and it came to hold the same ideas about authenticity that the folk music movement in Britain held.[41] Thus, rock music in Britain took on a suburban as opposed to urban character, a professional and creative demeanor in opposition to the amateurism of the earlier rock and roll years.[42]

The radio remained the listener's daily mode of access to rock music and its values. Yet the progression of rock and roll to "rock" was accompanied by a distressing regression in the availability of "rock" on the radio, a situation that the underground deemed counterrevolutionary. Radio One had a Top 40 format; Radio Two was its easy listening sister. Both stations were criticized for excluding a huge proportion of the music put out by rock bands that represented the counterculture's tastes. A sector of the music-buying public had grown up during the psychedelic era, and they were interested in singles only as a teaser toward buying an entire album.[43] There seemed to be almost no outlet for such musical window-shopping available in Britain after 1967.

Radio One was expected to cater to teenagers, but BBC polls showed that its main listeners were suburban housewives. Thus, its broadcasts were designed with this audience in mind. When it became obvious that the playlist format included too much Tom Jones and not enough Traffic, young listeners abandoned the station during the day. Radio One thus became the old Light Programme spread over a full broadcast day, which was not what anyone had in mind when the pirates went out of business.[44] As usual, Radio One was a compromise between the BBC's mission and the desires of its youth audience—and the counterculture despised the compromise. Disc jockeys were hired from the pirates and then shunted off into the nighttime hours, while the two daytime DJs, Jimmy Young and Terry Wogan, played the top thirty, pop crooners like Engelbert Humperdinck and orchestral ballads. Many of the pirate disc jockeys quit rather than put up with Radio One programming policies.[45]

International Times published the results of a probe into BBC censorship in late 1970, much of which dealt with radio broadcasting of music. The paper accused the BBC of "operating a policy of deliberate suppression & distortion on a far greater scale than recent public scandals suggest". It was designed to "'reduce the British people's collective consciousness to a level at which it can be controlled with maximum efficiency.'" According to a BBC-TV music producer, they imposed a "big clamp-down on modern music & head culture" that kept progressive music out of the public eye. Those who challenged the BBC's policies were subjected to subtle internal pressures and occasionally threatened with dismissal. The Free Communications Group began in 1970 to address such forms of censorship and investigate abuses of power in media-related corporate structures. Numerous members of the BBC's staff signed a petition for the group's creation, but when the petition was published in the *Guardian*, their signatures were blocked out so they would not lose their jobs.[46]

The BBC virtually ignored the increasing popularity of progressive and album-oriented rock, basically because it did not appeal to the audience its polls said was listening. That audience was clearly not attuned to the counterculture's values, as any perusal of the pop charts and the continually growing sales of singles seemed to prove. Yet without hearing the music on the radio, the audience for progressive and album-oriented rock could never grow, which aggravated the counterculture to no end. How could the revolution happen if its values could not be heard often enough on the radio? The counterculture simply could not understand why the cultural establishment it despised would not destroy itself and ignore the interests of a larger British constituency in favor of promoting a "revolution" that no one seemed to understand anything about. Not until the early 1970s was a progressive rock program launched, and even then, it was broadcast in a "ghetto slot", between 10 PM and 2 AM, featuring former Radio London DJ John Peel.[47]

Such discrimination encouraged the elitism of the progressive rock audience. If John Peel did not play a certain progressive rock song or band, it was not worth hearing, and if it was on the daytime shows, it was obviously a commercial sell-out to pandering tastes. The audience listening to Radio One fragmented between singles listeners and album listeners—or more tellingly, between the working-class teenage listeners who still listened to the Top Thirty along with housewives, and middle-class student listeners who had long abandoned "pop" music for "rock".[48] The counterculture and its adherents, virtually all of them from middle-class backgrounds, became hypercritical of rock music that showed up on Radio One's Top Thirty—if a record made the popular charts, it was virtually worthless. Only the occasional artist (of the caliber of the Stones, the Beatles, or Jimi Hendrix) would be granted a reprieve for producing a single that made it on *Top of the Pops*.[49]

It was recognized that Radio One broadcast music to fit its audience—as one writer for *Cream* put it, "how are you going to accuse fourteen million people of liking music you don't?"[50] But the counterculture still considered Radio One a miserable failure, because it did not broadcast music that the counterculture considered progressive, music that promoted positive youth values—music that had an elitist professionalism at its heart. The BBC was suddenly placed in a position of great irony. It had always wanted to create an intellectually discerning audience of young people who considered themselves to have refined tastes. Yet this selfsame audience damned the BBC for not recognizing their tastes and catering to them. The BBC simply did not notice or recognize rock music as having any sort of intellectual appeal.

The counterculture, in fact, measured its tastes according to the same questioned values as the BBC had before establishing Radio One. Was the music politically committed to the right cause? Did it express the folkish mentality of a mythical British public? Was it rooted in a traditional musical past? Was it exotic enough to expand the realm of the listener's tastes? Was the music spiritually uplifting? The standards that measured the answers were very different, but the source of the questions was the same. It was a Romantic mentality rooted deep in the British psyche, adhered to by the middle classes. Thus, the counterculture's values were retroactive; they adhered to cultural standards from the very same industrial past that the youth of the late sixties wanted to leave behind.

Another British Invasion

Progressive rock was above all else an especially "British moment". The United States produced virtually no progressive rock acts. Just as the aim of the folk movement in the early part of the century had been to find and propagate a truly British music, so progressive rock defined rock music in British terms, separate from original American rock and roll sources. Progressive rock carried with it an implicit nationalism in its influences: English, Irish and Scottish folk music, Anglican choral music, fantasy and science fiction novels, medievalism. Progressive rock was in some respect the new folk music, made for a new youth audience, and it came to hold the same ideas about authenticity as the folk music movement in England. Like their folk rock counterparts, progressive rock musicians were expected to maintain a suburban, professional and creative demeanor in opposition to the working-class amateurism of rock and roll's earlier years. Also like the folk rock bands, the original social roots of the music they made were ignored, since the current musicians and the audience members were one and the same intellectually, socially and culturally.[51]

Unlike the folk rock bands, however, the progressive rock bands sold albums, lots of them. Whether or not the music seemed exciting or dull to critics, audiences flocked to progressive rock concerts, bought progressive rock albums, and adopted progressive rock values as their own. If most progressive bands disdained the notion of making singles for the commercial pop music charts, they dominated the album charts in Britain and America, and occasionally even made appearances on the singles charts as well. They became immensely wealthy, and whatever the Romantic values they held as artists, they lived the lives of the most privileged aristocracy. It was not long into the seventies before the counterculture lost faith in the progressive rock bands' ability to transform British society into the new Romantic utopia. Progressive rock musicians moved quickly past the rhetoric of rebellion as artists, adopting the bourgeois values in which many of its musicians had been raised.

The bands' music seemed less and less relevant to the crumbling economic, social and cultural order in Britain, whereas they made absurdly large amounts of money in America. In fact, the nationalist elements in progressive rock contributed to its popularity in America, where critics and fans regarded British rock music as authentic when it displayed its most Anglophilic qualities. Bands with little commercial potential on the British charts were capable of commanding huge performance fees in America because of their image as brilliant musicians. At one time the spectacle, self-indulgence, exhibitionistic virtuosity and self-absorbed fantasy of English progressive rock had matched the times perfectly. Now, most of those same bands spent virtually all of their time in America, where their values were lionized—and where the money was.[52] Mike Pinder of the Moody Blues commented on the appeal across the Atlantic.

> In America everything is so much more now, more urgent, more important. They live in the present. Here we still live fifty years in the past. To feel that kind of excitement, that kind of now, makes the music come alive, because it's so much more pertinent to what's happening in America than to what's happening in England.[53]

British rock music had come to a new point by the beginning of the 1970s. The rhetoric was different, the society that rock music operated in was different, but the social divisions, commercial possibilities and cultural significance were nearly the same. In 1962, rock and roll had been a music dominated by the demands of professional, post-Victorian middle-class values, thoroughly tamed and not expected to push the boundaries of the public taste. America was the home of authentic rock and roll, and Britain was never expected to have a viable alternative.

In 1972, rock music was hardly tame, and it still had the ability to exceed the public taste, to push cultural boundaries to limits that the cultural establishment found unacceptable. The difference was in who made up the cultural establishment, and what they thought of rock music in general. Some of them—critics from the underground press, artists, young intellectuals—were younger, had grown up with professional values, and they applied those to the acts that they listened to, just as their parents had. They were more tolerant of the widened boundaries of popular culture, boundaries they themselves had pushed at in the later sixties. They considered some rock music to be art, something no one would have said in 1962. The music they liked was no longer merely American—in fact, the stamp of British nationalism had made British rock music an exportable commodity, to America in particular. America remained the most important market, however, whatever the social import of a group's success at home. Yet the British counterculture—the roots of a new cultural establishment—still held rock music to professional standards, no longer post-Victorian in outlook, but with the same Romanticism behind those standards.

Chapter 10
Heavy Metal and Hard Rock

In his book *The Young Meteors*, Jonathan Aitken identified a new young "talent" class emerging, parallel to the normal class system. It encompassed young people who rose in society based on merit and were not required to ape the mannerisms and ideals of the aristocracy in order to get ahead. Instead, they created their own aristocracy, one that people on all levels of society aspired to belong to with a hunger that seemed far more intense than that inspired by the old class system.

> The new "talent" class is basically a healthy development in our society, and for all its faults is an improvement on the old class structure. . . . One word of warning, however. The meritocracy is starting to create its own snobbery, and there are some signs to indicate that the new snobbery is almost as bad as the old one. The snobbery with the meritocracy is the concern with who has, or who does not have, status. . . . Status means popular esteem and, above all, envy, and reflects popular morality, or the lack of it. . . .

> What have they in common, these fortunate people? First, they are all young, or look young. In measuring status there are no longer three classes, the upper, the middle, and the working, but three walks of life, the young, the middle-aged, and the old-age pensioners. In an era which doesn't believe in heaven no one must die, so everyone must stay young. Secondly, probably because life is pretty good hell in spite of everything, the new people with status are inhabitants of cloud cuckoo land, inviting us to leave the pressing bills and the nagging wife and the disappointing children and join them in a dream world of television and show-biz and easy riches, the bingo world, the LSD world, the world of escape

and never-never. Thirdly, when they look at the past they must burst with rage. To be really well up you must be against everything that is meant by the British Empire, or Rupert Brooke, and "get your hair cut" and "send a gunboat". . . .

All this is not meant to be taken too seriously. Yet it would be regrettable if just at the moment when Britain appears to be getting a more reasonable sense of proportion about the importance of hereditary social distinctions, we simultaneously start to lose our heads over the importance of status. Society will always pay homage to the uncommon man, and rightly so, but let us hope that the younger generation will show a little more discrimination in whom it applauds for being uncommon.[1]

Aitken identified obviously with the older establishment, in its loss of control over the realities of social distinctions. Yet at the same time, he was hardly wrong. The counterculture was the virtual definition of Aitken's "young meteors", its alternative media and patronage of rock bands defining its aristocratic status among youth. Yet just as with the old class-based aristocracy, there were plenty of opportunities to question the counterculture's status and tastes, especially in music.

With the advent of the seventies, rock music's British audience fractured into a number of very different camps, based on class attitudes and their relationship to the music's aesthetics. Older listeners tended to like quieter rock music, and so listened mainly to singer-songwriters like Cat Stevens or Van Morrison; the more eclectic might listen to folk rock bands like Steeleye Span. Younger listeners, especially teenagers and preteens, went for pop. Those in the middle, usually college-aged, were the most wide-listening audience. They were the main audience for the progressive rock of the era, but many also came to prefer a heavier rock sound, often referred to as "heavy metal".

These bands' music was still blues-based, but loud and raucous, masculine, and often hypnotic. They provided an alternative to the elitism of the progressive bands and their audience, without abandoning the Romanticism that made the music appealing to a wide audience. Heavy metal represented the dark side of the Romantic vision. Influenced by Cream and Jimi Hendrix, the metal artists' desire was to create a droning, heavy, powerful sound that enveloped the listener in its sheer assault on the senses. Rock critics despised these bands, believing that they pandered to the public taste too much, that they lacked the requisite intelligence that progressive rock demanded from bands in the seventies. Only a very few critics realized that the rise of such acts and the critical hostility inherent marked a clear sociocultural change in music—that the old values of rock and roll were in decline. Bands like Led Zeppelin and Black Sabbath were often the only hope left in rebellion against a complacency that mirrored that of the adult establishment.

Led Zeppelin, Black Sabbath and the American Market

As a group, Led Zeppelin managed to bridge all of the divisions that had developed in rock music by 1970. They appealed to working-class and middle-class audiences; their music varied between the R&B of heavy metal and the Romantic artistic indulgence of progressive rock, between the hypertrophied masculinity of rock music and the delicacy of folk rock. Led Zeppelin was the culmination of the sixties' developments in British pop, rock and roll and rock music, and were simultaneously representative of the music's future in the seventies. The lyrics of singer Robert Plant and guitarist Jimmy Page were laden with images from ancient Celtic and Norse history and mythology, medievalism, fantasy, mysticism and magic.[2] Multiple-layered tracking of Page's guitar work—often upwards of ten tracks of guitar lines laid on top of each other—created a psychedelic drone that mesmerized listeners. Plant had an eerie voice that often ascended into the realms of a banshee-like wail, one of the most distinctive voices in rock. The band mixed heavy riffs with light acoustic folk as well; capable of immense power in sound, Zeppelin was all the more remarkable for the gossamer touch they applied to some of the most beautiful songs in rock music.

In short, no band was more Romantic than Led Zeppelin. They even combined the two geographical elements involved in the original rock and roll moment in England. Plant and drummer John Bonham were from Birmingham, while Page—an art school student—and bassist/keyboardist John Paul Jones were London session musicians. The ideals of the London underground would seem to have found their matching band.[3] Instead, the counterculture despised Led Zeppelin. So did British critics and some members of the progressive rock audience. Led Zeppelin exposed a great hypocrisy that the counterculture and its supporters preferred to ignore—that the values of the Romantic utopia they wanted to create were laden with commercialism and were eminently exportable.

Zeppelin was in fact a commercial creation, and a brilliant one at that. Manager Peter Grant rewrote the rules of rock music as a business, in contracts, touring arrangements, publishing deals and record packaging. Before the band had released a single song, Page promised that the "New Yardbirds", as his new band was often termed, would be one of the best-selling acts in the history of music. On that promise, Atlantic Records paid Led Zeppelin $200,000 to produce the first album, an unheard-of amount for an unknown act.[4] Page and Grant shunned the singles market, instead marketing the band by touring constantly and gaining a reputation as a live act, based on word of mouth, which made Led Zeppelin the top-selling band in Britain by 1970. Critics despised this calculated commercialism, and considered Led Zeppelin to be the embodiment of corporate values in music—especially because the band was popular with an "unsophisticated" audience of younger and working-class kids. Many chose to ignore the band's obvious talent in favor of lambasting its carefully crafted image.

The criticism was unfair. Led Zeppelin was the first band to do everything that the counterculture asked of it—to make music that was not meant to be teenaged, danceable, disposable, or even appealing to girls.[5] Zeppelin was, instead, adult, artistic, lasting and masculine, and with those values came an unmatchable marketability that the counterculture did not want to acknowledge. Jimmy Page was clearly proud of the accomplishment of directing the record industry's marketing of his band by playing live and selling albums, as opposed to simply following the industry's dictates. That allowed him to throw a bitchy retort at the hypocritical values of the London underground, who lambasted his new band as the very embodiment of record industry exploitation.

> I know you were referring to the underground in the sense of a collection of people and ideas existing within, but divorced from the society in which they live. That's an interesting concept but has little to do with our music. In this country, & this is just personally speaking, it seems to me to be something which has been distorted into an almost comical replica of the US. Take *IT [International Times]* for example. There's an example of the basic theory of the underground, the alternative society, the theory being lost behind the pounds shillings and pence. The underground is big business now and that's a pity.[6]

Page made his comments with the knowledge that the values his band espoused matched the counterculture's ideals; they also sold like crazy. Songs like "Ramble On", a partially acoustic song about the narrator's need to avoid being rooted, ended with a direct reference to Tolkien's *The Hobbit*—"Twas in the darkest depths of Mordor, I met a girl so fair/But Gollum and the evil ones crept up and slipped away with her". Zeppelin's dark Gothicism contrasted brilliantly with the progressivism of other bands of their era, and proved marketable as well. Page was fascinated by the life of Aleister Crowley, the demonologist, and rumors circulated that the entire band had sold their souls to the devil for their massive international success. No one in the band did anything to dispel such rumors, which only added to the mystique, and the amount of dollars and pounds.[7]

Future albums such as the folk-inflected *Led Zeppelin III* (1970) and the brilliant *Untitled* (1971), which featured "Stairway to Heaven", were among the best-selling albums of the 1970s. The band, however, was the very end of any notion of countercultural rebellion. Ultimately, for a British group to have a social impact at home, they had to stay in Britain and consider it the most important venue in which to succeed. Every rhetorical change that rock and roll had ushered in since 1963—in the way people discussed working-class participation in culture, in the creation of new standards of presentation in entertainment, in the acceptance of popular cultural media as art, in the notion that such media could change British society, and maybe the world—all of it hinged on the notion that the British market's acceptance of the product was the only acceptance that counted. Being a success in America was merely a bonus—in fact, for most bands it was considered a given that the American market was easy to crack once they had made it big at home.

Led Zeppelin, however, sold more records and made much more money on tour in the United States, much like the progressive rock bands. Though they craved acceptance from the British music press and public, Zeppelin knew where the money was and where the music press recognized their musical worth, despite any commercial intent. Gradually, Page and Plant abandoned the home market as an important source of revenue or acceptance. The inability of the counterculture in Britain to promote its youth revolution became explicit: Led Zeppelin, the epitome of their values in British rock music, toured the United States because the band made more money and got more respect than it did in Britain.[8]

As a music scene, Birmingham produced not just Plant and Bonham, but a plethora of good music acts like the Spencer Davis Group, the Moody Blues and the Move. Yet to 1970, the city had no distinctive musical sound associated with it, until the rise of heavy metal. At the time a grimy old steel town, Birmingham in the 1960s and 1970s produced half of Led Zeppelin, Black Sabbath and Judas Priest, not to mention the Electric Light Orchestra, a successor to the Move as a progressive/pop act. This was likely due to a distinctive atmosphere, according to journalist Rob Partridge.

> Birmingham . . . is dour and grubby, the biggest industrial city in Britain. Birmingham is flanked by coalfields, steel mills and car and engineering plants. Sometimes a little like Detroit, in fact. . . . [M]ost of all Birmingham is a strong working class community producing a culture, which has found contemporary substance in high-energy rock and roll.[9]

Black Sabbath was the first of the exclusively Birmingham-based heavy metal acts. The term "heavy metal", borrowed from the American act Steppenwolf, was aptly applied. As Sabbath's drummer Bill Ward noted, one could go to sleep in Birmingham tapping fingers in time with the beat of the sheet metal factories' machines. Guitarist Tony Iommi even lost the tips of two fingers in a sheet-metal cutting accident.[10] Beginning life as a jazz-fusion band, the band members hired singer Ozzy Osbourne and decided that the key to commercial success was to pursue the occult image of Led Zeppelin to the hilt. The band adopted the name of one of their darkest songs, turned up the volume, added ominous church bells and the sound of rain to the debut album, and became a major worldwide hit.

The first album stayed for three months in the UK album charts, based on its reputed connection with the black arts. The classic single, "Paranoid" (1970), even made number four in the British charts, a speed metal classic of its kind. Osbourne gained a reputation as a wild man on and off stage, a heavy drinker who sometimes showed up for concerts in a loincloth and was reputed to bite the heads off live doves and bats on stage.[11] Black Sabbath's appeal was almost exclusively to teenage boys in Britain, who transformed shows into virtual copies of fascist rallies. Only the band's unrelenting pacifism—filtered through night-marish images of nuclear catastrophe in their music—broke the image.[12]

Sabbath kept in touch with their audience more than most bands did, em-phasizing their provincial working-class roots on songs like "Back Street Kids" (1976). Judas Priest would as well. Singer Rob Halford understood the appeal of his band's version of heavy metal: "If you are working at British Leyland for eight hours a day putting nuts on machinery you need *some* relief."[13] Yet like Led Zeppelin, both these metal acts found there was much more money to be made in touring the United States than there was in Britain.

Hard Rock Bands

Heavy metal was not the only way to restore British rock music to its roots. "Hard rock" was the recycling of the old blues values of the sixties in a seven-ties context. It appealed to the entire rock audience in numerous ways. It had the musicianship of the progressives without its pretentiousness; it had the commer-ciality of the teenybopper groups without their crassness; it had the power of the major acts like the Who, the Stones or Led Zeppelin, but it was thoroughly Eng-lish in outlook. Thus, their English audience identified with these bands easily. Fans of the hard rock and heavy metal bands tended to be young working-class males. Rock music for these people was an escape from the pressures of closing factories, crumbling council estates, pollution, a divisive educational system, and frustration in general. Hard rock had none of the sophistication its progres-sive brethren aspired to, and far more energy and drive.[14]

Deep Purple became what might be termed the first "hard rock" band. Nev-er as heavy as Black Sabbath or as experimental as Led Zeppelin, Deep Purple was an act that found a formula of powerful riffs and tough lyrics that was strong enough to make them a popular concert draw. They were, in essence, Romantic lite, as were contemporaries like Stone the Crows, Free and Bad Company, Ten Years After, Status Quo, Humble Pie and the Faces.

Deep Purple began as a successful singles act, covering songs by other songwriters in the late sixties like "Hush" (1969). Because of the nature of what was termed "authentic" in British rock music at the time, they were thus a pop group in America and virtually unknown in their native England, a most unsatis-factory situation for band members that had been mainstays on the London ses-sion scene in the mid-sixties. They sacked two band members, replacing them with Ian Gillan, a powerful singer, and Roger Glover, one of London's most respected drummers. They then announced a change of direction with the public performance of organist Jon Lord's "Concerto for Group and Orchestra" in Sep-tember 1969. The band combined with the Royal Philharmonic Orchestra as conducted by Malcolm Arnold, and in the flurry of rock operas being produced at the time, the London press lavished the concerto with praise. The result was an effective turnaround in the group's fortunes.

The next album, *Deep Purple in Rock* (1970), established their formula, Gillan's rough, rugged vocals accompanied by the heavy guitar of Ritchie Blackmore and Lord's pounding organ work. It sold a million copies, but it also reestablished them as a singles band, with the song "Black Night", a UK number two single. Such pop success could get them questioned by the counterculture's mavens, but no one in the band seemed to mind, according to Jon Lord.

> I think the teenyboppers have gone heavy. It's very gratifying and it all adds life to a band. After all it is a young music and rock is running in danger of being over intellectualised and analysed. Its basic function is to entertain. If it gets over analysed it will die a painful death.[15]

Queen was a band of college graduates, a shocker in seventies Britain where it was assumed that all rock musicians were ambitious lower-middle-class or working-class kids right out of O-levels and looking for quick cash. Whenever the tabloid press wrote an article on them, it seemed as if their degrees got a mention as well. Freddie Mercury and his epicurean tastes filled the most column space. Queen thus gained the reputation of being "one of our most inventive bands", their intelligence a key link to their respectability.[16]

Status Quo, on the other hand, was a band that found the wrong side of the critics. Status Quo started life as a psychedelic pop band, specifically restructuring their sound to meet the needs of the moment. "Pictures of Matchstick Men" (1968) was a piece of psychedelic whimsy that used an eastern-tinged guitar riff as the center of a surreal set of lyrics, and it made the youthful band—no member was yet over twenty—into teen idols. It charted high in both Britain and the United States, but the band was unable to follow up their success. They decided to return to their roots, as a good time rhythm and blues-based act, and in 1970 returned to the charts with "Down the Dustpipe", a completely different sounding record dominated by the guitars of Rick Parfitt and Francis Rossi. They gigged incessantly up and down Britain, and stuck with this style of guitar boogie throughout the seventies, enjoying widespread and deserved commercial success. Yet progressive rock audiences hated them—they were not serious artists, they had once been teen idols and they wrote pop singles. The rock press lambasted them for being "musically atrocious" and "mindless". The band, to their credit, did not care. Said Rossi, "It was better to get up people's noses than to be ignored."[17]

The public did not care either. They bought Status Quo's records and packed concert halls. Status Quo remained one of the most popular groups in Britain throughout the seventies. As a select few critics noticed with the release of *On the Level* in 1975, the key to the band's very success was that they lacked the pretensions of the progressive rock bands. In an era when pop and rock stars in Britain seemed increasingly remote, Status Quo was a "people's band". The fact that such a label was necessary was not lost on a number of people in the rock audience in the seventies. *New Musical Express* found themselves required to ask, "Are Status Quo the worst band in the world or the true progenitors of working class punk heavy metal?" [18]

The "Sell-Outs"

Heavy metal and hard rock in particular threatened to expose the allegedly dirty, capitalist side of rock music. Bands like Deep Purple and Queen at least pretended to aspirations as artists, justifying the discerning fan's enjoyment of their music. Status Quo did not care about such distinctions; neither did Bad Company or Mott the Hoople, bands which played in order to have fun and make a good living doing it. Though the "revolution" was pretty well dead as a youth or cultural concept by the 1970s, it still was not acceptable to flaunt it—a future classless society dominated by youth had to be at least acknowledged as desirable, and its values as worthy of emulation. So the counterculture had taught, and so had it been established.

Yet it was obvious that rock stars made obscene amounts of money and hobnobbed in elite social and cultural circles in Britain and America. With the prevailing sense of authenticity abounding, many rock stars seemed to have lost their original bearings, killed artistically by the cash nexus. There could be nothing worse than the rock artist who had started out as a promoter of the values of youth and progress, and who had turned instead to making pounds and pence. Their outrageous wealth had placed them in the position of upholding the old class order rather than subverting it. They were labeled "sell-outs". Of no artist was this truer than Rod Stewart, singer for the raucous Faces, successor band to the Small Faces. Stewart was symptomatic of the rock musician's increasing distance from his audience—in particular, the working-class audience from which he came.[19]

Stewart grew up in a Scottish household in working-class Holloway in north London. In the mid-sixties, he was a journeyman singer and harmonica player on London's rhythm and blues circuit. His big break came when Jeff Beck of the Yardbirds asked him to sing for Beck's band in the late sixties. When that band broke up, he accepted an invitation to join the Small Faces with guitarist Ron Wood. The renamed Faces became a popular live act in Britain and America in the early seventies, putting out several albums of sloppy, good time rock and roll in the fashion of the old London clubs.

The Faces were a typical anti-artistic act, however. It was as a solo artist that Stewart truly found worldwide stardom. Unlike his work with the Faces, Stewart's albums were carefully crafted pastiches of folk, blues, and rock and roll songs. Stewart was a brilliant cover artist, selecting excellent material to highlight his grainy, battered-sounding voice. Yet it was his originals, like "Gasoline Alley" (1970), that were most beloved by fans and critics alike.[20]

Stewart, however, was never as committed to the "revolution" as other rock musicians of the day.

> I've apologised about ticket prices & called innumerable people bastards & greedy, but beyond that there's not much I can do about it. I want people to realise this is my job. I've got to make a living out of it. I'm not going to be doing it in 5 years time. I don't do anything for nothing. I'm quite materialistic really—I own up to it.[21]

Such statements were not calculated to impress his youthful audience, but most people never saw them. Instead, they heard his strong feeling for conveying lives and scenes on albums like *Every Picture Tells a Story* (1971). The album's greatest moments were all Stewart's compositions, and they told magnificent stories in folk acoustic arrangements that dripped with power and emotion. "Maggie May", a chart topping hit single on both sides of the Atlantic, was the story of a boy leaving the home of a prostitute he had moved in with to become an independent man. "Mandolin Wind" was the album's standout track next to the title song, a depiction of the life of a Montana homesteader attempting to ride out a powerful winter on the plains with his wife. For songs like this, Stewart was one of the most beloved performers in rock music, a working class lad with a feel for the simple life and human concerns that both reflected and transcended his origins.

> [Stewart] may drive home to Windsor in a Lamborghini, but he gives the impression as an artist that it could just as well be a bicycle ride in the cold, with a [Glasgow] Celtic scarf round his neck. Stewart's image may be that strange cross between a Dickensian figure, a loveable football fan, and council flats, but it's an image that has gone a long way in separating him from anyone else on the rock scene. Stewart's appeal is home grown. He couldn't have come from anywhere else but Britain. He's Saturday afternoons at Highbury [home of the Arsenal Gunners Football Club], mugs of tea, smokey old pubs and fish and chips.[22]

But it was not long before the profit-driven principles of the music industry seemed to catch up to Stewart's artistic instincts. In 1975, the Faces broke up when Ron Wood joined the Rolling Stones. The Faces's good time rock and roll had been very different from Stewart's solo albums in execution, but not in essence. Without a touchstone from which to derive his strengths as a rock and roller, Stewart gave up his acoustic folk roots to make easy electric singles with slick session players. The result was a series of hits that made a lot of money but abandoned any element of artistry or originality. His old audience abandoned him—it was devastating to listen to the singer of "Gasoline Alley" produce garbage like "Do Ya Think I'm Sexy?" (1978). Critical reviews were withering. In fairness, this was partly due to prevailing attitudes about authenticity and seriousness of intent in making music; like any other musician, no critic could possibly explain how Stewart could make music he didn't like just for the money.

Still, then, it was apparent that Rod Stewart liked songs like "Do Ya Think I'm Sexy", which was all for the worse. His jet-setting lifestyle, succession of Hollywood starlet girlfriends, and increasingly bland singles made him an obvious symbol of the corruption of rock music and its corporate values in the later seventies.[23]

On the other hand, Peter Frampton's career illustrated a number of changes in British rock music. Frampton recognized the need to maintain a façade of respectability in order to be taken seriously by the audience and critics, and therefore received less derision than Rod Stewart even though the results were the same in terms of profits.

Frampton began as the singer and guitarist in the Herd, a late sixties pop outfit. His good looks got him the label of "The Face of '68", and teenaged girls screamed at the band at numerous concerts all over Britain. But Frampton aspired to much more. In an era when musicianship was valued above all else, Peter Frampton wanted to be known as a great guitarist. With the Herd, his position as front for the band was so important that he usually sang at concerts with his guitar slung behind his back, not even bothering to play.

He left the Herd in 1969 to join former Small Faces singer Steve Marriott's new hard rock band, Humble Pie. The teen idol label stuck, however; Humble Pie was called a "teenybopper supergroup" when it was announced that Frampton had joined the band. Even worse, "we made a big mistake and released a single that made the chart. Of course, that got us exactly the kind of publicity we wanted to avoid."[24] Their successes as a touring group came mainly in the United States, where Frampton was unknown. He eventually quit Humble Pie at the height of the singer-songwriter craze of the early seventies, noting "[T]he other three are very much into rock and roll, hard exciting stuff. And while I enjoy that I needed the complete opposite as well and there really wasn't much room for the lighter things."[25]

Frampton recorded his first solo album, *Winds of Change* (1972). He studiously avoided releasing a single on the album for fear of earning the British audience's disdain. Above all, he could not appear to be overtly commercial.[26] Frampton had grown up listening to jazz guitarists like Kenny Burrell. His guitar style was original and melodic, and though he left a lot to be desired as a lyricist, he had a loose way with songwriting that proved winning, if bland. He was in great demand as a session guitarist, but he gave up this lucrative career to continue his solo career. Finally, a live album of his best songs, *Frampton Comes Alive!* (1976), became a huge hit in the United States and England, selling eight million copies. Frampton virtually invented the concept of corporate rock—the rock star who wasn't "very much into rock and roll" as opposed to acoustic and progressive songs, who disdained making money yet raked it in hand over fist. His next album, *I'm in You* (1977), flopped in comparison to its predecessor, selling only 1.5 million, and Frampton was never heard from again as a major artist. He instead became a valued session musician.[27]

Women in Rock Music

If one thing characterized and united heavy metal and hard rock groups, it was their general objectification of women. In reality, such was characteristic of British rock music in general, and had been since its inception. As early as 1965, an American folk group called the Womenfolk toured the country, and as a publicity stunt, a call went out in London newspapers for marriage proposals, as the bandmembers were allegedly very interested in finding husbands.[28] It was the heavy metal and hard rock acts, however, that reduced women to sexpots as a matter of lyrical intent and image-mongering. The more lascivious the lyrics, the wilder the rumors got, the nastier the leers looked in the papers, the more that these bands' teenaged working-class fans bought the albums.

Of course this was met with great anger on the part of the more enlightened section of the counterculture. In 1970, in the midst of the women's liberation movement, Germaine Greer released her famous work, *The Female Eunuch*. Greer was a mainstay in the underground newspapers, and her revealing tract allowed other women in the counterculture to question their roles in the coming revolution, as modeled on the alleged youth liberation represented by rock music. One was Arlene Brown.

> I think that rock music has changed a lot of things, released a lot of energy, created some good images for young people, emphasised enjoyment, sensual pleasure, relaxation, freaking-out, looking weird, turning on. But I also think that as far as the male-female relationship goes, as far as women's liberation goes, & the image a woman should have of herself, it is totally reactionary and must be changed. A woman can relate to rock music now only if she is a groupie—if not literally, than figuratively. As the drooling sex-hungry little girl dying for it from Pigpen, Jim Morrison, Pete Townshend. . . .

> To me the whole image of the rock scene is an image of a mod, "pretty", long-haired, mini/maxi-skirted, or bell-bottomed, passive, sweet chick, nice enough to be at the side of any strong, manly rock musician or business man. Or an image of a bra-less, long-skirted sweet mother earth, commune hippie chick. Both of these are distortions. And accepted roles. Just as the aggressive, dominant, creative genius is the role that men play, & what women LOOK UP to. And that's not my revolution![29]

Part of what Brown was referring to was the fact that British bands were surrounded by women who offered themselves up as sexual objects, known as "groupies". Groupies might be said to be representative of the entanglement of sex and power among young male musicians. Full of prestige and ambition, surrounded by adoring fans, few rock musicians were willing to resist the temptation of indulging in the sexual favors of the young women around them who were discovering their own independence at the same time. Some of the musicians had little power over their business affairs and sometimes had their musical content dictated by the record companies and their audiences, so they leapt at the opportunity to at least control a woman's body for a few hours, a seedy and exploitative compensation. Others, like the members of Led Zeppelin, had so much control over their own musical output and profits that manipulating a woman's sexuality for their own craven pleasure simply fit into their hedonistic lifestyle. The fact that most bands sold sex as a commodity on stage and on record did not hurt. As Mick Jagger once said, "There's no reason to have women on a tour unless they've got a job to do. The only other reason is to screw."[30]

Rock in the early seventies was still a male-dominated medium, and its sexual norms reflected those of the society it depicted (albeit with an exaggerated sense of the male's sexual attractiveness and prowess). Few bands had female members other than singers; only the British folk bands allowed those women to sing anything other than safe ballads. Even the folk acts dealt in a tradition-bound musical world, where women fulfilled the conventional stereotype of the "earth mother". They lacked the aggressive sexuality of their male counterparts: there was no female Mick Jagger, Roger Daltrey or Robert Plant. The audience embodied stereotypes as well, though less succinctly. Girls bought singles and boys bought albums. Girls joined fan clubs and bought posters, boys bought music journals. Male journalists got more respect from the music community, whereas female journalists were thought to be not as serious about rock and roll as they were enamored of the boys who played it. This was particularly insulting to women in the counterculture like Germaine Greer or Caroline Coon, who regularly dissected the sexism rampant in the rock music world. Rock was an expression of adolescent sexuality, and expressions of adolescent sexuality in music came from, and were expected to come from, males. Especially after the Beatles, girls were to respond to that sexuality rather than to the music itself.[31]

One pioneer arose from the hard rock genre to challenge these stereotypes in Britain. Suzi Quatro was a Detroit-born bass player but she became a star in Britain. She came to London in 1971 at the behest of Mickie Most, the former manager of the Animals, who saw potential in her excellent bass playing and leather-clad image. Most hooked her up with songwriters Nicky Chinn and Mike Chapman, and they produced several hit singles in Britain between 1972 and 1975. Quatro looked and acted like a Rocker, a tough biker girl—she was almost never seen without some sort of leather accoutrement, and her music was a rockabilly throwback to the fifties. "I guess parents figure I'd be a bad influence on their sons. We've had years and years of guys singing about what bad boys they are. I feel the same way, so I might as well sing about it."[32]

Heavy metal and hard rock were genres that reflected the emphasis on arena-sized sounds in the 1970s. The popularity of rock acts meant that they could be booked into stadiums holding upward of fifty to eighty thousand people and expect to fill them, and British acts dominated the arenas in the early seventies. Few American acts—Grand Funk Railroad, Alice Cooper, the Grateful Dead—had the drawing power of the Who, the Rolling Stones, the Moody Blues, Led

Zeppelin, Rod Stewart and the Faces, Black Sabbath, Pink Floyd, or Deep Purple.[33]

This was in part due to the attitude that British musicians had toward live performance. Like in America, in Britain, the musician was originally a live performer first and a producer of albums second; money was made in live performance. Bands like the Who, the Stones and Led Zeppelin considered their live shows to be the essence of their art. They judged their studio efforts mainly on their ability to capture the power of their live performances on record, and so did the critics.[34] The Rolling Stones produced their greatest albums once they landed the percussionist Jimmy Miller as their producer, who emphasized the elastic funk of bassist Bill Wyman and drummer Charlie Watts in the studio. The Who's *Who's Next* made the band sound entirely different, starkly powerful, due to the production and engineering of Glyn Johns.

Of no groups was this more true than the heavy metal and hard rock acts, whose powerful sound was almost designed to fill an arena. Yet the place to make money in live performance was America, not Britain, because America was bigger. The place to be lionized as artists was America, not Britain, because the critics were not as critical. The place to live the hedonistic, self-indulgent bohemian lifestyle of the artist was in America, not in Britain, because the economy and availability of women was greater. A rock journalist epitomized the limits of British indulgence in 1975.

> It is, perhaps, as a consequence of a certain adolescent commitment to rock music as a source of potential information about a contemporary social environment that it has become necessary to perpetuate the notion that the intrinsic strength and power of rock lies in the essentially primitive nature of its artistic expression.
>
> A standard vocabulary has been formulated which depends, for its future, upon maintaining a particular kind of heroism. The traditional "rock hero" is, largely, an inarticulate individual, who is, however, able to force into his work, through some mysterious artistic process, images and impressions which are interpreted, eventually, as pertinent and vivid perceptions.
>
> There is, then, a security in concentrating upon previously established impulses. The artist is inevitably more accessible, and his audience will not be disturbed since he is conforming to an image, however exciting it may initially appear, which is already stereotyped and therefore predictable.
>
> [Thus], there is a crucial lack of innovation.[35]

The professionalization of musicians in Britain meant social status, if you were a progressive rock act; largely, it meant castigation if you were not. A band like Humble Pie took a critical beating for launching into long guitar or drum solos in live performance; Keith Emerson of Emerson Lake and Palmer was accorded a grudging genius. In America, both groups would end up after any performance in hotels surrounded by young girls, record executives, celebrities and friends, all calling them superstars. There was little question where any one of them would want to make their money, regardless of their homes or social origins.

Chapter 11
Glamrock

In April 1970, an article by the Anglo-Indian poet and journalist Dom Moraes showed up in the *New York Times Magazine*, entitled "The Passing of the British Working Class". The article was a wistful travelogue as the author journeyed to pubs, Oxford colleges, high streets in the industrial north and strip clubs to figure out where the old working classes had gone. In such socially chaotic times, Moraes' lament revealed his conception of the working classes in their heyday—he believed that they had once been monolithically angry and organized, working and playing with equal measures of boisterousness and pride. In 1970, according to Moraes, they were now old, lost, and abandoned by their children. The children of the working classes had benefited from the Labour Party's creation of the welfare state and new educational opportunities, and now they seemed to want nothing more than to forget they were ever working-class.

> The heroes of the original working class were intellectuals, like [Thomas] Paine and William Cobbett. The heroes of their descendants are show-biz people, the Beatles, the Rolling Stones, Twiggy. They can be identified with by the young because they are mostly themselves working class. They are heroes because they have made it: they have achieved wealth, power, success, and become classless. They are heroes not because, like Paine and Cobbett, they are struggling for something. They are heroes because they do not have to struggle for anything. The class solidarity of the past has vanished. It is not that the young want to climb out of their class into another, but that they want to become classless.[1]

By 1970 such an archetype of the working classes was somewhat quaint, but Moraes still had the essence right on British youth. Many were now college students who played guitar, listened to rock music and the blues, and went to concerts on campus by any number of the top bands of the day during their tours of the island. "Pop" was now candyfloss music, apolitical, the stuff of housewives and teenaged girls, while "rock" was supposed to be intellectual, predominantly male and politically aware. New Romantic heroes emerged, guitarists and songwriters like Eric Clapton, Ray Davies and Pete Townshend. Everyone wanted to be Mick Jagger, or to sleep with him. Bands like Pink Floyd and Yes had created a new album market for the wealthier buyer; the more discerning fan who wanted his or her elitism on display bought albums by Renaissance, Lindisfarne or Curved Air.

Rock music in the early seventies was an album-oriented market. Audience and critics alike perceived it as music that was genteel, pretentious, artistic, bourgeois and expertly crafted. They also celebrated the music for most of these qualities—it was still not politically correct to be bourgeois, and better not to flaunt one's riches. In contrast, pop music's appeal was allegedly working class, a singles-oriented market. The rock audience and critics considered pop music banal, disposable, simple, and chart-oriented. Rock and pop were no longer simply separations of taste—they were also separations of class, age and sex, new social barriers that arose in place of the old ones that rock and roll had originally set out to destroy. Of course, these barriers were not hard and fast: but perception in British pop culture was always more important than reality.

The counterculture's elitism at the top of those social barriers seemed hollow to many in the early 1970s. College students and artists might feel as if they held a cultural superiority over the mass of British youth, but the economy dictated otherwise. The government devalued the pound twice, in 1967 and 1972. Trade unions broke out in wildcat strikes under both Labour and the Conservatives, mainly in response to inflating prices that threatened to dwarf wages. Britain finally joined the European Economic Community in 1973, but the results would be long in coming, and the OPEC oil crisis later in the year destroyed any positive economic development as the government was forced to place state employees on a three-day work week in early 1974. Under the circumstances, student demonstrations against nuclear proliferation and journals calling for cultural upheaval seemed simultaneously dangerous and frivolous—dangerous to the adult establishment, frivolous to working-class young people who wanted jobs, not a commitment to the "revolution". Rock music and its critics demanded cultural change, but with full wallets and comfortable backgrounds, the hypocrisies of such demands were more glaring than ever.

Rock, in sum, was a music that still defined itself in rebellion to an established adult, middle-class norm. Yet its popularity and the growing elitism of its audience threatened to replace that norm with another one, just as respectable, just as mainstream, and to many, just as boring. Critics ranked the Beatles with classical composers. Counterculture and music journalists solicited Pete Townshend's opinions on the political issues of the day, and Mick Jagger recited the poems of Shelley to huge audiences in Hyde Park. The music was more ambitious, but also far removed in image from the working-class roots by which rock and roll in Britain had once been defined. Rock music was the music of progress, and progress was, if often uneasy to handle, the mantra of the middle classes that had dominated British culture since the industrial era began.

There were now three broad groups of youth consumer, all of whom blended into one another, yet they were cohesive enough to allow the music industry to target them as markets. The young female buyer went for pop music and bought posters of young male idols and their singles as well. The older music buyer, often working class, bought singles that he or she liked, and listened to music on the radio during social occasions. Finally, the collegiate music buyer bought albums by "progressive" rock bands with both folk and artistic pretensions, attended concerts regularly, and could afford to buy records before ever hearing the music on them, based purely on the reputation of the act.[2]

The basic British pop audience ignored progressive bands like Yes, Genesis and King Crimson. In fact, many working-class teenagers quite preferred singles to albums, if for no other reason than that they were cheaper. They also liked showmanship, glamour, and fun, all qualities that the serious progressive rockers eschewed and which their audience hated.[3] A journalist with *Sounds*, a music paper that focused on progressive rock, found the pop audience's desire for fun a little tedious.

> The stock quote runs something like this: "We think people are tired of seeing all those musicians shambling up on stage dressed in levis and just playing their instruments. The kids want to see a show, and we're going to give them one, put some glamour back into this business." . . . [A]ll the contrived efforts of people trying to put a bit of glamour back into "the business" seem more than a little self-conscious and pathetic, because glamour—as I understand it—is not something you can take away, or put in. The legend of Hollywood tells you that stars are born and not made, and though I'm not sure I like the terminology, there's a certain amount of truth in the sentiment.[4]

Yet the desire to see glamour in music persisted, and like most consumer desires, there were plenty of musicians willing to meet the demand. A fusion of attitudes in the early 1970s produced the glamrock (as in glamour) subculture, focused on good times, androgyny and glitter. In opposition to the older, male-oriented, non-dance market, glamrock was pop music, pure and simple. It was danceable, accessible to teenagers and girls, and above all, fun.[5]

Glamrock bridged the gap between rock and pop music, largely because the most successful glamrock artists managed to straddle all of the buying public's categories at the same time. The gap between rock and pop was class-oriented, in reality if not in theory. Like previous bands, the adherents of glamrock emphasized their working-class origins. They likewise emphasized their relationship to commercial product to mock the hypocritical hippy-progressive stress on anti-material values. The market dictated all of glamrock's poses. One's clothes, music, and attitudes were the essence of the moment, and in turn, the most popular artists—David Bowie, T Rex, the Sweet, Elton John, Roxy Music—shaped those same attitudes themselves, changing music styles almost as often as they changed clothes.[6]

Some of the changes in style allowed bands to transcend their pop music images: for an artist like David Bowie, the production of singles was an artistic experiment with the limits of fame, consumer capitalism making money off the alienation of youth. Like Bowie, the best glam musicians established reputations as "album groups" who were also comfortable on *Top of the Pops.* Younger record buyers considered Bowie and Roxy Music to be singles artists, while older record buyers bought their albums and considered them rock performers. Glamrock, then, was the first musical genre to slip past the critical categorization of the counterculture, and to return the pop music-buying public's heroes to them.[7]

Skinheads

Glamrock arose from an unusual source—the combined ashes of the mid-sixties Mods and the Rockers. While it was apparently lost on the hippies that their anti-materialist rhetoric arose from their patronage of rock music's booming consumer culture, it was not lost on working-class teenagers who despised the hypocrisy of it all. Many of them hated the values of the hippies, the selling out of their own working-class ideals with the spread of Mod culture and the collapse of the Rockers. The result—the skinhead subculture—was the direct antithesis of the hippies, and a logical and long-lived extension of the values of the Mods and Rockers.

The skinheads were an oppositional subculture that thrived on their anger, and were exclusively working class, white and violent. In defiance of the predominance of hippiedom, they sheared their hair to an extremely short crop, sometimes a crewcut, sometimes no hair at all. They wore jeans and suspenders, or braces, and "bovver boots", steel-toed work boots that could bruise a shin easily. They rejected the lithe and light sounds of psychedelia for the tough, stabbing rhythms of ska. Moreover, more than any of their earlier or later subcultural brethren, for skinheads, violence was their creed. One of the skins addressed his atavistic hatred of hippies in an interview with *International Times*.

> We have also been put the question "why do we hate hippies?" We don't actually hate hippies but we think they are stupid cunts the way they dress. A lot of hippies say they get stoned because they have got problems or are depressed, but why don't they just get drunk? One of the reasons we have fights with hippies is because we think that they are always saying that we are trouble makers and so the only way we can get back at them is to give them a good pasting.[8]

The skinheads struck out at society, smashing hippies, immigrants (especially Pakistanis and Indians), rival soccer fans, and anyone else who excited their primitive, nihilistic protest against the world. Moreover, they hated mainstream rock, a major statement: they saw rock music as the music of the establishment in Britain by the late 1960s, and thus representative of their oppression.[9]

Ironically, the skinheads were everything that the rhetorical revolutionaries of the counterculture and its adherents believed that working class youth ought to be—violent, prepared for revolution, musically avant-garde and in thorough opposition to a consumer culture that threatened to consume them. It was therefore telling how much the counterculture held skinheads in abhorrence—apparently, if university-educated students and intellectuals could not control the revolutionary working classes, the revolution wasn't worth having. In reality, the skinheads upheld an order of working class values that they had made up themselves, just as the counterculture had, and frightened their social superiors a great deal more at the level of the street.

Unlike the Mods, the skinheads had few bands that catered to their tastes. While they patronized ska, they also would not think twice about launching a rain of fists and kicks on an Afro-Caribbean man in the street if it suited their purposes, and that did not lend to the extension of the brand in music. Many musicians simply went retrograde and appealed to the skinheads as a byproduct. There were still adherents of old subcultures and old musical styles around to appeal to, and where most musicians had long abandoned these audiences, there were others who called them out of the shadows to indulge in nostalgia. For example, the fifties has-been teen star Shane Fenton changed his name to Alvin Stardust, dressed like a Rocker and made a number of hits in 1974 and 1975.[10] David Essex, on the other hand, was a talented working class singer and actor from London's Docklands who had a number of hits as a Parnes-style teenage heartthrob. He was particularly renowned for having been on the dole before he won the role of Jesus in the London production of *Godspell* from 1971 to 1973. He also starred as a fictional fifties rock star in *That'll Be the Day* (1973), upon which his first single was released, "Rock On" (1973).[11]

Gary Glitter, meanwhile, was a hammy version of Elvis, with his gold lamé suits opened to expose a hairy chest and flabby belly, shaken in the most tastelessly lascivious manner possible. Glitter, the former Paul Gadd, had been on the British music scene since the days of the 2 I's coffee bar in London, and had been floating around beneath the national spotlight ever since. He had warmed up the crowd on *Ready, Steady, Go!*; he went to Hamburg in 1964 to emulate the Beatles' success. With the advent of glamrock, Paul Gadd dreamt up a new name, Gary Glitter, recorded the simplest pop song he could think of—"Rock and Roll (Parts One and Two)" (1971)—and created a smash hit, reaching number two in Britain and number seven in the United States. Glitter lived up to his name, sporting outrageous stage costumes and descending from old Hollywood staircases or motorcycles in his stage act. A huge publicity team recorded it all, and Glitter's camp sense and appeal registered eleven top twenty hits in Britain from 1972 through 1975.[12] Years later, he would be outed as a pedophile.

None of these groups actually made an effort to cater to skinheads, though. The one band that did failed, but in the process, they allowed for the transition to glamrock. Slade was a Midlands band, from Wolverhampton. They had flirted with progressive rock, soul and rhythm and blues and had a few minor hits in the sixties. As a way to single themselves out from the rest of the rock music scene in 1970, the band cropped their hair short, put on suspenders and boots, and called themselves skinheads. Suddenly, Slade were famous—or notorious, as it were, at once celebrated for their rebellion and reviled as dangerous advocates of skinhead violence. Naturally, it wasn't true, but Slade rode the wave of controversy to recognition, through interviews and news stories in the tabloids.

There was only one problem: all of their singles as a skinhead band flopped. So the band modified their look and their sound. They grew their hair long again, and made the rest of the skinhead look seem outlandish: high-heeled boots as opposed to work boots, rainbow suspenders, plaid suits and pants, top hats. They wrote their own singles for the first time, and in November 1971, they finally had their first number one with "Coz I Luv You".[13]

From then on, Slade rode this image and music to a number of hit singles in the early seventies, based on music principles that the working-class skinheads approved of—they represented good times, tribal loyalties, teenaged solidarity, anti-intellectualism.[14] Noddy Holder, the band's guitarist and vocalist, addressed their appeal.

> I'm very conscious that I'm a working class bloke. In this business, you meet a lot of people that are not working class and you know that you're different. Your outlook on life is different to what theirs is. You either decide you want to be part of that clique, or you don't. And I don't. I'm quite happy as I am. I don't want to move up into another sphere where I won't fit in. . . . I've just got no political interest, because I don't know anything about it.[15]

Slade created a sense of community in concert, a community of teenagers tired of the oppression of adult life. They even misspelled all of their song titles—"Cum On Feel the Noize" (1971), "Mama Weer All Crazee Now" (1973), "Gudbuy T'Jane" (1973)—largely to thumb a nose at the educational system that so many teenagers hated. The band could not buy better publicity when educational authorities angrily denounced them as a bad influence on youth. The BBC even asked Holder to participate in an educational program to try to counteract the influence of bad spelling. When questioned about the subject, Holder replied, "They say we're a bad influence on kids but we're from the Black Country and that's the way people there talk."[16]

Musically, Slade was raw, crude and simplistic. The idea of a Slade song was to sing along to it like a football chant, rather than to ponder the complexities of its musicians' indulgences. Over time, the band's following changed, coming from the younger brothers and sisters of skinheads rather than the skins themselves. Their warm-heartedness and boozy fellowship won them popularity, and they produced twelve top five singles and three number one albums in three years, one of the most successful British bands of their time. As Noddy Holder said, "The fans are fed up with paying to sit on their hands while watching musicians who clearly couldn't care less about the customers. What is wanted is more of a party atmosphere."[17] Over the first half of the seventies, Slade's fashion and musical sense, along with their attitude toward the purposes of their making music, would influence the growth of glamrock.

Glitter, Money and Marc Bolan

While the likes of Slade or Gary Glitter might challenge the status quo in rock or pop music, no one in the progressive audience looked at them and wondered what on earth pop music was coming to. They simply reflected the perception that the youth revolution could easily be hijacked by dross. Far more annoying and controversial were those musicians that the counterculture considered talented, who had all the cultural caché in the world to put forward as a challenge to the adult order, yet refused to maintain adherence to the counterculture's values, indulging in money, excess and outrage. Worse, by putting out singles, they dragged far too much of the audience with them, away from the revolutionary purposes of music.

Such a musician was, of course, branded a "sell-out". Every musician wanted to make money, every musician wanted to find an audience, and most of the counterculture's progressive rock heroes were swimming in American dollars from their expansive tours of North America. But the critical designation stuck, once a rock musician was so branded—a pop musician by definition was a "sell-out"—and most artists tried to avoid it like a terminal disease. To be popular was to be "pop", and to be pop was dangerous to a musician's reputation. Therefore, every rock and pop musician had to answer for his fans, and for the fact that they made money, as if they had stolen it from the public. Few if any had the guts to expose the hypocrisy of the question itself.

Others, however, simply rode the contradiction, flaunting their moneymaking power and irritating the sensibilities of the critical audience. The most flagrant violator was the musician most associated with glamrock, Marc Bolan, leader of the band Tyrannosaurus Rex, or T. Rex, as he abbreviated it. T. Rex sold a huge number of records in Britain between 1971 and 1974, and Bolan inspired insanity from his fans, especially screaming teenage girls. For a while, he was the closest phenomenon to the popularity of the Beatles in British rock music. The prince of glamrock, he teetered between teenybopper camp and rock respectability, a focus of critical consternation.

Bolan was the son of a truck driver from Stoke Newington. An early adherent to Mod, he became a model, his image used by department stores in the mid-sixties to sell Mod clothing. He was a "face" on the Mod scene of west London in 1964, one of the people who followed the Who around the London clubs. Bolan was an early master of publicity, able to get his face into a *Town and Country* magazine article about Mod as the very essence of what an ace face looked like. Yet his real ambition was to be a pop star himself, not one of the mere hangers-on. He joined a Mod band named John's Children for a while, and it became a fixture on the club circuit, but never broke through to the pop charts (which enamored John's Children even more to their Mod audience).

Bolan became very willing to change his lifestyle and his life story to provide imagination for his lyrics, fuel for his ambitions, and copy for his publicist. He lived in Paris for two weeks with an actor, for example, and recounted it instead as six months in a magical castle with a French wizard who taught him the black arts. This became the basis of his first single, "The Wizard", a flop in 1965. He became a folk rocker when the hippie scene became prevalent, and converted John's Children into a unit that dabbled in mysticism, Tolkien and any number of Romantic themes dear to the heart of the anti-establishment underground. When that didn't take, he formed Tyrannosaurus Rex as an acoustic unit at the height of the psychedelic folk era. Their songs centered on mystical and mythical themes: Nostradamus's predictions, legends of King Arthur, UFOs, and Tolkien. They were lumped in with the folk rock crowd, their first tour being as a supporting act for the Incredible String Band.

However, by 1969 it became clear that the electric rock bands were more successful. Bolan changed the musicians in the band and changed its sound as well. Frustrated with the inability of his act to gain any greater recognition, he decided to fill the void left in the singles market by bands that disdained the single as teenage whimsy. Bolan's first single with the snappier-named T. Rex was "Ride a White Swan" (1970), and it broke the glamrock sound at the same time that Slade helped define the glamrock look. It also broke his original audience. Bolan's clamoring for pop success galled earlier fans of his acoustic music, who proclaimed him a sell-out.

For Bolan, the entire goal of being a rock musician was to be a star, in the most glamorous Hollywood sense of the word. He created a veneer of commercial appeal which aggravated pompous rock critics to no end, but which also made him seem hipper than hip, mocking the record industry for making him rich while he took its money. He made everything he did seem bigger than it was, and did anything to keep his name in the public eye, often fabricating issues for the press. He invented feuds with David Bowie or Elton John, claimed he was a huge concert success in America, or asserted "I'm a better guitarist than Pete Townshend—and he knows it!"[18] The more hyperbolic his rhetoric became, the more records he sold, a Byronic figure just as important for his image as for his art.

His records sold well, based on rudimentary riffs, and earned him coveted spots on *Top of the Pops* that other rockers would have been horrified to play.[19] His audience crossed the entire spectrum of the youth movement—skinheads, young teenagers, hippies, and glamrock adherents—and the "cultural elite" of the progressive rock school thus hated him.[20] It hardly mattered: his audience hated the longhairs of the progressive rock spectrum as well. When bandmate Steve Took bumped into a girl at one of T. Rex's concerts in Lincolnshire, she didn't recognize him as one of the musicians she had come to see on stage—instead, she rounded on him and barked out "yeaaah—f__king longhair."[21]

Bolan himself did not see it this way. Having started out as a working class mod in the east end of London, he seemed determined to remember and hang on to his roots, and if it earned him a living, all the better.

> [Money] wasn't the reason I did it. Money buys freedom, I don't deny money, but the excitement is what I do it for, honestly, like fulfillment. I'd do what I'm doing now if I worked on a lathe producing nuts and bolts, and in the evening I'd probably play in a club somewhere, you know, or in the street. I mean, I started in the street.[22]

Unfortunately for Bolan, he did not seem to understand that great commercial success would limit his ability to sustain it for long. He barely dented the American charts at any time. Only one of his singles, "Bang a Gong (Get It On)", had any success whatsoever across the ocean. Which may well have contributed to his popularity—here was an artist that would not be poached by the American arena rock circuit. Yet at home, subcultures by their nature were fleeting; Bolan's popularity lasted only as long as glamrock seemed cool and teen-aged girls remained teenagers. He had earlier reveled in his fame, at one point saying, "the whole thing is a game of seduction between me and the audience . . . an orgiastic exercise. I've sort of become a rock and roll James Dean."[23] James Dean was dead, and Bolan himself was on his way there. His career took a quick nosedive in 1972, and rather morbidly, Bolan himself died in a car crash in 1977 in the midst of a career comeback.

David Bowie

David Bowie was always the most popular and powerful of glamrock's heroes. He symbolized the early 1970s in rock in the same way that Elvis symbolized the fifties and the Beatles the sixties. His continuing changes of character, informed by his dabbling in mime, painting, and acting, seemed to capture the decade's transitions in music, class, economics and gender. He even wrote a song about the subject, "Changes"—"turn and face the strange". He was associated with the glamrock subculture, but his intellect and experimental nature transcended any real musical categorization. Largely, he combined the adventurism of progressive rock with the image and commercial impact of the pop bands of the day. He essentially became the university student's glamrock artist, using stage presentation and image to pursue progressive rock ideals. As such, he excited violently opposing passions in rock fans and critics alike. He was undoubtedly an innovative and brilliant musician, yet his carefully crafted image, opportunistic bisexuality and flirtation with fascism made him anathema to an equally serious section of the rock audience.[24]

Bowie was a commercial artist at age seventeen. His job was as a junior visualizer in an advertising agency; he had to determine how a product was to be sold by determining what image it had on the market. As a musician, he traveled the club scene in London making a name for himself, using his birth name, David Jones. He caused a brief stir in early 1965 when he was scheduled to appear on BBC-2's pop show *Gadzooks!*, because his hair was apparently considered too long to show on television.[25] In general, though, he could not buy decent publicity. He even had to change his name: the Monkees had an English lead singer named Davy Jones as well. He chose the moniker "Bowie" from the American Bowie knife, to cut through to the truth.[26] His major vocal influence was the actor Anthony Newley, whose cabaret style and cockney accent attracted him. He also befriended Marc Bolan. However, continued chart failures pushed him out of the music business by the late sixties, when he became a Buddhist, learned mime and opened a multimedia art center in south London near Waterloo in 1968.

Bowie's inability to break through to a wider audience was because he was not of the same mindset as the counterculture that dominated public iterations and manifestations of youth culture in the late sixties. His lyrics always evoked emotions other than peace, love and understanding: Bowie delved into the darker mysteries of power, corruption, lies, hatred, and fear. By 1970, growing economic crises in Britain and the decline of countercultural media outlets like *International Times* and *Oz* meant that there was an opening for a cultural figure willing to challenge the growing youth establishment, and Bowie's moment had arrived.

He began with the single "Space Oddity", a parable about an astronaut, Major Tom, who chooses to leave his home and family on earth to roam the outer reaches of the universe, seduced by the emptiness of space. The song was released to coincide with the American lunar landing in the summer of 1969, and reached number five in the UK charts. Bowie was excited—he hoped to put the resulting profits into his arts center, to publicize its existence and open it up to a wider public.[27]

He was unable to consolidate the success of the single, however, and over the next three years searched for an angle for continued pop stardom. Along the way, he met and married an American design student named Angela Barnett. Her tastes in clothing tended to be futuristic: high boots, lots of vinyl and leather, colored hair and shoulder pads or shoulder ornamentations. They also coincided with the garishness of Marc Bolan or Noddy Holder. Angela's fashion style had a heavy influence on her new husband, who began to extrapolate a vision of his new rock music image from the clothes. His album cover sold the new image: *The Man Who Sold the World* featured Bowie in a dress, and was banned in the United States.

His next album, *Hunky Dory*, was released in January 1972. Despite critical acclaim, it was a surprising commercial flop. It failed to sell a hundred thousand copies, and it contained only one real hit (albeit a career-defining number), "Changes". Bowie needed an avenue through which to regain attention from the pop and rock markets or he would be ignored as yet another one-hit wonder in the long annals of rock music. He wrote a song called "Andy Warhol" for *Hunky Dory*, and met the artist in London a short time later at a concert. Warhol at the time was famous for his concept that anyone who wanted to be a star could be one by simply acting like a star, and Bowie accepted this concept wholeheartedly. With the release of the album, Bowie did an interview in *Melody Maker* where he announced he was gay, and created a media sensation in Britain.[28] Having created a media sensation, he now had to live up to it.

In fact, Bowie became rock's most outrageous image-monger, switching guises (and gender roles) with a regularity throughout the seventies that was exciting, if difficult to follow at times. He became rock's first Futurist, obsessed with technology and youth, determined to outrage and throw away the past in pursuit of the hedonism of the moment. "I feel so weird in the company of people who are actively and concretely behind their trains of thought. That destroys me. . . . I feel we're all in a fucking dead industry that really relates to nothing anymore."[29] Despite, and because of, the harsh attacks of a homophobic press on Bowie's androgyny, he was able to milk the publicity and sell more records than almost any other artist in the early seventies.

Bowie had found his niche—he would describe the oddities of the world, space or otherwise. *The Rise and Fall of Ziggy Stardust and the Spiders from Mars* (1972) defined its era and gave shape and definition to the glamrock movement in Britain. *Ziggy Stardust* was a concept album about a space alien who comes to a dying earth to become a rock and roll star and lead a massive youth revolt against the establishment. In the end, he cannot take the pressure and cracks under the strain, committing suicide. The world of rock and roll had changed since the Beatles; no artist, it seemed, could unite the British community of youth the way the Beatles had, including the solo Beatles themselves. The blues that had defined authenticity in the sixties were far removed from the popular charts, and the concept itself had been coopted by flaccid progressive rock bands whose values were distinctly Romantic and yet clearly at odds with the rebellious nature of rock and roll. With the personality of Ziggy Stardust, Bowie intended to present a vision of the rock and roll future: alien and alienated, fashionable and fascistic, byzantine and bisexual.

Ziggy Stardust produced a number of hit singles in Britain, extended Bowie's popularity into America, and earned critical acclaim that made him the most sought-after performer and producer of 1973. He wrote and produced the single "All the Young Dudes" for Mott the Hoople, produced Iggy and the Stooges' *Raw Power* and Lou Reed's *Transformer*, all of which were those artists' highest points of commercial and critical success.[30] Bowie had the golden touch in rock music, and it came from a Modernist vision of rock and roll apocalypse. Even better, he infuriated the pretensions of the progressive rock world, which demanded that its performers abandon old concepts of showbiz life. The creation and perpetuation of an image was inauthentic, and yet, no matter how loudly the

critical establishment proclaimed Bowie's compromised values, he sold more
records than ever and maintained a gigantic audience. Bowie was an actor—
read, poseur—on the rock scene, unlike contemporaries such as, perhaps, Pink
Floyd or Yes. Bowie was not "real". He always remained detached from the
image he presented on stage and screen, disdaining the pretensions of a singer-
songwriter like Van Morrison who wanted to bare his soul on record and stage.
Ziggy Stardust especially deflated the pose of the progressive rockers, whose
seriousness in a genre known for espousing the values of youth was perhaps
more dishonest and less authentic than Bowie's embrace of the popular market
and the idea that music should be, above all, fun and exciting.[31]

He extended that vision over the next two years. Immediately after establishing the image of a space alien rock star, Bowie trashed it in favor of a new
pose, of a ghost named *Aladdin Sane* (1973), the title of his next album. He announced his retirement from the stage, and decided to back off from the money
factory of an American tour. Instead, he moved to the Chateau d'Herouville
outside Paris in the French countryside to work on his next two albums.[32] He
soon returned to work on a collection of singles from the mod era called *Pin-
Ups* (1973), as if to revive the mod vision of speed and violence. He also
worked on scripts for a pair of musical productions, one an adaptation of *Ziggy
Stardust* and the other adapted from George Orwell's *1984*. When Orwell's wife
refused to grant him the rights to stage the musical, he took the script and released it as a new album, *Diamond Dogs* (1974).[33] It described a future world
where cities were beginning to collapse into urban decay, based on New York
City in the 1970s: "*This ain't rock and roll—this is genocide*".

Bowie moved on to films and new characters like the "Thin White Duke"
that became less and less commercial as the seventies moved on. He seemed
well attuned to the idea that the pursuit of affluence and material gain corrupted
and alienated people, especially in Britain. Bowie's image was the image of the
decadence and cynicism of the seventies. On the other hand, by 1975, his answer
to decadence and cynicism was the same one that Futurists had turned to in the
1920s and 1930s: fascism. In a number of statements made at the time, Bowie
compared himself to Hitler, seeing a perfectly correct, if critically lambasted,
parallel between the rock singer's appeal and the appeal of fascist ritual. After a
visit to Berlin, photographers snapped pictures of him leaving a limousine at
Victoria Station where he appeared to give the surrounding crowd a Nazi salute.[34]

> Dictatorship! There will be a political figure in the not too distant future who'll
> sweep this part of the world like early rock 'n' roll did. . . . You've got to have
> an extreme right front come up and sweep everything off its feet and tidy eve-
> rything up. Then you can get a new form of liberalism. . . . The best thing that
> can happen is for an extreme right front Government to come. It'll do some-
> thing positive at least to cause commotion in people and they'll either accept
> the dictatorship or get rid of it.[35]

Nevertheless, Bowie pointed to an uneasy parallel between rock music, modernist conceptions of art for the masses and fascist politics. Like a number of rock musicians influenced by him in the seventies, Bowie became obsessed with the image of Weimar Berlin and the decadence of life in 1930s Germany, as exemplified in the contemporary movie *Cabaret* (1972). *Cabaret*, about a flamboyantly sexual American cabaret singer in Weimar Berlin and her bisexual English boyfriend, asserted that the real inspiration for the "Me Decade" lay in the 1930s and 1940s, when life was austere and people aspired to Hollywood lifestyles in order to forget their poverty and the apocalyptic politics of the day. Life in Britain in 1973 was certainly not very different.

Bowie focused on Weimar Berlin for just this reason. It seemed to justify his fascination with fascism, and seemed more on the mark than his earlier predilections with right wing politics. Bowie's lyrics often depicted a future he saw as decadent and frightening, but which he embraced with abandon. To Bowie, the survivors of the decadent seventies would be those Nietzschean supermen who, through sheer will, could adopt the necessary personae to avoid persecution. If those personae meant that the next hit record went to number one, so much the better. It worked too; fans began to mine used clothing shops for wide-brimmed hats, golf sweaters, baggy Oxford pants. The images of Marlene Dietrich and Humphrey Bogart became popular, and all of these fashions sustained the clientele at Biba, a department store on Kensington High Street.[36]

Glamrock Mainstays and Elton John

One respect in which most of the stars of glamrock were similar was in their relative inability to cross the Atlantic and appeal to Americans. Bowie was a vast exception, but few of the rest scored hits or drove massive tours across the United States the way they did in Britain or Europe.[37] While the results didn't fatten wallets in Britain, it gave glamrock a provincialism that appealed to its fans—their heroes mostly would not disappear across the Atlantic. Rather, glamrock found its overseas outlet across the channel in Europe. One artist who addressed this was Bryan Ferry of Roxy Music.

> [Our image] is more English than most. Mind you, I've always been seduced by Americana, but I do probably come out quite English. In Europe, they tend to like that. As English, we're sort of quite restrained and conservative, though stylised, on stage. It seems to have met with very little opposition. They tend to like us most in Europe at the moment because of the intellectual aspirations we have—our literary bent. So therefore, the audience over there is probably much older than the audience over here. We've had a few singles out here as well, so the audience has been getting more and more of a mixture of young and old. On the continent we're not a discotheque-type band at all, it's much more of your heavy album group, I like the idea of being able to operate in both camps.[38]

Like Bowie, Ferry was beholden to the visual and lyrical image of doomed youth in Weimar Berlin. He was the son of a miner from Durham who swore he would never work down in the coal pits.[39] He instead attended the University of Newcastle as a fine arts student. One of his tutors was the Pop artist Richard Hamilton, and he took inspiration from the work of Marcel Duchamp. His standard outfit was a white dinner jacket and black bowtie, but he also wore tiger stripes and leopard spots, lamé suits, fascist leather, even GI greens and khakis. He cultivated an image as a lounge lizard, and lived up to it to the hilt, dating a succession of gorgeous models and regularly appearing in the tabloid gossip columns.[40]

Numerous other acts trod a similar path, including Mott the Hoople, Sparks, and Cockney Rebel. Cockney Rebel's star was Steve Harley, singer, songwriter and angry young man. Born and beaten up in Lewisham, Harley had a perpetual working-class chip on his shoulder. He considered himself a poet, and his continual pretensions as a star irritated the rock press to no end—especially since Cockney Rebel churned out one hit single after another in the era from 1974 to 1977. He often handed out roses to his audience at the end of concerts.

> And some people still get up and say, "Oh how SCHMALTZY, Harley, handing out roses to kids in the front row at the end of the show. Why do that? You're in rock, not entertainment." And I say: RUBBISH! I absolutely love those kids for standing by me, and for coming to my concerts and for spending their money on a ticket for Steve Harley and Cockney Rebel. I give them roses because I'm touched and I mean it, and it's a little piece of my heart, given symbolically to the whole audience via the front row kids. It's entertainment, sure, and what's wrong with that?[41]

Harley had a commanding stage presence, wearing a trademark bowler hat on stage in mockery of his alleged social superiors. His songs emphasized the circus atmosphere of being a rock and roll star—the women who threatened to command his life ["Loretta's Tale" (1974)], the loss of respect for rock and roll's roots ["Tumbling Down" (1974)] and how fame threatened to drive him insane ["The Psychomodo" (1974)].[42]

However, no one confounded the critics and intellectuals more than Elton John. Elton John became a focal point for the difficulties in dividing pop from rock in the seventies. Mostly, he was a rock and roll artist on the fringe of the glamrock cult, dressing in outrageous costumes and flaunting a jet-setting lifestyle. He started out, though, as a singer-songwriter type in the mold of Cat Stevens. John teamed up with lyricist Bernie Taupin to produce "Your Song" (1970), a sensitive, quiet, piano-driven paean to a lover needing reassurance of her importance in the singer's life. "Your Song" made the UK Top Ten, and two similar songs, "Take Me to the Pilot" and "Border Song", were also hits off the subsequent album, *Elton John* (1970); James Taylor produced similar work in Los Angeles at the time, and Elton John seemed like a British version of the same. With the rise of the glamrock subculture, however, he quickly abandoned his previous image as a serious entertainer for the glitzier image of the pop star extraordinaire. No one was more outrageous than Elton John in the early seventies, with his gigantic glasses, sequined stage suits and wild stage performances.[43]

Above all, he sold records by the boatload. Commercialism was indefensible, according to the critical standards of the time in Britain, and there was thus a lot of confusion for critics. Some of them liked Elton John, while most believed he had "sold out", as if he ever pretended to want to do anything other than make a lot of money. He was a huge success in America, where issues of authenticity were less intense, but in Britain, his success was always tempered by his blatantly commercial image.[44] The journalist Bob Edmands summed up the conundrum rather neatly.

> Elton John is altogether too healthy, prolific, energetic and shrewd for a big league rock star. His albums seem the product of a continuous adrenalin high. His career looks too much like an advert for the good old Protestant Ethic for him to find a comfortable niche in a culture with pretensions to decadence. Samuel Smiles would've dug Elton John, but what's he got to offer the average downer freak? . . . [W]hy does the man appeal to a hard rock audience which is normally hyper-sensitive to suggestions of impurity?[45]

The question seemed tough to answer in 1974. In hindsight, perhaps the key lay in the expectations of the rock audience as opposed to the image of the artists. The progressive crowd took themselves very seriously; Elton John did not. The hard rock musician disdained the idea of writing and releasing songs as singles; Elton John did not. Progressive rock musicians disdained the idea of music-making as a way of earning money; Elton John did not. Clearly, audiences in Britain and America were still more than pleased to have a star that was accessible, goofy and brilliantly tuneful at the same time. Elton John's popularity seemed to emanate in part from his unwillingness to toe the professional line of propriety and seriousness, as Michael Wale, a minor rock critic, pointed out.

> I'd never thought of Elton John as a pop star. That had been left to *Life* and *Time* magazines. They thought of him as a pop star. I thought of him more as a musician and composer. It was his music that was the thoughtful thing. His image had always worried me, and I suspect the comparatively reticent reception he gets in England is due to this. It is a case of the image not reflecting the man. His album *Honky Chateau* was one of the best of 1972.[46]

Meantime, John also openly admitted having a hair transplant, came out as bisexual in 1976 and admitted to attempting suicide twice. His honesty put the supposed "authenticity" of the progressive and hard rock acts to shame, and he sold more records than most of them combined. Furthermore, he indulged in his wealth, buying up an English soccer team as a hobby or paying to have the New York jeweler Cartier opened for him on a day off so he could shop for Christmas presents.[47] Like Bowie, he was an ambivalent figure—he did not conform to any of the established norms of taste and image for rock music. Yet the power of singles like "Levon" (1971), "Saturday Night's Alright for Fighting" (1972) and "The Bitch is Back" (1975) was undeniable. He addressed the confusion of the critics in an interview.

> The thing I like about rock and roll is that I don't have to take it seriously—I take it seriously enough but half the people you meet in America, for instance, take themselves far too seriously. I find that a pain in the arse. That's why I've always worn funny clothes on stage . . . it's been done in a humorous way because I couldn't compete with the Bowies or the Jaggers. I haven't got the figure for it. I'd look like Donald Dumpling from Dover, so I try to make people grin a bit. It's probably reacted against me a bit, but that's exactly the effect I wanted.[48]

Elton John and David Bowie together pointed up a number of the contradictions that the conception of rock music's authenticity was invested with, and both made a healthy living by dancing and singing all over them. When asked who his audience was, Elton responded, forthrightly, "Well who do you think they are? Bank clerks and Sainsbury's assistants I suppose."[49]

A writer for *Sounds* tried to pinpoint part of the difficulty in producing interesting new music for the seventies.

> In the mid Sixties the average age of professional group musicians was between 18 and 22—war babies in fact. Today the average age is considerably older. In fact, it is still the rock generation [the baby boomers who first inaugurated the explosion in British bands with the Beatles] that is dominating the rock market today. . . . The normal pattern is for a person to become conscious of rock music at the age of eleven or twelve and to lose interest in the early 20s. The rock generation has, to some extent, broken that pattern. Because pop music was so important to them, and because it was exclusively theirs, the generation has carried its interest over into their 20s and 30s.[50]

Many people did not like the new developments in rock music. They strained against the boundaries of authenticity, now considered a hard-won concept in the world of the money-conscious record industry. *Sounds* also interviewed four randomly selected music fans, all eighteen years old, for their music tastes and pronouncements on the state of rock music in 1974. Their assessments were generally negative, and the frustration of the music scene in 1974 was apparent. None of them felt as if they heard the music they wanted to hear on the radio. They tended to buy albums rather than singles, often on trust, without having heard anything off the album before simply because they liked the band. None of them made an effort to go and see new bands often—it cost too much money, outside of the pubs. Besides, a fan didn't find new music locally anyway—the record companies dictated what the best new music was, and made the consumer pay more and more for it. Smaller venues like the Roundhouse in

Camden gave way to big venues like Finsbury Park's Rainbow or Wembley. The four fans believed that the problems with rock music in 1974 stemmed from businessmen as opposed to the musicians themselves. Yet, as one interviewee said, "Well, sometimes I reckon people love it because they're determined to. They've paid money for it, so they've got to love it."[51]

Chapter 12
The Business of Rock

Heavy metal, glamrock, singer songwriters, folk rock, hard rock, all were prevalent in the early seventies music charts. Only glamrock really challenged the
counterculture's artistic terms, however—all the other genres' musicians were
just as determined not to "go commercial" and make music only for the profits.
The idea of being a "pop"—popular—musician was not a career killer, but popularity certainly meant that a musician could not be counted on to uphold the
values of youth rebellion. Therefore, in the counterculture's terms, the coming
revolution would see the pop musician up against the wall as opposed to leading
youth to utopia.

Critically, though, none of this would matter if it were not possible to make
a lot of cash as a popular musician—or to be more accurate, to make a lot of
cash by appearing to avoid being popular as a musician. Outside of a select few
perceptive music journalists in the early to mid-seventies, no one appeared to
notice that the British music industry was a smashing success as a profit-earner,
in particular at a time when the rest of the British industrial economy was in
decline. Singles, albums, tours, festivals, pub acts, radio airplays—no matter
how British listeners consumed their music, they did it by enriching the coffers
of the record companies, both majors and independents. Even more, the record
companies also exported the music to the United States, Europe, the Commonwealth and beyond, becoming perhaps the only industry in Britain to redress the
national economy's longstanding balance of payments deficit. "Selling out"
might be a thought crime in British rock music, but even being able to "sell out"

was a rather remarkable thing to accomplish for anyone involved in the British economy in the 1970s.

The coming of rock and roll to Britain had coincided with the settling-in of the social democratic welfare state designed by the Labour government of 1945 and the post-austerity economic recovery of the Conservative 1950s. "You've never had it so good" was the famous paraphrase of Prime Minister Harold Macmillan in the late 1950s, and few would argue otherwise. However, successive Conservative and Labour governments through the 1950s and 1960s focused on full employment of the working population, as opposed to the strength of the pound, the health of the exports market or inflating prices. None of this mattered much at the time. Though the Beatles won their MBEs in 1965 for their services to the British economy's balance of payments crisis, likely few fans would have been able to articulate the reason.

The wake-up call came in 1967. The Labour government under Harold Wilson devalued the pound for the second time in twenty years in order to be able to pay nationalized workers and avoid laying them off. For the first time, the news on the economy, on the possibilities of inflation and the balance of payments crisis hit home for the average British consumer. The shillings a teenager would spend to buy a Walker Brothers single were suddenly worth less than they were just days before, and a shudder ran through the entire music industry as a result.

By 1970, British voters had turned to the Conservative party of Edward Heath. Inflation remained high, economic planning by the government seemed to run on a day-to-day basis, trade union leaders could not control wildcat strikes by members, and crime statistics were rising. Heath's answer was to reapply for a third time for British membership in the European Economic Community; the application was accepted in 1972 and Britain joined in 1973. Nevertheless, the effort to conciliate the trade unions was ongoing and the national budget deficit was massive. Heath decided to float the pound on international currency markets to see how the markets would determine its worth—and shocked the country when the pound was devalued for the third time in twenty-five years, to $1.90. The devaluation helped exporters like the music industry sell product overseas by making records cost less, but did nothing for the problem of inflation at home.

The economic nadir of the period was 1973. Heath's Counter-Inflation Act created a price commission and pay board for nationalized industries, setting state controls on wages and prices. The OPEC oil crisis in October slammed Britain hard, especially when nationalized coal miners demanded higher pay since coal was in greater demand as a substitute fuel. They cut production to try to drive the price of coal up; businesses could not afford to heat their offices or run electricity, and Heath actually had to declare a state of emergency on January 1, 1974, cutting work time for all state employees to a three-day work week. In short, the economy was paralyzed.

The government called an election for February, resulting in a hung Parliament, and Labour negotiated its way into leading a minority government. Strikes subsided with the coming of a "social contract" between workers and the state, pledging to keep wages commensurate with inflation. As a result, Labour called another election in October 1974 and won an outright majority of three seats. For the next five years, the economy would continue to deteriorate as trade unions battled the Labour government over pay, while government spending was so out of control that Britain had to apply for an International Monetary Fund loan of £3.9 billion in 1976. The state of the British economy, particularly the industrial economy, was never worse than it was in the 1970s.

The British Record Industry in the 1960s

The record industry in Britain, however, continued to make a profit, despite every dire prediction made for its health, year after year, by the industry executives themselves. Consumers had less and less money; the British Musicians' Union threatened to derail the production of rock and pop music; moneymaking musicians could not afford to live in Britain because of the tax laws; at one point the companies could not even come up with enough vinyl to put out records. Yet again and again, projections of a coming decline in profits proved premature—if anything, the record industry boomed through most of the seventies.

Three issues defined the history of the music industry in Britain: the effects of technological change, the economics of producing popular music, and changes in the musical culture.[1] The first two were no different from issues faced by any major industry: new machinery and the balance between profits and costs were the essence of production values. However, the third issue was defining— Britain's music culture had exploded with the coming of rock and roll and rock music. In the 1970s, that change was still hugely profitable at a time when almost no other industry made profits, at home or abroad—and often in spite of efforts to stifle profit coming from every institutional angle.

At the beginning of the rock and roll era, government, industry and trade unions were in felicitous accord—all were dedicated just as much to the idea of full employment as anyone else involved in the British economy. The government-run BBC had rules as to how much airtime it allowed to be devoted to recorded music as opposed to live music, to be certain radio did not put musicians out of work. The record industry took its profits from rock and roll and used them to subsidize classical music, which employed many more musicians too. The British Musicians' Union had the legal right to copy musical product from other nations for British chart consumption, thus to maintain British jobs. A select few British singers—Craig Douglas, Frank Ifield, Jess Conrad and Mark Wynter among them—made careers out of mining the American charts with the BMU and covering certain appropriately tame American songs in a comfortably middle of the road fashion. Only Elvis escaped this butchering: he proved impossible to copy.

The constant pressure of full employment began to lessen just as British rock and roll acts were on the verge of exploding on the world market, however. On New Years' Eve 1962, taxes were lowered on records, creating a 10 percent drop in the price of singles and albums, and also making it cheaper to buy juke-boxes, radios, television sets and anything else that broadcast music. British consumers—especially teenagers—subsequently bought more music in more ways, putting more money in the average BMU-registered musician's pocket. This allowed the BMU to relax its rules such that most American rock and roll songs could enter the British charts without being covered by British musicians.[2]

Then came the Beatles, and an explosion in record industry profits. Up to January 1963, only three singles in British chart history had ever sold a million copies, all of them American—Harry Belafonte's "Mary's Boy Child" (1956), Bill Haley's "Rock Around the Clock" (1956), and Elvis Presley's "It's Now or Never" (1962). Now, the mining of music scenes in the provinces and the R&B scene in London, coupled with their vast sales overseas in the United States and the rest of the world, crowded pounds into the wallets of anyone associated with the industry, executives, musicians, writers or anyone else. By mid-1964, the Beatles' "Can't Buy Me Love" reached a million advance orders before its re-lease, and it passed the three million mark in the United States.[3] Instead, it was now the Americans' turn to complain about the economic consequences of the raiding of their pop charts. The American Federation of Musicians complained about "redcoats" replacing American musicians on the charts, and record com-pany executives were angered over their inability to book acts on CBS' *Ed Sul-livan Show* because British groups dominated bookings.[4]

The Beatles' success contributed heavily to the rise of EMI to become the biggest record company in the world at the time. Profits went up by £9.1 million between fiscal 1963 and 1964, and earnings rose another £8 million between 1964 and 1965. One in every four discs sold around the world were EMI records at the time, and half of the world's top ten singles of 1964 were by EMI artists.[5] The rest of the music industry saw its profits rise by £27.1 million over the course of only the first quarter of 1964. By the end of the year, total profits for the entire industry would exceed £100 million for the first time.[6] Thereafter, for the next several years, every standard of profit for the record industry exceeded expectations repeatedly, quarter by quarter, year by year.

Weathering the Economic Storm

However, as the decade wore on and the problems of the British economy began to set in, it seemed the bubble might burst. For the first time in 1969, record company executives began to prepare for a decline in sales. They assumed that economic conditions had to catch up with the record buying public, and compe-tition from American companies selling product in London had to cut into their profits in distribution.[7] Yet by June 1969, sales were up 37 percent over the previous quarter, and export sales climbed 27 percent as well.[8] By September 1970, Decca reported profits had risen 77 percent between March 1969 and March 1970, an astounding total.[9] The artists' Performing Rights Society reported that British musicians brought home a net profit of $5 million in 1970, thus doing their part toward redressing the balance of payments.[10] Songwriters' fees increased by 250 percent in nine years, and the Performing Rights Society actually won a Queen's Award for exports in 1971, as the "balance of musical payments with the United States was practically level—an impressive fact considering the differences simply in population and economic power at the time. Nearly everywhere else in the world, the same balance was well in Britain's favor too.[11]

In September 1971, the Department of Trades and Industry again reported that the British record industry's growth was slowing, and that the rise in exports was finally leveling off. The United States levied a 10 percent tariff on imports, and prices rose in part due to escalating production costs. The industry expected the boom to finally go bust.[12]

In fact, in every year of the first half of the decade, the record industry's economic prognosticators predicted problems, and for more reasons than just simple laws of supply and demand. One reason was that the British Musicians' Union had turned again to rock music as a place where their members' potential pay was hemorrhaging. It was hard for the BMU to assign a pound-defined work value to the making of a rock record and the increasing professionalization of its musicians. Rock musicians were not just artists, they were artisans: they were contracted as performers to produce unique works for an ephemeral audience. This was especially so as the technological changes of the era made their professionalization even more readily apparent.[13]

For example, synthesizers posed a problem for the British Musicians' Union: the instrumental sounds that a keyboard player could mimic on one synthesizer could put any number of trained musicians out of work. The Moody Blues' keyboard player, Mike Pinder, was briefly vilified in the early seventies for his work with the mellotron, an organ with a tape recorder in it that could reproduce sounds on keys that had been recorded into it. Pinder was an acknowledged master of the mellotron, not just by other musicians but also by the company that made them. The BMU howled at his use of a single instrument to replace the sound of many more instruments, and thus many more instrumentalists. Pinder finally had to bring BMU representatives to a studio and force them to try to play the mellotron, unsuccessfully, to get them to understand how he orchestrated it and what made it a unique instrument. The BMU dropped their claim.[14]

Later in the decade, the nature of prerecorded tapes used in live performance became a bugbear of the BMU. For example, Elton John refused to appear on *Top of the Pops* in March 1975 when the BMU would not allow him to record backing tracks for "Philadelphia Freedom" (1975). The song had an extensive orchestral backing that had taken arranger Paul Buckmaster weeks to put together, but the BMU insisted that John record exactly the same track in three hours with a BBC studio band and orchestra, an absurd demand designed to give BBC musicians an extra paycheck. It was legally enforceable according to a law put in effect at the beginning of the year, which disallowed the prerecording of television backing tracks by anyone other than the BBC studio orchestra and band. The Electric Light Orchestra—a band whose own members included classical instrumentalists—joined in Elton John's boycott.[15]

The oil crisis of the early seventies also threatened to cripple the industry—the plastic in vinyl records was made out of petroleum. In 1972 and 1973 there was a worldwide shortage of vinyl, which meant that even the major record companies were in trouble when they had hit singles with a lot of demand. As a representative for the British division of WEA (Warner/Elektra/Asylum) put it, "Record sales have gone up 40 per cent in the past few years. How could you have predicted that? If you don't have sufficient vinyl you're in trouble."[16] Some producing plants reported a 50 percent drop in capacity in 1972.[17] Without the ability to continue pressing records at will, the industry found it hard to meet rising demands. For example, the British and German company Polydor picked 1972 as the year they began releasing compilation albums with hits by original artists featured on Polydor labels. The first one was *20 Fantastic Hits*, put out on the Arcade label in July 1972. The idea was to copy the success of K-Tel in the United States. Demand was so high that Polydor found it necessary to rent space from other companies' pressing plants to meet the demand.[18]

The crisis got worse over time—promoters began to promise gallons of gasoline in contracts to ensure that bands could arrive at gigs on time. Rick Wakeman's second solo album had its release date pushed back two months to April 1974 because of the vinyl shortage. Smaller bands went out of business because they could not afford to drive their vans to gigs around the country. Nevertheless, the demand for product never waned. Sales were down only slightly in the first quarter of 1972, and were still 10 percent higher than they had been a year before.[19]

By March 1973, there had been little change in the record companies' profits, despite even the currency devaluation. The value-added tax substituted for previous British taxes when Britain joined the EEC in 1973, and it actually lowered record prices, which was a boon for exports. By the end of 1973, sales of records and tapes in the UK had broken the £150 million mark. More singles were sold in 1973 than in 1964, a stunning statistic considering that 1964 was the height of the British beat explosion. The Performing Rights Society collected nearly £12.5 million in 1973, including £4.5 million in profits from overseas, an increase of 8.5 percent over 1972.[20]

The 1974 holidays were again a banner period for the music industry, but as usual, they expected to see a major slump in sales in 1975, one dealer calling the Christmas season "customers' last fling".[21] The major record shop conglomerates decided that if there was going to be a "last fling", it was going to be held in their stores. In mid-1974 the major chains, such as Boots, Woolworth's and WH Smith all slashed record prices in response to a Labour government directive to return 10 percent of their profits to the consumer. The result was a small business disaster. Unable to meet the challenge from the majors and unable to pay their rent, numerous specialty shops—which often stocked hard-to-find records by groups not often heard on the radio—went out of business.[22]

Nevertheless, for all the worry and concern over the economy, the growth of the cassette industry meant that the British record industry made £170 million in total sales in 1975. British acts dominated the American charts, both in singles and albums. At one point in August, four of the top five songs on the American charts were by British acts—Elton John, 10CC, the Bee Gees and Olivia Newton-John. The album charts included Wings, Bad Company, David Bowie, the Rolling Stones and numerous others. British acts dominated the concert scene as well. No American band other than the Grateful Dead and the Beach Boys—both mainly nostalgia acts by 1975—could challenge the major British acts as concert draws on the arena circuit.[23]

In the end, the 1970s proved to be the decade in which the British record industry really came into its own. The three biggest selling albums of the decade were still to come, all products of British acts on British labels: Peter Frampton's *Frampton Comes Alive!* (1976), Fleetwood Mac's *Rumours* (1977), and the soundtrack to *Saturday Night Fever* (1978), which featured the Bee Gees. The last album sold 25 million copies worldwide, the highest selling album in history until Michael Jackson's *Thriller* (1982). It was not until 1978 that record sales even began to slump.[24] As a letter writer to *Melody Maker* made the point, "With the pound gradually becoming worth less than the dollar, Britain needs [Led] Zeppelin and [Jethro] Tull to earn valuable dollars—they're probably a better export than the entire British motor industry."[25]

Taxman

Led Zeppelin's sales may have proved a boon to British exports, yet the musicians in the band were exports themselves. Crushing taxation meant that many of Britain's most successful rock musicians, at the height of their profitability, had to flee the country in the 1970s just to keep their earnings intact. In some respects, this was ridiculously hypocritical; many of these selfsame stars were heavy players in the "rock-as-anti-capitalist-revolution" sweepstakes in the 1960s. On the other hand, it seemed the sort of choice that virtually any smart rich person would make under British governments determined to finance their own ineptitude out of the pockets of the wealthy.

A British resident in the top tax bracket in 1975 was a person living in Britain for more than three months a year, who earned over £20,000 a year. They paid 83 percent of their income out in taxes to the government. They also paid another 15 percent on unearned income such as investments and dividends from shares. Thus, major performers earning £200,000 a year, a not uncommon sum of money for the top rock stars of the day, contributed an overwhelming 98 percent of their income in taxes to the government. Out of that £200,000, they took home only £4000; any other earnings had to come from overseas. Starting in 1974, even those earnings were taxed at 90 percent owing to a finance bill introduced by the Labour government. [26]

Thus, numerous rock musicians fled Britain for destinations more accommodating to their pockets. The most popular destination was, of course, America, where so many of them made their biggest money. The IRS granted a 50 percent top tax rate as a concession to high earners who brought in foreign currency. Keith Moon of the Who moved to Los Angeles. John Lennon fought his long immigration battle with the Nixon Republican Party largely to avoid British taxes. Led Zeppelin's members moved to New York City. Eric Clapton was in the United States. Queen moved to Los Angeles in 1977. Even Slade, who never met with success in America, had to quit Britain, the band members complaining that they would pay a lot in taxes—but not 98 percent. As the publicist for Slade noted: "At the moment everyone loses. The country gets no tax at all, the fans get no concerts and the stars lose their freedom."[27]

Others moved to European countries that were willing to accommodate their incomes favorably. France made discreet deals with the accountants of the musicians and movie stars, so discreet that the tax ministers themselves would not admit they existed. In return, they got not only high amounts of money in taxes, they also received taxes on publishing, record company and distributor royalties. The Rolling Stones moved to France in the early seventies. Apparently, the islands off Britain had favorable tax rates as well. The Bee Gees held residence in the Isle of Man, their birthplace. Rod Stewart banked his money there and lived in Ireland. Ireland was briefly a popular place to live because the Irish Internal Revenue did not tax the earnings of people who "produc[ed] genuine original work of cultural artistic merit". The policy thus attracted rich celebrities to move to Ireland and spend their money there.[28]

Many of the acts, the Stones in particular, wanted to play in England, but were warned against it by their accountants—any stadium-level gig they played would lose money. Any act that would have signed on to headline these concert bills—British or American—would have earned up to £35,000, but they would have brought home less than £350 for all their trouble. On top of this, they would have had to use the £350 to pay all their roadies, agents, and other varied employees. The Stones offered to play a concert entirely for charity in 1975, but could not risk losing 98 percent of the band's income to the Inland Revenue. Major concerts at Wembley, Charlton Football Ground and the Crystal Palace Bowl were cancelled because so many of the major acts had to flee the country.[29] The nation was losing at least £100 million a year in taxes due to these tax laws.

Most stars, to their credit, decided to stay and put up with the horrible tax rate. Elton John remained in Watford and bought his local football team.[30] Paul McCartney continued to call his Scottish farm home. The members of Yes lived north of London in Hampstead. Pete Townshend, Roger Daltrey, and John

Entwistle all lived on the outskirts of west London. Most of them were unhappy with the current tax situation, but not so unhappy as to get them to leave. Townshend described how he had to answer to fans for the fact that *Tommy* sold in the millions: "[When] people really started to hit me with 'capitalist bastard', I was in debt and nobody would believe it."[31]

The "fame drain" in rock music was somewhat exaggerated—most of these stars could afford second homes in other countries, and they used them too. The recession of the mid-seventies made the differences between the top and the mid-level acts in Britain seem like a chasm. A class system seemed to be growing within the rock music industry itself. The Faces, in the midst of the economic crisis, went on tour and grossed £100,000; Pink Floyd achieved similar numbers by playing twenty venues in Britain over the course of the year. Meanwhile, semi-popular gigging bands like Sassafras and Bees Make Honey struggled desperately to keep themselves solvent, playing every night in an effort to afford better equipment and often slipping into debt when problems occurred, like a van's engine breaking down or an amplifier blowing up.[32] The easiest way to recognize who was making money and who wasn't was to look at which stars still lived in the country, and which ones didn't.

Nonetheless, as a public display of no confidence, those rock stars that left were a symbolic indictment of the economic problems of the era. They also marked the rock stars' removal from the atmosphere of daily life in the nation of their birth. Not until 1976 would a government committee recommend in a White Paper that the top tax rate be lowered to get Britain's top entertainers to move home again—and even then, the Labour government did not pass it into law.[33]

Success in the Seventies

Part of the reason the major record labels worried so much about their profits was that they still had little idea about the appeal of rock music. Label executives were never comfortable with pushing a product that they did not like themselves. Fear of having their ignorance exposed was not unfounded either. Decca Records, for example, suffered for its inability to understand changes in the music market. Having signed the Rolling Stones, the Who, the Moody Blues, Cat Stevens, Joe Cocker, David Essex, David Bowie and Van Morrison in the sixties and early seventies, they proceeded to lose them all to independent or American labels. Sir Edward Lewis, the chairman, never warmed to the idea of having rock artists supporting the profits of his company, which he still believed should be promoting classical and popular music to uplift the tastes of the British music audience. EMI, meanwhile, simply did not sign many new acts after the Beatles placed the company at the top of the world music market. Corporate executives clung to the Beatles as cash cows and held onto other old chart-toppers long after their hitmaking potential had run dry, due to an inability to understand market changes.

The result was an opening for independent music labels in Britain, displaying entrepreneurship that was often lacking in the British industrial economy in the seventies. The greatest success story of the early seventies was Virgin Records. Richard Branson and his partners started out running an independent record shop, which proved a rather dangerous proposition in the early seventies as many of them went out of business. Branson started a fledgling record label, and his first signing was a progressive rock keyboard player named Mike Oldfield. Oldfield was a pioneer with synthesizers whose sound straddled the rock and serious markets the way virtually no other artist of the time did. His first album, *Tubular Bells* (1973), quite literally made the label and built Branson's fortune when the music was chosen to score the popular American horror film *The Exorcist* (1973). Branson had miraculously landed one of the best-selling artists of the seventies. More important, Branson capitalized on Oldfield's success, signing only a few other new acts, lavishing attention on them, marketing them well and trying to assure that they sold in the British market.[34]

The major labels' struggle to maintain profits was successful, really, because regardless of how little their executives might like rock and pop music, they had actually managed to master its rhetoric. What was once "pop" in the sixties—Tom Jones, Engelbert Humperdinck, Cilla Black—was now being defined as "easy listening" or "middle of the road" music, often abbreviated as MOR. Certain artists like Elton John were capable of crossing over between rock, rock and roll and "easy listening", meaning they could sell to a much larger audience for the major labels, who duly marketed them as such. Other new performers like Leo Sayer, Gilbert O'Sullivan or 10CC were willing to play the old British showbiz game of turning into an entertainer, playing TV shows, pantomimes, and holiday camps. None of them could have arisen in Britain without the development of an adult audience attuned to rock music and its pretensions to respectability. The original buyers of Rolling Stones singles were now in their mid-twenties or thirties and less likely to show an interest in the antics of David Bowie. In fact, many of the people responding to the easy listening market were a "silent majority" of sorts who had been the very people who had made the early British rock acts such a success.[35] In such an atmosphere, with the British economy crumbling and social discord reaching a breaking point, the relaxed pop sound of such acts seemed a soothing balm to troubled minds and shaken attitudes, and it sold well enough to keep the record industry in the black.

Both O'Sullivan and Sayer indulged in unusual stage images. O'Sullivan dressed like a 1930s working-class schoolboy, complete with cloth cap, bowtie and short trousers. He aspired to be recognized as a working-class music hall throwback, and conducted his career as such, making sure that interviewers knew he had grown up the son of an East End butcher who played a £5 piano in a back garden shed.[36] He went to art school like many of his contemporaries, and had gone on to jobs working as a window cleaner and a clerk at the clothing store C&A. He was determined to hang onto the working class roots that he saw as central to his music. When he bought himself a £10,000 cottage in Surrey—getting back to nature—he had a room in it transformed to look like his old £8 a week bedsit in Bayswater, so he would not lose any inspiration.[37]

Leo Sayer, meanwhile, made himself up as a harlequin. He pandered shamelessly to the pop-buying public in a series of laughable television shows, yet he whined, "I want to be known as a rock singer—not a pop star. I know it's boring—the age old cry of the artist. But I want people to like me for my songs. Not just because I've got blue eyes."[38] Yet if he did not know by the seventies that he had to avoid television and singing to little girls, he was deliberately not paying attention.

10CC were a pop band fronted by two holdovers from the sixties—Graham Gouldman wrote hit songs for the Hollies and Herman's Hermits, while Eric Stewart sang with the Mindbenders, a band that had several hits in the mid-sixties—and two art school students, Lol Creme and Kevin Godley, who aspired to progressive rock critical standards. "All along we have insisted that we just want people to accept us for our music. We didn't want our success to depend on fashion—that kind of fame is just too short-term."[39] They put great time and effort into their recordings, a measure of the changes in pop music in ten years. "Often we'll spend days writing and recording a track for an album. Then we'll end up throwing the tape away because it doesn't sound quite as perfect as we want it to. . . . We like to have each number perfectly worked out in detail before we even go into the studio."[40] As a group, 10CC struck a good balance between the counterculture aesthetic and the cool professionalism of the pop charts.

Yet these new performers were not the cash cows of the music industry in the seventies—the old sixties rock and roll stars were now the artists they were most comfortable in promoting. They were also aging themselves and put out music that was now easier to recognize as respectable. Perhaps the king of the easy listening pop acts in Britain, for example, was the ageless Cliff Richard. Always with an eye on broadening his appeal to reach an ever-wider public, his efforts to sell himself as a wholesome pop crooner were highly successful. In 1975, he even asked the BBC to ban one of his singles, "Honky Tonk Angels", when he discovered that the lyrics he thought were about love and the pleasure of women were actually extolling the virtues of truck stop prostitutes.[41] His biggest-selling singles came in the seventies, particularly "Devil Woman" (1976), which even made the American charts that Richard had been trying to crack since the 1950s.[42]

By the seventies, his erstwhile replacements at the top of the charts, the Beatles, also maintained the same moneymaking balance between rock and easy listening. Once the definition of working class bravado, the Beatles broke up in 1970 and developed individual careers that virtually defined respectability and complacency in the 1970s. George Harrison's hitmaking potential virtually died after his triple album, *All Things Must Pass* (1970), proved that there was a reason his creative output was stifled in the Beatles. After releasing a couple of positively reviewed albums—*Beaucoup of Blues* (1971), a series of country songs, and *Ringo* (1973), which contained a couple of his singles—Ringo Starr settled into the role of being a professional celebrity, showing up in the occasional movie and doing session work for his friends.

Paul McCartney became a watchword for mediocrity in the seventies, probably the most maddening artist in rock. Singles like "Mary Had a Little Lamb" (1972), "My Love" (1974) or "Silly Love Songs" (1976) seemed to test the pop music public's patience—why would anyone buy a single version of "Mary Had a Little Lamb", by anyone? Even worse was the fact that his band, Wings, released the brilliant album *Band on the Run* (1973) and occasionally excellent rockers like "Junior's Farm" (1974) that reminded the public of just how talented McCartney could be.[43] The music critic Charles Shaar Murray called him to account in 1975.

> Up until the arrival of *Band on the Run* in the latter months of 1973, the prevailing assessment of Monsieur McCartney was that he was the possessor of a "basically bourgeois talent"—which meant that he was essentially uncommitted to rock-and-roll, was irremediably cutesy-pie, played and composed music with an unforgivably low *cojones* quotient, wrote songs that begged for Andy Williams to cover them, wimped around all over the place with a wife who seemed to have even less musical credibility than her fiendish Oriental opposite number, allowed an overwhelming facility for pleasant melody and easy-going charm to degenerate into vacuous glibness, angled his music at the mums and dads, came off poorly in comparison to the gritty honesty and commitment of John Lennon, the uplifting spirituality of George Harrison (or what looked like uplifting spirituality at the time) and the cloddish charm of Ringo Starr (from whom nobody expected anything better than cloddish charm anyway), was a swot and a teacher's pet and a soppy sneak who didn't even *pretend* to relate to a '70s which had taken him at his word about doing it in the road ["Why Don't We Do It in the Road", off *The Beatles* (1968)].[44]

John Lennon likewise attempted a solo career with middling success. His efforts earned him more respect from the critics, but far fewer sales. For the first few years of his relationship with Yoko Ono, both with and without the Beatles, he made a public spectacle of himself in chosen crusades for peace, revolution, and primal scream therapy. It was as if he had to exorcise the Beatles ghost, to destroy the love of his fans through strident criticism of their weaknesses, their political apathy and their psychological ills. Songs like "Imagine" (1971) sketched a utopian planet where, with no religions, politics, money or wars, all personal problems would be over. It was a pleasant vision, but it was impossible to achieve, and Lennon implied that the listener should "join us", as if he had already achieved it. Like his former bandmate George Harrison, Lennon believed himself to be more in touch with reality than his listeners, who should get smart and follow his lead. Such self-indulgence seemed misplaced when, for example, Lennon believed that there was nothing incongruous about an outrageously rich bohemian artist writing about himself as a "Working Class Hero" (1970) and telling his listeners "if you want to be a hero, well, just follow me". The album *Some Time in New York City* (1972) especially was an obnoxious series of musical lectures on political subjects of the day from a man sitting in a penthouse in Manhattan far removed from his subjects—Northern Ireland, the politics of the American justice system, and the lives of oppressed women around the world.[45]

The rebirth of the Bee Gees was also one of the major stories of the mid-seventies. In the sixties, they had been balladeers in the old Denmark Street style, the most syrupy band in Britain, a palatable, adult version of the Beatles that would fit right into the playlist at Radio Two. They made a career out of slow ballads like "New York Mining Disaster 1941" (1967) and "Massachusetts" (1967), generally avoiding any efforts to step up the rhythm. By the seventies, their careers were just as slowly moving—they sang dinner theater in Yorkshire. But with the rise of disco, they moved to America and engaged Arif Mardin, a noted R&B producer, to rework their sound. Their second album with Mardin, *Main Course* (1975), contained the disco hits "Jive Talkin'" and "Nights on Broadway", which became huge singles in both the United States and Britain. By 1977, the Bee Gees were engaged to write songs for the soundtrack of the movie *Saturday Night Fever* (1977), which would become the biggest seller of the seventies.[46]

Commercial Radio

Another contributing factor to the industry's profits was the establishment of commercial radio in Britain. Always sympathetic to the pirates, the Conservatives under Edward Heath intended to implement commercial radio as soon as possible when they came to power in 1970. They stopped jamming the transmission of non-British pirates in the North Sea, and within months, even more pirates returned to the oceans around Britain to broadcast pop music in a commercial format.[47]

In 1972, the Commons passed a Sound Broadcasting Act that created a series of commercial broadcast stations. It also proposed that local newspapers get a dominant share in their ownership, the idea being to provide them with an opportunity to make profits off a competing news media institution. Most local papers belonged to national media organizations, which catered to a middle-class suburban readership—clearly, the hope was that this same mentality might expand to the broadcasting of commercial radio too. The government also set up an Independent Broadcasting Authority to police the new stations for content.[48] Of course, the counterculture sniffed out the lack of revolutionary potential in the new stations—*Ink* called for the granting of commercial radio franchises to the hippie underground, which would pay for radio stations by appealing for subscriptions from listeners, or by selling records over the air.[49] The success of any such enterprise went unnoticed over the course of the early seventies.

Government regulation was not finished, however. The Commercial Radio Act of 1973 demanded that commercial stations broadcast only on a local basis, and that they broadcast fifty hours of needle-time out of ninety-five hours of broadcast time a week. In other words, almost half a station's broadcast time had to be filled by something other than records—presumably live music produced by unionized musicians. This was a major concession at the time, since Radio One broadcast only thirty-four hours a week of needle-time, thus having to fill sixty hours with live music. Amazingly, this was due to record industry pressure—despite their huge profits, the companies were convinced that continual plays of a record on the radio would lead to overexposure and a drop in demand. The British Musicians' Union was likewise determined to maintain full employment for its members, and believed that record plays put live musicians out of business. Said the trade union's general secretary, John Morton —

> The new stations must have obligations to musicians. There is a general acceptance within the Government and the record industry of the validity of our case—our interest is employment. Commercial radio is motivated by money. That's a perfectly acceptable motivation, but it needs social safeguards. We accept the decision to start commercial radio, but it must have obligations; our members, after all, are responsible for the records. Commercial radio must offer employment.[50]

In October 1973, London Broadcasting, a news channel, was the first commercial station on the air, followed by Capital Radio a week after. Capital became the model for all future rock music radio stations, commercial or otherwise. Its controller, Aidan Day, a former BBC employee, was confident that his hand was on the pulse of the British listening public. He was so confident that he threw away the top thirty format—a format dominated by the BBC anyway, since only records Radio One played had made the pop charts up until that time. Instead, Capital played what American stations called "adult-oriented rock", a combination of album tracks, oldies, and a few top thirty hits. Capital was staffed by former pirate disc jockeys and thus sounded more alive than the complacent Radio One, but its tastes proved to be little different from those at the BBC—pop music was what the singles-buying audience wanted, not progressive rock. Only one show, "Your Mother Won't Like It", programmed for the 6:30-8:30 pm time slot, appealed to a progressive rock audience. The rest of the music broadcast was, according to programmer Dave Cash,

> roughly equivalent to middle of the road FM—Paul Simon, Cat Stevens, James Taylor, and Carly [Simon] . . . that kind of stuff. I suppose the album that best represents the kind of thing we'll be playing during the day is Simon and Garfunkel's *Bridge Over Troubled Water* [1970]. . . . The thing is, we want to establish a completely new style in broadcasting. We've tried to develop a com-

pletely English format—and have spent thousands of pounds researching it in the process.[51]

Of course, that research would reveal that most people listened to Leo Sayer, Elton John and Paul McCartney, not Yes or Genesis or Edgar Broughton. By early 1975 an independent research organization found that Capital Radio had 1 million listeners, an estimate three times higher than what the BBC believed Capital's local audience to be.[52] Under pressure to increase listeners, the BBC conformed more and more to the tastes of its decidedly young audience, rather than the other way around. By late 1977, they had scrapped their wide-ranging playlist for the top forty format of the commercials.[53] Such programming met with the distaste of the record companies' executives, but certainly did a lot to fill up their checkbooks.

The State of Rock Music

In 1976, the *Daily Mirror* listed its first annual British Rock and Pop Awards for 1976. The poll distinguished between the best "rock" band and the best "pop" band—the *Mirror* had learned the rhetorical distinction between categories—but Paul McCartney and Wings won both categories. The outstanding personality was David Essex, who was also best male solo singer, with Rod Stewart following in both categories. Paul McCartney was the best group singer. The best instrumentalist was Eric Faulkner of the Bay City Rollers, giving a strong idea as to what was important to the fans: true musical talent or mere physical presence. The Bay City Rollers' *Dedication* (1976) was the best album of the year.[54] It would be hard to find a greater indictment of the failure of rock music to transform the values of its audience—if, of course, one required the music to do so. All that had really changed was how the audience talked about the music, and themselves, while the record industry followed along, however reluctantly.

Yet, succeeding in spite of itself, the British record industry navigated its way through the 1970s at full throttle. For all its continued dislike of rock music, it had mastered its presentation to the audience. The professionalism and artistic aspirations of the bands themselves lent themselves to marketability, and the industry reaped the benefits at a time when almost no other industry in Britain was making a profit. Yet for all this, everyone paying attention in the mid-seventies seemed to hate what rock music had become—critics, listeners, intellectuals, record company executives, sometimes even the artists themselves, and all of them were apparently paying for the privilege. One writer after another tried to peg what was wrong with rock music in the mid-seventies, why its values, for all their careful definitions, had not produced the cultural renaissance so

many seemed to be waiting for. Idris Walters was one such journalist; he
thought the problem lay in the rise of rock musicians to superstardom.

> Superstar systems put rock in danger of becoming totally isolated from its in-
> spirational causes and effects. . . . Rock, as people's music, is an exchange and
> a mart for the purpose of assimilating and disseminating popular imagery and
> ideas. Which feels good, has no doubt felt good for centuries: It is possibilities
> and opportunities open to thunderous celebrational debate. . . . But now it's
> highways and highways; for the byways have become almost inaccessible.
> There are fewer places to stop over without precision pre-arrangement. Which
> doesn't feel so good. . . . Out of rock 'n' roll came a predominantly "pop" lull.
> Then there were the Beatles and all that they entailed. And then another lull—
> more serious in concept—punctuated by the odd visionary figure. Now, in the
> mid-seventies, our "progressive" downer has become almost entirely predicta-
> ble, tired and listless.[55]

Others believed that the train of rock music might still be derailed. Things
on the music scene were so staid in 1975 that ATV began screening *The Jack
Parnell Show*, a sort of British Lawrence Welk, and it was an immediate hit. For
the first time in many years, the music and television industries began to pay
attention to the gap between the popular music and classical music listeners, and
tried to cater to them. Of course, bluenoses arose to celebrate the brief success of
the Reithian vision.

> What is evident is that the obnoxious, incomprehensible screamings of so many
> rock singers, flaunting their often degenerate life-styles and proud of their ama-
> teurish presentation, is rapidly losing its enchantment when put in competition
> once more with the music which, ironically, it replaced 20 years or more ago.
> As Joe Loss said, "If the big bands got equal air time on TV with the pop
> groups the public would soon choose what was best."[56]

Alan Price, one-time keyboard player with the Animals and a successful solo artist in his own right, became a writer for *Melody Maker* in 1975. His opening article was the sort of "state of the business" message that was ubiquitous in
British rock music in the mid-seventies. With the wild, working-class amateurism of the sixties corrupted and professional values dominant, Price joined a
legion of musicians and fans who believed that rock music in Britain had desert-
ed its purpose and audience to become another tool of a crumbling middle-class
adult establishment.

> The explosion of popular music that occurred in this country approximately 12
> years ago owed its strength to the simplicity, honesty and vitality of the per-
> formers. For the artists, three chords and more was an escape from industrial
> poverty and generations of ignorance. Likewise for the ordinary people they
> were working class heroes with whom they could identify.

But as is the way of all things, the more a successful artist learns about the business side of things, the more he is sucked into believing the music business ethic that profit equals art: and therefore if a thing is profitable let's have more of the same and don't experiment. . . . There is an inherent contradiction between business and art: the difference between making money and making music.

You can bet that with the economic climate as it is, record companies will be obliged to limit releases, and cut down on the exploitation of new talent. A new group will have to pray for a hit single which is not necessarily representative of their work, solely for the purpose of convincing a record company that they merit the finance required to cut an album. . . .

Perhaps our only hope is that where there is a vacuum between audiences and performers, something moves in to fill the space (as with pirate radio). If the space is filled with mindless unfeeling junk, it is all on our heads.[57]

Another commentator was Stanley Reynolds, a curmudgeonly whiner on the poor nature of pop music blaring from transistor radios in the hot summer of 1975. He was a Radio Three fan, one of the few and the proud. He also liked rock music, Frank Zappa in particular. Nevertheless, he despised the efforts of Tony Palmer, his counterpart at the *Observer*, and numerous others to make rock music seem like the single most significant cultural medium of the twentieth century.[58] Reynolds instead emphasized the trashy nature of rock music and how little of it was actually relevant to the lives of its listeners.

[I]n the fifties and early sixties we listened to trash: and we are listening to trash again. Musically the Beatles and what followed them was rather red hamburger joint cooking, lunch cart and road house fare, but this stuff, now this summer, is merely eating with your hands.

The woeful economic state is no doubt behind it. The discs are made of vinyl, an oil based product, and it is in short supply. Record buyers are also out of pocket. The big fat cat entertainment industry of the past decade is feeling the pinch: and just like any other hungry alley cat it is scrounging around the dustbins looking for garbage: in hard times they cannot take a chance on something new, different and possibly good—they must go for tried and true trash.

But it is an ill wind. If the record industry does backslide all the way back to the good old bad old days, well, we won't have to waste our time with it anymore. Pop music can become what it was like before the Beatles forced us all to start taking it seriously. There was something extremely undignified about that business, with distinguished music critics fingering the entrails of "Love Me Do" and "I Wanna Hold Your Hand" searching for greatness. They kept finding it too: I wonder if they ever blush! Pop music this summer has returned to its natural state. Pop music is like paper tissues. You use it once and then you throw it away. And it's probably all that much better for being like that. If only we didn't have to keep hearing it![59]

Never did this seem truer to the British rock audience than in the summer of 1975. Everyone seemed to be waiting for punk to happen.

Chapter 13
Punk

After a decade's worth of professionalization, Romantic artistic indulgence, and explosive cash growth, punk was an outspoken effort to restore working-class values in British rock and roll and rock music in the late 1970s. It articulated the frustrations of working-class British youth in an era of unemployment and inflation, through the development of a new subculture, manifested in music, fashion and attitude. The ability of punk musicians to challenge the boundaries of class culture through a new rhetoric was fundamental to the subculture's success. Subsequently, punk became the most stimulating, exciting and culturally significant music of the 1970s.

For all this, however, punk still assimilated into the mainstream of British culture. The workings of the music industry, punk's antecedents in earlier twentieth century art movements, negative publicity and especially the interpretation by less extreme musicians of what punk meant as culture and as music meant that punk's vague "revolutionary" moment would not last long. Terms like "revolution", "anarchy", "violence" and the like had no definition, and were useful mostly in that they made the average adult squirm. In general, punk was actually most coherent as an attack on the professionalization of music. At first, because of its amateur values and outré presentation, the ability of punks to shock their audiences into recognizing the routines of professional society was a success. Yet the longer trend of professional values dictating British social stratification and culture in the post-war era could not be avoided. Eventually, what it meant to be a part of the punk subculture became common knowledge, and thus its rhetoric dissolved, in the texts of language, business, even musical sound. In

225

other words, punk became a professional music itself, and musicians who made it were required to meet certain standards in the way they talked, dressed and sounded, just like any lawyer or doctor had to meet certain credentials set by the wider public.

As music, punk was an effort to recreate the original rebellious nature of rock and roll. At one time, that rebellion had been manifest in the music's presentation of newer, more egalitarian cultural values, derived from the social frontiers of class, race, and to a lesser extent, gender. As a result, rock music had already done much to upset the language of social stratification, particularly in the 1960s. Punk, however, developed as a musical genre in response to the increasing irrelevance of these cultural categories in the corporate climate of rock music in the 1970s. It reacted especially against the increasing detachment of rock musicians from their audience and social reality.[1] Bands that had once been great rebels against popular convention—the former Beatles, the Rolling Stones, the Who—had become pillars of respectability. Rock stars were now rich and far removed from their audiences. Eric Clapton toured Europe in 1977 in a customized train attached to the Orient Express, while at home, among the readers of the newspapers in which Clapton's tour was publicized, about one in ten adults were out of work.[2] *New Musical Express* correspondent Mick Farren considered this a problem in the opening days of 1976.

> There seems to be a kind of rule emerging that when rock and roll gets wrapped up in too much money, it begins to lose its guts. The kind of insulation that the corporate salesmen wrap around the musician tends to shut him off from the kind of essential street energy that is so vital to the best of rock and roll. . . . We are going through the worst depression since the 'thirties. In global terms, the fear of civil war is probably greater than it was even at the height of '60s paranoia, and in quieter moments I tend to wonder just how long the food, water, air, etc., are going to last. Do we hear any of this reflected in rock and roll? Not often. Most of the time it seems as though all either musician or audience want to deal with is pure escapism.[3]

Malcolm McLaren

Change came through the auspices of a pair of fashion designers with a shop called Sex, at World's End on the King's Road in Chelsea. Malcolm McLaren was an art school student who had been fascinated by the politics of the French Situationist International. The Situationists engineered "situations" designed to provoke an audience into confrontation with itself and society, with all its attendant social repressions. McLaren and his fashion designer girlfriend, Vivienne Westwood, set out to create similar situations in London. At first, they thought the best way to be provocative was by designing outrageous fashions. They were fascinated by the images that had given birth to rock and roll fashion in the

1950s, especially that of the Teddy Boys subculture, with the danger it represented. They also liked fetish gear for the shock it represented on the street. Together they opened a clothing store called Let It Rock that catered to what was left of the Teds, and they even managed to provide clothing for the motion pictures *That'll Be the Day* (1972) and *Mahler* (1973).[4]

On a marketing trip to New York, McLaren and Westwood's clothing attracted the attention of a rock and roll band, the New York Dolls. Seeing an opportunity to put a situation into practice, McLaren became the Dolls' manager. He dressed them in red leather with Soviet flags draped behind them on stage, in an effort to attract intense media attention. But McLaren's efforts were wasted on a band that was rather wasted itself—the Dolls were renowned drug addicts at the end of their careers. McLaren's efforts were a failure, but he did not give up on the idea of managing a rock and roll act. Another interesting figure to him was Richard Hell, a bass player and singer in the band Television, who dressed in torn T-shirts held together with safety pins and had his hair chopped short and spiky. McLaren decided to form a band of his own in Hell's image, an image described in New York music circles as "punk".[5]

Back home in Britain in 1975, many working-class teenagers had a hard time finding their first jobs because of the recession. Eight million people, fifteen percent of Britain's population, were between ages thirteen and twenty-one. Two thirds of them were working-class, and a quarter of their total was on the dole. Many left school early with no qualifications for a job, which only reinforced the hopelessness they felt in the current economic situation. In some places, there was an average of ten school leavers—graduates or otherwise—for every available job. Not surprisingly, then, many teens were gloomy and fatalistic. It seemed there was little hope of a future in 1975 if you were young and working-class, and there was little question that the rock music they listened to did nothing to reflect their plight.[6] Like just about every entertainment medium, rock music was more about escapism than reflection, but to a core group of working-class youth, the economic privations of 1975 demanded that their music reflect their values more exclusively.

From this nexus of music, class, cash and politics, McLaren conceived what he eventually called the "great rock and roll swindle" to exploit these circumstances. By getting a subversive rock band signed to a major label and marketing its subversive songs about cultural revolution, the Situationist message could spread to the widest possible audience. What that revolution would involve was difficult to say—punks and Situationists alike seemed to use the term to describe changes in everything from who topped the pop charts to the overthrow of the monarchy. Regardless, the punk band McLaren wanted to form would propose an alternative social system—youth domination—and alternative politics— "anarchy", another vague term that essentially meant little more than chaos— designed to destroy the very society that produced major record labels. Essentially, a rock and roll band could fool the established order into bringing it into the system, and then its members would violently overthrow it. It was a ridiculously naïve idea, but one which McLaren decided to pursue at home, in London, with a pair of unemployed working-class teenaged musicians who had been hanging around Westwood's shop for several months.[7] Dozens of other bands and musicians would contribute to the definition and redefinition of punk terms over the next three years.

Steve Jones and Paul Cook were in the process of forming a rock and roll band, so McLaren decided to use them to create his image of a pop group. McLaren recruited a shop assistant, Glen Matlock, to play bass, and John Lydon, an impoverished, green-haired Irish teenager, became the lead singer. Lydon took the stage name "Johnny Rotten" in deference to the decayed state of his teeth. McLaren named the band the Sex Pistols, and even renamed Westwood's shop Sex to capitalize on the name. Matlock wrote the music, and Lydon wrote the lyrics he would sing, often assisted with phrases from McLaren, who taught him Situationist slogans to use in the lyrics. He also encouraged Lydon to place his class circumstances in words.[8]

McLaren wanted his new band to fuse avant-garde art with commercial culture. The Sex Pistols accomplished this, and inspired numerous aspiring musicians to do the same. At its popular height, punk rock matched the artistic avant-garde's desire to be revolutionary in the changing of society through art. Like avant-garde artists of the past, punks saw no boundary between art and life, provoked their audiences and felt that spontaneity in performance and a lack of training were assets in artistic production.[9] Amateurism especially inspired the audience, as Subway Sect lead singer Vic Godard noted—"The Pistols don't play great and, as such, a kid in the audience can relate to that . . . he can visualise himself being up there on stage."[10]

Art, Punk and Art Punks

Artistic rebellion, to the punks and many other artists, was social rebellion. Like the Russian futurists, punks espoused ugliness, loved to be offensive and detourned traditional symbols of deviance such as the swastika or fetishist clothing. Punks declared the society around them to be nonsensical, and the performer confronted the audience with this fact, like the Dadaists. Punk was German expressionist in its espousal of sado-masochism and anarchy. The only major differences between punk and avant-garde art movements were the nationality of the ordinary street kids who adhered to such ideals and the medium they chose to express them in.[11]

McLaren's new band was also supposed to be a billboard for Westwood's shop. The Sex Pistols wore ripped T-shirts, safety pins, leather trousers and spiked hair, like Richard Hell, and numerous other bands contributed to punk style too. Most fans learned to do-it-themselves, however, as opposed to buying the expensive styles on display at Sex. Punk fashion became an escape from conventional personalities and roles; it was a measure of authenticity to be completely impossible to copy. In McLaren's cosmology, such resistance to the dictates of commercial influence would destroy the power of commerce from within—"we wanted to create a situation where kids would be less interested in buying records than in speaking for themselves".[12]

Lydon's working-class background provided an agenda too, as did the backgrounds of the dozens of musicians inspired by the Pistols. Critics and fans alike interpreted Johnny Rotten's lyrics as a reaction against the detachment of rock stars from their social backgrounds, but they were also an effort to provide symbolism for Britain's economic recession.[13] Johnny Rotten meant punk to be the voice of working-class youth, calling on them to have fun and rebel against a society that had ignored their interests for too long. Certain buzzwords were particularly useful in declaiming his philosophy, and were coincident with McLaren's ideals. "Anarchy", "pop" and "violence" were a few of the many terms thrown around in opposition to the concepts of "authority", "rock" and "middle-class society", and in support of the notion that Britain was in the midst of a broad political, economic, social and cultural crisis. Such terms shocked the public and the wider rock music audience that had noticed this new musical movement.[14] According to McLaren, punk was supposed to be a return to consciousness of working-class kids, and the vanguard of a new youth movement meant to change the existing society, or at least the pop charts.

> Writing a song like "Anarchy in the UK" is definitely a statement of intent—it's hard to say something constructive in rock these days. It's a call to arms to the kids who believe very strongly that rock and roll was taken away from them. And now it's coming back. "Anarchy in the UK" is a statement of self-rule, of ultimate independence, of do-it-yourself, ultimately.[15]

Yet the connection between punk and the avant-garde also represented the first challenge to the subculture's authenticity. Most of the punk musicians who understood the connections between punk as a subculture and European art movements were art students. They saw the music as a vital new artistic statement on the problems of British society, found in the parallels between the punk lifestyle and the art movements they learned about at their colleges. Meanwhile, working-class street punks saw the music and the rebellion it represented as primarily fun instead of revolutionary. The working-class punk was unemployed because he could not find work, and punk was his angry protest against his lot in life. Art student punks claimed that they understood the capitalist values behind work and that they would not adhere to them—they didn't have jobs because they didn't want jobs.[16]

Both statements shocked public opinion. However, the ability of art students to adopt the mantle of the punk subculture removed the music from its roots in an alleged working-class anger. Of course, there was no chance that McLaren's "revolution", whatever it was, would ever occur through music. But to expose the reality so blatantly divided the punk subculture between its working-class and art school elements.[17] The Sex Pistols were perhaps the greatest punk band because they married these two ideals briefly—the bitter and bilious anger of Johnny Rotten and Steve Jones coupled with the intellectual art school rebellion of Glen Matlock and manager Malcolm McLaren. Other bands, the Clash in particular, understood and espoused these values as well, on stage, on record and in image. So long as the punk subculture presented a united social front in rhetoric and attitude, it could become a force for agitation, and perhaps change.

Much of the rhetoric and attitude that all punks espoused came from reggae, the music of a socially outcast Afro-Caribbean population that also prophesied doom for British society in an era of economic decline. Especially important was reggae's overtones of Rastafarian religion. Rastafarians expected a battle with whites to take place with the fate of the world at stake, after which all victorious black men would return to Africa to live in peace and harmony—and significantly, it would take place in "the year when the two sevens clashed", 1977.[18] Punks adopted Rastafarian rhetoric easily, seeing modern British society as the "Babylon" that Rastas castigated. The punk answer to the Rastafarian assault on Babylon was the espousal of anarchy, a white version of Rastafarian ideology. The safety pins, clips, chains, ripped shirts and the like all represented the damage that a culturally barren professional society had foisted upon their bodies and their lives. By adopting such language, punks could launch their own attacks on the predominant adult establishment culture. The feeling of oppression that blacks felt in a white British society mirrored the sense of oppression that punks felt in a bankrupt society determined to impose its cultural authority on them at all turns. By 1976, with the economy in a shambles, oppression by the white man easily translated into the authoritarian dominance of the cultural establishment.[19]

Punk was a rebellion not just against the rock establishment, but also against the establishment at large. It was clearly the most focused political challenge rock had yet produced; many punk musicians became known for their explicitly left-wing politics. The punk subculture also addressed sexism; young women became heroines of the subculture, as fans and as musicians, and sexual politics was a popular topic in the lyrics of female punks.[20] The punk movement was a major release for women in British pop music. In punk, amateurism was a virtue, and since anybody could be incompetent on an instrument, women who had never learned to play found an opening into the rock world beyond simply singing in front of a bunch of men. Musicians such as Poly Styrene of X-Ray Spex sang songs about body odor, being fat and the pressures on adolescent girls from advertising, television and other media sources. She was a revelation, and she inspired numerous similarly minded girls to follow her lead.

The seventies were a period of political ferment in the UK concerning women's issues, and punk was one of the major beneficiaries in this change in political intent. Abortion laws were relaxed, squatters argued for their right to decent housing, and opposition to racism and sexism was militant. Such issues united men and women, and punk proved to be a useful artistic outlet for such unity.

The Slits were among the top heroines of the punk era, an all-female band influenced by reggae and uninhibited on stage.[21]

Thus, punk was never a respectable working-class movement in the Victorian sense, but rather representative of a new vision of what being working-class meant—to be angry, politically focused and violent in rhetoric. Punks accurately represented the feelings of disenfranchised working-class youth in 1976 and 1977, if they represented them in an extremely radical fashion.[22]

How that radicalism would take effect beyond music was, of course, a very different story. Punks themselves often identified their politics as anarchic, if not socialist. The music's heart was certainly anarchic, especially as seen in the ubiquitous phrase "no future". Its intentions were socialist, as manifested in its constant rhetoric about the failures of the British government and economy to go further in bringing working-class youth and minorities into the system of employment and sociocultural equality. Nevertheless, its practices never went far beyond the rhetorical.[23] Punk was about protest, not change—and since music was its primary medium, perhaps that was enough. As one commentator put it, "[T]ruly punk rebelliousness is ambivalent, symbolic and rather well founded and expressed. It is time that rock became political, as befits a mass art-form; it hardly matters that it[s politics] is also confused."[24]

1976: The Beginning

On stage, the Sex Pistols soon built a reputation as one of the most exciting bands playing the universities and clubs of London. Their alleged frustrations as working-class teenagers were taken out on the audience, and often returned in kind. Whatever McLaren's original intent, he clearly had no control over the artistic statements his band made on stage. "You're all so fucking boring! You make me fucking sick!" Rotten would howl at his audience; they would spit back at him in affirmation.

The music press began to notice the band in February 1976, and the rest of the year saw a series of reviews of the band's gigs marking them as The Great Working Class Rock and Roll Hope. The announcement that "We're not into music—we're into chaos!" in *New Musical Express* was too provocative to miss. The generation gap began to reopen, between parents and older siblings who despised this new music and younger kids, especially working-class kids and art students, who heard the most exciting sound of their young lives. Charles Shaar Murray described the atmosphere at a September gig in Islington.

> [The Sex Pistols] have [an] air of seething just-about-repressed violence . . .
> and watching them gives that same clenched-gut feeling that you get walking
> through Shepherds Bush just after the pubs shut and you see The Lads hanging
> out on the corner looking for some action and you wonder whether the action
> might be you. . . . The Pistols are all those short-haired kids in the big boots

and rolled-up baggies and sleeveless T-shirts. Their music is coming from the straight-out-of-school-and-onto-the-dole deathtrap which we seem to have engineered for Our Young: the '76 British terminal stasis, the modern urban blind alley.[25]

The Sex Pistols inspired imitators, some of whom adhered to their allegedly political agenda, others of whom loved punk for its iconoclasm. The most prominent and talented of them were the Clash, who took their fashion inspiration from Jackson Pollock and the abstract expressionists, and their musical inspiration from the pub rock groups with whom band member Joe Strummer had originally played. The Clash were the most politically committed of the punk bands, featuring songs angrily denouncing the United States, dole queue politics, racism and the apathy of people in opposition to these problems. Managed by an associate of Malcolm McLaren, Bernard Rhodes, they quickly became darlings of the London music critics' set.[26] On the opposite end of the spectrum was the Damned, an entertainingly sloppy band that saw punk mainly as obnoxious fun that irritated their social superiors. They hired their lead singer, Dave Vanian, merely because he looked and dressed like a vampire. They took on pseudonyms like Rat Scabies and Captain Sensible, often wore dresses on stage, and hung dead rats from the drum kit. Their only concession to a socio-political agenda was the often-repeated admission that Ray Burns (Captain Sensible) had once been on the dole.[27]

In an effort to combine forces and present a unified front to the media—to create a situation—McLaren organized the first and only "Punk Rock Festival" at the 100 Club on Oxford Street in late September 1976. It featured the core of punk music for the next year: the Sex Pistols headlined the first night with Subway Sect, Siouxsie and the Banshees and a French band, Stinky Toys, backing them up. The second night featured the Damned with the Vibrators and the Buzzcocks.[28] The different bands represented the range of punk culturally, musically and socially. Subway Sect was among the more avant-garde of the punk bands, representative of the art school end of punk, middle-class pub rockers who caught onto the new sound.[29] Siouxsie and the Banshees were members of the "Bromley Contingent", walking advertisements for Westwood's fashions and McLaren's attitudes. The band played the 100 Club as its first gig, having only learned to play instruments the week before. The band members did a long, cacophonous version of "The Lord's Prayer" set to something approximating music, interspersed with any lyrics Susan Dallion—rechristened Siouxsie Sioux—could remember. They then went home to practice and learn to play properly.[30] The Buzzcocks were a Manchester band, representing the provincial version of punk. Despite a hurricane of powerful chords, the songs of Howard Devoto and Pete Shelley were about love, as traditional a subject as there was in rock and roll. One writer compared Devoto to Samuel Beckett in his obsession with "the absurdity of existence".[31]

The festival brought punk to the nation's attention, as McLaren wanted, but not for the reasons he expected. A young girl lost her eyesight when a glass was smashed during the Damned's set, thrown by one John Beverley, who had just adopted the punk alias Sid Vicious. The incident was highly publicized, and turned most of the public that was paying attention against punk. The subculture became identified as violent, an unfair association but one that lone individuals like Sid Vicious would keep alive through the seventies. Working-class subcultures like the Teddy boys, the mods, the rockers and the skinheads had all been associated with violence, and the music attached to them gained all the more in reputation as a result. Punk proved to be no different.[32]

For the moment, though, the incident at the 100 Club did not keep major and independent record labels from signing punk bands. The Pistols signed with EMI in October 1976, receiving a two-year contract and a £40,000 advance. The Damned signed with a growing independent label, Stiff Records, in November 1976, with records to be distributed by the much larger independent label, Island Records. The Clash signed a record contract with a major American label, CBS. Many fans and sympathetic critics believed that the signing of punk groups to established record labels was a sure disaster. It seemed that the music's original rebellious energy was about to be dissipated in a hurricane of pounds and pence. Small independent labels did not sign any of the most popular punk bands, and the music papers did not fail to notice the idea that money talked just as loudly to the punk bands as it did to any other rock acts of the seventies, regardless of their sociocultural politics.[33]

Thus, punk was presented with a paradox as old as the sixties bands the punks hated. The music was fundamentally anti-commercial in principle, but its bands sought commercial success. To overcome this paradox, punk musicians claimed that they played "pop" music, a term meant to sound ironic. By the mid-1970s, even consistent hit-making acts like Gilbert O'Sullivan or Leo Sayer, without a rough number in their entire catalogues, would sooner be labelled "soft rock" than as "pop" acts, only out to make a pound. By placing a single in the pop charts—EMI printed the Sex Pistols' first single, "Anarchy in the UK" (1976), soon after signing them—the band expected to bring anarchy to the radio airwaves and into the streets too. Pop music, the most prominent cog in the wheel of the corporate music establishment, would become the engine of social and political change, or at least—and more likely—a source of irritation to established cultural sensibilities.

Such was McLaren's intention. He spelled out his philosophy in an interview with the *Daily Mirror*.

Punk is the gross enemy of apathy. The Sex Pistols created a spark of life and energy which has now turned into a forest fire. The everyday lives of the street kids were poverty-stricken garbage—financially and spiritually.

Punk action then turns into an outright frontal attack on the system.

Don't forget this was a generation brought up on distant pop stars who sang about sex and love from their tax havens. . . . Long established stars are fright- ened. We constitute a basic challenge to the whole way the record business is organised.[34]

Yet McLaren was less the revolutionary id, and more the rhetorical ego. He was not the final arbiter of the band's actions on stage or on record—Johnny Rotten held that role. Rotten had little sympathy with McLaren's Situationist objectives, even while he played them out to the letter. He was far more inter- ested in what he considered the traditional working-class joys of rock and roll— rebellion, wildness, shocking the establishment and being paid well to do it. He too outlined his strategies in the *Mirror*.

Do not think I am for violence. . . . [Rather] what we produce is a climate of controlled frenzy. . . . Our songs are anti-God, anti-the Queen, anti-the palsied values of present day society. I am a revolutionary. . . . An anarchist. I want to stir people up to think for themselves. That's all. . . .

Yet all of the excitement of his actions came from being a dirty-toothed Irish kid who might soon be rich and dominate the music world. In the same inter- view, he swore off McLaren's artistic program and admitted that he had exactly the same aspirations as any of his forebears in British rock music.

I am against the whole of the middle-class bit: tellies, cars, possessions. But that don't mean I won't get corrupted by middle-class values too. I've just bought a pad near Chelsea football ground. I gotta live somewhere. I was living in a place with water running down the wall not that long ago. I gotta have a washing machine too. I'm sick of going to the launderette. I've had my teeth fixed. That costs money and was middle class. But I'd knocked the whole bloody lot out one day biting the microphone in a fit of excessive enthusiasm.[35]

The punk project, then, was just as compromised by wealth as that of any previous efforts made by British rock musicians to change their society through music. But at least for a short time longer, punk would have the effect of making an anarchic youth rebellion against society, class and culture seem somewhat real—or at least, real enough to have an impact in British mass culture in 1977 and 1978.

Anarchy, Pop and Violence

After recording "Anarchy in the UK", the Sex Pistols went off on a tour of Eng- land, where the band's stage antics quickly got them banned from nearly every venue they had booked—and also got them into the tabloids. Looking to ride the wave of publicity, EMI managed to get the band a last-minute interview on Thames Television's *Today* show with Bill Grundy on 1 December. Obviously disgusted with the band's appearance and attitude, Grundy prodded the Pistols with provocative and occasionally insulting remarks. Finally, Steve Jones used the word "fuck" while castigating Grundy for making a sexual innuendo toward Siouxsie Sioux, who had joined the Pistols in the studio. The Sex Pistols thus became the top story in the nation's tabloids for 2 December 1976. Newspaper reports described men kicking in television sets, elderly women having strokes, and children repeating dirty words they had heard on television the other night.[36] Thames TV suspended Grundy. The other voice of the working classes expressed itself when staff at EMI's pressing plant refused to press any more copies of "Anarchy in the UK" as it climbed the national charts. The Transport and General Workers' Union had meetings with EMI to ask them to drop the band. Bournemouth, Preston, Lancaster and Newcastle scrapped local concert bookings. Soon after the interview, ITV postponed the airing of a documentary series on teenaged violence, fearing that "violence was being made attractive and glamorous"—as if the Pistols had beaten Grundy with clubs. The BBC imposed a blanket television ban on the Pistols, the director of variety programming claiming, "People do not want to see such things."[37] Punk had become a cultural phenomenon literally overnight.

At first EMI sprang to the Pistols' defence. The managing director of EMI, Leslie Hill, agreed with a number of people who believed that Grundy had egged the Pistols on to prove his point about these "foul-mouthed bunch of yobs", as he termed them.[38] But the development of the Pistols' second single proved too much for the company. "God Save the Queen" (1977) was the band's response to the Queen's upcoming Jubilee, a mockery of everything the monarchy stood for. After issuing a warning, chairman Sir John Read decided that the offences the group caused were too outrageous. The record company cancelled the Pistols' contract in January 1977 and allowed them to keep the £40,000 advance.[39]

Numerous record companies lined up to sign the Pistols. Finally, they landed with A&M Records, who had the band members sign their contracts outside Buckingham Palace in March 1977, as if the company sympathized with the band's cultural project. However, A&M were a middle-of-the-road corporation, founded by jazz bandleader Herb Alpert to produce and market safe, family-oriented acts. The effort to sign the Pistols was probably an effort to improve the company's image with younger record buyers, but it was an effort doomed to a short life. The press reception following the signing degenerated into a hailstorm of abuse and squabbles between the band and record company representatives. Within a week, A&M dropped the Pistols as well, and the group left with another free advance of £75,000, without recording a single thing for A&M.[40] By March 1977 the band had recorded one song, made a free £115,000 from two multinational record companies and the tabloids believed the Pistols were heralds of the coming youth armageddon. So far, McLaren's Situationist project looked to have some merit.

The fact that the Pistols had not disappeared was an irritation to media critics. As the *Daily Express* noted of the signing bonus the band received from
A&M, "The little beasts have gone from strength to strength".[41] The *Mirror*
called for readers to send them jokes about the punks, claiming: "The prize for
the best jokes will be a Sex Pistol record. The worst ones will win TWO Sex
Pistol records."[42] The *Evening Standard* printed a definition of "punk" from
Partridge's Dictionary of Slang—"Worthless, decidedly inferior, displeasing,
rotten."[43] The public clearly responded to this sentiment too. When Bill Grundy
was suspended by Thames Television for his on-screen antics with the Pistols,
many people wrote letters to the *Mirror* applauding Grundy for showing up the
Pistols as best he could, and for bringing parents to see the dangers of punk rock
for their children.[44]

Suddenly punk was everywhere, the most frightening subculture to arise
since rock and roll had shown up in Britain. Punks were categorized as dole-
queue kids, bored and frustrated. They took out their aggressions on their guitars, on themselves and on their audiences. Captain Sensible of the Damned and
Johnny Rotten were the exemplars of the movement, both renowned for harangu-
ing their audiences and accepting limitless abuse in return. It seemed but a matter
of time until they turned on the respectable public as well. The mother of Dee
Generate, the fifteen-year-old drummer of Eater, was quoted as saying "I can see
what they're trying to do", making herself the archetype of poor parenting
throughout the land. Above all, the bands horrified the average consumer, which
was exactly what an agitator like McLaren wanted. A select few took the punk
call for anarchy very seriously. One *Melody Maker* reader saw the punks as a
fifth column for the coming Red Chinese invasion.

> Has anybody really asked themselves honestly what these punks are part and
> parcel of? . . . With the gradual infiltration of Trotskyites and left-wingers of all
> sorts into our Labour Party, bands of the Sex Pistols' ilk are all very welcome.
> After all, what better creation in existence is designed to bring about the normal
> downfall of the teenage warriors of England than the Sex Pistols at the mo-
> ment?
>
> . . . [The] Utopia of Pistolery seems to be one of anarchic bliss, but of course
> it's little more than a false euphoria cunningly set up by subversives. Of course
> "they" want youth to revolt and smash the hated so-called capitalistic dogs, as
> they are termed. They want all our traditions broken, our democracy toppled.
>
> Of course, when the majority of our revolutionary youth are all in the phony
> state of advanced karma lolling on their psychiatric couches, copulating in the
> streets, pumping themselves with as much dope as they can lay their hands on,
> and anarchy is in its prime, the little yellow men from the East will cross the
> English Channel and with outstretched fingers push us all over.
>
> I wonder what sort of music they'll be playing then?[45]

Such responses seemed ridiculous both then and now, but the punk message of anarchy, pop and violence occasionally seemed very literal due to the few incidents where anarchy and violence became explicit. In February 1977, the Sex Pistols' bass player, Glen Matlock—the group's major songwriter and most talented musician—left the band. His replacement was John Beverley, aka Sid Vicious, the Sex Pistols' most visible and outrageous fan. Vicious was inclined to mindless aggression, directed against himself and other people. He had thrown the shattered glass that put a girl's eye out at the 100 Club festival, and he assaulted members of the press at other Sex Pistols gigs. He mutilated himself on a regular basis, cutting his body with glass and looking to get into fights where he would come away bruised and battered.[46]

There was always plenty of aggression at punk concerts. Audience members bounced around doing a dance called the "pogo", slamming into one another and the band, with both sides spitting on each other copiously. Thus far, it had been confined to the concert hall, and to punks themselves, and rarely did anyone get hurt. In the person of Sid Vicious, the punk subculture made what had been implicit violence explicit, random and often frightening. Universally acknowledged by friends as an intelligent person, Vicious clearly cared only about the opportunity to vent his own aggressions and the excesses that a rock star's life afforded him, aggressions and excesses that other punks were trying to expose as evil, bloated and hedonistic. Vicious was a prime example of the ability for anyone to find anything they wanted in the punk subculture. "Anarchy", "pop" and "violence" were useful in scaring up a reaction from a complacent music audience, but when interpreted on the street or in the studio, the results were at first dangerous, then debilitating for the subculture.

Also problematic was the flaunting of swastikas in punk fashion. Most punks were interested in the swastika as a symbol, as an image that retained its ability to alarm people. They would go to great lengths to state that they did not adhere to the ideas behind the swastika; wearing swastikas was a way of upsetting the sensibilities of the average person on the street, to wake them up to more recent and more real horrors of an affluent society gone awry. Nevertheless, at a time of high youth unemployment comparable to the 1930s, and the resurgence in popularity of the National Front, the swastika could not help but be taken as a statement of punk political principles. It did not help that a few punks used the swastika specifically to terrify people into believing they were Nazis, merely for a laugh. Sid Vicious was the worst offender, as he strolled through a Jewish neighbourhood in Paris while wearing a swastika T-shirt in the film *The Great Rock and Roll Swindle* (1978). Punks used Nazi imagery because it brought attention to social problems, but no punk knew how to handle the righteous backlash such imagery elicited from people.[47] There clearly came a point at which the detournment of texts in the punk project went too far.

The dangers of such symbolism became manifest with the revival of the skinheads. Skinheads wanted to reassert "traditional" working-class values in

British culture, as they read them. To many skinheads—and by no means all—resorting to violence against other races was a conscious political act, and even worse, their embracing of the National Front and the British Movement gave their politics a violent coherence that the punks did not have. They identified what they thought were "deviant" groups among the British working classes—Asians, hippies, homosexuals—and targeted them for abuse, in what they saw as an effort to preserve their sense of community and their traditions.[48] The worst assertion of racist skinheads was the mistaken notion that violence was a working-class virtue and a working-class reality, and not the rhetorical instrument of the punks.

In general, punks were anti-racist. The founding of Rock Against Racism became a central unifying factor bringing art students and street kids together in large outdoor concerts to declare their opposition to problems of racism in Britain.[49] Nevertheless, the swastika as a symbol did all the damage necessary to the reputation of punks, damage that the wider public had been looking for in the subculture since it had become well known publicly.

Chaos and Commerce

In spring 1977, the Sex Pistols signed with Virgin Records to record the band's first album. The single "God Save the Queen" protested the Queen's Jubilee celebration, and it reached the number two spot in the singles chart in June 1977—with virtually no airplay, since the BBC and most of the independent radio stations banned the record. According to Virgin Records, the song actually reached number one, but was kept out of the top spot to avoid embarrassing Queen Elizabeth. Their third single "Pretty Vacant" (1977) became a top ten hit in July, and their album, *Never Mind the Bollocks, Here's the Sex Pistols* was released in October 1977 and sold well.[50]

However, by the middle of 1977, the band was coming apart. Rotten did not want to pursue McLaren's idea of doing a movie about the band [later released as *The Great Rock and Roll Swindle* (1978)]. Hoodlums assaulted the band on stage in Stockholm, egged on by Vicious. Clubs shut down when the Pistols were scheduled to play at them.[51] And without Matlock to write for the band, it had lost its creative energy.

Other punk acts likewise saw their unity fragment. An intense rivalry had grown between the various groups, spawned by managerial one-upmanship, provincial prejudices and the growing divide between art school students and working-class punks. A punk tour in 1977, the White Riot Tour, broke down quickly. The police harassed the headliners, the Clash, at many stops. The Jam, a second line act at the time, left the tour halfway through to promote its first album. Beyond the tours, bands like the Pistols and the Clash derided acts like the

Damned for lacking any political intent in their music, and the Buzzcocks and other provincial acts were considered outsiders by the London mainstream.[52]

The punk subculture these bands represented, however, grew in energy throughout 1977, particularly in the way of new enterprises beyond the making of music. If punk was mainly a rhetorical exercise in the transformation of social stratification, there were many efforts to start alternative businesses to cater to the potential reality behind the rhetoric. For example, hundreds of independent record labels were set up to press and promote punk records and preserve punk values. Stiff Records was one of the great success stories of the punk era, despite its reputation for promoting the label itself over its own artists. Between Stiff's founding in 1976 and its eventual demise, the label released 200 singles and saw almost 50 of them reach the UK charts, an outrageously successful percentage that was four times the rate of the majors at the time.[53] Independent labels became the life's blood of punk music. The creation of an alternative music production system and an alternative music industry highlighted the opposition between art and the standard practices of corporate capitalism.[54] As one of the co-founders of Stiff, Jake Riviera, put it: "For far too long, there has been a gap between the million quid advance and scuffling about in a cellar. There has to be a middle ground. I believe Stiff is it."[55]

Likewise, thousands of punk fans started alternative music magazines, disgusted with the lack of coverage of their favourite bands in the censored national press. A fan named Mark Perry started the most famous punk magazine, titled *Sniffin' Glue*. He took on the pseudonym Mark P. so he would not have to answer to the authorities about the profits he made off the magazine, since Perry was on the dole. John Sage, a London law student, produced a magazine called *London's Outrage. London's Outrage* focused on the dangers of punk and the punk lifestyle, in a climate of hostility. Fanzines captured the nature of punk and its adherents in Britain. They were generally rough and crudely produced, and pitched at young working-class kids as opposed to art school students. They emphasised community, especially in the fans' oneness with musicians who usually could not play instruments any better than they could, and were self-effacing as a result. Fanzines only enhanced the punk reader's sense that it was "us vs. them", and the constant attack on punk by the mainstream media contributed to this attitude as well.[56]

New Wave

By the time of the Jubilee in 1977, however, punk music was fast becoming the sound of the moment. Any number of acts began to change their songs, their fashion style and their attitudes to try to catch on to the wave and capture an audience, not to mention a record deal. In the process, punk was interpreted and reinterpreted by dozens of new musicians and new fans, and could not help but become a more acceptable music to a wider public. Journalists and musicians gave this reinterpretation a new name, "new wave", the most prominent rhetorical term used to defuse the radical elements in punk music.

Few people had ever been happy with the term "punk", which had once been the term used to refer to a pubescent male prostitute. As an adjective to convey decay, disease, and worthlessness, it seemed more appropriate, but it lacked political intent.[57] "Dole queue" was preferred, but as bands became popular and wealthy, the term lost its meaning. Furthermore, too many punk band musicians were the same art students who had driven British rock music from its beginnings, and their motivations did not come from the frustrations inherent in the dole queue. Therefore, "new wave" described bands that were classless, artless, thrashed their guitars and professed a hatred for the Rolling Stones.

Furthermore, as opposed to the punk acts, the best "new wave" acts were all singles chart mainstays of 1977. For all their tabloid publicity in 1976 and 1977, the punk bands had not captured the majority of people's ears. The "Turkey of the Year" band in *New Musical Express*'s Readers Poll of 1976 was the Sex Pistols. The winners of *Melody Maker*'s Readers Poll Awards in late September 1976 were Yes, Genesis, Kiki Dee, Thin Lizzy, Rick Wakeman and Mike Oldfield, not a punk in the bunch. Punk was never dominant on the British popular charts at any point. Numerous singles did make a large splash, but at no time was the music popular enough to drive Wings, ABBA, or any number of disco or easy listening acts off the charts. The real popular phenomenon of 1976 was the Bay City Rollers, whose tours of Britain inspired scenes of Beatles and Stones-like frenzy on the part of teenaged girls on both continents. At the end of 1977, neither the Pistols, the Clash, nor the Damned made a single dent in the *Daily Mirror*'s readers' poll of the top performers of the year. Not one of the year's best selling singles was by an identified punk band. Their albums sold better; the Pistols' *Never Mind the Bollocks, Here's the Sex Pistols* (1977) made number twelve in the list of the year's best-selling albums, but no other punk act's debut album made a similar showing.[58]

New wave, in contrast, was the sophisticated alternative to punk, a professional version of punk with which adolescents of all social persuasions could identify. It took punk challenges to middle-class politics, gender and sexuality, and made them seem glamorous in a way that punks never intended them to be. Though bands like the Jam positively seethed with political intent, they were far less controversial than their punk predecessors, and thus easier on the consciences of major music critics. Critics in general had never responded to the Sex Pistols' baiting of the establishment, though a select few celebrated the band in print. However, there was almost universal approval of "new wave", one critic calling it "the healthiest event in popular music this decade".[59] By 1977, music critics were able to separate all versions of this new pop music from the social implications involved in its creation. They also began to distinguish between the more "respectable", experimental, art school elements in the punk and new wave movements, and the working-class rebels whom they eventually came to ignore.[60] Without massive chart successes, such detachment did not bode well for the continued impact of punk on the consciousness of British society.

The Jam was the paradigm for new wave acts arriving in the wake of punk. The band members revamped the old Mod look and sound of the early sixties, exemplified by the Who. The Jam was also overtly political. Paul Weller, the band's front man and songwriter, had spent his earliest years in Woking in a council house with no hot water and no indoor bathroom. His songs about working-class life were about anger and repression, and he clearly thought of his band's espousal of mod values as original and in congruence with punk ideals. However, the Jam was unwilling to slay the influences that had built the music, a crucial element in being a punk band. If punks had no future socially, they were also supposed to have no past musically. Mod was similar to punk, but it was not the same, whatever Weller's values. The Jam, a truly terrific and politically committed act, was still a step away from punk rebellion and into new wave respectability.[61] Their retro sound and values placed them squarely in the professional tradition—you had to know and master the mod sound to make it acceptable to a new pop audience. The Jam thus represented a death knell for punk's efforts to make a revolutionary sociocultural impact on British life.

Other acts added to the sense that new wave was classless and professionalized. Elvis Costello had all the anger and cynicism of British punks with an added measure of literacy to boot. He was lumped in with the punk movement with the release of his debut album, *My Aim is True* (1977). Still, he lacked the anarchic nature of the Damned or the Sex Pistols. His next effort, the album *This Year's Model* (1978), included the brilliantly dangerous song "Radio Radio", a scathing attack on the broadcasting establishment in Britain and its efforts to shape the public taste.[62]

The Stranglers were fast lumped in with other punk acts by the press when the band signed a record contract in December 1976, just days after the Pistols had appeared on the *Today* show. The band's attitude at gigs seemed to back up that assessment.

> The Stranglers get up onstage at the Marquee and rant about its obsolescence and tell the audience to smash the place up after the gig. . . . [They] see the Marquee as a major stanchion of the system which they reckon has repressed their talent. Like most of their punk/dole-queue/new-wave rock cohorts, they are martyrs and rebels.[63]

Yet the Stranglers were really a pub rock act, and Hugh Cornwell's misogynistic lyrics set the band apart from the rest of the punk acts. Yet such outrageous lyrical attitudes gave the band a certain pre-eminence as rebels, and they had a tough sound honed in the bars of London. It served them well enough on the pop charts throughout 1977 and 1978.[64]

"Ever Get the Feeling You've Been Cheated?"

In January 1978, the Sex Pistols crossed the Atlantic to play an American tour. Punk was returning from Britain to the place where it had begun, now under an entirely different guise. The social and cultural circumstances that inspired its beginnings and its intents now lent London punk an aura of authority in comparison to its New York predecessor. In New York, punk was born of affluent boredom; in London, punk sprang from truly desperate economic circumstances. Both saw rock and roll, a musical genre that should have been reflective of the self-expression necessary to voice such emotions, as artistically bankrupt.[65] In London, though, the subculture had a much truer social resonance. As one New York journalist noted, "the discontented over here are PhDs who can't find jobs."[66]

The Sex Pistols were booked into as many country and western clubs as McLaren could find in the American South, for maximum offensiveness. The band played Atlanta, Memphis and Baton Rouge in succession, but the reaction was less than expected; a Memphis police lieutenant tagged them as "run of the mill" in terms of the crowd reaction.[67] The British working-class youth revolution was less than exportable in a country where class was less of an issue. Vicious spent most of the tour covered in blood from his continually battered nose and cut body. Rotten and Vicious finally left the band after the last date in San Francisco; McLaren took Cook and Jones to South America to record some songs with Ronnie Biggs, the escaped Great Train Robber. The entire Sex Pistols enterprise, once truly rebellious and frightening in its intensely accurate commentary on England's decline, descended into farce. Rotten went on to form a new band, Public Image Limited. Vicious murdered his girlfriend in New York and died while out on bail of a heroin overdose. McLaren went on to record albums of his own, detourning world music and opera.

Eventually, all of the actors in the last great rock and roll cultural rebellion were professionalized and brought to heel. Punk turned out to be the greatest subculture, the one that lasted the longest without being entirely assimilated into the mainstream of British youth culture. But its music had been recodified as new wave, which dominated the pop charts in Britain in 1978 and beyond. Especially critical was the return of ska to British clubs, played by both white and black musicians and combining punk and reggae in both attitude and raucousness. Fashion designers mainstreamed punk fashions, and Vivienne Westwood became a lasting celebrity and innovator in British fashion circles. By 1978, the punk look was essentially uniform—spiky hair, jeans or bondage trousers, leather jackets with slogans on them, T-shirts, studs and chains. A punk in London was no more a standout by the 1980s than a mod, a Ted or a skinhead.[68] They also made great fodder for postcard photographers looking to make a killing in the tourist trade.

Some new wave bands in the late seventies began to emphasise the use of the synthesizer too. The synthesizer was the perfect punk instrument: a musician did not have to know how to play an instrument at all, yet he could press a key and sound like a complete orchestra. It cost approximately the same amount of money to buy as an electric guitar, and you could get innumerably more sound effects to work with on a synthesiser, without years of painstaking practice (or weeks, as the case might be).[69] However, the sound was infinitely less harsh and abusive, and thus abandoned the sound by which punk had been proselytized. The synthesizer was the ultimate way for kids of all social persuasions to get into music as well, and thus effectively killed the punk subculture's spirit in Britain.

By 1982, five years after the original punk heyday, the old punk idols—Siouxsie Sioux, the Clash, Johnny Rotten and the like—were now rock's biggest stars, the new "aristocracy of rock". They had achieved respectability, and now they wanted to keep it. Younger bands considered some of the older punks their heroes (particularly John Lydon in Public Image, LTD), but most of the old punks now seemed hypocritical. Punk was just another recycled idea, exploited by the rock and pop music business machine.[70]

Conclusion

Another poll, this one even further removed in time from the punk era. In March 2011, the *Independent on Sunday* dedicated an issue to the changing conception of class in Britain. Using a newer polling group called BritainThinks and asking polling groups to answer more specific questions, the issue noted that seven out of ten Britons now consider themselves middle class. People defined their social status first by their education level, then their parents' background, then the nature of their job before they then defined it in terms of income.[1]

The poll seems to show that the British people have caught up with the decline of industrialism in their nation. Yet it also reinforces some other conceptions about the nature of how they define their society. For one thing, class is still relevant. Many an academic has rightfully contended that class is outmoded and that there's a need to repackage social relationships in western societies—none have come up yet with an acceptable definition for the average public, particularly to the writers of newspapers like *The Independent* that might popularize such ideas. Furthermore, readers of *The Independent* now define class in mostly cultural terms—when asked to provide an object from their homes that symbolized their class status, the most popular item people came with was a French coffee press. "[O]ther objects included a book about Mozart, theatre tickets, a Kindle e-reader, an expensive bottle of brandy, a box of specialty teas, a Cath Kidston bottle warmer and a ski hat"—not a paystub or tax return in the bunch.[2] On the other hand, there weren't any CDs by the Beatles, Yes, Elton John or the Clash, either. It is certain, if such groups aren't exactly prominent on British radio any longer, that they no longer represent an alleged version of working-class values more than three decades after their popular relevance in British culture. In fact, they likely don't represent much in terms of class distinctions at all;

at best they are retro-chic, at worst they are musical dinosaurs who reveal the fossilized cultural tastes of one's parents, and even grandparents.

Much has changed in British culture since the period this book covers. Thatcherism divided much of the rock and pop music community from the real political gravity of the country, the same way it attacked the unity of the working classes and their unions. The result was the exposure of the irrelevance of music as a mode of rebellion against the establishment: when the mode of the music changed, only the discos in the city shook. New wave was an exciting change in rock music, but despite the commitment of musicians like Paul Weller, Billy Bragg or Jimmy Sommerville, its power to move people to take social and political change seriously was nonexistent—and more importantly, it appeared to be nonexistent, as nonexistent as that of the sixties counterculture and its favorite artists.

As the nineties began, British rock music even gained a classless sheen as the pop culture world indulged itself in the brilliance of "cool Britannia", a second wave of cultural production equal to the first in the sixties and seventies. That was not to say that groups like Oasis, Blur, or Pulp did not address cultural and social distinctions in British society. However, their origins, their messages, their dress and their politics counted less than the music itself to the reading public; what mattered about "cool Britannia" was the profits it made. People now recognized culture as an industry, and as an export, and rock music was again at its forefront. Now, however, the seemingly dangerous social barrier of class did not provide a straw fortress to assault in the effort to gain headlines. When social commentators among "the establishment" had grown up in a postpunk era, no one was impressed with the cheeky quality of Pulp's "Common People", so much as they shook their heads knowingly at the stereotypes it pilloried.

What to say, then, of the sixties and seventies, of a time when it was still possible to shock the adult British public into thinking that its values were under fire? It's a long time ago, to begin with. It was also an exciting time to be alive, and to be a fan of rock music and musicians in Britain. Who today would not miss the joy of having to hide an album under your arm when you walked into the house for fear your mother would see it, and tell you that the values it represented were unacceptable under your roof? Never mind that those values might be invented, hypocritical or even cynical. playing them on your turntable connected you to a generation of young people in Britain across all social boundaries, and made you a rebel.

Yesterday's rebels are today's establishment. It's harder to shock today's cultural establishment when people like Julie Burchill are writing for *The Independent*. Perhaps the point is that that is a good thing. Britain is a better place today for having chosen a forum, rock music, in which to address its industrial divisions and provide a language with which to overcome them. Of course, those divisions still exist—riots in British cities in 2011 lend to the idea that issues of race have gone too long ignored, and Britain is more like the United States than its own politicians might care to admit. But at least it seems possible to talk about them through cultural media like music, should British young people so decide—whether such will raise their parents' eyebrows in the future, none can say for sure.

Notes

Introduction

1. "Most Britons are working-class and proud of it", *Guardian*, 21 August 2002.
2. Steve Winwood, "Down Home with Mr. Fantasy", interview by Steve Peacock, *Sounds,* 4 August 1973, 7.

1   Society, Culture and Music in Britain Before 1963

1. Georgina Boyes, *The Imagined Village: Culture, Ideology and the English Folk Revival* (Manchester: Manchester University Press, 1993), 7e, 29-32.
2. Ian Watson, *Song and Democratic Culture in Britain: An Approach to Popular Culture in Social Movements* (New York: St. Martin's Press, 1983), 30-35.
3. Boyes, *The Imagined Village*, 41-85.
4. Dave Russell, *Popular Music in England, 1840-1914* (New York: Manchester University Press, 1997), 79-80.
5. Russell, *Popular Music in England*, 19-21; Peter Bailey, *Leisure and Class in Victorian England: Rational Recreation and the Contest for Control, 1830-1885* (London: Routledge and Kegan Paul, 1978), 147-157; Andrew Blake, *The Land Without Music: Music, Culture and Society in Twentieth Century Britain* (New York: Manchester University Press, 1997), 79-86; James Walvin, *Leisure and Society 1830-1950* (New York: Longman Books, 1978), 111-112.
6. Russell, *Popular Music in England*, 83-86.
7. D. L. LeMahieu, *A Culture for Democracy: Mass Communication and the Cultivated Mind Between the Wars* (Oxford: Clarendon Press, 1988), 1-17.

8. Walvin, *Leisure and Society*, 134-137; Simon Frith, *Sound Effects: Youth, Leisure and the Politics of Rock and Roll* (New York: Pantheon Books, 1981), 46; Jonathan Rose, *The Intellectual Life of the British Working Classes* (New Haven, CT: Yale University Press, 2001), 361.

9. Walvin, *Leisure and Society*, 137-139; Simon Frith, *Music for Pleasure: Essays in the Sociology of Pop* (New York: Routledge and Kegan Paul, 1988), 25-26.

10. Frith, *Music for Pleasure*, 30-34.

11. Asa Briggs, *The BBC: The First Fifty Years* (Oxford: Oxford University Press, 1985), 61, 150.

12. Frith, *Music for Pleasure*, 36-38.

13. Briggs, *The BBC*, 187, 247.

14. Frith, *Sound Effects*, 191-192; Robert Wohl, *The Generation of 1914* (Cambridge, MA: Harvard University Press, 1979), 105, 109-121.

15. David Fowler, *The First Teenagers: The Lifestyle of Young Wage-earners in Interwar Britain* (London: Woburn Press, 1995), 7-12.

16. John Davis, *Youth and the Condition of Britain: Images of Adolescent Conflict* (Atlantic Highlands, NJ: Athlone Press, 1990), 67-79.

17. Bill Osgerby, *Youth in Britain since 1945* (Oxford: Basil Blackwell, 1998), 30-50; Fowler, *The First Teenagers*, 102-105, 124-128.

18. Frith, *Sound Effects*, 185.

19. Michael Brake, *Comparative Youth Culture: The Sociology of Youth Culture and Youth Subcultures in America, Britain and Canada* (London: Routledge and Kegan Paul, 1985), 30-31; Davis, *Youth and the Condition of Britain*, 100; Dick Bradley, *Understanding Rock 'n' Roll: Popular Music in Britain 1955-1964* (Philadelphia: Open University Press, 1992), 84, 86-88; Frith, *Sound Effects*, 186.

20. Osgerby, *Youth in Britain since 1945*, 2-3.

21. Daren Garratt, "Youth Cultures and Sub-Cultures", in *Youth and Society: Contemporary Theory, Policy and Practice,* eds. Jeremy Roche, Stanley Tucker, Rachel Thomson and Ronny Flynn (London: Sage Publications, 2004), 148.

22. Bradley, *Understanding Rock and Roll*, 80-81; Meredith Veldman, *Fantasy, the Bomb and the Greening of Britain: Romantic Protest, 1945-1980* (New York: Cambridge University Press, 1994), 4-6.

23. Andrew Blake, "Americanisation and Popular Music in Britain", in *Issues in Americanisation and Culture*, eds. Neil Campbell, Jude Davies and George McKay (Edinburgh: Edinburgh University Press, 2004), 151; Bradley, *Understanding Rock and Roll*, 107, 116-120.

24. Bradley, *Understanding Rock and Roll*, 12-16.

25. Blake, *The Land Without Music*, 76.

26. Davis, *Youth and the Condition of Britain*, 118-129.

27. Frith, *Sound Effects*, 189-190.

28. Garratt, "Youth Cultures and Sub-Cultures", 145; Dick Hebdige, *Subculture: The Meaning of Style* (London: Methuen and Co., 1979), 17-19.

29. Brake, *Comparative Youth Culture*, 60-64; Bradley, *Understanding Rock and Roll*, 95-100.

30. Hebdige, *Subculture*, 50-51; Frith, *Sound Effects*, 184; Geoff Mungham and Geoff Pearson, "Introduction", in *Working-class Youth Culture*, eds. Geoff Mungham and

Geoff Pearson (London: Routledge and Kegan Paul, 1976), 5; Brake, *Comparative Youth Culture*, 73-74; Davis, *Youth and the Condition of Britain*, 129-141.

31. Ian J. Knight, "Generation Landslide", *The History of Rock* 6, no. 70 (1983): 1384; Bradley, *Understanding Rock and Roll*, 86; Frith, *Sound Effects*, 187.

32. Knight, "Generation Landslide", 1384; Davis, *Youth and the Condition of Britain*, 142-165.

33. Christopher Booker, *The Neophiliacs: A Study in the Revolution in English Life in the Fifties and Sixties* (London: Collins, 1968), 37; Linda Martin and Kerry Segrave, *Anti-Rock: The Opposition to Rock 'n' Roll* (Hamden CT: Archon Books, 1988), 32-38.

34. Bradley, *Understanding Rock and Roll*, 64-71.

35. Bradley, *Understanding Rock and Roll*, 60-61.

36. Lonnie Donegan, "As 3-chord Lonnie scores again ...", interview by Adrian Mitchell, *Daily Mail,* 11 April 1963, 14; Dave Laing, "Rock Around the Maypole", *The History of Rock* 7, no. 74 (1983): 1461.

37. Ian Anderson, "Blue Britannia", *Folk Roots* 7, no. 11 (1986): 23-25, 35.

38. Karl Dallas, "Lonnie Donegan and Skiffle", *The History of Rock* 1, no. 7 (1982): 125-127.

39. Bradley, *Understanding Rock and Roll*, 62-63.

40. Colin Irwin, "English Folk Revival: The Early Years 1957-1961", *Southern Rag* 5, no. 3 (1984): 25.

41. Dave Laing, "Roll Over Lonnie (Tell George Formby the News)", in *The Beat Goes On: The Rock File Reader*, eds. Charlie Gillett and Simon Frith (London: Pluto Press, 1996), 11-12; Frith, *Sound Effects*, 96.

42. Rob Finnis, "The Bermondsey Backbeat", *The History of Rock* 1, no. 7 (1982): 130-131.

43. Rob Finnis, "The Elvis Followers", *The History of Rock* 1, no. 7 (1982): 135-136.

44. Ashley Brown, "The U.K. Rocks", *The History of Rock* 1, no. 7 (1982): 122.

45. Rob Finnis, "Gee Whizz It's Cliff", *The History of Rock* 2, no. 19 (1982): 365-366.

46. Finnis, "Gee Whizz It's Cliff", 367-368.

47. Cliff Richard, "Cliff Richard: He's Happy, Healthy and Still Nearly Famous", interview by Jeff Tamarkin, *Goldmine,* no. 61 (June 1981): 20-21; Colin Shearman, "Rock on TV", *The History of Rock* 4, no. 43 (1982): 850.

48. Cliff Richard, "Me and My Code of Living", interview by Kenneth Allsop, *Daily Mail,* 5 January 1963, 6.

49. Shearman, "Rock on TV", 850.

50. Adrian Mitchell, "Cliff Outpops Elvis", *Daily Mail*, 22 March 1963, 20.

51. Bradley, *Understanding Rock and Roll*, 89; Chris Hutchins, "Yanks Dominate British Jazz", *Billboard*, 12 October 1963, 33; Greg Shaw, "Sounds, Worldwide", *The History of Rock* 2, no. 20 (1982): 393; Don Wedge, "Establishment Not Easy to Enter", *Billboard*, 22 December 1962, 29-30.

52. Bradley, *Understanding Rock and Roll*, 72-79.

2   The Beatles

1. Watson, *Song and Democratic Culture in Britain*, 45-62; Ian Inglis, "Men of Ideas? Popular Music, Anti-Intellectualism and the Beatles", in *The Beatles, Popular*

Music and Society: A Thousand Voices, ed. Ian Inglis (New York: St. Martin's Press, 2000), 4-5.

2. Kenneth Hudson, *The Language of the Teenage Revolution: The Dictionary Defeated* (London: Macmillan Press, 1983), 46-50.

3. Robert Pattison, *The Triumph of Vulgarity: Rock Music in the Mirror of Romanticism* (New York: Oxford University Press, 1987), 82.

4. Dave Marsh and James Bernard, *The Book of Rock Lists* (New York: Fireside Press, 1994), 20.

5. Sara Cohen, *Rock Culture in Liverpool: Popular Music in the Making* (Oxford: Clarendon Press, 1991), 9-17; Bill Harry, "Why Liverpool?" *The History of Rock* 3, no. 27 (1982): 522.

6. Liverpool musician, *The Mersey Sound*, BBC-TV, December 1963.

7. Briggs, *The BBC*, 342.

8. Adrian Mitchell, "Crawling Up—The Beatles with a Fierce New Noise", *Daily Mail*, 1 February 1963, 10. Mitchell was unimpressed by their first efforts; he characterized "Please Please Me" as "a record which is almost incoherent except for its solid, battering beat." Obviously, the accolades would have to come later.

9. Harry, "Why Liverpool?" 522-523.

10. Chris Roberts, "The Beat Boys!" *Melody Maker*, 23 March 1963, 8-9.

11. Pete Best, "Pete Best: A Beatle Talks", interview by Jeff Tamarkin, *Goldmine*, no. 76 (September 1982): 6-8.

12. Bill Harry, *The Mersey Sound*, BBC-TV, December 1963.

13. Maureen Cleave, "Disc Date", *Evening Standard*, 12 June 1965, 5.

14. Chris Roberts, "If you want to get ahead—get an accent", *Melody Maker*, 29 June 1963, 8-9.

15. Watson, *Song and Democratic Culture in Britain*, 45-62.

16. Martin and Segrave, *Anti-Rock*, 130-131; Philip Norman, *SHOUT! The Beatles in Their Generation* (New York: Fireside Books, 1981), 187-188; Mike Gross, "Beatles' Net Shows Fans' Love", *Billboard*, 12 September 1964, 3.

17. George Harrison, "George Talking", interview by Kenneth Passingham, *Daily Sketch*, 22 October 1963, 16.

18. Dixon Scott, "Beatlemania: Why It Makes You Tick", *Daily Mirror*, 6 November 1963, 6.

19. "A Doctor Tries to Answer: What Makes the Screamers Scream?" *Melody Maker*, 25 September 1965, 10; Letters, *Melody Maker*, 9 October 1965, 16; Nat Hentoff, "Still Trying to Explain Beatles", *New Musical Express*, 6 March 1964, 12.

20. Herman, "The Press Gang", 1335.

21. Peter Chippindale and Chris Horrie, *Stick It Up Your Punter! The Uncut Story of the Sun Newspaper* (London: Pocket Books, 1999), 42-43.

22. Donald Zec, "The Beatles", *Daily Mirror*, 10 September 1963, 12.

23. Donald Zec, "Viewpoint: Your Angle on Events", *Daily Mirror*, 14 September 1963, 9.

24. Fergus Cashin, "The Man With Tears to Shed", *Daily Sketch*, 13 November 1963, 4.

25. Bob Dawbarn, "Why I Dig the Beatles", *Melody Maker*, 23 October 1963, 5.

26. "We've Got to Beat the Beatles!" *Daily Mirror*, 5 December 1963, 16; Patrick Doncaster, "But Can You Beat This? On Hit Parade They Now Have Nos 1, 2, 11, 17, 19", *Daily Mirror*, 5 December 1963, 16.

27. "The Beatles Needle Bob Hope", *Daily Sketch*, 13 February 1964, 7.

28. "Beatles Cut Banned", *Daily Sketch*, 18 November 1963, 12.

29. "A Beatle Haircut Cost Boy His School Prize", *Daily Mirror*, 6 December 1963, 15.

30. "200 Beatle Off", *Daily Sketch*, 19 November 1963, 2.

31. Paula James, "Mock Beatles Start a Riot", *Daily Mirror*, 20 December 1963, 3.

32. Patrick Doncaster, "If You Can't Beat 'Em ...", *Daily Mirror*, 28 November 1963, 23.

33. Chris Hutchins, "Richard, Beatles Poll Win Show Buy-British Impact", *Billboard*, 28 December 1963, 3. Chris Hutchins, "Britons Put Yanks in the Horsecollar", *Billboard*, 1 February 1964, 29

34. Derek Johnson, "Beat-Alls Again! Highest Score Ever", *New Musical Express*, 3 January 1964, 2-3.

35. "Britain Tops the Pops", *Daily Express*, 3 March 1964 (no page number available); "Top Records Are British Again", *Daily Telegraph*, 10 March 1964 (no page number available); Derek Johnson, "77 Per Cent of Top Sellers are British", *New Musical Express*, 3 July 1964, 3.

36. Tom Hibbert, "Britain Invades the World", *The History of Rock* 3, no. 35 (1982): 681; Nat Hentoff, "Beatles: 'Gold Drain'...", *New Musical Express*, 21 February 1964, 13; Blake, *The Land Without Music*, 91-94; Barnard, "The Beatles", 543.

37. Ralph J. Gleason, "Like a Rolling Stone", *The Age of Rock: Sounds of the American Cultural Revolution*, ed. Jonathan Eisen (New York: Random House, 1969), 64.

38. Fergus Cashin, "A Lesson from the Beatles", *Daily Sketch*, 14 February 1964, 4.

39. Ian MacDonald, *Revolution in the Head: The Beatles' Records and the Sixties* (London: Pimlico, 1995), 9-12; Devin McKinney, *Magic Circles: The Beatles in Dream and History* (Cambridge, MA: Harvard University Press, 2003), 46-48.

40. Nat Hentoff, "Can't Understand It", *New Musical Express*, 14 February 1964, 2.

41. Letter, "The Amateurs", *Daily Mirror*, 7 July 1964 (no page number available).

42. Monica Furlong, "TV", *Daily Mail*, 4 August 1964, 3.

43. Monica Furlong, "Seven Deadly Virtues", *Daily Mail*, 23 September 1964, 18.

44. Martin and Segrave, *Anti-Rock*, 114.

45. Inglis, "Men of Ideas?" 11; "A Comedy of Letters", *Times Literary Supplement*, 26 March 1964, 250; Booker, *The Neophiliacs*, 234-235.

46. Judith Simons, "John and Paul: Hitting the Bull Every Time!" *Daily Express*, 3 August 1964, 4.

47. Francis Wyndham, foreword to *David Bailey's Box of Pin-Ups*, by David Bailey and Francis Wyndham (London: Weidenfeld and Nicolson, 1965), 36.

48. Derek Johnson, "Bank Holiday Bonus from John and Paul", *New Musical Express*, 26 August 1966, 3.

49. Michael Wood, "John Lennon's School Days", in *The Age of Rock: Sounds of the American Cultural Revolution*, ed. Jonathan Eisen (New York: Random House, 1969), 125.

50. Charles Hamblett and Jane Deverson, eds., *Generation X* (London: Anthony Gibbs and Phillips Ltd., 1964), 137-139.

51. "Dame Barbara is Backing the Beatles", *Evening News*, 17 March 1964, 1.

52. "Mersey Beat a New Culture Says Minister", *Daily Sketch,* 20 February 1964, 3.

53. "Honour the Beatles!" *Melody Maker,* 6 March 1965, 1; "What the Papers Say" *Melody Maker,* 13 March 1965, 10-11; Norman, *SHOUT!,* 246; Hudson, *The Language of the Teenage Revolution,* 45-46. The same people would be even more insulted when Lennon would return his MBE to the crown himself in 1969, in protest over the Wilson government's support of the wars in Biafra and Vietnam. Martin and Segrave, *Anti-Rock,* 117-118.

54. John Lennon, "How Does a Beatle Live? John Lennon Lives Like This", interview by Maureen Cleave, *Evening Standard,* 4 March 1966, 10.

55. Gleason, "Like a Rolling Stone", 74.

56. Cleave, "How Does a Beatle Live?" 10; Stephen Barnard, "Beatlemania", *The History of Rock* 3, no. 28 (1982): 558-560.

57. Derek Johnson, "Group Sound Comes from All Over Britain", *New Musical Express,* 21 February 1964, 5.

58. Cohen, *Rock Culture in Liverpool,* 103-104; Stephen Barnard, "Beat Rules UK?" *The History of Rock* 3, no. 31 (1982): 601.

59. Stephen Barnard, "Ferry Across the Mersey", *The History of Rock* 3, no. 27 (1982): 524-527; Chris Roberts, "It's Gerry—Balladeer", *Melody Maker,* 19 October 1963, 12.

60. Bob Woffinden, "From Cavern to Cabaret", *The History of Rock* 3, no. 27 (1982): 529-530. The Beatles, as prolific a group as ever recorded a rock and roll album, put out one album every ten months.

61. Cilla Black, "What Comes Next?" interview by John Sandilands, *Daily Sketch,* 11 October 1963, 13.

62. Cilla Black, "The Time I Sang with the Beatles", *Daily Sketch,* 25 February 1964, 8; Ann Leslie, "My Kind of Heaven: For Cilla Black, It's an Island", *Daily Express,* 2 June 1964, 6; Stephen Barnard, "Simply Cilla", *The History of Rock* 3, no. 32 (1982): 629; Cilla Black, "Swinging Cilla", *Daily Sketch,* 24 February 1964, 10-11; Trudi Pacter, "I Had to Learn to be Tough", *Daily Express,* 12 October 1967, 10.

63. Jerry Dawson and Chris Roberts, "Liverpool v Manchester", *Melody Maker,* 1 June 1963, 8-9; Barnard, "Beat Rules UK?" 602-603.

64. Barnard, "Beat Rules UK?" 603.

65. Barnard, "Beat Rules UK?" 603; "Cheers for the Zombies", *Evening News,* 6 April 1964, 4; Dave Gillard, "Educated Zombies!" *New Musical Express,* 21 August 1964, 8; Cordell Marks, "Our Problem Parents and Us by the Zombies", *New Musical Express,* 4 September 1964, 14; Pete Frame, "Time of the Zombies", *The History of Rock* 3, no. 35 (1982): 688-691; "Troggs Look Set for Another Great Year in '67", *Melody Maker,* 7 January 1967, 7.

66. Maureen Cleave, "Disc Date", *Evening Standard,* 9 October 1965, 7.

67. Alan Smith, "Don't Blame Us, Please!" *New Musical Express,* 25 March 1966, 9; Don Short, "There's a Chip Off the Old Iron Duke in Tin Pan Alley", *Daily Mirror,* 30 September 1963, 23; Stephen Barnard, "Brits on Broadway", *The History of Rock* 3, no. 35 (1982): 693-694.

68. Bob Dawbarn, "Pop—For Export Only", *Melody Maker,* 16 January 1965, 11.

69. International Music Charts, *Billboard,* 4 April 1964, 22, 30; George Melly, *Revolt into Style: The Pop Arts in Britain* (London: Penguin 1970), 72-73; International

Music Charts, *Billboard*, 11 April 1964, 76; Chris Hutchins, "Stones Roll to UK Championship", *Billboard*, 15 January 1966, 8.

70. Gary Herman, "Turn On, Tune In, Drop Out", *The History of Rock* 6, no. 70 (1983): 1381.

71. Ashley Brown, "The Long and Winding Road", *The History of Rock* 5, no. 58 (1983): 1143.

72. Joan Peyser, "The Beatles and the Beatless", *The Age of Rock: Sounds of the American Cultural Revolution*, ed. Jonathan Eisen (New York: Random House 1969), 129-130.

3 London

1. Jerry White, *London in the Twentieth Century: A City and Its People* (New York: Viking, 2001), 341-345; Davis, *Youth and the Condition of Britain*, 198-199.

2. Pattison, *The Triumph of Vulgarity*, 151-154.

3. Melly, *Revolt into Style,* 82; Simon Frith and Howard Horne, *Art into Pop* (New York: Methuen, 1987), 80-81.

4. Barnard, "Beat Rules UK?" 603.

5. "Folk Cellar", *English Dance and Song* 24, no. 4 (1961): 128-129.

6. Sue Pemsel, "Young Folk", *English Dance and Song* 31, no. 3 (1969): 106.

7. Director's editorial, *English Dance and Song* 24, no. 3 (1960): 76-77.

8. Bob Dawbarn, "Well—what is R&B?" *Melody Maker,* 30 March 1963, 6.

9. John Pidgeon, "UK Blues", *The History of Rock* 3, no. 30 (1982): 583-585; Paul Oliver, "Blue-eyed Blues: The Impact of Blues on European Popular Culture", in *Approaches to Popular Culture*, ed. C. W .E. Bigsby (London: Edward Arnold, 1976), 232.

10. Chris Roberts, "Trend or Tripe", *Melody Maker*, 5 January 1963, 5; Melly, *Revolt into Style,* 82; Pidgeon, "UK Blues", 588.

11. Pidgeon, "UK Blues", 586-588; John Pidgeon, "Heart of Stone", *The History of Rock* 4, no. 45 (1982): 887.

12. Jon Fitzgerald, "Lennon-McCartney and the Early British Invasion, 1964-1966", in Inglis, *The Beatles, Popular Music and Society*, 81.

13. Ray Coleman, "Can YOU Tell the Difference?" *Melody Maker,* 29 February 1964, 7.

14. Stevie Winwood of the Spencer Davis Group: "Groups are sick of the word R&B . . . We are sick of it and prefer this term 'Negro pop'." "Last of the R&B groups?" interview by Chris Welch, *Melody Maker,* 12 June 1965, 8; Ray Coleman, "Just What is R&B?" *Melody Maker,* 9 May 1964, 7.

15. Judith Simons, "On the Top of the World! But Beware of Imitations", *Daily Express,* 18 August 1964, 5.

16. Bob Dawbarn, "Stones Stoned!" *Melody Maker,* 23 May 1964, 8-9; Ray Coleman, "Hands Off", *Melody Maker,* 23 May 1964, 8-9; "Curses! Stoned Again", *Melody Maker,* 30 May 1964, 8-9.

17. Mark Williams, "Through the Past Darkly", *The History of Rock* 4, no. 45 (1982): 889-890; Stanley Booth, *The True Adventures of the Rolling Stones* (New York: Vintage Books, 1984), 82-96; Pete Goodman, *The Rolling Stones: Our Own Story* (London: Corgi Books, 1964), 11-43.

18. "With a Tycoon Aged 20", *Daily Sketch*, 23 May 1964 (no page number available); Williams, "Through the Past Darkly", 891.

19. Margaret Horrigan, "Rough? They're All Nice Young Men", *Daily Sketch*, 13 March 1964, 13; Iain Chambers, *Urban Rhythms: Pop Music and Popular Culture* (New York: St. Martin's Press, 1985), 64-68; Frith, *Sound Effects*, 78.

20. "'It's Over' is Still Top Pop", *Daily Express*, 23 June 1964, 4.

21. Ned Grant, "No-Tie Rolling Stone is Told 'No Lunch'", *Daily Mirror*, 12 May 1964 (no page number available).

22. "Rolling Stones the Ballroom Wreckers", *Daily Express,* 25 July 1964, 1; "Pop Fans Put in Straitjackets", *Daily Mail*, 1 August 1964, 1; "Rioting Fans Wreck Stones Concert", *Daily Express*, 1 August 1964, 1; "Scores Faint at Pop Show", *Daily Express*, 3 August 1964, 1; "Rolling Stones in Riot", *Daily Express*, 10 August 1964, 6.

23. "YEAH, YEAH, YEAH!" *Daily Mirror*, 6 November 1963, 2.

24. "Yellow Ribbons for the Boys", *Daily Express*, 18 July 1964, 7; "The Rolling Stones—Complete Morons", *Evening Standard*, 30 June 1965, 11.

25. Mick Jagger, "The Rolling Stones Gather Speed", interview by Chris Roberts, *Melody Maker*, 29 June 1963, 8-9.

26. Ian Marlowe, "'The Beatle War' …It's How You Look As Well As How You Sound", *Daily Sketch*, 4 January 1964, 8-9; Mick Jagger, "Rebels with a Beat!" interview by Ray Coleman, *Melody Maker*, 8 February 1964, 10-11.

27. Quoted in Patrick Doncaster, "Discs", *Daily Mirror,* 17 November 1964, 21.

28. Cliff Ash, "It's Only Rock and Roll", *The History of Rock* 4, no. 45 (1982): 881.

29. Maureen Cleave, "But Would You Let Your Daughter Marry One?" *Evening Standard*, 11 May 1964, 7.

30. Jack Hutton, "Stateside Snub for Stones", *Melody Maker*, 13 June 1964, 8-9.

31. "Good Day's Work for a 'Hard Day's Night'" *Daily Express*, 14 July 1964, 1.

32. Richard Green, "Rolling Stones Defend Their 'Juke-Jury' Stint and Discuss New Disc", *New Musical Express*, 17 July 1964, 4; Ray Hill, "The Rolling Stones Run Into Television Row", *Daily Mirror*, 30 November 1964, 6; Martin and Segrave, *Anti-Rock*, 120-123, 147; Ian Murray, "The Girl Who Loved a Rolling Stone", *News of the World*, 16 January 1966, 4.

33. "A Fighting Duke—And Mick Jagger's Hair", *Daily Mirror*, 27 November 1964, 15; "'Pop' Vocalist Fined", *The Times*, 11 August 1964 (no page number available); "£32 Car Fine on Rolling Stone", *Daily Telegraph*, 11 August 1964 (no page number available).

34. "Three of the Rolling Stones Summoned", *Evening Standard*, 1 July 1965, 11; "3 of the Stones Fined, Rebuked", *Evening Standard*, 22 July 1965, 11; Brian Hogg, "Everybody Needs Somebody", *The History of Rock* 4, no. 45 (1982): 896-897.

35. Blake, "Americanisation and Popular Music in Britain", 151-153.

36. Melly, *Revolt into Style,* 84-88; Maureen Cleave, "Mick Jagger—Bad Joke into Social Lion", *Evening Standard*, 4 February 1966, 8.

37. Fowler, "Still Going Solo", 722-723.

38. Gary Herman, "Shout!" *The History of Rock* 3, no. 32 (1982): 635-636; David Wigg and Jackie Modlinger, "Why Sandie Shaw Is Fed Up with Clothes and Wants to Learn to Sing", *Daily Express*, 2 June 1977, 15; Michael Watts, "Barefoot in the Charts", *The History of Rock* 3, no. 32 (1982): 626-628; Harron, "Puppets on a String", 621-622;

George A. Ingram, "The Springfields: A Three Year Success Story", *Goldmine*, no. 69 (February 1982): 8-10.

39. Colin Irwin, "English Folk Revival: The Boom Years, 1962-1967", *Southern Rag* 5, no. 4 (1984): 16-18.

40. Karl Dallas interview with Ewan MacColl, "Focus on MacColl", *Melody Maker*, 18 September 1965, 23.

41. "D. D." [Ian Campbell], "Pop and Folk—and How to Tell the Difference", *Melody Maker*, 21 August 1965, 10. In a display of the most unforgivable hypocrisy, Campbell promptly cut a cover version of "The Times They are A-Changin'" (1964) and released it as a single—where it fortunately was eclipsed by Dylan's own version of the song, which became a Top 30 chart hit.

42. Bob Dawbarn, "Donovan", *Melody Maker*, 20 February 1965, 13.

43. Alan Beckett, "Stones", *The Age of Rock*, 112-117.

44. Gleason, "Like a Rolling Stone", *The Age of Rock*, 71-72; Martin Cloonan, *Banned! Censorship of Popular Music in Britain: 1967-1992* (Brookfield, VT: Ashgate Publishing Co., 1996), 123.

45. Keith Richards, "Stones Reveal Secrets", interview by Keith Altham, *New Musical Express,* 23 September 1966, 3.

46. Wyndham, *David Bailey's Box of Pin-Ups*, 36.

47. Stephen Barnard, "Folk+Rock+Protest=Dollars", *The History of Rock* 3, no. 34 (1982): 676-677.

48. Adrian Gilbert, "Shapes of Things . . ." *The History of Rock* 3, no. 33 (1982): 642-643.

49. Robert Palmer, *Rock & Roll: An Unruly History* (New York: Harmony Books, 1995), 116, 118, 119.

50. Maureen Cleave, "Disc Date", *Evening Standard*, 22 May 1965, 7; Jeff Tamarkin, "The Animals", *Goldmine*, no. 89 (October 1983): 26-33.

51. John Pidgeon, "Guitar Gods and Other Divinities", *The History of Rock* 5, no. 52 (1983): 1021-1022.

52. "Clapton quits Yardbirds—'too commercial'", *Melody Maker*, 17 March 1965, 5; Brian Hogg, "Flying High", *The History of Rock* 3, no. 33 (1982): 650-651.

53. Keith Relf, "Yardbirds—Why We Went 'Commercial'", interview by Nick Jones, *Melody Maker,* 17 July 1965, 7.

54. Jonathan Bellman, "Indian Resonances in the British Invasion, 1965-1968", in *The Exotic in Western Music*, ed. Jonathan Bellman (Boston: Northeastern University Press, 1998), 294-297; "The Quiet Revolution", *Melody Maker*, 16 October 1965, 7; Hogg, "Flying High", 651-653.

55. Robert Bickford, "Top-pop Kinks", *Daily Mail*, 8 September 1964, 3; Ray Davies, *X-Ray* (London: Penguin Books, 1994), 72-73.

56. Laing, "Roll Over Lonnie", 14.

57. Keith Altham, "Kinks Keep to Humour on Discs", *New Musical Express*, 17 June 1966, 9; Phil Hardy, "Well Respected Men", *The History of Rock* 4, no. 38 (1982): 753; Blake, "Americanisation and Popular Music in Britain", 150.

58. Maureen Cleave, "Disc Date", *Evening Standard*, 28 August 1965, 7.

59. Steve Lake, "The Kinks: Muswell's Hillbilly Satirists", *Melody Maker*, 26 January 1974, 25.

60. Hardy, "Well Respected Men", 752; Keith Altham, "Kinks Don't Mind 'Formby Quartet' Tag", *New Musical Express,* 18 March 1966, 3.

4 Mods

1. Graham Murdock and Robin McCron, "Youth and Class: The Career of a Confusion", in *Working-class Youth Culture*, eds. Geoff Mungham and Geoff Pearson (London: Routledge and Kegan Paul, 1976), 11-14; Davis, *Youth and the Condition of Britain*, 129-135.

2. Paolo Hewitt, "Editor's Introduction", in *The Sharper Word: A Mod Anthology*, ed. Paolo Hewitt (London: Helter Skelter Publishing, 1999), 6-7.

3. Frith, *Sound Effects*, 219.

4. Brake, *Comparative Youth Culture*, 72-73; Hebdige, *Subculture: the Meaning of Style*, 73-80.

5. Howard Parker, "Boys Will Be Men: Brief Adolescence in a Down-Town Neighborhood", in *Working-class Youth Culture*, eds. Geoff Mungham and Geoff Pearson (London: Routledge and Kegan Paul, 1976), 27-31; Peter Willmott, *Adolescent Boys of East London* (Harmondsworth, UK: Penguin Books 1969), 15-19; Brake, *Comparative Youth Culture*, 68-70.

6. Murdock and McCron, "Youth and Class", 20-21.

7. Quoted in Hamblett and Deverson, *Generation X*, 11.

8. Charles Curran MP, "The Face of Violence", *Evening News*, 22 May 1964, 10.

9. Mungham and Pearson, "Introduction", 4; Davis, *Youth and the Condition of Britain*, 134; E. Ellis Cashmore, *No Future: Youth and Society* (Aldershot, UK: Gower Publishing Company Ltd., 1985), 9; Brake, *Comparative Youth Culture*, 63-64.

10. Mungham and Pearson, "Introduction", 6-7.

11. Brake, *Comparative Youth Culture*, 65-72.

12. Murdock and McCron, "Youth and Class", 15; Frith, *Sound Effects*, 217-218.

13. Brake, *Comparative Youth Culture*, 74-75.

14. Quoted in Hamblett and Deverson, *Generation X*, 21-22.

15. Quoted in Hamblett and Deverson, *Generation X*, 56. The "Profumo lark" was a cabinet-level sex scandal where the Minister of War, John Profumo, had an affair with a model and sometime prostitute, Christine Keeler, who was simultaneously involved with an official of the Soviet Embassy.

16. Kevin Davey, *English Imaginaries: Six Studies in Anglo-British Modernity* (London: Lawrence and Wishart, 1999), 81.

17. Hebdige, *Subculture: The Meaning of Style*, 52-53.

18. Michael Wale, *Voxpop: Profiles of the Pop Process* (London: Harrap, 1972), 120-121.

19. Cathy McGowan, "Boy Meets Girl", *Daily Sketch*, 31 October 1963, 13.

20. Cathy McGowan, "We Are the Teenagers", *Daily Sketch*, 29 October 1963, 12; Pete Fowler, "The Mod Generation", *The History of Rock* 4, no. 41 (1983): 801-802.

21. Cathy McGowan, "With-It Cathy", interview by John Sandilands, *Daily Sketch*, 12 October 1963, 6.

22. Cathy McGowan, "What We Think of Adults", *Daily Sketch*, 30 October 1963, 8.

23. Brake, *Comparative Youth Culture*, 75; Chambers, *Urban Rhythms*, 80; McGowan, "We Are the Teenagers", 12; Fowler, "The Mod Generation", 801.

24. "The 'Mod' Rocks Them", *Evening News*, 14 May 1964, 11.

25. John Edwards, "The Night They Rounded Up the Teenagers in Soho", *Daily Mirror*, 7 December 1964, 16-17.

26. Hamblett and Deverson, *Generation X*, 21-22; John Pidgeon, "Jamaican Soul", *The History of Rock* 4, no. 41 (1983): 812-813.

27. Roy Blackman, "Mods and Rockers", *Daily Mirror*, 11 November 1963, 9.

28. Stanley Cohen, *Folk Devils and Moral Panics: The Creation of the Mods and Rockers* (New York: St. Martin's Press, 1980), 27-44; "Terror on Beach: Youth Shot and Stabbed As 'Sawdust Caesars' Are Sentenced", *Evening News*, 18 May 1964, 1; Harry Jones, "Brighton Violence—And Stones Start to Fly", *Evening News*, 18 May 1964, 1.

29. Quoted in Hamblett and Deverson, *Generation X*, 9. The authors declared his statement "an extreme case", believing that his sentiments were expressed in an "artificial, studied" fashion because they were writing a book.

30. Frith, *Sound Effects*, 220; Davis, *Youth and the Condition of Britain*, 190-195.

31. Dave Marsh, *Before I Get Old: The Story of the Who* (New York: St. Martin's Press, 1983), 66-67.

32. George Gilpin, *The Art of Contemporary English Culture* (New York: St. Martin's Press, 1991), 2-3.

33. Jonathan Reed, "Pop Goes the Easel", *The History of Rock* 6, no. 65 (1983): 1296-1297.

34. Jonathan Aitken, ed., *The Young Meteors* (London: Secker & Warburg, 1967), 199.

35. Alex Seago, *Burning the Box of Beautiful Things: The Development of a Postmodern Sensibility* (New York: Oxford University Press, 1995), 139-140.

36. Simon Frith and Howard Horne, *Art into Pop* (New York: Methuen Books, 1987), 1-25.

37. David Allan Mellor, "'Tomorrow Starts Now': Utopian Visual Culture in Britain", in *The Sixties: Britain and France, 1962-1973*, eds. David Alan Mellor and Laurent Gervereau (London: Philip Wilson, 1997), 12-29; Seago, *Burning the Box of Beautiful Things*, 19; Reed, "Pop Goes the Easel", 1297; Marsh, *Before I Get Old*, 45.

38. Davey, *English Imaginaries*, 3; Peter Lloyd Jones, "The Pop Art of Living", *The Listener*, 11 August 1977, 170.

39. Chambers, *Urban Rhythms*, 82.

40. Marsh, *Before I Get Old*, 20-35, 46-49; Davey, *English Imaginaries*, 80.

41. Chambers, *Urban Rhythms*, 54; Davey, *English Imaginaries*, 80; John Pidgeon, "Who's Who", *The History of Rock* 6, no. 64 (1983): 1265.

42. Mitch Howard, "The Working-class Heroes: Pete Townshend", *Cream*, December 1972, 27-31, 49-50; Marsh, *Before I Get Old*, 124-126.

43. Clark, "The Seeker", 1279.

44. Pete Townshend, "Miles Interviews Pete Townshend", interview by [Barry] Miles, *International Times*, 13-26 February 1967, 5.

45. Pidgeon, "Who's Who", 1265.

46. Ray Tolliday, "Well, What Would You Have Done After *Tommy*?" *Cream*, October 1971, 28-31, 53-54.

47. Peter Townshend, "Born Under a Bad Sign", *Oz*, no. 21 (May 1969): 28.

48. Pete Townshend, "Disc Date", interview by Maureen Cleave, *Evening Standard*, 29 May 1965, 7.

49. Mitch Howard, "The Working-class Heroes: Pete Townshend", *Cream*, December 1972, 27-31, 49-50.

50. Booker, *The Neophiliacs*, 283-284.

51. Davey, *English Imaginaries*, 80.

52. Pete Townshend, "Disc Date", interview by Maureen Cleave, *Evening Standard*, 29 May 1965, 7.

53. Fowler, "The Mod Generation", 803.

54. Ian McLagan, *All the Rage: A Riotous Romp Through Rock & Roll History* (New York: Billboard Books, 2000), 45-118; John Pidgeon, "Facing the Music", *The History of Rock* 4, no. 41 (1983): 806-807.

55. Keith Altham, "Steve Marriott: Everyone's 'Luv' and 'Mate'", *New Musical Express,* 9 September 1966, 2; McLagan, *All the Rage*, 52-54.

56. Brian Hogg, "Where the Action Was", *The History of Rock* 4, no. 41 (1983): 819-820.

57. John Pidgeon, "Funky Butt Live", *The History of Rock* 4, no. 41 (1983): 811.

58. Quoted in Hamblett and Deverson, *Generation X*, 22.

59. Murdock and McCron, "Youth and Class", 10.

60. Davis, *Youth and the Condition of Britain*, 118-129.

61. Quoted in Aitken, *The Young Meteors*, 264.

62. Ibid.

63. "Every So Often, A Group is Poised on the Brink of a Breakthrough. Word Has It It's the Who." *Melody Maker*, 5 June 1965, 7; Nick Jones, "Well, What is Pop Art?" *Melody Maker,* 3 July 1965, 11.

64. Pidgeon, "Who's Who", 1265.

65. Michael Heatley, "Ready Steady Who!" *The History of Rock* 6, no. 64 (1983): 1261.

66. Marsh, *Before I Get Old*, 125; Maureen Cleave, "Disc Date", *Evening Standard*, 29 May 1965, 7.

67. Townshend, "Miles Interviews Pete Townshend", 5.

68. Alan Smith, "What a Way to Talk about Your Own Fans!" *New Musical Express,* 14 January 1966, 3.

5 Marketing a Lifestyle

1. Aitken, *The Young Meteors*, 13.

2. Quoted in Aitken, *The Young Meteors*, 51-52.

3. *Billboard*, 25 May 1968, L-10 (special supplement).

4. Malcolm Keogh, "Call Them Spendagers!" *Daily Mirror*, 2 October 1963, 9; Melly, *Revolt into Style*, 11; Bradley, *Understanding Rock and Roll*, 85-86; Davis, *Youth and the Condition of Britain*, 160-165.

5. Platt, "Swinging London", 743.

6. Chris Hutchins, "Barry Exits EMI to Light Embers", *Billboard*, 13 July 1963, 33.

7. Bob Woffinden, "BBC Blues", *The History of Rock* 2, no. 19 (1983): 376-377; Frith, "1967", 7.

8. Mike Raven, "Lid Off the Pop Pirates", *News of the World*, 23 October 1966, 3.

9. Quoted in Aitken, *The Young Meteors*, 255-256.

10. Chris Hutchins, "Bill's Shelving Puts Pirates Back at Helm", *Billboard*, 30 May 1964, 14; "'Pirate' Caroline May Sail North in Merger", *Daily Express*, 23 June 1964, 7; Stephen Barnard, "Piracy in the Air", *The History of Rock* 4, no. 38 (1983): 744; Clifford Davis, "Radio Pop Ship in New Bid to Beat the BBC", *Daily Mirror*, 8 January 1965, 9.

11. "Radio 'Pirates' to be Warned", *Daily Express*, 1 June 1964, 1; "Bevins: 'Pirate' Ban Must Wait", *Daily Express*, 3 June 1964, 20; Omer Anderson, "Radio Luxembourg's Success Brings Broadcast Reappraisal", *Billboard*, 13 June 1964, 32; "Radio Caroline Buoyant", *Billboard*, 31 October 1964, 3; "The 'Pirates' Are Banned", *Daily Mirror*, 23 January 1965, 14; "Radio Pirates Claim Victory", *Daily Mirror*, 8 February 1965, 2; Barnard, "Piracy in the Air", 744-745; Chris Hutchins, "Pirates Forcing UK Govt to Walk Legislative Plank", *Billboard*, 6 November 1965, 1, 58.

12. "Pirates in Peril—New Act Planned", *Melody Maker*, 9 July 1966, 4; Frith, *Sound Effects*, 96-97; Barnard, "Piracy in the Air", 745; Raven, "Lid Off the Pop Pirates", 3.

13. Martin Jackson, "Pop Around the Clock", *Daily Express*, 23 June 1964, 1; "BBC-TV Exec Blasts Pop Groups, Producers", *Billboard*, 29 May 1965, 20; "'Top Gear' Pop Show Goes Flop", *Daily Mirror*, 3 November 1964, 4.

14. Bob Dawbarn, "Is the BBC Anti-Pop?" *Melody Maker*, 29 May 1965, 8.

15. "3d of UK 'Captives' of Buoyant Pirates", *Billboard*, 30 April 1966, 30.

16. "Pop Pirates Cry 'Stand By to Repel Boarders!'", *Daily Mirror*, 31 December 1964, 5; Don Wedge, "Luxembourg Going to Pirates' Format", *Billboard*, 10 September 1966, 1, 26, 30-31; Raven, "Lid Off the Pop Pirates", 2; Barnard, "Piracy in the Air", 745-746.

17. Graeme Andrews, "BBC Gets OK to Bow Pop Service in Rap at Pirates", *Billboard*, 31 December 1966, 4,12; "BBC Opening Fire v. Pirates", *Billboard*, 18 February 1967, 1,8; Martin Jackson, "'Pop' Pirates Told: Ban on Aug. 15", *Daily Express*, 14 July 1967, 1-2; Barnard, "Piracy in the Air", 746; John Edwards, "State Plan for Pop Radio and Adverts", *Daily Mirror*, 21 September 1966, 1; "Radio Caroline will defy new ban", *Daily Express*, 1 September 1967, 1; Graeme Andrews, "Pirate Radio in Hot Water", *Billboard*, 16 December 1967, 1, 10.

18. "New BBC Program Boasts Top Knights of Turntable", *Billboard*, 16 September 1967, 66; "Blueprint for Free Radio", "Radio Andorra the Blueprint for Action", *International Times*, 18-31 July 1969, 10; Barnard, "Piracy in the Air", 746.

19. Felix Dennis, "Jimmy Page", *Oz*, no. 20 (April 1969): 38.

20. Brake, *Comparative Youth Culture*, 65-67.

21. Chambers, *Urban Rhythms*, 57.

22. Brian Hogg, "Mod Managers", *The History of Rock* 4, no. 41 (1983): 816.

23. Booth, *The True Adventures of the Rolling Stones*; Andrew Loog Oldham, *Stoned* (New York: St. Martin's Press, 2000).

24. McLagan, *All the Rage*, 96-98; Hogg, "Everybody Needs Somebody", 896-897.

25. Ian Dove, "I Couldn't Afford to Sign Stones!" *New Musical Express*, 3 July 1964, 14; Hogg, "Mod Managers", 816.

26. Marsh, *Before I Get Old*, 103-110, 249-252.

27. Quoted in Aitken, *The Young Meteors*, 248-249.

28. Bob Woffinden, "Hit or Miss?" *The History of Rock* 2, no. 19 (1983): 378-380; Briggs, *The BBC*, 305; Colin Shearman, "Rock on TV", *The History of Rock* 4, no. 43 (1983): 849; "Now It's Two-Point-Foive", *Daily Mirror*, 19 August 1963, 1; Norman, *SHOUT!* 173.

29. Booth, *The True Adventures of the Rolling Stones*, 335-336; Shearman, "Rock on TV", 849.

30. Marsh, *Before I Get Old*, 153; Shearman, "Rock on TV", 850.

31. Bob Woffinden, "Celluloid Rock", *The History of Rock* 2, no. 22 (1983): 429; John Blair, "Early Rock Cinema, 1956-1960", *Goldmine,* no. 40 (September 1979): 8A-12A.

32. Bob Woffinden, "Hard Day's Night", *The History of Rock* 4, no. 43 (1983): 854-855.

33. Dadomo, "Reeling & Rocking", *The History of Rock* 4, no. 43 (1983): 844-845; Weston Taylor, "Herman the Hermit Hits Hollywood", *News of the World*, 30 January 1966, 15; Marsh, *Before I Get Old*, 282; Booth, *The True Adventures of the Rolling Stones*, 273.

34. Aitken, *The Young Meteors*, 300-301.

35. "Beatles as a World Commodity", *Billboard*, 5 December 1964, 3.

36. "Beatles Gross 17 Mil. Plus in 6 Months", *Billboard*, 29 February 1964, 1, 8.

37. Jack Maher, "Nobody Loves the Beatles 'Cept Mother, Capitol, Etc." *Billboard*, 14 March 1964, 3.

38. "Beatles Share £17,875,000—Without Selling One Record", *Daily Sketch*, 20 February 1964, 3.

39. "Beatlemania Makes the Hatters Mad", *Evening News and Star*, 9 March 1964, 2.

40. Patrick Doncaster, "1980—And the Beatles Will Still Be Winning . . ." *Daily Mirror*, 5 October 1964, 23.

41. Robert Head, "How Safe Are the Beatles?" *Daily Mirror*, 16 February 1965, 17.

42. "Want to Share Two Beatles?" *Daily Mirror*, 19 January 1965, 2; "Beatles Want an Upbeat Budget", *Daily Mirror*, 12 February 1965, 21.

43. Frederick Ellis, "Northern Songs Reports Brightly—But Price Slips", *Daily Express*, 26 October 1967, 12.

44. Chris Hutchins, "British Retailers Seek Industry Support for 'Better Music' Drive", *Billboard*, 6 February 1965, 3.

45. Mike Gross, "UK Teen Leanings Bring Lean Class Artist Pickings, Says Newell", *Billboard*, 11 June 1966, 1, 14.

46. Ed Hanel, "Revolutions in Sound", *The History of Rock* 6, no. 70 (1983): 1393; "Best Chart Year Ever for Our Artists", *New Musical Express*, 7 January 1966, 2; Chris Hutchins, "Jolly Good '66 Seen for UK", *Billboard*, 1 January 1966, 1.

47. Wale, *Voxpop*, 98-99; "Will Cheap LPs Knock Single Sales?" *Melody Maker*, 18 September 1965, 17. Oddly, American music corporations have seemingly only just started to pick up on this market strategy in the 1990s, with the growth of Rhino Records and Rykodisk.

48. Graeme Andrews, "British Labels Reissuing Major Teen Record Acts on Budget", *Billboard*, 28 January 1967, 66; Graeme Andrews, "UK Steps Up Raids on US", *Billboard*, 25 March 1967, 1, 3; "British Record Sales Climb 9%, April Production Up", *Billboard*, 5 August 1967, 36.

49. "UK Record Sales Up 11% in 1967", *Billboard*, 23 March 1968, 49.

50. Graeme Andrews, "London: Capital of the Music World", *Billboard*, 25 May 1968, L-3 (special supplement).

51. Melly, *Revolt into Style*, 91, 101.

52. Chris Welch, "Spencer—Group Who Just Had to Hit", *Melody Maker,* 18 December 1965, 9.

6   Psychedelia

1. Quoted in Aitken, *The Young Meteors,* 270-271.
2. Alan Bisbort and Parke Puterbaugh, *Rhino's Psychedelic Trip* (San Francisco: Miller Freeman Books, 2000), 15.
3. Edward Macan, *Rocking the Classics: English Progressive Rock and the Counterculture* (New York: Oxford University Press, 1997), 17; Palmer, *Rock & Roll,* 165-166; Alan Smith, "How 'Paperback' Came About", *New Musical Express,* 24 June 1966, 3; MacDonald, *Revolution in the Head,* 157; Mark Teahan, "The Byrds, 'Eight Miles High', the *Gavin Report,* and Media Censorship of Alleged 'Drug Songs' in 1966: An Assessment", *Popular Musicology Online* (2010) http://www.popular-musicology-online.com/issues/04/teehan.html (accessed May 24, 2012).
4. Melly, *Revolt into Style,* 111, 116.
5. Camille Paglia, *Sexual Personae* (London: Penguin Books Ltd., 1991), 358; John Street, *Rebel Rock: The Politics of Popular Music* (Oxford: Basil Blackwell, 1986), 72-73; James F. Harris, *Philosophy at 33 1/3 RPM: Themes of Classic Rock Music* (Chicago and Lasalle, IL: Open Court Publishing Co., 1993), 65; Herman, "Turn On, Tune In, Drop Out", 1381-1382.
6. George Harrison, "The Way Out is In: Miles Interviews George Harrison MBE", interview by [Barry] Miles, *International Times,* 19 May-2 June 1967, 9; Bellman, "Indian Resonances in the British Invasion", 293-294.
7. Bellman, "Indian Resonances in the British Invasion", 297-305.
8. Pattison, *The Triumph of Vulgarity,* 66-69; Michael Watts, "The Call and Response of Popular Music: The Impact of American Pop Music in Europe", in *Superculture: American Pop Culture and Europe,* ed. C. W. E. Bigsby (Bowling Green, Ohio: Bowling Green University Popular Press, 1975), 123-124.
9. Macan, *Rocking the Classics,* 69-76; Bigsby, "The Politics of Popular Culture", 9.
10. Booth, *The True Adventures of the Rolling Stones,* 337-338.
11. Harris, *Philosophy at 33 1/3 RPM,* 183-185; Colin Shearman, "The Inner Light", *The History of Rock* 6, no. 70 (1983): 1396-1397.
12. Veldman, *Fantasy, the Bomb and the Greening of Britain,* 94-98, 107-113.
13. Harris, *Philosophy at 33 1/3 RPM,* 194.
14. Graham Bond, "Graham Bond", interview by Mark Williams, *International Times,* 26 September - 9 October 1969, 17-18.
15. Donovan, *All My Loving,* Tony Palmer, director (1968).
16. Dick Hebdige, *Subculture: The Meaning of Style* (New York: Routledge, 1988), 55; Frith, *Sound Effects,* 220-221.
17. Murdock and McCron, "Youth and Class", 22-26.
18. Peyser, "The Beatles and the Beatless", 129-130.
19. Jim Miller, *Flowers in the Dustbin: The Rise of Rock and Roll, 1947-1977* (New York: Simon & Schuster, 1999), 250-251.
20. Norman, *SHOUT!,* 282-283; MacDonald, *Revolution in the Head,* 170-179.
21. Frith, "1967", 4.
22. Philip Phillips, "Beatles Song Banned by BBC", *Sun,* 20 May 1967, 1; Cloonan, *Banned!* 122-127; Street, *Rebel Rock,* 114.

23. Frith, "1967", 5.

24. Bisbort and Puterbaugh, *Rhino's Psychedelic Trip*, 77.

25. Narration, *All My Loving*, Tony Palmer, director (1968).

26. Macan, *Rocking the Classics*, 15.

27. Mike Nevard, "*Sgt. Pepper* has a 41-Piece Band", *Sun*, 23 May 1967, 15; Melly, *Revolt into Style*, 112-115.

28. Norman, *SHOUT!*, 292-293.

29. Paul McCartney, *All My Loving*, Tony Palmer, director (1968).

30. Burgess, "Donovan", 1134.

31. Melly, *Revolt into Style*, 110; "What Has Happened to the Folk Folk?" *New Musical Express, Summer Extra Special* [1967-no date given], 49; Stephen Barnard, "Donovan", *The History of Rock* 5, no. 58 (1983): 1135-1136.

32. Phil Hardy, "Art on Their Sleeves", *The History of Rock* 6, no. 65 (1983): 1292-1293.

33. Frith, "1967", 5-7.

34. Macan, *Rocking the Classics*, 21; Stephen Barnard, "Flower Power or Money Power?" *The History of Rock* 5, no. 55 (1983): 1081-1085; Stephen Barnard, "Times A-Changin'", *The History of Rock* 5, no. 57 (1983): 1123-1124.

35. David Sinclair, "Wheels of Fire", *The History of Rock* 5, no. 52 (1983): 1027-1028.

36. Charles Shaar Murray, "Eric Clapton: Being God Has Its Hangups, Too", *Cream*, May 1973, 31-35.

37. Wale, *Voxpop*, 44-45.

38. Ken Hunt, "Winwood", *The History of Rock* 5, no. 60 (1983): 1188; Steve Winwood, "Steve Winwood", interview by Gene Kalbacher with Lynn DeLotto, *Goldmine*, no. 64 (September 1981), 13-15; Chris Welch, "Why I Quit", *Melody Maker*, 4 March 1967, 10-11.

39. "Time for a New-Look Spencer", *Melody Maker*, 11 February 1967, 3; Frith, "1967", 8; "Winwood—New Group, New Identity", *Melody Maker*, 10 June 1967, 7.

40. "Steve Winwood: First Single", *Melody Maker*, 29 April 1967, 1.

41. John Morthland, "Jimi Hendrix", in *Rolling Stone Illustrated History of Rock & Roll*, 276-280; Bisbort and Puterbaugh, *Rhino's Psychedelic Trip,* 63-64; Miller, *Flowers in the Dustbin*, 267.

42. Martin and Segrave, *Anti-Rock*, 126.

43. Jane de Mendelssohn, "Hendrix as Experienced by Jane de Mendelssohn", *International Times*, 28 March-10 April 1969, 13-14.

44. Peter Clark, "Welcome to the Machine", *The History of Rock* 6, no. 66 (1983): 1307-1308.

45. Tom Hibbert, "Crazy Diamond", *The History of Rock* 6, no. 66 (1983): 1319; Reed, "Pop Goes the Easel", 1297.

46. Jody Breslaw, "A Hard Rain's Gonna Fall: Visions of the Apocalypse", *International Times*, 26 August-9 September 1971, 14.

47. Ian MacDonald, "Lookin' Back: The Soft Machine", *New Musical Express*, 25 January 1975, 32.

48. Steve Lake, "The Softs Parade . . ." *Melody Maker*, 3 April 1976, 17.

49. Chris Schuler, "I Hear a Symphony . . ." *The History of Rock* 8, no. 85 (1983): 1681.

50. Macan, *Rocking the Classics*, 22, 32; Graeme Andrews and Mike Hennessey, "Harum's 'Pale' Captures Europe", *Billboard*, 1 July 1967, 1, 50; Paul Kendall, "Procol Harum", *The History of Rock* 5, no. 55 (1983): 1086-1088; Frith, "1967", 8.

52. MacDonald, *Revolution in the Head*, 187, 199; Miller, *Flowers in the Dustbin,* 253.

53. Herman, "Turn On, Tune In, Drop Out", 1381-1383.

54. Anthony Burgess, *All My Loving*, Tony Palmer, director (1968).

55. MacDonald, *Revolution in the Head*, 17-34.

56. Cloonan, *Banned!* 159-171.

57. Martin Cloonan, "Popular Music and Censorship in Britain: An Overview", *Pop Music and Society* 19 (Fall 1995): 76.

58. "Beat-Club Evil Spreading, Says Lord Parker", *Sun*, 4 February 1967, 7.

59. John Orman, *The Politics of Rock Music* (Chicago: Nelson-Hall, 1984), 12, 95-96.

60. "Young Britain and the Influence of Pop Stars", *Sun*, 26 April 1967, 6.

61. Booth, *The True Adventures of the Rolling Stones*, 337, 367-383.

62. [William Rees-Mogg,] "Who Breaks a Butterfly on a Wheel?" *The Times*, 1 July 1967, 11.

63. "Is This Fair to Rolling Stones?" *Sun*, 20 May 1967, 8; Robin Turner, "I'll Still Take Pills—Jagger", *Daily Express*, 1 August 1967, 1; Williams, "Through the Past Darkly", 893.

64. Chambers, *Urban Rhythms*, 101-106.

65. Frith, *Sound Effects*, 190.

66. Graham Keen, John Sheppard et. al, interview by Jonathon Green, *Days in the Life*, 95-103.

67. Platt, "Going Underground", 1303-1304.

68. Noel Whitcomb, "This Music Is Bad for Your Eyes", *Sun*, 6 March 1967, 7.

69. Sue Miles, John Hopkins et. al., interview by Jonathon Green, *Days in the Life*, 131-140, 203-206.

70. Platt, "Going Underground", *The History of Rock*, 1307.

71. Frith, *Sound Effects*, 196-197.

72. Ian Birchall, "The Decline and Fall of British Rhythm and Blues", in *The Age of Rock: Sounds of the American Cultural Revolution*, ed. Jonathan Eisen (New York: Random House, 1969), 98-101.

73. Alan Walsh, "The Danger Facing Pop", *Melody Maker*, 20 May 1967, 3; Nick Logan, "Traffic Want to Push Albums Now", *New Musical Express*, 16 March 1968, 2; Richard Green, "Or Do We Need Something New?" *New Musical Express*, 4 May 1968, 16; Birchall, "The Decline and Fall of British Rhythm and Blues", 94-96.

74. Stephen Barnard, "Saturday Night Out", *The History of Rock* 3, no. 31 (1982): 618-620.

75. Philip Phillips, "Beatles in World TV Link", *Sun*, 19 May 1967, 3.

7   Folk Rock

1. Karl Dallas, "Those Revivalists Who Won't Get Their Feet Wet", *Morning Star* 20 September 1968 (no page number available).

2. Laing, "Roll Over Lonnie (Tell George Formby the News)", 15.

3. Watson, *Song and Democratic Culture in Britain*, 38-42.

4. Blake, *The Land Without Music*, 86-90.

5. Veldman, *Fantasy, the Bomb and the Greening of Britain.*

6. Boyes, *The Imagined Village*, 184, 196-199.

7. Paul Oliver, "Blue-Eyed Blues: The Impact of Blues on European Popular Culture", *Approaches to Popular Culture*, C. W. E. Bigsby, editor (London: Edward Arnold, 1976), 230.

8. Boyes, *The Imagined Village*, 204-206, 222-223; Colin Irwin, "English Folk Revival: The Boom Years, 1962-1967", *Southern Rag* 5, no. 4 (April 1 to June 30 1984): 17.

9. Letters, *English Dance and Song* 24, no. 5 (September 1961): 172.

10. Laing, "Rock Around the Maypole", 1461; Louis Killen, "Pop or Trad", *English Dance and Song* 26, no. 5 (October 1964): 111.

11. Sydney Carter, "Folk and the Beatles", *English Dance and Song* 26, no. 1 (December 1963): 3.

12. Letters, *English Dance and Song* 26, no. 2 (February 1964): 43.

13. Letters, *English Dance and Song* 31, no. 1 (Spring 1969): 17.

14. Boyes, *The Imagined Village*, 231-234; Karl Dallas, "Folk? No Boom Here, Says Dusty Springfield", *Melody Maker*, 14 September 1963, 18, Irwin, "English Folk Revival", 16.

15. Ray Coleman, "Can There Ever Be a Folk Boom?" *Melody Maker*, 13 February 1965, 10-11.

16. Steve Benbow, "What Happens When Folk Goes POP!" *Melody Maker*,25 January 1964, 11; Max Jones, "US-Type Folk Boom? Not Here!" *Melody Maker*,18 January 1964, 6.

17. Ewan MacColl, "Focus on MacColl", interview by Karl Dallas, *Melody Maker*, 18 September 1965, 23.

18. Laing, "Rock Around the Maypole", 1462.

19. Jean Aitchison, "Growing Up", *English Dance and Song* 30, no. 4 (Winter/Christmas 1968): 113.

20. Steve Peacock, "Incredible String Band Part 2", *Sounds*, 27 March 1971, 8.

21. Robin Williamson, "Celtic Stringman", interview with Dave Davies, *Folk Roots* 7, no. 6 (December 1985): 11-12.

22. Steve Peacock, "The Incredible String Band", *Sounds*, 20 March 1971, 14.

23. Irwin, "English Folk Revival", 18.

24. "Child That I Am I Do", *Oz*, no. 20 (April 1969): 34-35.

25. Chris Gardiner, "Some Records for Schools", *English Dance and Song* 30, no. 3 (Autumn 1968): 106.

26. Adrian Bull, "Half a Kaleidoscope", *English Dance and Song* 29, no. 2 (Summer 1967): 55; "Festival at Royal Albert Hall", *English Dance and Song* 29, no. 1 (Spring 1967): 22; "Record Rack", *English Dance and Song* 29, no. 1 (Spring 1967): 26, 28; "Record Rack", *English Dance and Song* 30, no. 4 (Winter/Christmas 1968): 142; Irwin, "English Folk Revival", 17; Nick Logan, "Pentangle Plead for 'Open Ears'", *New Musical Express*, 7 February 1970, 10.

27. Irwin, "English Folk Revival", 17.

28. Simon Nicol, "Fairport Convention Present the New English Electric Sound", interview with Tony Wilson, *Melody Maker*, 26 July 1969, 16; Patrick Humphries, "Fairport's Full House", *The History of Rock* 7, no. 74 (1984): 1465; Irwin, "English Folk Revival", 18.

29. Humphries, "Fairport's Full House", 1465-1466.

30. Letter, *New Musical Express,* 28 March 1970, 17.

31. Dave Laing, "Steeleye Span", *The History of Rock* 7, no. 74 (1984): 1471-1472.

32. Ashley Hutchings, interview by Ian A. Anderson and Lawrence Heath, *Southern Rag* 4, no. 1 (1 July – 30 Sept 1982): 10-13.

33. Karl Dallas, "Steeleye, Spanning the Pop-Folk Gap", *Melody Maker,* 25 July 1970, 31.

34. Ashley Hutchings, "Spanning the Scene", interview by Andrew Means, *Melody Maker,* 30 October 1971, 46.

35. Jerry Gilbert, "Maddy Prior", *Sounds,* 15 December 1973, 27.

36. Laing, "Roll Over Lonnie (Tell George Formby the News)", 16-17; Dave Laing, "Rock on the Tyne", *The History of Rock* 7, no. 74 (1984): 1475; Jerry Gilbert, "Lindisfarne in Newcastle", *Sounds,* 7 October 1972, 22-23.

37. Steve Clarke, "Hats Off to Harper", *The History of Rock* 7, no. 74 (1984): 1478; Dave Laing, "No Man's Land: Between Folk and Rock", *Ink,* 7 August 1971, 17.

38. Irwin, "English Folk Revival", 17-18; Clarke, "Hats Off to Harper", 1479-1480; Martin Hayman, editor, "Music People", *Sounds,* 7 August 1971, 13.

39. Roy Carr, "Matthews Southern Comfort", *New Musical Express,* 21 March 1970, 10; Richard Green, "Renaissance: They Want You to Listen", *New Musical Express,* 21 March 1970, 12; Karl Dallas, "Electric Folk", *Melody Maker,* 26 September 1970, 37.

40. *English Dance and Song* 32, no. 4 (Winter/Christmas 1970): 119.

41. Letter, *English Dance and Song* 32, no. 3 (Autumn 1970): 107.

42. Diane Easby, "Community Culture and Folk Festivals", *Morning Star,* 1 July 1974, 4.

43. Andrew Means, "The Folk Revival", *Melody Maker,* 18 March 1972, 31.

44. Bob Dawbarn, "There's Nowt as Queer as Folk", *Sounds,* 23 September 1972, 25.

8   The Counterculture

1. Herbert Lomas, "Workless Society: 3—How to Get It", *International Times,* 1-16 Jan 1969, 8-9.

2. Mick Farren, "Alternatives: Politics", *Ink,* 23 September 1971, 5.

3. Colin Campbell, *The Romantic Ethic and the Spirit of Modern Consumerism* (Cambridge, MA: Basil Blackwell, 1987), 2-6, 195-201.

4. McDonald, *Revolution in the Head,* 17-26.

5. Frith, *Sound Effects,* 195-196; Macan, *Rocking the Classics,* 12-13; Davis, *Youth and the Condition of Britain,* 185.

6. Mick Farren, "Pop in the Police State", *International Times,* 2-16 June 1967, 14.

7. Mark Williams, "Pop Protest: The Media is the Message", *International Times,* 9-22 May 1969, 22.

8. Roland Muldoon, "Subculture: The Street-Fighting Pop-Group", *Black Dwarf,* 15 October 1968, 8.

9. MacDonald, *Revolution in the Head,* 223-234, 237-238.

10. Orman, *The Politics of Rock Music;* 105, 107.

11. Felix Dennis, "'One Thing You Can't Hide is When You're Crippled Inside'", *Ink,* 2 November 1971, 17.

12. John Hoyland, "An Open Letter to John Lennon", *Black Dwarf*, 27 October 1968, 6.

13. Orman, *The Politics of Rock Music*, 97-102; Martin and Segrave, *Anti-Rock*, 159-161.

14. Mick Jagger, "Jagger on Stage", interview by Keith Altham, *Melody Maker*, 22 March 1969, 14-15.

15. Mick Jagger, "I'm a Rock and Roll Singer, So I Don't Really Care What 'They' Think About Me", interview by Keith Altham, *Melody Maker*, 15 March 1969, 14-15.

16. Germaine Greer, "Mozic and the Revolution", *Oz*, no. 24 (October 1969): 27-28.

17. Richard Neville, "Sympathy for the Holy Ghost", *Ink*, 29 May 1971, 1, 5.

18. Gilbert, "Shapes of Things . . ." 642-643.

19. Townshend, "Born Under a Bad Sign", 28.

20. Marsh, *Before I Get Old*, 249-284.

21. Pete Townshend, "*Tommy*: The Who", interview by [Barry] Miles, *International Times*, 23 May-5 June 1969, 16.

22. "Birth of the First Rock Opera", *Sunday Telegraph*, 18 May 1969 (no page number available).

23. John Entwistle, "The Who by Numbers", interview by Roy Carr, *New Musical Express*, 17 July 1976, 25.

24. Pete Townshend, "Why the Who Aren't Pop Anymore", interview by Chris Welch, *Melody Maker*, 19 April 1969, 16.

25. Felix Dennis, review of *Arthur, or the Decline and Fall of the British Empire*, *Oz*, no. 24 (October 1969): 30.

26. Hardy, "Well Respected Men", 753-754.

27. Steve Lake, "Kinks: We're Not English", *Melody Maker*, 19 April 1975, 3.

28. Colin Shearman, "Barefoot in the Park", *The History of Rock* 6, no. 63 (1983): 1245.

29. Bisbort and Puterbaugh, *Rhino's Psychedelic Trip*, 95; Dafydd Rees, "Festivals Diary", *The History of Rock* 6, no. 63 (1983): 1242.

30. Martin and Segrave, *Anti-Rock*, 137; [John Hopkins,] "Free Concerts: The Aftermath", *International Times*, 1-14 August 1969, 10.

31. Sarah [?], "Pop on a Summer's Day", *International Times*, 18-31 July 1969, 16.

32. Mitch Howard, "They Won't Let Edgar Do It in the Park", *Cream*, October 1971, 7-8.

33. Cliff Ash, "The Dream Goes Sour", *The History of Rock* 6, no. 63 (1983): 1259.

34. Steve Peacock and Marian Partington, "Festival of All Time", *Sounds*, 3 July 1971, 14.

35. Mick Farren, Charles Shaar Murray and Paul Lewis, "Glastonbury Fair to Independence Day", *International Times*, 15-29 July 1971, 11-14.

36. Tim Heald, "To Feed the Pop Festival—50 Tons of Chips!" *Daily Express*, 25 July 1970 (no page number available).

37. Howard, "They Won't Let Edgar Do It in the Park", 7-8.

38. Mick Farren, "Magic Triangle: Broughton's Band", *International Times*, 11-24 April 1969, 17.

39. Dave Williams, "Music for the Hell of It", *International Times*, 10-23 October 1969, 21.

40. Howard, "They Won't Let Edgar Do It in the Park", 8.

41. Steve Peacock, "Edgar: Fighting for a Cause", *Sounds,* 3 April 1971, 6.

42. "It's All a Wank: Peter Jenner of Blackhill", *International Times,* 20 November—3 December 1970, 11.

43. Tony Palmer, "Pop Must Stand on Its Own Two Feet", *Melody Maker,* 4 January 1969, 10-11.

9 Progressive Rock

1. Booker, *The Neophiliacs,* 239-240.

2. "The Broad and the High", *Times* 20 July1968 (no page number available).

3. Ronald S. Milner, "Rock and the Classics", *Guardian,* 14 September 1970 (no page number available).

4. Booker, *The Neophiliacs,* 239-240; Langston Jones, "*IT* New Music Supplement", *International Times,* 2-15 February 1968, 7-8; Macan, *Rocking the Classics,* 12-13.

5. Macan, *Rocking the Classics,* 12-13, 32, 40-42, 69, 144-148.

6. Macan, *Rocking the Classics,* xi, 19-23, 76-78, 153.

7. Macan, *Rocking the Classics,* 3.

8. (Barry) Miles, "Two Thirds Nice", *International Times,* 25 April-8 May 1969, 10.

9. Keith Dewhurst, "'The audience for pop music will accept as normal standards of presentation that would drive any other sort of audience out of the building' etc." *Guardian,* 11 November 1970 (no page number available).

10. Brian Harrigan, "Threshold of Success", *The History of Rock* 5, no. 60 (1983): 1194-1195.

11. Bellman, "Indian Resonances in the British Invasion", 301-302; "A Lot Less Moody—So No More Blues?" *Melody Maker,* 21 January 1967, 15.

12. Tony Stewart interview of Ray Thomas, "Moody Music: The Place of Electronics", *New Musical Express,* 3 June 1972, 8.

13. Quoted in Wale, *Voxpop,* 136.

14. Quoted in Wale, *Voxpop,* 137.

15. Peter Clark, "Welcome to the Machine", *The History of Rock* 6, no. 66 (1983): 1311.

16. Pete Erskine, "Dave Gilmour", *Sounds,* 6 October 1973, 20.

17. Wale, *Voxpop,* 139.

18. Erskine, "Dave Gilmour", 20-21.

19. Richard Williams, "Robert Fripp . . . Super Stud?" *Melody Maker,* 18 August 1973, 8.

20. Tony Mastrianni interview with Robert Fripp, "Robert Fripp: The Crimson King Speaks Harshly About His Court", *Goldmine,* no. 52 (September 1980): 18-19.

21. Macan, *Rocking the Classics,* 23; Williams, "Super Stud?" 8; B.P. Fallon, "Give King Crimson Six Months", *Melody Maker,* 5 July 1969, 7.

22. Robert Fripp, "Looking at the World Thru Crimson Coloured Glasses", *International Times,* 29 August—11 September 1969, 18.

23. Alan Kinsman, "Air Conditioned", *The History of Rock* 7, no. 79 (1983): 1575-1576.

24. Charles Shaar Murray, "Brown Shoes Don't Make It", *Oz,* no. 31 (May 1970): 22.

25. Miles, "Two Thirds Nice", 9.

26. "'Controversial' Single by Nice", *Billboard,* 20 July 1968, 53, 55.

27. Chris Welch, "ELP v. the Critics", *Melody Maker,* 26 January 1974, 9.

28. Mick Farren, "Why Bother? Asks the Oblivion Kid", *International Times,*10-24 Feb 1972, 17.

29. Mark Williams, "Twice as Nice", *The History of Rock* 8, no. 85 (1983): 1687-1688; Macan, *Rocking the Classics,* 175.

30. Graham Fuller, "The Musical Box", *The History of Rock* 8, no. 88 (1983): 1751-1753; Macan, *Rocking the Classics,* 79-81; Steve Clarke, "The Genesis Guide to Genesis", *New Musical Express,* 1 January 1977, 6-7; Chris Welch, "Masked Idol", *Melody Maker,* 19 January 1974, 28-29.

31. Mark Williams, review of *Yes, International Times,*18-31 July 1969, 13.

32. Peter Clark, "Yes", *The History of Rock* 8, no. 85 (1983): 1690-1691.

33. Steve Peacock, "Bill Bruford in the Talk-In", *Sounds,* 18 November 1972, 11.

34. Ray Telford, "Yes: So Far So Good", *Sounds,* 20 October 1973, 14.

35. Mark Plummer, "Classical Heads", *Melody Maker,* 19 December 1970, 17.

36. Chris Welch, "Sentimental Journey", *Melody Maker,* 19 January 1974, 8.

37. Chris Welch, "The Caped Crusader", *The History of Rock* 8, no. 85 (1983): 1697.

38. John Blake, "Is Rick Still Skating on Thin Ice?" *Evening News,* 28 May 1975, 13.

39. Frith, *Sound Effects,* 168; Frith, "1967", 10; Macan, *Rocking the Classics,* 51, 57.

40. David Paul, "Pop, First a Social Phenomenon, Grows Into an 'Art Music'", *Morning Star,* 29 December 1969 (no page number available).

41. Frith, *Sound Effects,* 72-75.

42. Frith, *Music for Pleasure,* 4.

43. James Hamilton, "Are We Really What We Hear?" *Cream,* July 1971, 8.

44. Stephen Barnard, "Sounds, of the 70s", *The History of Rock* 9, no. 98 (1984): 1958.

45. Peter French, "Big Brother at the BBC: An *IT* Enquiry into the Extent of Censorship", *International Times,* 3-17 December 1970, 11-12.

46. Peter French, "Big Brother at the BBC: An *IT* Enquiry into the Extent of Censorship", *International Times,* 3-17 December 1970, 11-12.

47. Blake, *The Land Without Music,* 108-113.

48. Barnard, "Sounds, of the 70s", 1958-1959.

49. Steve Turner, "First Get Yourself on the Telly . . ." *Cream,* June 1972, 6-7; Graham Jones, "Anyone for Cosmic Reggae?" *Cream,* July 1971, 15.

50. Charles Shaar Murray, "Does Tony Blackburn Hang You Up?" *Cream,* December 1971, 17, 49-50.

51. Sue Francis, "They're Just Wild About the British", *Evening News,* 9 August 1975, 16; Letter, *Melody Maker,* 16 October 1976, 19; Blake, *The Land Without Music,* 146-149; Macan, *Rocking the Classics,* 151-155; Frith, *Sound Effects,* 4, 72-75.

52. Paul, "Pop, First a Social Phenomenon, Grows Into an 'Art Music'"; Macan, *Rocking the Classics,* 176-177.

53. Andrew Means, "Moody Views", *Melody Maker,* 18 March 1972, 15.

10 Heavy Metal and Hard Rock

1. Aitken, *The Young Meteors*, 272-275.

2. Harris, *Philosophy at 33 1/3 RPM*, 186; Veldman, *Fantasy, the Bomb and the Greening of Britain*, 82, 86.

3. Stephen Davis, *Hammer of the Gods: The Led Zeppelin Saga* (New York: Berkley Boulevard Books, 1997), 43-55; Elizabeth Jane Wall Hinds, "The Devil Sings the Blues: Heavy Metal, Gothic Fiction and Postmodern Discourse", *Journal of Popular Culture* 26 (Winter 1992): 151-164.

4. "Atl. Rides $200,000 on Zeppelin, UK Act", *Billboard*, 30 November 1968, 4.

5. Frith, *Sound Effects*, 213.

6. Felix Dennis, "Jimmy Page", *Oz*, no. 20 (April 1969): 38.

7. Francis King, "Sympathy for the Devil", *The History of Rock* 6, no. 69 (1983): 1373; Davis, *Hammer of the Gods*, 1-3.

8. Chris Welch, "Why Led Zeppelin Took Off in America and Not Britain", *Melody Maker*, 22 March 1969, 10.

9. Rob Partridge, "Brum Beat", *Melody Maker*, 26 January 1974 (no page number available).

10. Andrew L. Cope, *Black Sabbath and the Rise of Heavy Metal Music* (Burlington VT: Ashgate Publishing, 2010), 28-31.

11. Luke Crampton, "Children of the Grave", *The History of Rock* 6, no. 69 (1983): 1369-1371.

12. Chris Charlesworth, "Sabbath Daze", *Melody Maker*, 12 February 1972, 15.

13. Anne Nightingale, "The High Priest of Heavies", *Daily Express*, 14 June 1977, 20.

14. Chris Welch, "British Steel", *The History of Rock* 9, no. 100 (1984): 1981-1982; Marcus Tybalt, "Rockin' the Seventies", *The History of Rock* 8, no. 87 (1984): 1721.

15. Chris Welch, "Lord of the Deep", *Melody Maker*, 18 March 1972, 13.

16. Pauline McLeod, "Queen Race Home in Style", *Daily Mirror*, 29 November 1976, 23.

17. Neville Wiggins, "Again and Again", *The History of Rock* 8, no. 87 (1984): 1731-1733.

18. Wiggins, "Again and Again", 1733-1735.

19. Pattison, *The Triumph of Vulgarity*, 157-158; Frith, *Sound Effects*, 79-81.

20. Dave Morley, "Rod", *The History of Rock* 8, no. 87 (1984): 1723-1726.

21. James Mandelkau, "Rod the Mod", *International Times*, 17-31 December 1970, 17.

22. Penny Valentine, "The Singer and the Songs", *Sounds*, 25 November 1972, 11.

23. Morley, "Rod", 1726.

24. Royston Eldridge, "A Humble Offering of Rock and Roll", *Sounds*, 3 July 1971, 7.

25. Penny Valentine, "Now Frampton Faces It Alone", *Sounds*, 2 October 1971, 10.

26. Tony Norman, "Frampton: The Musician Who Beat a Pretty Face", *New Musical Express*, 3 June 1972, 6, 40.

27. Steve Clarke, "The Face of '76", *The History of Rock* 9, no. 102 (1984): 2038-2040.

28. "Britain Takes to Womenfolk", *Billboard*, 20 November 1965, 16.

29. Arlene Brown, "Has Anyone Reading This Article Met a Woman Bass Player", *International Times*, 27 August –10 Sept 1970, 13.

30. John Dennis, "Groupies", *The History of Rock* 5, no. 54 (1983): 1073-1074.

31. Simon Frith, "Girls Don't Make It in Rock, Except on Their Backs Maybe" *Cream*, October 1971, 22-25.

32. Gordon Coxhill, "Suzi and the Mamas Who Don't Like It", *Sun*, 31 January 1975, 20; Tom Hibbert, "Suzi Q", *The History of Rock* 8, no. 92 (1984): 1829-1831; Charles Shaar Murray, "For Your Information, She Happens to Be a Lady." *New Musical Express*, 25 January 1975, 7.

33. Nat Freedland and Bob Kirsch, ""British Acts Master Hard Rock", *Billboard*, 12 May 1973, 21.

34. Frith, *Sound Effects*, 79-81.

35. Allan Jones, "Eno—Class of '75", *Melody Maker*, 29 November 1975, 14.

11 Glamrock

1. Dom Moraes, "The Passing of the British Working Class", *New York Times Magazine*, 5 April 1970, 32, 60-72.

2. Frith, *Sound Effects*, 213-215.

3. Stephen Barnard, "All that Glitters", *The History of Rock* 6, no. 72 (1983): 1422.

4. Steve Peacock, "Glitterbiz", *Sounds,* 1 July 1972, 23.

5. Frith, *Sound Effects*, 214.

6. Mungham and Pearson, "Introduction", 7.

7. Dave Rimmer, "Oh! You Pretty Things", *The History of Rock* 8, no. 91 (1983): 1802; Wale, *Voxpop*, 10; Taylor and Wall, "Beyond the Skinheads", 112-120.

8. Mick and Jan Povey, "Thanks for Nothing", *International Times*, 26 Sept—9 Oct 1969, 13.

9. Knight, "Generation Landslide", 1386.

10. Patrick Humphries, "Stardust Memories", *The History of Rock* 7, no. 76, 1514-1515; Bob Hart, "Why Alvin Has Lost His Smile", *Sun*, 17 January 1975, 22.

11. Robert Partridge, "Jesus Rocks On!" *Melody Maker,* 1 September 1973, 3.

12. Annette Kennerley, "Leader of the Gang", *The History of Rock* 6, no. 72 (1983): 1430-1432.

13. Tom Hibbert, "Feel the Noize", *The History of Rock* 6, no. 72 (1983): 1428.

14. Barnard, "All that Glitters", 1422.

15. Bob Edmands, "The Working Class Heroes: Noddy Holder", *Cream*, January 1973, 22-27.

16. Ray Telford, "So You Think Slade are Simple?" *Sounds,* 18 November 1972, 15

17. Hibbert, "Feel the Noize", 1427; Martin Hayman, "Slade: Scruff Bags Who Made It . . ." *Sounds,* 9 December 1972, 12.

18. Christopher North, "Born to Boogie", *The History of Rock* 6, no. 72 (1983): 1436-1440; Ivan Kolmarek, "Marc Bolan: Punk Palladin of Pop", *Goldmine,* no. 83 (April 1983): 18-19.

19. Barnard, "All that Glitters", 1422.

20. Charles Shaar Murray, "Hello. I'm Marc Bolan. I'm a Superstar. You'd Better Believe It." *Cream*, May 1972, 27-31, 47-50.

21. Steve Peacock, "Took's Ballad of the Mountain Grill", *Sounds,* November 25 1972, 8.

22. Quoted in Wale, *Voxpop,* 128.

23. Barnard, "All that Glitters", 1422.

24. Taylor and Wall, "Beyond the Skinheads", *Working Class Youth Culture,* 111; Barnard, "All that Glitters", 1422-1423; Chris Schuler, "Ringing the Changes", *The History of Rock* 7, no. 82 (1983): 1622.

25. "Row Over Davy's Hair", *Daily Mirror,* 4 March 1965, 2.

26. Christopher Sandford, *Bowie: Loving the Alien* (New York: Da Capo Press, 1998), 36.

27. Mary Finnigan, "An Interview with David Bowie", *International Times,* 15-21 August 1969, 15.

28. Chris Charlesworth, "Bowie", *The History of Rock* 7, no. 82 (1983): 1625.

29. Andrew Lycett, "David Bowie: A Rock Oddity", *Cream,* November 1971, 17.

30. Fletcher, "A Decade of Changes", 12-14; Charlesworth, "Bowie", 1626.

31. Schuler, "Ringing the Changes", 1622.

32. Martin Hayman, "David Bowie—In Search of Lost Time", *Sounds,* 4 August 1973, 10.

33. Fletcher, "A Decade of Changes", 13.

34. Schuler, "Ringing the Changes", 1622.

35. Miles, editor, *Bowie In His Own Words* (London: Omnibus Press, 1980), 126.

36. Ian MacDonald, "Will David Bowie Commit Rockanroll Suicide to Become a Superstar?" *Cream,* 10-13, 41-42; Rimmer, "Oh! You Pretty Things", 1803.

37. Barnard, "All that Glitters", 1423.

38. Rob Randall, "There's Nothing More Boring Than Blatant Nostalgia—Bryan Ferry", *Melody Maker,* 2 March 1974, 13.

39. Deborah Thomas, "Ferry Brings Back the In Crowd", *Daily Mirror,* 16 July 1974, 23.

40. Bob Edmands, "The Last Bus Has Gone But the Millenium Has Arrived: Roxy Music in the Sticks" *Cream,* May 1973, 14-16; Graham Fuller, "For Your Pleasure", *The History of Rock* 8, no. 91 (1983): 1805.

41. Ray Coleman, "Harley: A Rose in a Fisted Glove", *Melody Maker,* 17 May 1975, 24.

42. Graham Fuller, "Cockney Rebel", *The History of Rock* 8, no. 92 (1983): 1838-1840.

43. Chris Charlesworth, "Rocket Man", *The History of Rock* 7, no. 84 (1983): 1665-1667.

44. Barnard, "All that Glitters", 1423.

45. Bob Edmands, "Mr. Clean—Taking the Hard Rock Audience (By Strategy)", *New Musical Express,* 7 December 1974, 20.

46. Wale, *Voxpop,* 50.

47. Charlesworth, "Rocket Man", 1667-1668.

48. Steve Peacock, "The Rise and Rise of Fat Reg from Pinner", *Sounds,* 6 July 1974, 7.

49. Peacock, "The Rise and Rise of Fat Reg from Pinner", 7.

50. Ray Hammond, "The Rock Generation", *Sounds,* 6 January 1973, 14.

51. Steve Peacock, "The Kids Are Alright", *Sounds,* 18 May 1974, 28-29.

12 The Business of Rock

1. Frith, *Music for Pleasure*, 6.

2. "Govt. Price Cut Boosts Disk Mart", *Billboard*, 19 January 1963, 38; Chris Welch, "The Boy Next Door", *The History of Rock* 2, no. 19 (1982): 374; Don Wedge, "Presley on Rise Again (Natch)", *Billboard*, 1 September 1962, 17.

3. Christopher Tugendhat, "Golden Discs in a Golden Age", *Financial Times*, 13 June 1964 (no page number available).

4. "Musicians Union Watching Invasion of British Groups", *Billboard*, 28 March 1964, 10; "Manager Takes Ed to Task", *Billboard*, 23 May 1964, 3.

5. Wale, *Voxpop*, 106; Harry Weaver, "Even With All This It Isn't All Gravy", *Daily Mail*, 7 October 1964, 15; "Beatle Bonus from EMI", *Daily Mail*, 22 September 1964, 17.

6. Tugendhat, "Golden Discs in a Golden Age".

7. "Pye's Benjamin Sees Darker Days Ahead for UK Industry", *Billboard*, 4 October 1969, 79, 83.

8. "June's Disk Sales Soared in England", *Billboard*, 25 October 1969, 85, 88.

9. "Profits Up 77% at UK Decca", *Billboard*, 12 September 1970, 1.

10. Phillip Palmer, "5 Million Gain by UK PRS", *Billboard*, 10 July 1971, 1, 42.

11. Sheila Black, "How Music to Remember Earns £12½ m a Year Between the Supermarket and the Albert Hall", *Times*, 14 August 1974 (no page number).

12. "UK Record Sales Up, Exports Down", *Billboard*, 11 September 1971, 53.

13. Bradley, *Understanding Rock 'n' Roll*, 82-83.

14. Thomas, "Moody Music", 8.

15. Bob Hart, "Exit Angry Elton as the Pop Battle Heats Up", *Sun*, 20 March 1975, 15.

16. "Plastics Crisis Hits Records", *Melody Maker*, 20 October 1973, 5.

17. Brian Mulligan, "UK Carrying On In Darkest Hour", *Billboard*, 26 February 1972, 1, 40.

18. "Gem/Levens' 'Fantastic Hits' Use K-Tel's 'Dynamic' Buildup Concept", *Billboard*, 15 July 1972, 44.

19. "We're Back in the Middle Ages", *Melody Maker*, 5 January 1974, 15; Philip Palmer, "British Crisis over Pressing", *Billboard*, 29 July 1972, 1, 71; "Sales Dip in UK, March", *Billboard*, 1 July 1972, 44.

20. "UK Dollar Devaluation Has Little Immediate Effect", *Billboard*, 10 March 1973, 46; "VAT Seen Lowering UK Retail Price", *Billboard*, 24 March 1973, 52, 55; Brian Mulligan, "UK Disk-Tape Boom Sales Boom", *Billboard*, 13 July 1974, 4; Robert Partridge and Edward Jones, "Music and Money", *Melody Maker*, 22 November 1975, 28; Black, "How Music to Remember Earns £12½ m a Year Between the Supermarket and the Albert Hall".

21. "UK Dealers Have Bumper Yule, Cautious on Future", *Billboard*, 18 January 1975, 64.

22. Mike Flood Page, "Plight of the Street Corner Record Shop", *Sounds*, 10 August 1974, 8.

23. Partridge and Jones, "Music and Money", 28; Francis, "They're Just Wild about the British", 16.

24. Steve Clarke, "Crisis? What Crisis?" *The History of Rock* 9, no. 102 (1984): 2026.

25. Letter, *Melody Maker*, 16 October 1976, 19.

26. Edward Jones, "Rock and the Taxman", *Melody Maker*, 11 October 1975, 18, 44.

27. Ian Mather, "Are We Off Our Rockers?" *Daily Mail*, 4 July 1975, 6; David Wigg, "Queen to Abdicate", *Daily Express*, 10 June 1977, 24; John Blake, "Why You Can't See the Stones for Money or Love", *Evening News*, 20 August 1975, 12.

28. Mather, "Are We Off Our Rockers?" 6; Jones, "Rock and the Taxman", 18, 44.

29. Blake, "Why You Can't See the Stones for Money or Love", 12.

30. John Blake, "Elton John Plans to Quit the Pop Scene for His New Love—Football", *Evening News*, 12 June 1975, 3.

31. Mitch Howard, "The Working-class Heroes: Pete Townshend", *Cream*, December 1972, 27-31, 49-50.

32. "Rockin' Inflation", *Melody Maker*, 18 January 1975, 8-9.

33. Jones, "Rock and the Taxman", 18, 44; Kenelm Jenour, "Sing Up Fellas, They're Playing Your Song", *Daily Mirror*, 15 January 1976, 3.

34. Clarke, "Crisis? What Crisis?" 2026-2027.

35. Stephen Barnard, "Family Favourites", *The History of Rock* 9, no. 98 (1984):1941-1942; Dave Laing, "Behind a Painted Smile", *The History of Rock* 9, no. 102 (1984): 2034.

36. Desmond Zwar, "But If Gilbert O'Sullivan Happens, He's the One Who'll Be Laughing . . . All the Way to the Bank", *Daily Mail*, 30 October 1970 (no page number available).

37. Don Short, "Gilbert O'Sullivan[?]", *Daily Mirror*, 8 October 1970 (no page number available).

38. Bob Hart, "Why Leo Is Turning His Back on the Teenies", *Sun*, 28 February 1975, 21.

39. John Blake, "Why Those Minestrone Men Won't Get All Souped Up", *Evening News*, 7 May 1975, 17.

40. Jack Lewis, "How 10CC Made a Hit with the Law", *Daily Mirror*, 6 January 1976, 19.

41. Roderick Gilchrist, "Cliff Says: Please Ban My Happy Hooker Disc", *Daily Mail*, 7 October 1975, 3.

42. Steve Turner, "Rock 'n' Roll Juvenile", *The History of Rock* 9, no. 98 (1984): 1950-1951.

43. Patrick Humphries, "Baby You're a Rich Man", *The History of Rock* 9, no. 99 (1984): 1963-1966.

44. Charles Shaar Murray, "The Raps of Wacky Macca", *New Musical Express*, 26 July 1975, 20.

45. Steve Peacock, "Exile on Sunset Strip", *Sounds*, 17 November 1973, 7.

46. Steve Turner, "Children of the World", *The History of Rock* 9, no. 106 (1984): 2104-2107.

47. "Pirate Radio Set Via Tory Victory", *Billboard*, 4 July 1970, 1, 67; "Pirates Back in Business", *Billboard*, 15 August 1970, 55.

48. Andrew Lycett, "And Now, Over to You, Hughie", *Cream*, December 1971, 12-13.

49. Alan Ereira, "Alternatives: Radio", *Ink*, 23 September 1971, 4.

50. Robert Partridge, "Rock and the BBC", *Melody Maker*, 7 July 1973, 36.

51. Peter Erskine, "Capital: Middle of the FM Road", *Sounds,* 6 October 1973, 10.

52. "Cap Radio Bites Into BBC; Has 1 Mil Listeners", *Billboard,* 18 January 1975, 64.

53. Peter Jones, "UK Radio 1 Publishing 1st Playlist", *Billboard,* 10 December 1977, 4, 72.

54. "Here Are the Stars You Named the Greatest!" *Daily Mirror,* 16 November 1976, 18-19.

55. Idris Walters, "God Gave Rock 'n' Roll to You", *Melody Maker,* 19 April 1975, 16.

56. Roderick Gilchrist, "The Hit of the Week", *Daily Mail,* 27 September 1975, 6.

57. Alan Price, "The Price of Success", *Melody Maker,* 4 October 1975, 1.

58. Stanley Reynolds, "No Grand Claims, No High Praise Has Been Too Much. etc", *Guardian,* 19 April 1975 (no page available).

59. Stanley Reynolds, "'There was something extremely undignified about that business etc'", *Guardian,* 16 August 1975 (no page number available).

13 Punk

1. Frith, *Sound Effects,* 75, 158-159.

2. Anne Nightingale, "Clapton's 6-5 Special . . ." *Daily Express,* 20 June 1977, 16-17.

3. Mick Farren, "Is Rock 'n' Roll Ready for 1976?" *New Musical Express,* 3 January 1976, 18-19.

4. Jon Savage, *England's Dreaming: Anarchy, Sex Pistols, Punk Rock, and Beyond* (New York: St. Martin's Press, 1992), 57-58.

5. Tricia Henry, *Break All Rules! Punk Rock and the Making of a Style* (Ann Arbor MI: UMI Research Press, 1989), 8, 38-45, 59; Neil Nehring, *Flowers in the Dustbin: Culture, Anarchy and Postwar England* (Ann Arbor, MI: University of Michigan Press, 1993), 269-272; Giovanni Dadomo, "Sex Pistols", *The History of Rock* 9, no. 103 (1984): 2045; Savage, *England's Dreaming,* 88-92.

6. Cashmore, *No Future,* 4-9.

7. Pattison, *The Triumph of Vulgarity,* 151.

8. Chris Brazier, "Apathy in Wolverhampton", *Melody Maker,* 24 December 1977, 9; Henry, *Break All Rules!* 75; Brake, *Comparative Youth Culture,* 80.

9. Greil Marcus, *Lipstick Traces: A Secret History of the Twentieth Century* (Cambridge, MA: Harvard University Press, 1989), 5-7.

10. Chris Salewicz, "Anarchy in the UK", *The History of Rock* 9, no. 103 (1984): 2043.

11. Henry, *Break All Rules!* 1-6; Marcus, *Lipstick Traces,* 208-211.

12. Brake, *Comparative Youth Culture,* 78-80; Marcus, *Lipstick Traces,* 437.

13. Chambers, *Urban Rhythms,* 175-176, 184.

14. Nehring, *Flowers in the Dustbin,* 273; Savage, *England's Dreaming,* 255.

15. Malcolm McLaren, "Meet the Col Tom Parker of The Blank Generation", interview by Nick Kent, *New Musical Express,* 27 November 1976, 27.

16. Brake, *Comparative Youth Culture,* 78-79.

17. Frith, *Sound Effects*, 160-162.

18. Paul Gilroy, *The Black Atlantic: Modernity and Double Consciousness* (Cambridge, MA: Harvard University Press, 1993), 33.

19. Cashmore, *No Future*, 41-44; Karl Dallas, "Burnin' and A-Lootin'", *Melody Maker*, 9 October 1976, 36; Nick Kimberley, "Cooling Down the Pace", *The History of Rock* 8, no. 95 (1983): 1883-1884; Chambers, *Urban Rhythms*, 178.

20. Chris Schuler, "The Politics of Punk", *The History of Rock* 9, no. 108 (1984): 2158-2160.

21. Sue Steward, "Making Waves", *The History of Rock* 9, no. 104 (1984): 2070-2072.

22. Chambers, *Urban Rhythms*, 181.

23. Street, *Rebel Rock*, 175-176.

24. Richard North, "Rock of All Ages", *The Listener* 98, no. 2521 (1977): 185.

25. Charles Shaar Murray, "Rebel Fun Page", *New Musical Express*, 11 September 1976, 41.

26. Penny Valentine, "Combat Rockers", *The History of Rock* 9, no. 104 (1984): 2066; [Barry] Miles, "Eighteen Flight Rock and the Sound of the Westway", *New Musical Express*, 11 December 1976, 14.

27. Russell Miller, "Who Are These Punks?" *Daily Mirror*, 2 December 1976, 9.

28. Savage, *England's Dreaming*, 217-221.

29. Chris Salewicz, "1977—Two Sevens Clash", *The History of Rock* 9, no. 104 (1984): 2062.

30. Savage, *England's Dreaming*, 218-219.

31. Chris Schuler, "Buzzcocks", *The History of Rock* 9, no. 104 (1984): 2073-2074; Paul Morley, "They Mean It M-a-a-a-nchester", *New Musical Express*, 30 July 1977, 6.

32. Henry, *Break All Rules!* 83-84.

33. Miller, "Who Are These Punks?" 9; Bert Muirhead, "The Stiff Story", *The History of Rock* 9, no. 97 (1984): 1939; Street, *Rebel Rock*, 144-145; Valentine, "Combat Rockers", 2067; Phil McNeill, "So You Thought Ollie Garky and Ty Ranny Were the Rhythm Section for a Heavy Metal Band . . ." *New Musical Express*, 4 December 1976, 5; Robert Partridge, "Punk Rock: There's Money in Anarchy", *Melody Maker*, 23 April 1977, 3.

34. Gloria Stewart, "The Punks' Mr. Fix-it", *Daily Mirror*, 20 December 1977, 10-11.

35. Gloria Stewart, "I'm a Revolutionary!" *Daily Mirror*, 19 December 1977, 12-13.

36. Stuart Greig, Michael McCarthy and John Peacock, "TV Fury at Rock Cult Filth", *Daily Mirror*, 2 December 1976, 1.

37. Barry Wigmore, John Jackson and Stuart Greig, "OFF! Sex Pistols Are Sent Packing", *Daily Mirror*, 3 December 1976, 1; Kenneth Tew and Norman Leith, "Women's Demo Hits Punk Discs", *Evening Standard*, 3 December 1976, 6; Martin Jackson, "Teeny Thugs!" *Daily Mail*, 12 November 1977, 19; Cloonan, "Popular Music and Censorship in Britain", 86-87; John Peel, "What's So Funny?" *The Listener* 98, no. 2516 (1977): 6.

38. John Jackson, "The Night of the Nasties", *Daily Mirror*, 3 December 1976, 16-17; Stuart Greig, "Yobs!" *Daily Mirror*, 3 December 1976, 16-17.

39. Michael Kilbane, "Clean It Up! Pistols Get EMI Ultimatum", *Evening Standard*, 7 December 1976, 5; Cloonan, "Popular Music and Censorship in Britain", 77, 96-98; Dadomo, "Sex Pistols", 2046-2047.

40. John Hayward, "Fire the Pistols", *Billboard*, 22 January 1977, 3, 102; Steve Clarke, "V-Sign at Queen's Pad Fails", *New Musical Express*, 19 March 1977, 11; Savage, *England's Dreaming*, 314-321.

41. "Grundy's a Top Job Tip—Sex Pistols Permitting", *Daily Express*, 19 May 1977, 13.

42. "Yuk, Yuk", *Daily Mirror*, 3 December 1976, 16-17.

43. James Johnson, "The Punks—Rotten and Proud of It!" *Evening Standard*, 2 December 1976, 3.

44. "What YOU Say about Those Punk Shockers", *Daily Mirror*, 8 December 1976, 15.

45. Letter, *Melody Maker*, 25 December 1976, 13.

46. Savage, *England's Dreaming*, 116-118, 177-178.

47. Brake, *Comparative Youth Culture*, 80; Chris Schuler, "Siouxsie and the Banshees", *The History of Rock* 9, no. 108 (1984): 2148; Henry, *Break All Rules!* 37.

48. Cashmore, *No Future*, 32-34, 64-65.

49. Brake, *Comparative Youth Culture*, 78; Orman, *The Politics of Rock Music*, 169-171; Chris Brazier, "Out, Racists, Out!" *Melody Maker*, 5 November 1977, 46; Street, *Rebel Rock*, 77.

50. Anne Nightingale, "Pop", *Daily Express*, 14 June 1977, 20; Cloonan, *Banned!* 121; "Courts Clear the Pistols", *Melody Maker*, 3 December 1977, 5; Cloonan, "Popular Music and Censorship in Britain", 80; "Pistols Cover Ruled Decent", *Billboard*, 10 December 1977, 70.

51. Cloonan, *Banned!* 164.

52. Salewicz, "1977—Two Sevens Clash", 2062-2063.

53. Muirhead, "The Stiff Story", 1939.

54. Eric Robson, "A Night Out with the Punks", *The Listener* 98, no. 2520 (1977): 145; Frith, *Sound Effects*, 159; Cloonan, *Banned!* 71-73.

55. Roy Carr, "On the Down Home, Dusty Flip Side of the Record Biz, Something Stirs . . ." *New Musical Express*, 6 November 1976, 25.

56. Leana Pooley, "All the Punk That's Fit to Print", *Evening Standard*, 14 January 1977, 14; Savage, *England's Dreaming*, 201-202; Henry, *Break All Rules!* 93-111.

57. Henry, *Break All Rules!* 7.

58. Pauline McLeod, "Punk Gets Junked!" *Daily Mirror*, 31 December 1977, 11; "*NME* Readers Poll", *New Musical Express*, 19 February 1977, 24; Chris Welch, "Derek and Clive—Live at the MM Poll Awards", *Melody Maker*, 2 October 1976, 8-9; Paul Callan, "With the Roller Fans", *Daily Mirror*, 21 September 1976, 17; Charles Catchpole, "Rotten Year for Punk", *Evening Standard*, 4 January 1978, 7.

59. Brake, *Comparative Youth Culture*, 76-80; Street, *Rebel Rock*, 178-179; James Johnson, "They're Still the Kings of Punk . . . But How Long Can It Last?" *Evening Standard*, 31 December 1976, 26; Anne Nightingale, "Watery Rave!" *Daily Express*, 17 May 1977, 20.

60. Herman, "The Press Gang", 1335-1336.

61. Colin Shearman, "That's Entertainment", *The History of Rock* 10, no. 113 (1984): 2244-2248; "Testament of Youth: Paul Weller", *Flexipop!* no. 11: 11-12; Brian Harrigan, "Spreading the Jam", *Melody Maker*, 23 April 1977, 8.

62. Steve Jones, "The Other Elvis: Elvis Costello, A Brief History", *Goldmine,* no. 80 (January 1983): 22-23; Allan Jones, "I'm Not Angry", *The History of Rock* 10, no. 110 (1984): 2192-2195.

63. McNeill, "So You Thought Ollie Garky and Ty Ranny Were the Rhythm Section for a Heavy Metal Band . . ." 5.

64. James Johnson, "£40,000 Contract for Another Punk Group", *Evening Standard,* 6 December 1976, 4; Graham Fuller, "The Stranglers", *The History of Rock* 10, no. 110 (1984): 2188-2189.

65. "Yanks Spike Sex Pistols' Guns", *Daily Mirror,* 29 December 1977, 1; Henry, *Break All Rules!* 69.

66. Jenny Rees, "Punk or Bunk...?" *Daily Mail,* 16 November 1977, 35.

67. David Douglas, "Rotten and Co. 'Run of the Mill'", *Evening Standard,* 6 January 1978, 3.

68. Mick Mercer, "The Punk Collection", *The History of Rock* 9, no. 103 (1984): 2053-2055.

69. Johnny Black, "Metal Machine Music", *Flexipop!* no. 19: 16-17.

70. Johnny Black, "Ring Out the Old, Ring In the New", *Flexipop!* no. 14: 24-25.

Conclusion

1. John Rentoul and Matt Chorley, "Class Exclusive: Seven in 10 of Us Belong to Middle Britain", *The Independent,* 20 March 2011: 1.

2. Rentoul and Chorley, "Class Exclusive", 1.

Select Bibliography

Addison, Paul, and Harriet Jones, editors. *A Companion to Contemporary Britain*
   1939-2000. Malden, MA: Blackwell Publishing, 2007.
Adonis, Andrew, and Stephen Pollard. *A Class Act: The Myth of Britain's Classless Society*. London: Penguin Books, 1997.
Aitken, Jonathan, ed. *The Young Meteors*. London: Secker & Warburg, 1967.
Appleford, Steve. *The Rolling Stones—Rip This Joint: The Stories Behind Every Song*. London: Da Capo Press, 2001.
Barber, Michael. *The Making of the 1944 Education Act*. New York: Cassell, 1994.
Bernstein, George L. *The Myth of Decline: The Rise of Britain since 1945*. London: Pimlico, 2004.
Bigsby, C.W.E., ed. *Approaches to Popular Culture*. London: Edward Arnold, 1976.
_____. *Superculture: American Pop Culture and Europe*. Bowling Green, Ohio: Bowling Green University Popular Press, 1975.
Bisbort, Alan, and Parke Puterbaugh. *Rhino's Psychedelic Trip*. San Francisco: Miller Freeman Books, 2000.
Bourdieu, Pierre. *Distinction: A Social Critique of the Judgement of Taste*. Translated by Richard Nice. Cambridge, MA: Harvard University Press, 1984.
Bourke, Joanna. *Working-Class Cultures in Britain 1890-1960: Gender, Class and Ethnicity*. New York: Routledge, 1994.
Blake, Andrew. *The Land without Music: Music, Culture and Society in Twentieth Century Britain*. New York: Manchester University Press, 1997.

Booker, Christopher. *The Neophiliacs: A Study in the Revolution in English Life in the Fifties and Sixties.* London: Collins, 1968.

Booth, Stanley. *The True Adventures of the Rolling Stones.* New York: Vintage Books, 1984.

Boyes, Georgina. *The Imagined Village: Culture, Ideology and the English Folk Revival.* Manchester: Manchester University Press, 1993.

Bradley, Dick. *Understanding Rock 'n' Roll: Popular Music in Britain 1955-1964.* Philadelphia: Open University Press, 1992.

Brake, Michael. *Comparative Youth Culture: The Sociology of Youth Culture and Youth Subcultures in America, Britain and Canada.* London: Routledge and Kegan Paul, 1985.

Breckman, Warren. *European Romanticism: A Brief History with Documents.* Boston: Bedford/St. Martin's, 2008.

Campbell, Colin. *The Romantic Ethic and the Spirit of Modern Consumerism.* Cambridge, MA: Basil Blackwell, 1987.

Campbell, Neil, Jude Davis and George McKay, editors. *Issues in Americanisation and Culture.* Edinburgh: Edinburgh University Press, 2004.

Cannadine, David. *The Rise and Fall of Class in Britain.* New York: Columbia University Press, 1999.

Chambers, Iain. *Urban Rhythms: Pop Music and Popular Culture.* New York: St. Martin's Press, 1985.

Clark, Anna. *The Struggle for the Breeches: Gender and the Making of the British Working Class.* Berkeley, CA: University of California Press, 1995.

Cloonan, Martin. *Banned! Censorship of Popular Music in Britain: 1967-1992.* Brookfield, VT: Ashgate Publishing Co., 1996.

Cohen, Stanley. *Folk Devils and Moral Panics: The Creation of the Mods and Rockers.* New York: St. Martin's Press, 1980.

Cohn, Nik. *Awopbopaloobop Alopbamboom: Pop from the Beginning.* London: Paladin, 1969.

Cope, Andrew L. *Black Sabbath and the Rise of Heavy Metal Music.* Burlington VT: Ashgate Publishing, 2010.

Davey, Kevin. *English Imaginaries: Six Studies in Anglo-British Modernity.* London: Lawrence and Wishart, 1999.

Davies, Ray. *X-Ray.* London: Penguin Books, 1994.

Davis, John. *Youth and the Condition of Britain: Images of Adolescent Conflict.* Atlantic Highlands, NJ: Athlone Press, 1990.

Davis, Stephen. *Hammer of the Gods: The Led Zeppelin Saga.* New York: Berkley Boulevard Books, 1997.

Dworkin, Dennis. *Cultural Marxism in Postwar Britain: History, the New Left, and the Origins of Cultural Studies.* Durham, NC: Duke University Press, 1997.

Echols, Alice. *Shaky Ground: The '60s and Its Aftershocks.* New York: Columbia University Press, 2002.

Eisen, Jonathan, ed. *The Age of Rock: Sounds of the American Cultural Revolution*. New York: Random House, 1969.

Fairlie, Henry. *The Spoiled Child of the Western World: The Miscarriage of the American Idea in Our Time*. London: Sheldon Press, 1976.

Fast, Susan. *In the Houses of the Holy: Led Zeppelin and the Power of Rock Music*. New York: Oxford University Press, 2001.

Frank, Thomas. *The Conquest of Cool: Business, Culture, Counterculture, and the Rise of Hip Consumerism*. Chicago: University of Chicago Press, 1997.

Frith, Simon. *Music for Pleasure: Essays in the Sociology of Pop*. New York: Routledge and Kegan Paul, 1988.

_____. *Performing Rites: On the Value of Popular Music*. Cambridge, MA: Harvard University Press, 1998.

_____. *Sound Effects: Youth, Leisure and the Politics of Rock and Roll*. New York: Pantheon Books, 1981.

Frith, Simon, and Howard Horne. *Art into Pop*. New York: Methuen Books, 1987.

Garratt, Daren. "Youth Cultures and Sub-Cultures". In *Youth in Society: Contemporary Theory, Policy and Practice*, ed. Jeremy Roche, Stanley Tucker, Rachel Thomson and Ronny Flynn. London: Sage Publications, 2004.

Gillett, Charlie. *The Sound of the City: The Rise of Rock and Roll*. London: Souvenir Press, 1971.

Gillett, Charlie, and Simon Frith, eds. *The Beat Goes On: The Rock File Reader*. London: Pluto Press, 1996.

Gilpin, George H. *The Art of Contemporary English Culture*. New York: St. Martin's Press, 1991.

Gilroy, Paul. *The Black Atlantic: Modernity and Double Consciousness*. London: Verso, 1993.

Green, Jonathon, ed. *Days in the Life: Voices from the English Underground 1961-1971*. London: Pimlico, 1988.

Greer, Germaine. *The Female Eunuch*. New York: McGraw-Hill, 1971.

Hamblett, Charles, and Jane Deverson, eds. *Generation X*. London: Anthony Gibbs and Phillips Ltd., 1964.

Harris, James F. *Philosophy at 33 1/3 RPM: Themes of Classic Rock Music*. Chicago and Lasalle, IL: Open Court Publishing Co., 1993.

Hebdige, Dick. *Subculture: The Meaning of Style*. New York: Routledge, 1988.

Hewitt, Paolo, editor. *The Sharper Word: A Mod Anthology*. London: Helter Skelter Publishing, 1999.

History of Rock, The, volumes 1-10, 1981-1984.

Hoggart, Richard. *The Uses of Literacy: Changing Patterns in English Mass Culture*. Boston: Beacon Press, 1961.

_____. *The Way We Live Now*. London: Chatto and Windus, 1995.

Hoskyns, Barney. *Glam! Bowie, Bolan and the Glitter Rock Revolution.* London: Faber and Faber Ltd., 1998.

Hudson, Kenneth. *The Language of the Teenage Revolution: The Dictionary Defeated.* London: Macmillan Press, 1983.

Inglis, Ian, editor. *The Beatles, Popular Music and Society: A Thousand Voices.* New York: St. Martin's Press, 2000.

Inglis, Ian, editor. *Popular Music and Television in Britain.* Burlington, VT: Ashgate Publishing, 2010.

Joyce, Patrick. *Visions of the People.* New York: Cambridge University Press, 1991.

LeMahieu, D. L. *A Culture for Democracy: Mass Communication and the Cultivated Mind Between the Wars.* Oxford: Clarendon Press, 1988.

Mabey, Richard. *The Pop Process.* London: Hutchison Educational, 1969.

Macan, Edward. *Rocking the Classics: English Progressive Rock and the Counterculture.* New York: Oxford University Press, 1997.

MacDonald, Ian. *Revolution in the Head: The Beatles' Records and the Sixties.* London: Pimlico, 1995.

McKibbin, Ross. *The Ideologies of Class: Social Relations in Britain, 1880-1950.* Oxford: Clarendon Press, 1990.

McKinney, Devin. *Magic Circles: The Beatles in Dream and History.* Cambridge, MA: Harvard University Press, 2003.

McRobbie, Angela. *In the Culture Society: Art, Fashion and Popular Music.* New York: Routledge, 1999.

Marsh, Dave. *Before I Get Old: The Story of the Who.* New York: St. Martin's Press, 1983.

Martin, Linda, and Kerry Segrave. *Anti-Rock: The Opposition to Rock 'n' Roll.* Hamden, CT: Archon Books, 1988.

Marwick, Arthur. *Culture in Britain since 1945.* London: Basil Blackwell, 1945.

Mays, John Barron. *The Young Pretenders: A Study of Teenage Culture in Contemporary Society.* New York: Schocken Books, 1967.

Melly, George. *Revolt into Style: The Pop Arts in Britain.* London: Penguin, 1970.

Miller, Jim. *Flowers in the Dustbin: The Rise of Rock and Roll, 1947-1977.* New York: Simon & Schuster, 1999.

Miles, [Barry,] editor. *Bowie in His Own Words.* New York: Omnibus Press, 1980.

Mungham Geoff, and Geoff Pearson, eds. *Working-class Youth Culture.* London: Routledge and Kegan Paul, 1976.

Norman, Philip. *SHOUT! The Beatles in Their Generation.* New York: Fireside Books, 1981.

Orman, John. *The Politics of Rock Music.* Chicago: Nelson-Hall, 1984.

Osgerby, Bill. *Youth in Britain since 1945.* Oxford: Blackwell Publishers, 1998.

Paglia, Camille. *Sexual Personae.* London: Penguin Books Ltd., 1991.

Pattison, Robert. *The Triumph of Vulgarity: Rock Music in the Mirror of Romanticism.* New York: Oxford University Press, 1987.

Perkin, Harold. *The Rise of Professional Society: England since 1880*. London: Routledge and Kegan Paul, 1989.

Perkin, Harold. *The Third Revolution: Professional Elites in the Modern World*. New York: Routledge, 1996.

Reynolds, Simon, and Joy Press. *The Sex Revolts: Gender, Rebellion and Rock 'n' Roll*. Cambridge, MA: Harvard University Press, 1995.

Richards, Keith, with James Fox. *Life*. New York: Little, Brown and Co., 2010.

Roche, Jeremy, Stanley Tucker, Rachel Thomson and Ronny Flynn, editors. *Youth and Society: Contemporary Theory, Policy and Practice*. London: Sage Publications, 2004.

Seago, Alex. *Burning the Box of Beautiful Things: The Development of a Postmodern Sensibility*. New York: Oxford University Press, 1995.

Street, John. *Rebel Rock: The Politics of Popular Music*. Oxford: Basil Blackwell, 1986.

Turner, Steve. *A Hard Day's Write: The Stories Behind Every Beatles Song*. London: Collins, 1999.

Veldman, Meredith. *Fantasy, the Bomb and the Greening of Britain: Romantic Protest, 1945-1980*. New York: Cambridge University Press, 1994.

Wale, Michael. *Voxpop: Profiles of the Pop Process*. London: Harrap, 1972.

White, Jerry. *London in the Twentieth Century: A City and Its People*. New York: Viking, 2001.

Wicke, Peter. *Rock Music: Culture, Aesthetics and Sociology*. New York: Cambridge University Press, 1987.

Wiener, Martin. *English Culture and the Decline of the Industrial Spirit 1850-1980*. New York: Cambridge University Press, 1981.

Williams, Raymond. *Culture and Society*. London: Chatto and Windus, 1960.

Index

21201316R00190

Printed in Great Britain
by Amazon